THE SCALAWAGS

"Secret Meeting of Southern Unionists," *Harper's Weekly*, August 4, 1866

THE

SCALAWAGS

~

Southern Dissenters
in the
Civil War and Reconstruction

JAMES ALEX BAGGETT

LOUISIANA STATE UNIVERSITY PRESS
BATON ROUGE

Designer: Melanie O'Quinn Samaha
Typeface: Minion
Typesetter: Coghill Composition, Inc.
Printer and binder: Thomson-Shore, Inc.

Library of Congress Cataloging-in-Publication Data
Baggett, James Alex.
   The Scalawags : southern dissenters in the Civil War and Reconstruction / James Alex Baggett.
      p. cm.
Includes bibliographical references (p.) and index.
   ISBN 0-8071-2798-1 (cloth)
      1. Confederate States of America—Politics and government.   2. Dissenters—Southern States—History—
19th century.   3. Unionists (United States Civil War)—History.   4. Politicians—Southern States—History—
19th century.   5. Whites—Southern States—Politics and government—19th century.   6. Southern States—
Politics and government—1775–1865.   7. Southern States—Politics and government—1865–1950.
8. United States—History—Civil War, 1861–1865—Public opinion.   9. Public opinion—Southern States.
10. Reconstruction.   I. Title.
   E487 .B34   2002
   975'.03—dc21

                                                                                      2002001390
ISBN 0-8071-3014-1 (pbk.)

The paper in this book meets the guidelines for permanence and durability of the Committee on Production
Guidelines for Book Longevity of the Council on Library Resources. ∞

To Lillian

Contents

Illustrations

Preface

Having always felt a part of what Carl N. Degler called the Other South, I found my attention drawn years ago to the most dissenting southerners of them all, the scalawags, white supporters of Congressional Reconstruction. My description of their origins began with a dissertation about those from Texas. Later I wrote an article on scalawag origins in the Upper South, which like this book used a collective biography approach. Those studies, plus additional archival research and new works by a handful of scholars, laid the foundation for the generalizations underlying this work.

Like most politicians, scalawags did not suddenly enter politics, win office without previous political experience, or rise from the lower class. As pro-Union political activists, they found themselves in the minority in the 1850s, in the presidential election of 1860, and in the referendums over secession in 1861. They supported the minority Whig Party (and its later iterations: American Party, Opposition Party, and Constitutional Union Party) a nationalist faction in the Democratic Party, or an anti–Democratic Party faction composed of both. Their most common characteristic was opposition to secession in 1861. Once war came, they generally backed the Confederacy to a lesser degree than other southerners and often engaged in resistance to that government, actively as well as passively. For example, some served as Union army officers and public officials of wartime Reconstruction governments.

Original unionists' numbers were depleted from loyalists' ranks during 1861–65 because many identified with the Lost Cause. So die-hard loyalists lost the peace during 1865–66 because of their minority status and the government's unwillingness to disfranchise large numbers of Confederates. Being familiar with the tradition of political coalition building, hard-core loyalists reluctantly accepted black enfranchisement and limited white disfranchisement as a means of gaining power and protecting themselves. At the same time, the federal government used them as officeholders under the Reconstruction Acts because of their record of opposition to secession and the Confederacy, the same record that predisposed them to accept Congressional Reconstruction.

Some original unionists who supported the Confederacy converted to the Republican Party after 1867. They believed it hopeless for the South to continue to resist the will of the victorious North after Ulysses S. Grant's election as president in 1868. Moreover, they hoped to prevent a carpetbagger-black coalition from ruling their state by seizing control of state Republican Parties. Several of these individuals—James L. Orr of South Carolina, Lewis E. Parsons of Alabama, and James L. Alcorn of Mississippi—had wide political followings, some of which they led into the Republican Party. They were joined by a few former Confederate leaders, such as Joseph E. Brown, and their followers, holding similar opinions.

Despite the continued party loyalty of blacks and many whites, who were undeterred by factional fights, the Republican Party in the South—outside of the Upper South—was doomed to failure. As more and more whites returned to the polls, the redeemer Democrats drove the scalawags into obscurity. The redeemers and their advocates left only memories of the scalawags' worst exemplars, associating the scalawags with corruption and the black man in politics, historically the kiss of death in southern politics. The purpose of this book is to rescue those early white southern Republican leaders from the shadows, to see their origins in the light of circumstances surrounding them.

Acknowledgments

I have been researching, writing, and revising this book longer than I care to admit, a protraction partially caused initially by the heavy teaching load of a small liberal arts college and later by administrative tasks and the researching and writing of two other books. No one can accuse me of rushing to press with *The Scalawags*, which I think has led to a better book. It certainly embodies the perspective of time.

My intense interest in the Civil War era began while studying under Jack B. Scroggs, a Reconstruction revisionist and realist who directed my dissertation on the Texas scalawags. During the early stages of research on this broader Southwide study, the National Endowment for the Humanities facilitated my pursuit of sources with grants to two college faculty seminars. The faculty sponsors of those seminars, Dewey Grantham of Vanderbilt University, always a great encourager and friend, and Jerome Clubb of the University of Michigan, assisted me in clarifying my purpose and methodology. I also received a faculty development grant from Union University to continue my research. Two fellow panelists from a Southern Historical Association meeting—Lawrence N. Powell and Sarah Woolfolk Wiggins—have made constructive and illuminating comments on parts of the book.

I appreciate the permission granted by three presses to incorporate material from articles I published with them. These include "Origins of Early Texas Republican Party Leadership" in the *Journal of Southern History*, and "Birth of the Texas Republican Party" and "The Constitutional Union Party in

Texas," in *Southwestern Historical Quarterly.* Part of another article, "Origins of Upper South Scalawag Leadership," published in *Civil War History,* is used with permission of Kent State University Press. The editors of these journals helped me focus on the essentials of my study.

Because in numerous instances I wanted the scalawags to speak for themselves, I quote freely from many manuscript sources. Among the archives granting me permission to quote from their collections were the Alabama Department of Archives and History, Montgomery; Arkansas History Commission, Little Rock; Austin History Center, Austin Public Library, Austin, Texas; The Center for American History, University of Texas at Austin; Houghton Library, Harvard University, Cambridge, Massachusetts; Louisiana and Lower Mississippi Valley Collections, LSU Libraries, Louisiana State University, Baton Rouge; Louisiana State Museum Historical Center, New Orleans; Mississippi Department of Archives and History, Jackson; North Carolina Department of Archives and History, Raleigh; South Carolina Department of Archives and History, Columbia; Southern Historical Collection, Wilson Library, University of North Carolina at Chapel Hill; Tennessee State Library and Archives, Nashville; Tracy W. McGregor Library, Albert H. Small Special Collections Library, University of Virginia Library, Charlottesville; University Archives and Special Collections, University of Tennessee, Knoxville; West Virginia and Regional Collection, West Virginia University Library, Morgantown; and Rare Book, Manuscript, and Special Collections Library, Duke University, Durham, North Carolina.

Finally, I wish to thank those who have been most closely connected with the many revisions of a book twice this size. Charlotte Van den Bosch, my administrative assistant during the 1990s, keyboarded several revisions in between our other tasks and discussions about politics, the latter about which we almost always amiably disagreed. My wife, Lillian Faulkner Baggett, the love of my life and a colleague at Union University, suffered through many holidays and vacations, which I turned into half-time research trips, as my research assistant. Recently she has served as keyboarder and critic. Our chief assistant lately has been Jonathan Waller, more like a son to us than a nephew. He is our computer consultant in Atlanta, where we have retired.

Abbreviations

AlaHQ	*Alabama Historical Quarterly*
ArkHQ	*Arkansas Historical Quarterly*
BDTGA	*Biographical Directory of the Tennessee General Assembly*
BDAC	*Biographical Directory of the American Congress*
DAB	*Dictionary of American Biography*
DNCB	*Directory of North Carolina Biography*
ETHSP	*East Tennessee Historical Society Publications*
FHQ	*Florida Historical Quarterly*
GHQ	*Georgia Historical Quarterly*
JMH	*Journal of Mississippi History*
JSH	*Journal of Southern History*
KKK Report	Report of the Joint Select Committee to Inquire into the Condition of Affairs in the Late Insurrectionary States
LH	*Louisiana History*
LHQ	*Louisiana Historical Quarterly*
NCHR	*North Carolina Historical Review*

OR   *The War of the Rebellion: A Compilation of the Official Records*
            of the Union and Confederate Armies. 128 vols. Washington,
            D.C., 1880–1901. All citations are to series 1.

PAJ   *The Papers of Andrew Johnson*

SwHQ   *Southwestern Historical Quarterly*

THQ   *Tennessee Historical Quarterly*

VMHB   *Virginia Magazine of History and Biography*

WTHSP   *West Tennessee Historical Society Papers*

THE SCALAWAGS

Introduction

In Search of the Scalawags

For the first time since Reconstruction, Republicans during the 1990s controlled the administration of several former Confederate states. Their rule followed election campaigns waged against federal involvement in regional issues—the type of judicial and administrative involvement often encouraged by the area's original Republicans. They rose to power despite the opposition of blacks, who gave Republicans their earliest electoral success in the South. Bitter memories have stemmed any romanticizing of the initial Republican reign. Only blacks recall Reconstruction with any fondness, and they for the most part have not been Republicans for decades. Still GOP control of southern statehouses may at least remind some that the party once controlled these states through a coalition of white southern Republicans called scalawags, newcomers from the North called carpetbaggers, and newly freed blacks. As Mikhail M. Bakhtin states, "Nothing is absolutely dead: every meaning will have its homecoming festival."[1]

This study offers a more charitable image of scalawags than the one created by their enemies, who described them as "ignorant, incompetent, vicious and corrupt men." *Scalawag* is an old epithet, springing from the 1600s. Although obscure in origin, the word has connotations consistent with terms from which it likely derived, such as the word *scollowag*, originally used by Scots in

---

1. Mikhail M. Bakhtin, *Speech Genres and Other Late Essays,* trans. Vern W. McGee, ed. Michael Holquist and Caryl Emerson (Austin, Tex., 1986), 170.

the Shetland Islands to denote inferior livestock. Applied to an individual, *scollowag* meant a scamp—an idle, impish rascal or rogue. Another possible etymological source used in the Hebrides, west of the Shetlands, is the Gaelic *scallag,* a person without stature, a drifter, a doer of menial tasks. Brought from abroad by Scotch-Irish emigrants, these terms, or one of them, became *scalawag* (spelled variously—scalawag, scallawag, skalleway, scallywag). By the Civil War, Americans used the word throughout the nation, although perhaps not often, considering its infrequency in print. John Russell Bartlett's *Dictionary of Americanisms* (1859) describes a scalawag as "a compound of loafer, blackguard, and scamp."[2]

Although *scalawag* retained prior connotations, during 1867 it began being used widely and exclusively to depict white southerners (and longtime residents) who supported Congressional Reconstruction and the Republican Party. Published testimony from congressional hearings and newspaper accounts shows that their opponents distinguished scalawags from recently arrived carpetbaggers—that is, northerners who settled in the South following the war and supported the Republican Party—and that they intended both as terms of "political opprobrium." Reconstruction mythmaker Thomas Dixon, whose novel was made into the film *Birth of a Nation,* summarized the scalawag as a "Judas Iscariot who sold his people for thirty pieces of silver, which he got for licking the feet of his conqueror and fawning on his Negro allies."[3]

Stereotypical scalawags appear repeatedly in older works about Reconstruction. Usually they are limited to a handful of individuals. Invariably they were opportunists and scoundrels involved in the types of corruption endemic in the mid–nineteenth century: fraud, graft, and bribery. For example, South Carolina had more than its share of corrupt scalawags. First among them stood Governor Franklin J. Moses Jr. of Sumter—the most frequently presented scalawag caricature. He managed to fill all of his offices as a Republican unscrupulously, with what Hodding Carter colorfully called "progressive degeneracy." In turn, Moses was a bribe taker, a swindler, and a thief. As governor, he sold appointments, pardons, and legislative support. True to the

2. Hilary A. Herbert, ed., *Why the Solid South? Or, Reconstruction and Its Results* (reprint; New York, 1969), 350; Sarah Woolfolk Wiggins, "What Is a Scalawag?" *Alabama Review* 25 (January 1972): 57–58; John Russell Bartlett, *Dictionary of Americanisms: A Glossary of Words and Phrases Usually Regarded as Peculiar to the United States,* 2d ed. (Boston, 1859), 382.

3. *KKK Report,* Ala., 233, Ga., 764–65, Miss., 871; Thomas Dixon, *The Sins of the Fathers: A Romance of the South* (New York, 1912), 207.

caricature, he eventually became a penniless vagabond and drug addict who served several jail terms. But these practices varied by degree from state to state, and they did not owe their origins to Republican state governments. Republicans, for example, did not initiate political corruption in Louisiana, a subject well documented in the state's prewar newspapers, nor did the redeemers end it.[4]

Most often an individual scalawag was vilified after he began to support Congressional Reconstruction—about the only exceptions being occasional remarks concerning a person's past: that he was a ne'er-do-well before the war, a slave trader, a slave beater, or that he lied about his antisecessionist record. Much of the original criticism represented an effort to ostracize white Republicans from polite society. In most cases, otherwise good reputations were damaged because the men were considered traitors to their community and race, tainted by their close cooperation with lowly blacks in the work of Reconstruction. Before the war, scalawags generally exhibited the same commendable character traits and civic consciousness as their redeemer counterparts. Both valued middle-class morality and lodge and church memberships, with the only difference being that redeemers more often belonged to denominations associated with status and wealth. Each group had its share of those who were friends of "temperance, missions, the Sabbath-school and every good work." Both engaged in reform movements such as campaigns for temperance and for public schools.[5]

After Reconstruction, scalawags and their friends continued to defend their status as a group. Oliver P. Temple contended that unionist scalawags proved equal "with their opponents in every element that constitutes an intelligent, a moral and a respectable people." One of Temple's works, *Notable Men of Tennessee*, which includes about an equal number of Republicans and Democrats he had known in East Tennessee, shows a composite picture of Republican leaders who were middle-class men upholding middle-class morality.[6] An

4. Joseph Woodruff Diary (photostats), Rare Book, Manuscript, and Special Collections Library, Duke University, Durham, N.C.; *BDAC,* 275–76; Hodding Carter, *The Angry Scar: The Story of Reconstruction* (Garden City, N.Y., 1959), 268–70; Ella Lonn, *Reconstruction in Louisiana after 1868* (New York, 1918), 88.

5. Kenneth Stampp, *The Era of Reconstruction, 1865–1877* (New York, 1965), 160.

6. Oliver P. Temple, *East Tennessee and the Civil War* (Cincinnati, Ohio, 1899), 542; Temple, *Notable Men of Tennessee, from 1833 to 1875: Their Times and Their Contemporaries,* comp. Mary B. Temple (New York, 1912); William W. Holden, *Memoirs of W. W. Holden,* introduction by William K. Boyd (Durham, N.C., 1911), 97.

aging William W. Holden remembered that "in a social sense" he and other scalawags were "in the eyes of society, ignorant and awkward." But he saw the outlook as politically motivated. The same had been the case a generation before, he said, with North Carolina Democrats. John R. Lynch, a black man from Natchez who went on to serve two terms in Congress, spoke favorably of his former colleagues in *The Facts of Reconstruction* (1913). Lynch saw an auspicious brand of Mississippi Republican leadership rising to the fore after 1871, after blacks no longer had to cast their ballots for "such material among the whites as . . . available." Lynch said blacks preferred the former aristocrats entering the Republican Party in large numbers after 1871. Besides, he said, it was "a rare thing" to find men of the poor white class who "had any political ambition or manifested any desire for political distinction or official recognition."[7]

Following Reconstruction and some reflection, earlier opponents wrote respectfully of some scalawags. Colonel U. R. Brooks in *South Carolina Bench and Bar* credits most scalawag state judicial officials with ability, "integrity and good intentions." For example, he reports that Robert F. Graham shared "the opinion with [some] other distinguished men of the state that its redemption could be best secured by affiliation with the Republican party." Former Confederate general Isaac W. Avery, who later edited the *Atlanta Constitution,* divided the state's Republicans into those "who were sincere in their politics and enjoyed personal esteem" and those "whose names have become very familiar" in a negative sense. He believed that if the advice of moderate Republicans had been followed, Georgia could have avoided many afflictions while undergoing Reconstruction. Several Mississippi scalawag judges received praise from their enemies. James D. Lynch, certainly no friend of Reconstruction, in *The Bench and Bar of Mississippi* describes some of those judges as "learned, upright and fearless." Such accounts question the simplistic idea that scalawags on the whole sold their souls for the spoils of public office.[8]

Departures from the stereotypical view of scalawags have appeared slowly because of lack of interest about supposedly despicable scalawags. Any more

7. John R. Lynch, *The Facts of Reconstruction* (New York, 1913), 35–37, 106–9.

8. U. R. Brooks, *South Carolina Bench and Bar* (Columbia, S.C., 1908), 195; I. W. Avery, *The History of the State of Georgia from 1850 to 1881, Embracing the Three Important Epochs: The Decade before the War of 1861–5; The War; The Period of Reconstruction* (New York, 1881), 375, 383, 396, 519; James D. Lynch, *The Bench and Bar of Mississippi* (New York, 1881), 185.

than cursory comments about them are rare in works published before the 1940s. Turn-of-the-century graduate students studying Mississippi scalawags at the local level found many white Republicans of the 1870s to have been quite respectable. Building on the foundation of such research, later historians found "the Republican leadership in Mississippi contained an unusually large number of prominent white men who were old residents of the state."

Scalawags received serious, focused, and prolonged treatment initially in the 1944 article "The Scalawag in Mississippi Reconstruction," by David H. Donald. According to Donald, that state's scalawags were predominately conservative, business-minded planter-Whigs from the fertile Black Belt who desired reunion with the nation, if necessary even on Republican terms (black suffrage and so on). They were determined to take the initiative before their old enemies, the Democratic leaders of the small farmers, gained dominance. Thus, many Mississippi Whigs reluctantly joined hands with newly enfranchised blacks, expecting to manipulate them and thereby prevent a takeover by either the Democrats or a carpetbagger-black coalition. Later, Donald extended his Whig theory to include all the former Confederate states except North Carolina and Alabama, where he contended scalawags mostly were unionist farmers who continued to oppose the planter-Whig element.[9]

Donald's thesis received support, at least by implication, from Thomas B. Alexander, who repeatedly identified white native Republicans as former Whigs. Donald's ex-Whig interpretation remained unchallenged, except from a few traditionalists, until the 1963 appearance of Allen W. Trelease's "Who Were the Scalawags?" In a county-by-county quantitative analysis of the 1872 presidential election in the Confederate states, Trelease locates white Republicans geographically strongest in prewar Democratic strongholds of hill-county farmers—precisely where Donald had argued they were weakest. Trelease asserts that in the 1872 election "wherever the percentage of Republican votes significantly exceeds the percentage of Negro population by at least twenty percent . . . we may expect to find native white Republicans." He argues that in only three states—Tennessee, North Carolina, and Virginia—is it possible to identify correctly Republicans with antebellum Whigs. Then, in a 1970 article based largely on his "identification of 140 active scalawags," William

9. Vernon Lane Wharton, *The Negro in Mississippi, 1865–1890* (Chapel Hill, 1947), 157; David H. Donald, "The Scalawag in Mississippi Reconstruction," *JSH* 10 (November 1944): 447–60; James G. Randall and David H. Donald, *The Civil War and Reconstruction,* 2d ed. (Boston, 1961), 627–28.

C. Harris contends that insofar as Mississippi is concerned, scalawags "were of a varied lot and were products more of the convulsion produced by the Civil War and Reconstruction than of past political or socio-economic ties."[10]

Harris's view closely parallels that of Sarah Woolfolk Wiggins in *The Scalawag in Alabama Politics,* the first book-length study about the group. Since 1970, others have approximated Donald's ex-Whig thesis or, favoring neither his nor Trelease's thesis, have simply demonstrated, as did Harris, that scalawags were of varied origins—politically, socially, and economically. Many, perhaps unintentionally, avoided definitiveness by covering all bases; that is, they describe so many different types that classifying scalawags by origin becomes virtually meaningless. In any case, their descriptions are an improvement over accounts that never question redeemer portrayals of scalawags as loathsome opportunists.[11]

Opportunists abound among politicians, whatever their party label, their generation, their class, or even their individual circumstance. The Confederate government had hundreds, albeit they were individuals connected with a popular cause rather than an unpopular one like that of the scalawags. The line between opportunism and the desire to affect public policy (including building a winning coalition to do so) is not so easily drawn. Nor is the line between opportunism and finding a political home that is philosophically comfortable and effective. For some, failure to accept political office with the help of blacks meant surrendering to their worst enemies. On the other hand, taking office under the Republicans also meant facing political risk, forever being disowned by the white man's party, enduring the ostracizing of one's family, the boycotting of one's business, and having one's life threatened. Trelease's *White Terror* abounds with examples of scalawags who were beaten, wounded, or killed because they supported Reconstruction by joining the Republican Party. Such men would hardly have taken the gamble without important issues being involved.[12]

10. Thomas B. Alexander, *Political Reconstruction in Tennessee* (Nashville, 1950); Allen W. Trelease, "Who Were the Scalawags?" *JSH* 29 (November 1963): 445–68. Donald responded to Trelease's article, claiming that "Trelease's method excludes, by definition, virtually all counties with a heavy Negro population as possible sources of scalawag strength." Donald, "Communication to the Editor of the *Journal of Southern History,*" *JSH* 30 (May 1964): 254–56. William C. Harris, "A Reconsideration of the Mississippi Scalawag," *JMH* 32 (February 1970): 27n, 39–40.

11. Sarah Woolfolk Wiggins, *The Scalawag in Alabama Politics, 1865–1881* (Tuscaloosa, 1977); David G. Sansing, "The Role of the Scalawag in Mississippi Reconstruction" (Ph.D. diss., University of Southern Mississippi, 1969), 67–68.

12. Allen W. Trelease, *White Terror: The Ku Klux Klan Conspiracy and Southern Reconstruction* (New York, 1971), 76–79, 232–33.

What follows is an analysis of scalawag origins in the entire South, using a collective biography approach, with a well-defined universe and a uniform set of questions asked about each individual. This approach is what Lawrence Stone defines as "the investigation of the common background of a group of actors in history by means of a collective study of their lives." After compiling the information and formulating questions, the information is "examined for significant variables." In this present study, only the most prestigious, best-salaried, highest-ranking officeholders and the Republican Party nominees for such offices were examined. Below those ranks, information is thin. As Stone points out, "At all times and in all places, the lower one goes in the social system the poorer becomes the documentation."[13]

The number of scalawags examined for each state depended upon the total high-level state and federal offices available there (state cabinet sizes varied little, but other high-level position totals varied greatly). Numbers differed also because the total positions filled by carpetbaggers and blacks varied greatly from state to state. Carpetbaggers occupied more than one-third of the offices in Arkansas, Florida, and Louisiana and about one-fourth in other Lower South states—except for Georgia with less than one-fifth—as was the case in the Upper South. Blacks filled even fewer high-level positions, occupying a significant number only in Louisiana, Mississippi, and South Carolina, approximately 10 percent of the total. In those three states, blacks also occupied a large number of seats in the states' legislatures.

The length of time Republicans ruled in each state was also important. The time ranged from only a few months in Virginia to approximately a decade in the four Lower South states of South Carolina, Florida, Mississippi, and Louisiana. Individuals included were officeholders and candidates during Reconstruction and redemption (defined here as 1863–80). They served as governors, congressmen, state supreme court and circuit court judges, heads of state executive departments; were party candidates for one of these offices; or were high-ranking federal officeholders (internal revenue collectors, customs collectors, or United States judges, attorneys, and marshals). Their salaries and the attitudes of politicians toward each position reflect large political plums. Twenty percent of the individuals in the categories enumerated are excluded because they are largely unidentified except as being scalawags.

Biographical studies often inquire about the place of birth, ethnic identity, family background, level of education, religious affiliation, occupation, mili-

13. Lawrence Stone, "Prosopography," *Daedalus* 100 (winter 1971), 46–79.

tary experience, economic condition and interest, and social class of the individuals studied. Information for some of these categories is naturally more accessible than for others; some categories are more relevant than others, depending on the study. The questions asked here focus on the origins of white southern Reconstruction Republican leaders and are answerable for the overwhelming majority of scalawags. The book examines both the origins of their postwar party affiliation and the origins of their high standing within that party, making it an investigation of the elite. Certain assumptions characterize such a study, especially that an "elite is not a collection of—a mere statistical artifact." Rather the "individuals in the elite know each other well, have similar backgrounds and . . . share similar values, loyalties, and interests." Also it is assumed that the technique will "free the historian from dependence on the haphazard generalizations of journalists, novelists, and biographers of famous men."[14]

Questions are asked about traditional claims that scalawags were largely poor, uneducated, and politically inexperienced ne'er-do-wells. Other inquiries look at their prewar political affiliation, Whig or Democratic, and the depth of their unionism. Questions asked of each, as well as of the group, include the following: Where were they born and reared? Did being born in the North cause some to become Republicans? What was the extent of their formal education? What were their occupations, wealth, and slaveholdings in 1860? What had been their prewar political experiences? Had most belonged to pre-Reconstruction unionist political parties or factions? Were a majority former Whigs, as many historians have claimed? Were those who once had been Democrats Douglas or Breckinridge supporters in 1860? Were they unionist Democrats or secessionist Democrats in 1861? What role, if any, did the short-lived Constitutional Union Party or other 1860 state party coalitions (such as those supporting Stephen A. Douglas for president) play in creating groups from which future Republicans were drawn? How did scalawags react to secession and the Civil War? Did they strongly support secession and the early war effort, merely acquiesce and adjust to the times, or resist the new Confederacy actively or passively?

Other important questions concern the circumstances that brought scalawags into the Republican Party during the war or predisposed them to joining the party later. Early resistance to the Confederacy, for example, took place in

14. Ibid.

East Tennessee with the meeting of two regional unionist conventions, and major opposition to the new government continued for some months. Hundreds of white southerners associated with secret anti-Confederate resistance orders such as the Heroes of America in North Carolina. Later in the war, many associated with the Union League of America, introduced into the South by individuals in the invading army. These and other groups supported peace party movements there and in Alabama and Georgia. The leaders of these parties, such as William W. Holden and Joshua Hill, and many of their followers later became Republicans. To what extent did these experiences lead others into the Republican Party? Some refugees traveled from afar, such as those from Texas who traveled to the North; some traveled a short distance, crossing the Potomac River; and others fled to cities in their own or a nearby state. Nashville, New Orleans, Memphis, Little Rock, and to a lesser degree Key West and a few other towns, served as gathering points for unionists. Did large numbers of unionist refugees also become Republicans after the war? Some southern towns had loyalist undergrounds, places such as Austin, Montgomery, Mobile, Atlanta, Raleigh, and Richmond. Did their members later support the Republican Party?

Many unionists joined the Union army as it invaded the South. In some cases, such as in Alabama, Arkansas, and Florida, they formed friendships with Union army officers. Did they create alliances that continued into Reconstruction under the Republican Party banner? At least 100,000 white southerners from the Confederate states served in the United States Army, ranging from a high of more than 30,000 from Tennessee and Virginia units, to 5,000 or more from Arkansas, Louisiana, and North Carolina, to a low of 400 from Georgia. The officers of some of these fighting Federals became Republican officeholders after the war, especially in Tennessee, Arkansas, and Texas. As one historian has shown regarding Republicans of southern Appalachia, not only their unionism but also their veterans' benefits later tied many to the national Republican Party. Did southerners who served in the Union army also join the Grand Army of the Republic (a supporter of the Republican Party in 1867–68)? Wartime Reconstruction occurred in Virginia, Tennessee, Louisiana, and Arkansas through the election of constitutional conventions, legislatures, and state officials. Did coalitions develop in these states that foreshadowed later state Republican Parties? Also, United States congressional elections took place in these states. Only a few congressmen were seated, but almost all those seated voted with the Republicans. And these states met in political conventions to elect delegates to the 1864 Republican Convention. Not all wartime unionists became Republicans, but the majority did. Why did some accept the leadership of Lincoln and others reject it? What part did issues such as emancipation and political proscription have in determining who would join the Republican Party?[15]

Even if the evidence shows scalawags shared certain characteristics, however, little is signified unless it can be demonstrated that their traits, opinions, and decisions differed substantially from those of their postwar political enemies, the Conservative-Democratic Party. Therefore, the 742 scalawag Republicans are compared and contrasted with their counterparts, a group of 666 redeemer Democrats who opposed and replaced them. In each state, comparisons are made of like officeholders; it is nonproductive to compare governors with county judges.

Backgrounds of scalawag and redeemer leaders are examined in all categories studied: nativity, vocation, estate, slaveholdings, education, political antecedents and experience, stand on secession, war record, and immediate postwar political activities. That a particular leader was a scalawag rather than a carpetbagger, black, or redeemer is ascertained with certainty by identifying his postwar politics as Republican, his race as white, and his antebellum residence as the South. Included in the scalawag category are a few northern-born whites who had resided in the South since antebellum days and later became Reconstruction Republicans. Redeemers were simply identified by state party label—Conservative or Democratic, or Conservative-Democratic, all of whom identified with the national Democratic Party.

Unlike studies that describe scalawag officeholders or voters in a single state, or Trelease's statistical study that portrays white Republican voters in all of the former Confederate states, this study analyzes separately the scalawag leadership of particular southern regions—the Upper South, the Southeast, and the Southwest—as well as scalawag elite Southwide. The Upper South is defined as North Carolina, Tennessee, Virginia, and West Virginia; the Southeast is limited to Alabama, Florida, Georgia, Mississippi, and South Carolina; and the Southwest includes only Arkansas, Louisiana, and Texas. These geographical divisions were not fashioned arbitrarily but followed an extensive examination of the Republican Party's emergence in the entire South, which

15. Gordon B. McKinney, *Southern Mountain Republicans, 1865–1900: Politics and the Appalachian Community* (Chapel Hill, 1978), 30; Gordon B. McKinney, "The Rise of the Houk Machine in East Tennessee," *ETHSP* 45 (1973): 72–73.

demonstrated a greater commonality within each grouping than could be found Southwide. In addition to being contiguous states, other significant factors existed in the determination of these regions. The physical terrain, the ratio of blacks to whites, the 1860 strength of the two-party system, the percentage of incoming nonsoutherners in recent decades, the wartime occupation of the invading Union army, and the influence of carpetbaggers and black politicians were all factors.

West Virginia Republicans are included in the early part of this study, despite the fact that most of the counties of the area (state after 1863) supported the Union in the Civil War. Some of the southern and eastern counties of what later became the state of West Virginia favored and fought for the Confederacy. It is practically impossible to separate the history of scalawag origins in Virginia from antebellum and wartime events in West Virginia, where Virginia's Republican Party and the state's first Reconstruction government originated. And the particular wartime issues—separate statehood, the emancipation of the slaves, and the degree of disfranchisement—which divided the unionist political factions in West Virginia and Tennessee, were largely of the same substance and origin. Finally, the lack of scalawag leadership in Virginia can partially be accounted for by the creation of West Virginia.[16]

The chronological scope of the narrative spans the 1850s to the 1870s. The first part describes the scalawags before the war, particularly their community status, their political affiliation and experience, and their secession stand. This is followed by the story of their lives during the war years, especially their relationship with the Confederacy and their role in the creation of the Republican Party in the South.

The study is constructed upon separate yet complementary research methodologies. First came the creation of the composite biographical profile of the 742 scalawags, along with that of the control-group profile of 666 redeemers. Included in the profiles is information about nativity, age, and status, as well as the response of each group to several key political issues. For the most part,

16. For a description of political conditions in West Virginia during the Civil War and Reconstruction, see Richard Orr Curry, *A House Divided: A Study of Statehood Politics and the Copperhead Movement in West Virginia* (Pittsburgh, 1964). Elsewhere, Curry says, "The issues Congress attempted to resolve by military intervention in the South constituted the basis of intrastate, party power struggles throughout the border land." Curry, ed., *Radicalism, Racism, and Party Realignment: The Border States during Reconstruction* (Baltimore, 1969), xv.

names of the scalawag and redeemer officials and their prior political experience were located in numerous manuscript lists of public officials and election
statistics and published directories, legislative journals, and convention proceedings. In almost all cases, the source for individual estate and slaveholdings
was the Eighth Census of the United States. National and state collective biographical sources, county histories, congressional reports, newspapers, and
manuscript collections supplied most of the information for the other categories.

Beyond the biographical profile, which may be viewed as the study's frame-
work, further archival research helped capture the flavor of the times and the
attitudes of the participants. One of the failures of a purely statistical approach
to history has been that of expecting statistics to speak for themselves. Historians cannot satisfactorily interpret data without being aware of the time and
context within which events occurred. The painting of such a broad canvas,
including hundreds of individuals and a multitude of events, of course, required some reliance on other historians. The order of this study was largely
dictated by geographical considerations (Upper South, Southeast, and Southwest); by chronological ones, especially antebellum, wartime, and postwar;
and by topical ones, antisecession, anti-Confederate, wartime Reconstruction,
and Congressional Reconstruction.

This work recognizes that individuals most often act in concert with their
fellows rather than in isolation. Although many scalawags were loners, often
acting on a sense of nationalism, which in some cases was like a religion, the
vast majority acted only with the assurance of others with common beliefs,
ideals, and interests. While this work dwells on the general rules, it does not
ignore the ever-present exceptions in pragmatic American politics. Many of
these pragmatic leaders had followers who were also exceptions to the general
pattern. Scalawags were as much coalition builders as other successful politicians before and after them have been. Indeed, in a sense, it can be said they
were introducing blacks to politics in much the same way as others had helped
to bring the Irish into the system or in the South, such groups as the French
of Louisiana and the Mexicans of Texas. Exceptions to the general rule or
pattern also include individuals at the local level who became Republicans
because their opponents were Democrats or because they saw their only opportunity to control the political power of local blacks (often the majority
race locally) lay in becoming a Republican leader.

The work describes the social and political origins of scalawags and demonstrates that they were by a large margin opposed to secession and that on the whole they were far less loyal to the Confederacy than their redeemer counterparts. In dealing with wartime Reconstruction, it shows, as many Reconstruction revisionist accounts have before, that Reconstruction started long before 1867. It describes the failure of ultraunionists to gain control over each of the former Confederate states and how original unionists-turned-Confederates easily won that control before being turned back by the tide of Congressional Reconstruction, a plan favored by the vast majority of scalawags. Then it outlines the development of the Republican Party in the states where Republicans had existed since the war (in the Upper South and Southeast) and the birth of the Republican Party in the Southeast. A close relationship is shown between the ideology of individuals and their desire for the rewards of politics and the necessity of both to build a political party and attract political leaders (in this case, the scalawags).

Next, the victory of the Republican Party in each of the states and the seeds of its future defeat are traced, along with situations in some states that caused Congressional Reconstruction to start late, especially in Mississippi, where many of the scalawags were latecomers to the Republican Party. Most important, this study demonstrates why individuals joined the party and became Republican leaders despite bitter opposition by most whites. Finally, the work describes some of the tensions within the carpetbagger-black-scalawag coalition as well as tensions among the opposition Democrats that caused some Democrats to go over to the Republicans.

1

~

Antebellum Origins

Why did some southern whites become Republicans during the Civil War and Reconstruction? Answers to this question are contradictory. Explanations include their class status, high as well as low; their political antecedents, Democratic as well as Whig; their being reformists as well as opportunists; their unionist convictions; and combinations thereof. Scalawags are seen by some as individuals who "smarted under a system that gave every advantage to the planter class" and consequently punished their adversaries when the opportunity came with the military occupation of the South. Others portray them to be the opposite: mainly planters, with a sprinkling of middle-class lawyers and merchants. They are viewed as men whose antisecessionism and loyalty to the United States isolated them from others and consequently predisposed them to Republicanism (which stood for the preservation of the Union). Or they are seen as merely an unprincipled lot in all seasons, war and peace.[1]

Examples of why individual scalawags became Republicans include all of the above, but in what proportions? To what degree did different motives, operating simultaneously, cause the men to become Republicans? And how did their predisposition differ, if any, from those of their postwar Democratic

1. Donald, "Scalawag in Mississippi," 447–60; Trelease, "Who Were the Scalawags?" 445–68; Otto H. Olsen, "Reconsidering the Scalawags," *Civil War History* 12 (December 1966): 304–20; John Hope Franklin, *Reconstruction: After the Civil War* (Chicago, 1961), 98; W. E. B. Du Bois, *Black Reconstruction in America* (New York, 1935), 350; Herbert, *Why the Solid South?* 350.

opponents? Balanced, coherent answers to these questions are needed. A range of reasons considered singularly and in combination will explain more than a simple rationale about why white southerners became Republicans. Recent revisionism simply reversing the roles of scurrilous scalawags and righteous redeemer Democrats will not suffice. As Gerald N. Grob aptly comments: "To read about heroes and villains . . . makes for considerable excitement; that it illuminates the past is more questionable."[2]

Scalawags and redeemers differed to a degree in some features of their antebellum backgrounds: place of birth, formal educational level attained, primary vocation, and amount of wealth and slaveholdings. In some categories the gulf between them was not as wide as often imagined. In others, the difference was significant. For example, twice as many scalawags as redeemers were born outside of the South, either in the North or abroad (especially Germany). One fifth of them, compared with one-tenth of redeemers, were non-southern natives. Although this may seem a minor difference, when scalawags of nonsouthern birth are combined with carpetbaggers (northern Republican newcomers after 1860), the number of nonnative Republicans proved significant everywhere. Among the high-ranking officeholders in this study, non-natives dominated Reconstruction in Arkansas, where they were mainly former army officers; in Florida, centered in Jacksonville; and in Louisiana, centered in New Orleans.[3]

Before the war, future scalawags who had been born and reared in the North often maintained ties with family, old friends, and classmates. Some of their northern friends became prominent politicians. For example, Abraham Lincoln knew several such individuals in the Southwest, most from southern families who sojourned in the Midwest. He once practiced law in the same Illinois circuit as Alexander P. Field and on occasion campaigned alongside the man who later served as attorney general of Louisiana. Ulysses S. Grant and Rutherford B. Hayes had college classmates who became scalawags. Still, too much should not be made of such relationships regarding subsequent political decisions. Most of these scalawags lived the greater part of their lives in the South. As young men, many married southern belles, reared their children in Dixie, and loved the region. When given an option in 1861 of remaining or returning to the North, most stayed. Some had lived in the South "so long

2. Gerald N. Grob, "Reconstruction: An American Morality Play," in *American History: Retrospect and Prospect,* ed. George A. Billias and Gerald N. Grob (New York, 1971), 220.

3. Eighth Census of the United States, 1860, RG 29, National Archives, Washington, D.C.

as to be generally considered a native." Many fought for the South. Georgia, for example, had several northern-born high-ranking Confederate officers who later became Republicans.[4]

Elisha W. Peck of Tuscaloosa, Alabama, a native of New York, was very much part of his community as the town's most successful attorney, as an Episcopalian churchman, as "a kind neighbor," and as a giver, "without ostentation," of charity to the needy. Born during the Washington administration, he considered himself a Federalist, as his father before him had been. So he had become accustomed to being in the minority. After experiencing wartime persecution, he left the Alabama home he had known since the 1820s and settled in Illinois. But Peck soon returned, having grown "homesick for the old red hills of Alabama."[5] Jason Niles left Kosciusko, Mississippi, and slipped out of the Confederacy during June 1861 for what he feared would be his final visit to his native Vermont. On his return trip south, he mailed several letters at Louisville as it was his "last chance before plunging into the 'Southern Confederacy.'" To his friends in Mississippi, he seemed southern enough. He had married his wife while teaching in Tennessee, and four of his children had been born in Mississippi. His neighbors, who had elected him to represent them in the state's constitutional convention of 1851, chose him as mayor of Kosciusko in 1864.[6]

In the Upper South, most northern-born scalawags had settled in the upper fringes of Virginia, where several served as local officeholders before 1860. Others, mostly young teachers, journeyed to the South, where they eventually achieved success as attorneys. One such individual was Horace

4. Theodore C. Pease, ed., *Collections of the Illinois State Historical Library,* vol. 18 (Springfield, Ill., 1923), 504–5; Lincoln to Alexander P. Field, 1 May 1839, in *The Collected Works of Abraham Lincoln,* ed. Roy P. Basler (New Brunswick, N.J., 1953–90), 1: 149–50; William Garrett Piston, *Lee's Tarnished Lieutenant: James Longstreet and His Place in Southern History* (Athens, Ga., 1987), 4; Fletcher M. Green, *The Role of the Yankee in the Old South* (Athens, Ga., 1972), 5, 37; Whitelaw Reid, *After the War: A Southern Tour, May 1, 1965 to May 1, 1866* (Cincinnati, Ohio, 1866), 268; *DAB,* 1: 133; William S. McFeely, "Amos T. Akerman: The Lawyer and Racial Justice," in *Region, Race, and Reconstruction: Essays in Honor of C. Vann Woodward,* ed. J. Morgan Kousser and James M. McPherson (New York, 1982), 398.

5. Thomas McAdory Owen, *History of Alabama and Dictionary of Alabama Biography* (Chicago, 1921), 4: 1333; E. A. Powell, "Fifty-five Years in West Alabama," *AlaHQ* 4 (winter 1942): 636–38.

6. Diary entries, June and July 1861, 2 May, 16 October 1864, Jason Niles, Diaries, Journals, and Scrapbook, Southern Historical Collection, Wilson Library, University of North Carolina at Chapel Hill; newspaper clipping, *Kosciusko Chronicle,* 27 May 1869, Niles Papers; Eighth Census, RG 29.

Maynard of Massachusetts. According to one observer, he had "a magnetic hold upon the people of East Tennessee." Following graduation from Amherst College in 1838, he moved to Knoxville, where he taught college before beginning the practice of law and entering politics as a Whig. When the war came, Maynard was serving his second term in Congress. Another such individual was Amos T. Akerman who turned from teaching to law while tutoring the children of John M. Berrien of Savannah, once the nation's attorney general.[7]

Some scalawags moved to the South as children. At age two, Samuel F. Phillips arrived in Chapel Hill, "a small, isolated village without a primary school," with his well-educated parents from New York City. Later he graduated from the University of North Carolina, where his father chaired the Department of Mathematics and Natural Philosophy. Maynard, Akerman, and Phillips gained recognition during the 1870s and 1880s as members of Republican administrations. Postmaster General Maynard became his party's dispenser of federal patronage in the South during the final year of the Hayes administration, 1880–81. Attorney General Akerman led a crusade against the Ku Klux Klan in the Carolinas during 1871. He won about one-half of the Klan cases prosecuted under his watch, quite an accomplishment given the circumstance of southern juries. And Solicitor General Phillips served as the government attorney in several significant civil rights cases before the Supreme Court during his lengthy term, from 1872 to 1885.[8]

Settlers from outside the South represented one-third of the scalawags in the Southwest. Because of their numbers and ability, they had greater influence than did others like them elsewhere. Included among them were governors—Isaac Murphy of Arkansas, Michael Hahn and Benjamin F. Flanders of Louisiana, and Elisha M. Pease of Texas—and others who served as congressmen, judges, and state and federal officials. Nonnative southerners dominated the wartime-occupied Louisiana administration, which had only one state native, James Madison Wells, a wealthy Rapides Parish planter. All the others

7. Especially helpful was George A. Atkinson and Alvaro F. Gibbens, *Prominent Men of West Virginia* (Wheeling, W. Va., 1890); *BDTGA*; Sidney Andrews, *The South since the War as Shown by Fourteen Weeks of Travel and Observation in Georgia and the Carolinas* (Boston, 1866), 138; Temple, *Notable Men of Tennessee*, 137–39; Samuel S. Cox, *Union—Disunion—Reunion: Three Decades of Federal Legislation, 1855 to 1885* . . . (Providence, R.I., 1885), 73.

8. Temple, *Notable Men of Tennessee*, 142; McFeely, "Amos T. Akerman," 397, 404–10; Trelease, *White Terror*, 402–7; Robert D. Miller, "Samuel Field Phillips: The Odyssey of a Southern Dissenter," *NCHR* 43 (July 1981): 262–70, 276–77; Kenneth Coleman and Charles S. Gurr, eds., *Dictionary of Georgia Biography* (Athens, Ga., 1983), 1: 218–19.

were either foreign-born or northern-born men with longtime residency in Louisiana, especially in the New Orleans area. One historian, who claims "that contact with the North . . . [was] a consistent theme in Southern dissent" before and during the Civil War, identifies 172 wartime Louisiana unionists, including almost all of the state's earliest Republicans. He found that 65 percent were either northern-born or foreign-born. For comparison, he checked sixty prominent state Confederates and found that 77 percent were born in states that joined the Confederacy.[9]

Yankee schooling may have been one of the reasons several southern-born Louisiana politicians became Republicans. According to Judge William H. Hunt's son, his father's Connecticut education made him "never again the Southerner but the American." When his family left Charleston, South Carolina, in 1839, William Hunt continued his education at Yale College. While visiting the Hudson River Valley area in 1864, he met and married Elizabeth Ridgely, a daughter of Commodore Charles G. Ridgely. Although Hunt fought secession, he retained his position as a New Orleans judge in 1861. Once the city fell to the Federals in 1862, he immediately displayed his true colors by making friends with General Benjamin F. Butler and Admiral David G. Farragut. During 1864, Hunt became a Republican and supported Lincoln for president in 1864.[10]

Most nonnative scalawags in the Southwest practiced professions such as law, journalism, or medicine. They hailed from the North, the Midwest, or Germany, from which thousands sailed to New Orleans and Galveston following the 1848 revolution. Most settled in New Orleans, in the small towns of north Arkansas, or south of a line running from Houston to Austin. Several German natives who settled in Texas as children or young men became prominent Republican officeholders. Except for a few individuals in Arkansas who arrived shortly before 1860, almost all nonnative scalawags had settled in the Southwest more than a decade earlier as young men seeking opportunities. Pease of Connecticut, for example, sailed to Texas shortly before the 1836 revolution, served as the provisional government's secretary, and helped draft the republic's constitution before becoming a highly successful Austin attorney and a two-term Democratic governor in the 1850s. After sailing to Louisiana

---

9. Ted Tunnell, *Crucible of Reconstruction: War, Radicalism, and Race in Louisiana, 1862–1877* (Baton Rouge, 1984), 21; Thomas Hunt, *The Life of William H. Hunt* (Brattleboro, Vt., 1922), 56, 116–22; Joe Gray Taylor, *Louisiana Reconstructed, 1863–1877* (Baton Rouge, 1974), 30.

10. Hunt, *William H. Hunt*, 56, 116–22.

in 1837, folk humorist Thomas B. Thorpe of Massachusetts married and reared a family, penned two collections of tall tales, made a living as a newspaper editor and sometime postmaster, and twice ran as Whig candidate for state school superintendent.[11]

Elsewhere in the South, scalawags originally from above the Mason-Dixon Line outnumbered nonnative redeemers almost three to one. They accounted for more than one-third of scalawags in Florida and exceeded one-fourth of those in Georgia, where they guided the constitutional convention of 1867–68. For the most part, they practiced professions—primarily as lawyers and businessmen in towns such as Augusta, Atlanta, Jacksonville, and Vicksburg. Politically, most identified with the Whig Party, with only one in five a Democrat. And philosophically, few expressed antislavery feelings, which might have propelled them into the Republican Party. Many, in fact, owned slaves.

Among Southwest scalawags, German-Americans were about the only ones openly antislavery before the war. These included Edward Degener and Charles N. Riotte, who along with others at an 1854 San Antonio meeting declared slavery "an evil, the abolition of which is a requirement of democratic principles." Riotte became one of several antislavery exiles from Dixie who identified with the Republican Party before or during the Civil War and who received federal appointments from the Lincoln administration. The president appointed Riotte minister to Costa Rica in early June 1861. Degener later served as a Texas Republican congressman. Valentine Dell, of Fort Smith, Arkansas, was "an outspoken Abolitionist" driven out of Kansas in the mid-1850s. And physician Maximilian F. Bonzano of New Orleans, so "strongly opposed to the institution of slavery, [that] out of his limited means . . . [he] purchased and emancipated several negroes."[12]

In the Upper South, some scalawags born outside of Dixie openly opposed the institution. Mostly they came from the ranks of farmers and businessmen in the area between the Rappahannock and Potomac Rivers and the Virginia

11. Roger A. Griffin, "Connecticut Yankee in Texas: A Biography of Elisha Marshall Pease" (Ph.D. diss., University of Texas, Austin, 1973); Milton Rickels, *Thomas Bangs Thorpe: Humorist of the Old Southwest* (Baton Rouge, 1962); *DAB*, 5: 18; Stanton Garner, "Thomas Bangs Thorpe in the Gilded Age: Shifty in a New Country," *Mississippi Quarterly* 36 (winter 1982–83): 35–52.

12. Rudolph L. Biesele, "The Texas State Convention of Germans in 1854," *SwHQ* 33 (April 1929): 249–55; Walter Prescott Webb et al., eds., *The Handbook of Texas* (Austin, 1952–76), 1: 683–84; *The Encyclopedia of the New West* . . . (Chicago, 1880), 56; George S. Denison to Chase, 28 June 1862, *Diary and Correspondence of Salmon P. Chase,* Annual Report of the American Historical Association, 1902 (Washington, D.C., 1903), 2: 308.

Panhandle. John C. Underwood first ventured into Virginia as a teacher in the 1830s. After marrying his student Marie Gloria Jackson of Clarksburg, a cousin of Thomas "Stonewall" Jackson, Underwood returned to his native New York. During the 1840s, he and his wife settled on an 800-acre estate in Clarke County, Virginia, and turned to farming, using white rather than slave labor. Because of his involvement in antislavery politics—first in the Liberty Party, then in the Free-Soil and Republican Parties—Underwood on more than one occasion quickly exited Virginia. By 1857, Underwood worked for the American Emigrant Aid and Homestead Company, organized by Congressman Eli Thayer of Massachusetts. They hoped to colonize Virginia with hardy free white laborers from the North and Europe on cheaply bought land, make a profit, and revolutionize the state.[13]

About the only native scalawags challenging the institution of slavery before the war were some Virginians from the northwestern part of the state, a few Virginia Quakers, and several North Carolina Whig free-soilers from Rowan and other nearby counties. Some became early Republicans and expatriates in the North. North Carolinians predisposed toward the Republican Party by their attitude toward the "peculiar institution" included Hinton R. Helper, author of *The Impending Crisis of the South*, a widely circulated statistical treatise advocating free soil; his brother, Hardie H. Helper; their friend, Daniel R. Goodloe, a self-exiled newspaperman residing in Washington, D.C., since the 1840s; and an expatriate named Benjamin S. Hedrick, a chemistry professor vilified by the press for expressing pro-Fremont sentiments and driven from his position at the University of North Carolina. These men, all recipients of patronage from the Lincoln administration, applauded the Emancipation Proclamation and identified with the Republican Party prior to Reconstruction. All but Hinton R. Helper returned to North Carolina in 1865 and became active in Tarheel politics. In 1867, they helped found the state's Republican Party.[14]

13. Charles H. Ambler and Festus P. Summers, *West Virginia: The Mountain State*, 2d ed. (Englewood Cliffs, N.J., 1958), 254–57; Richard H. Abbott, "Yankee Farmers in Northern Virginia, 1840–1860," *VMHB* 66 (January 1968): 56–63; Richard Lowe, "The Republican Party in Antebellum Virginia, 1856–1860," VMHB 81 (July 1973): 261; Walter M. Merrill and Louis Ruchames, eds., *The Letters of William Lloyd Garrison* (Cambridge, Mass., 1976), 4: 440; Richard H. Sewell, *Ballots for Freedom: Antislavery Politics in the United States, 1837–1860* (New York, 1976), 314–16.

14. Atkinson and Gibbens, *Prominent Men*, 347; Theodore F. Lang, *Loyal West Virginia from 1861 to 1865* (Baltimore, 1895), 129; Granville Parker, *The Formation of the State of West Virginia*

William H. Brisbane of South Carolina also possessed good antislavery credentials. As a wealthy Beaufort planter and an ordained Baptist minister, he started out orthodox enough on the slavery issue to please fellow Carolinians. Yet influences around him such as the system's cruelty caused him to doubt his proslavery arguments. His antislavery sister and brother-in-law and Francis Wayland, president of Brown University in Rhode Island, contributed to Brisbane's self-doubts. After freeing his slaves in the summer of 1835, he and his wife decided to settle in Ohio. During the next twenty years, Brisbane was a tireless antislavery advocate in the pulpit, in the press, and on the political platform. He moved to Arena, Wisconsin, in 1853, where he served as clerk of the Wisconsin senate. In 1862, Secretary of the Treasury Salmon P. Chase, an old Ohio friend, appointed Brisbane as one of the three direct tax commissioners to serve in his old home district of Beaufort, recently occupied by Federal troops.[15]

But the appeal of "Free Soil, Free Labor, Free Men" that attracted northerners to the Republican Party in the mid-1850s repelled almost all southerners. Only in a few rare cases did a clear connection exist between antislavery convictions and affiliation with the Republican Party. Indeed, some Republicans championed the peculiar institution. William G. "Parson" Brownlow of Knoxville, a successful editor, defended slavery from the pulpit and press as being scriptural, civilizing, and profitable. And William W. Holden, editor and publisher of the *(Raleigh) North Carolina Standard,* often rose to the defense of the institution, being, according to his own words, "jealous for the . . . rights of the South on the question of slavery." Many, perhaps most, in their views resembled Brownlow's friend, attorney Oliver P. Temple, a self-described "moderate friend of African slavery." Admitting his conscience had not troubled him, Temple said, "I was a slave-owner, as my father and grandfather had been."[16]

---

and Other Incidents of the Late Civil War (Wellsburg, W. Va., 1875), 230; W. H. T. Squires, *Unleashed at Long Last: Reconstruction in Virginia, April 9, 1865, to January 26, 1870* (Portsmouth, Va., 1939), 63–64; Carl N. Degler, *The Other South: Southern Dissenters in the Nineteenth Century* (New York, 1974), 71, 74, 135, 144; B. S. Hedrick to Abraham Lincoln, 23 September 1862, Abraham Lincoln Papers, Library of Congress; Douglas C. Dailey, "The Election of 1872 in North Carolina," *NCHR* 40 (summer 1963): 339.

15. Blake McNulty, "William Henry Brisbane: South Carolina Slaveholder and Abolitionist," in *The Southern Enigma: Essays on Race, Class, and Folk Culture,* ed. Walter J. Fraser Jr. and Winfred B. Moore Jr. (Westport, Conn., 1983), 120–25.

16. E. Merton Coulter, *William G. Brownlow: Fighting Parson of the Southern Highlands* (Chapel Hill, 1937), 95–109; Holden, *Memoirs,* 10; Temple, *East Tennessee,* 547–48.

Some scalawags held reservations about slavery, as did other southerners, but before the war they had not gone public with their feelings. Later, many did, especially in states undergoing wartime Reconstruction—Arkansas, Louisiana, Tennessee, and Virginia—and in West Virginia, eventually admitted as a free state. Some freed their slaves before emancipation. So, given different circumstances and some encouragement, antislavery expressions developed. But attitudes among unionists were mixed and often changed within a few months. Some sought and received exemptions from freeing slaves in their areas under the provisions of the Emancipation Proclamation. One reason future Republicans in the South were not antislavery was, of course, that they owned slaves. Although fewer of them were slaveholders than were redeemers (two-thirds), still fully one-half of the scalawags owned slaves (see tables 1, 3, and 5). When the South is broken into regions, then a slightly different pattern emerges.[17]

One-third of scalawags from the Upper South owned slaves in 1860, compared with more than one-half of the section's redeemers. Fewer scalawags came from families residing in fertile agricultural areas, especially in the eastern section of Virginia and of North Carolina and of Middle and West Tennessee. With rare exceptions, only in North Carolina did planters, owners of twenty or more slaves, later become prominent Republicans. A similar situation existed in the Southwest, where most scalawags resided in nonplantation areas: northwestern Arkansas, southwestern Texas, and urban New Orleans. In the Lower South, a majority of both scalawags and redeemers held slaves in 1860. In Alabama, Florida, and Mississippi, the number of large slaveholders in the two groups varied less than in Georgia and South Carolina, where only one-half as many planters became scalawags as became redeemers. That there were fewer slaveholders among scalawags related only slightly to antagonism toward the peculiar institution; largely it reflected the location of their livelihood and to a lesser extent, less wealth and its trappings, including slaves.[18]

17. Local Citizens of the State of Tennessee to Abraham Lincoln, 4 December 1862, W. G. Brownlow to Lincoln, 25 December 1862, T. B. Thorpe and B. F. Flanders to Salmon P. Chase, 29 November 1862, W. D. Snow to Lincoln, 29 February 1864, Lincoln Papers; A. P. Dostie, *Freedom Versus Slavery, Address Delivered before the Free State Union Association of New Orleans, January 2, 1864* (New Orleans, 1864); Reid, *After the War*, 232–33; W. W. Clayton, *History of Davidson County, Tennessee, with Illustrations and Biographical Sketches of Its Prominent Men and Pioneers* (Nashville, 1880), 125; Frank Moore, ed., *The Rebellion Record: A Diary of American Events . . .* (New York, 1861–71), vol. 3, pt. 1: 100.

18. In most cases the source for the individual's estate and slaveholdings was the Eighth Census, RG 29.

At a time when slaves sold for $1,000 to $2,000 (and a workingman earned less than $10 a week), many scalawags as well as redeemers held small estates worth less than $10,000 in 1860, and these figures differ little from section to section. In a middle bracket of wealth, from $10,000 to $20,000, scalawags constitute only a slightly lower percentage in each section. Thirty-seven percent of redeemers compared with 26 percent of scalawags possessed over $20,000. The figure of $20,000 or more was later used by President Andrew Johnson to define one of the groups of Confederates who should be granted a presidential pardon.[19]

In the Upper South, North Carolinians accounted for more of the well-to-do among both groups, followed by Tennesseans, Virginians, and West Virginians. Not only did the estates of North Carolina scalawags exceed those of redeemers in other Upper South states, but they exceeded those of redeemers in five other states as well. Several scalawags from North Carolina possessed more than $100,000 (equivalent to considerably more than $1 million today). In the Southwest, scalawags and redeemers from Louisiana had estates in 1860 almost identical at all wealth brackets—perhaps because of the ten-year lower median age of redeemers—but in Arkansas and Texas, estate values of the two varied considerably, with scalawags having fewer large estates and more modest estates. Arkansas scalawags proved to be the poorest group of all; only Asa Hodges of Crittenden County, a planter with large slaveholdings near Memphis, was very wealthy. In the Lower South, only Alabama scalawags turned out to be as prosperous as their opposition (an explanation for why many of them later sought presidential pardons). As with Louisiana redeemers, the younger median age of Alabama redeemers may explain why the pattern varied from those of other states. Judges accounted for the greatest number of wealthy scalawags in Mississippi, mostly Whigs and planters—fitting David H. Donald's profile and black reconstructionist John R. Lynch's description of the judges as being "to the manor born."[20]

A larger universe, or sample, including less significant postwar officeholders might show a greater gulf between the estates of scalawags and redeemers. One study finds more difference in North Carolina in a larger sample than in a smaller one. Another comparing a large group of Alabama scalawags with the state's antebellum officeholders, however, finds little difference in their

19. Walter L. Fleming, ed., *Documentary History of Reconstruction: Political, Military, Social, Religious, Educational, and Industrial, 1865 to the Present Time* (New York, 1906–7), 1: 170.

20. Lynch, *Facts of Reconstruction*, 35, 37, 109; Lynch, *Bench and Bar*, 127, 185, 358, 361; Sansing, "Role of the Scalawag in Mississippi," 172–91.

economic status. Other works contend that white Republican voters, not just their leaders, were poorer than Democratic voters. Allen W. Trelease's study of the 1872 presidential election vote in the South shows that most scalawags resided in the less affluent areas of the South. Supporting this view is another work that finds a split along class lines occurred among Tennessee's Whigs in the postwar era, with the more affluent becoming Democrats and the less affluent becoming Republicans, regardless of their domicile. Studying southern Appalachian Republicans as a whole though, Gordon B. McKinney finds little, if any, appreciable difference between white supporters of the two parties.[21]

Both groups, scalawags and redeemers, included politicians who neither inherited nor accumulated large estates. While more scalawags came from the ranks of the less affluent, they were not poor. On the contrary, some were exceedingly wealthy. In several states, they were more prosperous than redeemers in other states. For example, the estates of North Carolina and Alabama scalawags exceeded those of redeemers in at least half of the states. And, significantly, because of a greater loss of slaves by redeemers, along with more ill-fated investments in the Lost Cause, the financial differential between them narrowed before 1866. Some redeemers were really rich only by reputation.

The greatest gap between the two political groups appears in the level of education attained (see tables 1, 3, and 5). Forty percent of scalawags attended college, compared with 60 percent of redeemers. Of those whose schooling ended at the academy stage (used here to describe college preparatory or classical studies), only a slight difference occurred between the groups. So while scalawags on the whole received fewer years of formal education, they were by no means ignorant or illiterate, as has been claimed by some. Their schooling exceeded that of southerners generally, and their professions, such as law, medicine, newspaper editing and publishing, and teaching, all demanded "book learning." Although fewer scalawags attended college, among those who did were graduates of Harvard, Yale, Princeton, and the finest medical schools. At least six scalawags were honor graduates of the University of North Carolina.

Several scalawags gained a degree of literary distinction. Their writings cov-

---

21. James L. Lancaster, "The Scalawags of North Carolina, 1850–1868" (Ph.D. diss., Princeton University, 1974), 350, 367–71; Milton Henry, "What Became of the Tennessee Whigs?" *THQ* 11 (March 1952): 61–62; McKinney, *Southern Mountain Republicans*, 15–16; Trelease, "Who Were the Scalawags?" 445–68. For a view of scalawag leaders in a few select counties, see Randolph B. Campbell, *Grass-Roots Reconstruction in Texas, 1865–1880* (Baton Rouge, 1997).

ered a wide spectrum of subjects, such as agriculture and antiquity, autobiography and biography, fraternal orders and folklore, history and politics, and economics and the law. Dr. Noah B. Cloud of Macon County, Alabama, whom Walter L. Fleming mistakenly labeled "without character, without education, and entirely without administrative ability," was a graduate of what later became the University of Pennsylvania School of Medicine. Cloud was a humane reformer interested in education and the well-being of southern slaves and a highly successful organizer of agricultural conventions and state fairs who wrote extensively about scientific farming in his *American Cotton Planter* and other agricultural journals. According to his biographer, "he possessed a flair for writing and at times a pen dipped in venom." Shortly before the Civil War, he served a term as a vice president of the United States Agricultural Society.[22]

Buckingham Smith of Saint Augustine ranged widely in his writing. Smith, born in the South of northern parents, graduated from Harvard Law School and followed his father into the diplomatic corps before returning to Florida in 1858. He wrote of the Florida Everglades, Giovanni da Verrazano's expedition, and Native American languages, in addition to translating for publication numerous Spanish and Portuguese works. Thomas B. Thorpe of Baton Rouge wrote, among other works, two popular collections of folk stories about frontier life. During the 1850s, after a twenty-year southern sojourn in Louisiana, he was able to make his livelihood as a writer in New York. And former congressman John F. H. Claiborne of Mississippi penned works of biography and history about the people of his state. Other scalawags wrote autobiographies, among them well-known Confederate generals turned Republicans James Longstreet and John S. Mosby. Some wrote books about secession and the war. Temple described his area before, during, and after the war, especially the origins of political parties, in *East Tennessee and the Civil War*. In *Notable Men of Tennessee*, he sketched the lives of unionists he knew.[23]

22. Weymouth T. Jordan, "Noah B. Cloud and the *American Cotton Planter*," *Agricultural History* 31 (October 1957), 44–49; Walter L. Fleming, *Civil War and Reconstruction in Alabama* (New York, 1905), 607.

23. *DAB*, 17: 243–44, which, however, incorrectly identifies Smith as attending the 1864 Democratic Convention; *The American Annual Cyclopaedia and Register of Important Events of the Year 1861, Embracing Political, Civil, Military, and Social Affairs; Public Documents; Biography; Statistics; Commerce; Finance; Literature; Science; Agriculture and Mechanical Industry* (New York, 1864–78), 4: 378–79; Rickels, *Thomas Bangs Thorpe*; James Longstreet, *From Manassas to Appomattox: Memories of the Civil War in America* (Philadelphia, 1896); John S. Mosby, *Mosby's War*

Then, as now, would-be officeholders, including scalawags, often were attorneys (see tables 1, 3, and 5). Overall, about 70 percent of scalawags and in
excess of 80 percent of redeemers studied law, passed the bar examination,
and practiced law. The percentage of scalawag lawyer officeholders ranged
from a bare majority of all scalawag officials in the Upper South to a slightly
higher percentage in the Southeast, to a high of almost 70 percent in the
Southwest. The combination of law and politics existed for several reasons.
Attorneys already were engaged in the business of law and accustomed to ar-
guing for a cause or a client, useful skills in the making of law. Attorneys often
represented a particular community constituency and thereby had a following
(in the case of scalawag lawyers, it often consisted of unionists and/or blacks).
They belonged to a profession that perpetuated its influence in politics. Perhaps most important of all, attorneys' work could be performed, if necessary,
intermittently, especially if they had law partners. Several law firms in the
South had more than one significant scalawag officeholder during Reconstruction. For example, Joseph E. Brown's firm in Atlanta contributed two
state supreme court justices and a federal attorney; Lewis E. Parsons's firm in
Talladega, Alabama, provided a lieutenant governor, a speaker of the state
house, and a congressman.[24]

Numerous newspapermen from antebellum Dixie eventually became Republicans, including two proverbial bootstrappers: Brownlow of the *Knoxville*

Reminiscences and Stuart's Cavalry Campaigns (Boston, 1887); William G. Brownlow, *Sketches of the Rise, Progress, and Decline of Secession: With a Narrative of Personal Adventures among the Rebels* (Philadelphia, 1862); James W. Hunnicutt, *The Conspiracy Unveiled: The South Sacrificed; or the Horrors of Secession* (Philadelphia, 1863); John M. Botts, *The Great Rebellion: Its Secret History, Rise, Progress, and Disastrous Failure* (New York, 1866); Henry S. Foote, *War of the Rebel-lion; or, Scylla and Charybdis: Consisting of Observations upon the Causes, Course, and Conse-quences of the Late Civil War in the United States* (New York, 1866); Alexander H. Jones, *Knocking at the Door: Alex H. Jones, Member-Elect to Congress; His Course before the War, during the War, and after the War* (Washington, D.C., 1866); George W. Paschal, *A Digest of Decisions of the Su-preme Court of Texas and of the United States upon Texas Law*, 3 vols. (Washington, D.C., 1872–75); William H. Bailey, *The Effects of the Civil War upon the Rights of Persons and Property* (Raleigh, N.C., 1867). Robert W. Hughes edited five volumes of federal circuit and district court reports.

24. Fannie Memory Farmer, "Legal Education in North Carolina, 1820–1860," *NCHR* 28 (July 1951): 271; Joseph H. Parks, *Joseph E. Brown of Georgia* (Baton Rouge, 1977), 467; Sarah Woolfolk Wiggins, "Five Men Called Scalawags," *Alabama Review* 17 (January 1964): 47, 50, 52–55; Barnett A. Elzas, *The Jews of South Carolina, from the Earliest Times to the Present Day* (Philadelphia, 1905), 197; Francis Butler Simkins and Robert Hilliard Woody, *South Carolina during Reconstruction* (Chapel Hill, 1932), 126–27; Brooks, *Bench and Bar*, 171, 195; *New Orleans Times*, 1 May 1865.

Whig, which with fourteen thousand subscribers enjoyed the largest circula-
tion in East Tennessee, and Holden, editor and publisher of the *(Raleigh)
North Carolina Standard* and sometimes state public printer. Holden, according to his own account, "cleared between 1850 and 1860 $8,000 per anum" (a
handsome sum for that day). Every southern state had scalawags who had
been antebellum editors; most had several, including Texas, where some edited German-language newspapers. Most of these editors, after stopping their
presses during the war, later resumed careers as publishers of Republican
newspapers. Scalawags also had been professors at public colleges, such as
those of North Carolina, Tennessee, Alabama, Mississippi, and Louisiana, or
at private institutions. In addition, scalawags once served as headmasters in
towns such as Charleston, New Orleans, and Austin. Of course, many scalawags (probably more than one hundred), as was true of so many young professional men, had once taught school.[25]

Since scalawags are often assumed to have been ne'er-do-wells thrust up-
ward by circumstance, some individuals have claimed scalawags never would
have been elected or appointed to public office by white men. To what extent,
if any, is this viewpoint valid? Had they had any political experience before
the beginning of Congressional Reconstruction in 1867? Had they been politi-
cal-party activists, delegates, officials, or candidates? Had they held public office during antebellum days? If so, how did the number of offices occupied by
scalawags compare to the number held by redeemers before the war? And how
do the two groups compare concerning the types and/or levels of the positions
held? Did this differ from state to state or from section to section (Upper
South, Southeast, and Southwest)? Had those who later became Republican
officeholders been Whigs or Democrats? Finally, was there a relationship between the number of offices held and the fact that many scalawags had once
belonged to a minority party, the Whigs, or to a minority faction in the majority Democratic Party?

Most scalawags had political experience before the beginning of Congressional Reconstruction in 1867 (see tables 2, 4, and 6). Newspaper accounts of
the 1860 presidential campaign, the 1861 secession crisis, and the postwar
contests of 1865 and 1866 show that most ran for office, campaigned for others, or supported their political party's rallies. For example, in Austin, Texas,

25. Granville D. Hall, "Hon. Archibald W. Campbell," in Parker, *Formation of the State of
West Virginia,* 202–6; *DAB,* 7: 390–91, 9: 357–58; Holden, *Memoirs,* 98; *DNCB* 1: 103; Temple,
Notable Men of Tennessee, 137.

among those active in the 1860 presidential election who later became Republican officeholders were two postwar governors, one United States senator, four state supreme court judges, six state cabinet members, and several federal officials. Much the same could be said of New Orleans scalawag officeholders. About one-fourth of the southern delegates to the 1860 Constitutional Union Party National Convention were future Republicans. Most of the leading campaigners for that party in Texas later became Republicans. Such was also the case with Douglas Democrats in North Carolina, where all surviving Douglas presidential electors running in 1860 joined the Republican Party during Reconstruction. Few redeemers could rival the political exploits of Henry S. Foote, who served as a senator from Mississippi, as that state's governor after defeating Jefferson Davis, and as a Confederate congressman from Nashville, Tennessee.[26]

Further evidence that many scalawags had political experience appears in pardon applications requesting Congress to remove office-holding sanctions from those "having previously taken an oath" as officeholders "to support the constitution of the United States" later "engaged in insurrection or rebellion against the same, or given aid or comfort to the enemies thereof." In 1868, Congress lifted the sanction for 1,350 prewar officeholders who later aided the Confederacy, primarily so Republicans recently elected or appointed could hold office again. In Alabama alone, for example, about two hundred officeholders sought congressional relief.[27]

On the whole, however, fewer scalawags than redeemers held office before the war, especially in the highest positions. Many scalawags had served at the district or local level, 40 percent compared with more than 50 percent of the redeemers. But less than 10 percent had served in federal or state positions, compared with 20 percent of redeemers. Scalawags had occupied lower offices typically occupied by less prominent individuals. But they were not strangers to politics or office. More often than not during the 1850s, scalawags were affiliated with a minority party or a small minority faction within the majority party espousing reforms or losing causes. This caused fewer of them to be

26. "Henry S. Foote Autobiographical Sketch," John Francis Hamtramck Claiborne Papers, Southern Historical Collection.

27. Jonathan T. Dorris, *Pardon and Amnesty under Lincoln and Johnson: The Restoration of the Confederates to Their Rights and Privileges* (Chapel Hill, 1953), 67–68; James Wilford Garner, *Reconstruction in Mississippi* (New York, 1901), 272n; William McKinley Cash, "Alabama Republicans during Reconstruction: Characteristics, Motivation, and Political Activity of Party Activists, 1867–1880" (Ph.D. diss., University of Alabama, 1973), 77–78.

elected to public office. In a few cases, of course, individuals who simply had been unsuccessful in their quest for public office before the war seized the opportunity, becoming Republicans during Reconstruction. Neither group, scalawags nor redeemers, had really arrived politically in 1860. But as the 1860s dawned, redeemers rather than scalawags were more likely candidates for the highest offices.

The greatest contrast in officeholding occurred in the Upper South, where 40 percent of scalawags, compared with 70 percent of redeemers, were prewar officeholders. Only nine scalawags (all Whigs), compared with twenty-six re-deemers, had been antebellum members of Congress. Neither group had held many state offices; scalawags were outnumbered by about two to one. But in North Carolina, about the same number of each group had held state posi-tions. There, as in Alabama, some scalawags served as officeholders before, during, and immediately after the war as well as during Congressional Recon-struction. Many scalawags, especially those from East Tennessee and western Virginia, served as local officials before they engaged in a "true" civil war. One-half of Southeast scalawags were prewar officeholders, compared with three-fourths of Southeast redeemers. Some scalawags held several offices over an extended period. More than one-third of Alabama and Mississippi scala-wags occupied seats in the state legislature before the war, as did a few from Georgia. Several from Georgia also once served locally, including a number of mayors.

Other scalawags held office during the war and shortly thereafter, well be-fore Congressional Reconstruction. Blocs of future scalawags not only served in the wartime unionist governments of the Virginias, Tennessee, Louisiana, and Arkansas and parts of those administrations that extended into the post-war period, but also many scalawags served within blocs in the postwar con-stitutional conventions of North Carolina, Alabama, and Texas and in the postwar legislature of North Carolina. According to one study, "a pervasive characteristic" of Alabama's scalawag leaders was "continuity in office holding from antebellum times through war and Presidential Reconstruction into the Congressional Reconstruction years." This seemed to have been especially the case for those from north Alabama.[28]

Some South Carolinians had been influential local politicians before be-coming Republicans after the Civil War. Such was James L. Orr's law partner,

28. Cash, "Alabama Republicans," 381.

Jacob P. Reed, described by a conservative historian as "a gentleman of high character and high standing." Their firm for many years accounted for almost half the law practice in Anderson County. Reed, like Orr a part-time planter and a "staunch Democrat," served his party and his community as a state and national party convention delegate, circuit court solicitor, secession convention delegate, and congressional candidate. York County included such future Republicans as Alexander S. Wallace, a popular politician and farmer from Turkey Creek whose followers had elected him to the state legislature. Wallace obtained credit for his supporters at a friend's store in Yorkville, and his supporters in turn created a business boom The store became a gathering site for Wallace and his flock. Samuel W. Melton, the town's postmaster and publisher of the *Yorkville Inquirer,* was also a leading local opinion maker before joining the law firm of his brother Cyrus D. Melton, a member of the state legislature, at Chester in 1857.[29]

Scalawags from the Southwest stacked up alongside their opponents in officeholding slightly better than did scalawags elsewhere. Forty percent served in some government position before the war, compared with about 55 percent of redeemers. While scalawags from the Southwest may have held somewhat lower-level offices, they were hardly strangers to government. The postwar Republican Texas governors were during the 1850s Congressman Andrew J. Hamilton and Governor Elisha M. Pease of Austin and Judge Edmund J. Davis of Corpus Christi. Scalawags from Louisiana had been councilmen or school board members at the local level and legislators or judges at the district level. One-third of Arkansas scalawags in this study served as legislators during the 1850s. Most were natives of the Upper South; some were Democrats and others Whigs. Among them were future governors Isaac Murphy of Huntsville, Alabama, and Elisha Baxter of Batesville, Arkansas; state supreme court justices; and Confederate generals turned postwar federal officeholders. Some from the Southwest brought office-holding experience from elsewhere.[30]

29. Brooks, *Bench and Bar,* 171–95; John S. Reynolds, *Reconstruction in South Carolina, 1865–1877* (Columbia, S.C., 1905), 295; Elzas, *Jews of South Carolina,* 197–99; Eighth Census, RG 29; Anne King Gregorie, *History of Sumter County, South Carolina* (Sumter, S.C., 1954), 228; *Cyclopedia of Eminent and Representative Men of the Carolinas of the Nineteenth Century* (Madison, Wis., 1892), 1: 98–99, 565; Lacy K. Ford Jr., *Origins of Southern Radicalism: The South Carolina Upcountry, 1800–1860* (New York, 1988), 90, 187, 316, 319–20; Joel Williamson, *After Slavery: The Negro in South Carolina during Reconstruction, 1861–1877* (Chapel Hill, 1965), 368, 374.

30. Edward C. Billings, *The Struggle between the Civilization of Slavery and That of Freedom, Recently and Now Going on in Louisiana* (Hatfield, Mass., 1873), 29; E. Russ Williams, "John Ray: Forgotten Scalawag," *Louisiana Studies* 13 (fall 1974): 241–62; "Ex-Governor Isaac Murphy,"

Many younger scalawags without government experience in 1861 had politics rub off on them from their kinfolk. A number of Alabama scalawags, for example, were sons of state judges or legislators. Several also had grandfathers who had held political offices; others had brothers, cousins, nephews, and uncles involved in politics. Kinship ties through blood and through marriage abounded among scalawag officeholders; nepotism was common, perhaps at times necessary, to find qualified Republicans. Many families had more than one member who held an office as a Republican. For example, in the Upper South, prominent scalawag families included the family of Senator John F. Lewis of the Shenandoah Valley in Virginia; in North Carolina, there were Alfred Dockery and Daniel L. Russell and their sons; and East Tennessee had the Brownlows of Knoxville, headed by Parson Brownlow; and West Tennessee had the Hawkins clan of Huntingdon, including Governor Alvin Hawkins.

Among questions often asked about scalawags is what was their previous political party affiliation, the answer to which was thought to have implications about their social status and their loyalty to the Union. Donald first seriously raised the issue. According to Donald, of those scalawags serving in Mississippi government, "almost every one . . . had before the war been an old-line Whig and a bitter opponent of the Democrats." Their joining the Republican Party, he writes, "is not hard to understand. The Whigs were wealthy men—the large planters and the railroad promoters—who naturally turned to the party which in the state as in the nation was dominated by business interests." Later he extended his Whig thesis of scalawag origins to include all the former Confederate states except North Carolina and Alabama (ironically, two of the states in addition to Tennessee in which others have shown that Whigs dominated the Reconstruction Republican Party). He says that in those two states scalawags "appear to have been largely hill-county farmers, who had been opposed to the plantation-slavery system before the Civil War and had been disaffected toward the Confederacy during the war," that is, they were former Democrats. Eventually many other historians adopted his conclusions.[31]

What can be made of Donald's seemingly strange claim that these individuals formerly belonged to the political party of greater social standing if, as almost everyone had claimed, scalawags came from a lower social level than did their redeemer counterparts? The apparent contradiction may not be one

---

newspaper clipping, n.d., James R. Berry Papers, Arkansas History Commission, Little Rock; John Hallum, *Biographical and Pictorial History of Arkansas* (Albany, N.Y., 1887), 300, 412–14.

31. Donald, "Scalawag in Mississippi," 448.

at all. Despite a once widely held view that the Whig Party was almost exclusively a rich man's party, both political parties consisted of all classes. The degree of difference, however, may have varied from region to region within a state, thereby producing a stable and competitive two-party system. Scholars have shown, for example, that North Carolina Whigs were "broadly based both geographically and socially" and that Alabama Whigs were "no more exclusively the 'silk stocking' party . . . than the Democracy was exclusively the party of the 'common man.'" Otherwise, Whig politicians never could have been elected.[32]

Family party identification generally fixed individual loyalty to a political party before the Civil War; party affiliation, like religious affiliation, usually passed from father to son. What Dr. Joseph E. Manlove of Nashville said about himself was, in principle, true of others: "My youthful political prejudices . . . were formed in 1824 . . . for no reason of my own, but . . . in favor of my father's choice . . . I became then, an Adams' man." Then he summarized thirty-five years of identifying as a Whig: "With that party in its various names and phases I have always been associated. In 1860 I voted for Bell & Everett— with their short but significant platform." Although Whig identifiers during the 1850s declined slightly in numbers because of the slavery issue intensifying and because some Whigs resented the nativistic platform of Know-Nothingism, individual party affiliation generally remained the same. Though the Whig Party ran no more presidential candidates under its label after 1852, the faithful, such as Manlove, still considered themselves Whigs whichever appellation—American, Opposition, or Constitutional Union—was used to attract adherents. In classifying individuals by their party affiliation during the 1850s, this work therefore follows *The Anatomy of the Confederate Congress:* "Members of the American and Constitutional Union Parties are considered Whigs (since, in the South, the former parties were essentially the latter under different nomenclature) unless they had a Democratic party affiliation between 1848 and the time they became Know-Nothings or Constitutional Unionists."[33]

32. Max R. Williams,"The Foundations of the Whig Party in North Carolina: A Synthesis and a Modest Proposal," *NCHR* 47 (spring 1970): 129; Alexander, *Reconstruction in Tennessee,* 13; Grady McWhiney, "Were the Whigs a Class Party in Alabama?" *JSH* 23 (November 1957): 522; William H. Adams, "The Louisiana Whig Party" (Ph.D. diss., Louisiana State University, 1960); David N. Young, "The Mississippi Whigs, 1834–1860" (Ph.D. diss., University of Alabama, 1958), 157.

33. Manlove to Genl. Gillem or Gov. Johnson, 28 January 1863, in *Papers of Andrew Johnson,* ed. Leroy P. Graf and Ralph W. Haskins (Knoxville, 1967–), 6: 128–31; Thomas B. Alexander and Richard E. Beringer, *The Anatomy of the Confederate Congress: A Study of the Influences of Member Characteristics on Legislative Voting Behavior, 1861–1865* (Nashville, 1972), 350.

Following their party's demise, southern Whigs voted for the new coalition, or new party, identified with the defunct Whigs, the American Party (1856–57), the Opposition Party (1858–59), and the Constitutional Union Party (1860). In 1856, they voted for Millard Fillmore and the American Party (commonly called the Know-Nothing Party). However, that party's nationalistic/nativistic platform failed. It did not distract the country from the issue of slavery as members had hoped. The American Party crashed on the same rock that earlier destroyed the "Conscience Whigs" and "Cotton Whigs" coalition: slavery's expansion. From the 1856 Whig wreckage emerged Opposition Party spokesmen hoping to coalesce the nation's conservatives. They offered a haven for Whigs isolated by tradition from the Democratic Party and repelled by the Republican Party's sectional and radical nature. These Whigs championed the so-called Opposition Party (that is, opposition to the Democratic Party), which ran candidates in state elections. Results for Opposition candidates proved negative in the North, where most Whigs and Know-Nothing holdouts became conservative Republicans. But in the South, the Opposition Party captured seats in the legislatures, elected some congressmen, and controlled the ballots of Whigs.[34]

Opposition Party leaders received in December 1859 the blessings of the dormant, but still official, national executive committees of the Whig and American Parties to form the Constitutional Union Party. The following May at Baltimore, the Constitutional Union Party National Convention nominated John Bell of Tennessee, a former Whig senator, for president. They also endorsed a brief platform calling for support of the Constitution, the Union, and the law, and left to state parties the adoption of platforms suitable for their constituencies. Most scalawags supported the Constitutional Union Party, some as national convention delegates, including at least twenty from the Upper South; many as state or district convention delegates; and others as presidential electors. They helped the party to win a majority in Virginia, Kentucky, and Tennessee; to run a close race in North Carolina; and to exceed 30 percent of the vote in another four states. The vote really continued along traditional party lines. Altogether, the vote for Bell was 41 percent, only 4 percent less than the 1856 vote for Millard Fillmore.[35]

34. John B. Stabler, "A History of the Constitutional Union Party: A Tragic Failure" (Ph.D. diss., Columbia University, 1954).

35. Stabler, "History of the Constitutional Union Party," 459–60; *Marshall Harrison Flag,* 20 July 1860; William B. Hesseltine, ed., *Three against Lincoln: Murat Halstead Reports the Caucuses of 1860* (Baton Rouge, 1960), 126, 285–96; Dwight Lowell Dumond, *The Secession Movement,*

One historian contends the reputation of the Constitutional Union Party for antisecessionism "derives from a fallacious interpretation of the campaign of 1860 as a referendum on secession in the South." He holds that the party voiced strong sentiments for federal protection of slavery in the territories. Moreover, he concludes that all contending political parties in the South contained lovers of the Union and that large numbers of them voted for Democrat John C. Breckinridge. Such claims are true but are not the total story.[36] By denying differences existed between the Democratic and the Constitutional Union Parties, he confuses campaign rhetoric with a record of conservatism and nationalism. Appeals to voters often brought the pronouncements (and perhaps outlook) of political parties closer together; still, this did not make the parties identical. Of course, many unionists voted for Breckinridge, but most did not. Moreover, the secessionist leadership came from the Democrats, and in the crisis of 1860 antisecessionist leadership came mostly from former Whigs.[37]

In the Upper South during Reconstruction, of almost six hundred politicians, more than three-fourths of the scalawags and more than one-half of the redeemers had been prewar Whigs (see table 2). A combination of circumstances, including disillusionment, disfranchisement, and disqualification from office, kept former secessionist Democrats from wielding the power they exercised before the war. Because former Whigs dominated both postwar parties in the Upper South, a schism must have occurred within their ranks in each state. A survey of the 1860 Upper South national convention delegates and presidential electors shows the following: Breckinridge and Douglas Democrats from Tennessee and Virginia remained Democrats after the war, whereas Douglas Democrats from North Carolina became Republicans. Whig leaders in North Carolina and Tennessee divided into Democrats and Republicans; and most 1860 Whig leaders of Virginia became Democrats, leaving the door open for less prominent Whigs and a few antebellum Republicans.[38]

1860–1861 (New York, 1931), 93–94; Thomas B. Alexander, "Whiggery and Reconstruction in Tennessee," *JSH* 16 (August 1950): 294–95; J. G. de Roulhac Hamilton, *Reconstruction in North Carolina* (New York, 1914), 243–44; Jack Maddex Jr., *The Virginia Conservatives, 1867–1879: A Study in Reconstruction Politics* (Chapel Hill, 1970), 38; Richard Orr Curry, "A Reappraisal of Statehood Politics in West Virginia," *JSH* 28 (November 1962): 421; Walter Dean Burnham, *Presidential Ballots: 1836–1892* (Baltimore, 1955).

36. John V. Mering, "The Slave-State Constitutional Unionists and the Politics of Consensus," *JSH* 43 (August 1977): 395–410.

37. James Alex Baggett, "The Constitutional Union Party in Texas," *SwHQ* 82 (January 1979): 233–34.

38. Hesseltine, *Three against Lincoln,* 284–92.

ANTEBELLUM ORIGINS
35

If three-fourths of the Upper South's scalawags had been Whigs, then, of course, all of the others, with the exception of a few prewar Republicans and a few who had not reached adulthood, once were Democrats. One study of more than two hundred North Carolina scalawag officeholders whose prewar politics could be identified found that about 20 percent had been Democrats, more than one-third of whom had supported Stephen A. Douglas in 1860, several as party delegates or electors. Many friends of Raleigh publisher Holden (himself a secret supporter of Douglas) were founders of the Republican Party in North Carolina. Fewer outspoken secessionist Democrats found their way into Republican circles. Indeed few tried. But among those who did were two North Carolina Coastal Plain attorneys and former Confederate colonels, William B. Rodman of Beaufort County and Edward Cantwell of Wilmington.

Other Douglas Democrats emerged as leaders in the West Virginia Republican Party. In Virginia and Tennessee, former Democrats remained a negligible factor, representing fewer than 15 percent of Republican Party leaders during Reconstruction. The lone former Democrat of significance among Virginia scalawags seems to have been future federal judge Robert W. Hughes, *Richmond State Journal* editor and son-in-law of onetime governor John B. Floyd. One study of eighty-seven leaders in East Tennessee with known political party affiliations in 1861 found that of the unionists at least two-thirds were Whigs and one-third Democrats. About one-fourth of the wartime unionist Whigs eventually became Conservatives (and afterward Democrats), "while only one of the pre-war Democrats who became a Unionist is known to have changed to the Radical party and later to the Republican party."[39]

Even fewer scalawags, of course, had been prewar Republicans. Although the Republican Party had emerged nationally by the mid-1850s, it had barely penetrated the South before the war. Lincoln got fewer than 30,000 votes in five border states, one-half of which came from Missouri (he was not on the ballot in the Lower South). Of the seceding states, Virginia alone had an organized antebellum Republican Party, which existed almost completely in the northwestern section, founded by Free-Soilers in the mid-1850s. In 1856 and 1860, Virginia Republicans had sent delegates to the national conventions and

39. Atkinson and Gibbens, *Prominent Men*, 271–72, 585–89; Granville D. Hall, *The Rending of Virginia: A History* (Chicago, 1901), 227, 251; Ambler and Summers, *West Virginia*, 249; *DAB*, 9: 357–58; Verton M. Queener, "The Origins of the Republican Party in East Tennessee," *ETHSP* 13 (1941): 75–76; Jon L. Wakelyn, *Biographical Dictionary of the Confederacy* (Westport, Conn., 1977), 501.

presented presidential electoral tickets. Also with northern financial support, they had published a few party-backed newspapers, such as the *Wheeling Intelligencer*, the *Wellsburg Herald*, and the *Ceredo Crescent*. In the presidential election of 1860, their candidate, Abraham Lincoln, received almost 2,000 votes in the state. A few scalawag officeholders were prewar Virginia Republicans. Still, by no means did prewar Republicans compose more than a small percentage of Reconstruction leaders.[40]

In the Southeast as a whole, former Whigs were less numerous among scalawags. But excluding South Carolina, a one-party Democratic state, former Whig Republicans outnumbered former Democratic ones in states other than Florida. Former Whig Republicans were especially numerous in Mississippi and Alabama. Generally these men had greater feelings of nationalism, and after the war they were more likely than Democrats to affiliate with another party. Although Donald may have exaggerated Whig-Republican connections in Mississippi, former Whigs figured more prominently there than elsewhere in the Lower South (see table 4), outnumbering former Democrats two to one. Mississippi scalawags may have been "a varied lot" politically, as has been claimed, but in what proportions? Lumping them together—including local officeholders and nonofficeholders along with high-level officials—proves far less than does a well-defined universe. According to another study, one with a well-defined universe, Alabama Republicans were twice as likely to have been Whigs.[41]

Many scalawags strongly identified with the Whig Party. The author of *James Lusk Alcorn: Persistent Whig* claims that Alcorn's "temperament, beliefs, and ambitions" drew him to the Whig Party and that he "never really lost his political identification with the Whigs, any more than he did his class identification." His vision in the early 1870s was to rally former Mississippi Whigs under the Republican banner. He thought of himself as a Whig into the 1890s, fifty years after that party ran its last presidential campaign. Congressman Joshua Hill of Morgan County, Georgia, clung to his "Whig faith" out of hatred for the Democratic Party. He was said to be "one of a few gentlemen in

40. Lowe, "Republican Party in Antebellum Virginia," 259–79; *Proceedings of the First Three Republican National Conventions, 1856, 1860, and 1864, as Reported by Horace Greeley* (Minneapolis, 1893), 10, 123–24; *Wheeling Intelligencer*, 1 October 1856; Republican Party of Virginia broadside, 1 October 1860, John C. Underwood to Lyman Trumbull, 6 December 1858, Lincoln Papers.

41. Harris, "Reconsideration of the Mississippi Scalawag," 39; Cash, "Alabama Republicans," 313.

the South so utterly anti-democratic that they would have gone anywhere on earth before they would have affiliated with the Democratic party on any terms." Other Georgia Republicans felt so close to their Whig roots that in the 1870s they called their party's state newspaper the *Atlanta Whig*.[42]

Yet Whiggery among Republicans should not be exaggerated. As well as constituting a majority in South Carolina and Florida, former Democrats accounted for a large minority elsewhere among white Republicans. Some served as 1860 national convention delegates or as presidential electors, mostly for Stephen A. Douglas. A number of Douglas leaders hailed from the northern part of Alabama, a few until 1860 having identified with the Whigs. Most of these unionist Democrats had been active in antisecessionist fusion parties during the 1850s, including several congressmen who later became Republicans. In one-party South Carolina during the 1850s, many future scalawags, including Orr and some of his Upland friends, who were known as National Democrats, opposed the states' rights wing of the state's party. They saw the National Democratic Party as the best hope for serving their state's interests and for keeping it in the Union. Nationally, they hoped to create a coalition of proslavery Democrats to control the party in Congress and at the national conventions. These goals were partially realized with the presidential nominees of the 1850s and Orr's election as Speaker of the House of Representatives in 1856. Within South Carolina, the men wanted to promote democratic reform and to further the Upland area's interests, which they thought had been overlooked and underrepresented.[43]

In the Southwest, as elsewhere, many scalawags took pride in their former association with the Whig Party and its onetime advocate Henry Clay, their "beau ideal of public men." Biographical sketches of scalawags include such comments as "brought up at the feet of old Henry Clay" and "early drawn into politics as a Whig." Texans showed their Whiggery before the Civil War by supporting the national party, fielding gubernatorial candidates in 1851

---

42. Lillian A. Pereyra, *James Lusk Alcorn: Persistent Whig* (Baton Rouge, 1966), 8; Powell, "Fifty-five Years in West Alabama," 638; Judson C. Ward Jr., "The Republican Party in Bourbon Georgia, 1872–1890," *JSH* 9 (May 1943): 208; *KKK Report*, Ga., 765; Olive Hall Shadgett, *The Republican Party in Georgia, from Reconstruction through 1900* (Athens, Ga., 1964), 58.

43. James Q. Smith to Stephen A. Douglas, 29 April, 31 October 1859, Joseph C. Bradley to Douglas, 31 August 1860, David C. Humphrey to Douglas, 28 October 1860, Stephen A. Douglas Papers, University of Chicago, Chicago, Ill.; Laura A. White, "The National Democrats in South Carolina, 1852 to 1860," *South Atlantic Quarterly* 28 (October 1929): 370–89; Lillian A. Kibler, "Unionist Sentiment in South Carolina in 1860," *JSH* 4 (August 1938): 346–66.

and 1853, and advocating a policy of "Union, internal improvements, disbursement of public revenue for education, and amendment of the state constitution to permit the chartering of banks," positions all later espoused by Texas Republicans. They and their contemporaries thought it natural, or at least understandable, for them to move from the Whig Party to the Republican Party, because they disliked Democrats and had never forgiven them for secession and the war.

Anthony B. Norton, onetime publisher of the *Fort Worth Whig Chief*, a supporter of Sam Houston, and one of the founders of the Texas Republican Party, unequivocally deserves the distinction of being the most extreme example among this group by virtue of his oath during the election of 1844. While still an Ohio resident, he swore "before God and man" he "would neither shave nor have his hair cut until Henry Clay was elected president." Given a silver-dollar-headed ash walking cane by a grateful Clay, Norton proved to be a man of his word: when he died in 1893, "his hair and beard were yet untrimmed."[44]

Because non-Democrats in Texas were too few in the mid-1850s to win elections alone, the Know-Nothings (former Whigs) combined with Sam Houston's disaffected union Democrats. In 1859, the coalition, which included hundreds of Germans who felt that Houston had renounced his Know-Nothingism of the mid-1850s, triumphed over the fire-eater Democratic regulars. Next they pushed for a Houston nomination to head the newly formed Constitutional Union Party ticket—an effort lost on the second ballot at Baltimore in 1860. Eventually Houston and his die-hard followers formed a state fusion party with the supporters of Constitutional Unionist John Bell and those of Democrat Stephen A. Douglas, including the many German admirers of Douglas. The state party "pledged to vote for the most available candidate to defeat Lincoln." Significantly, as far as Reconstruction is concerned, most of these Constitutional Union campaigners eventually became Republicans, including former Whigs as well as prominent union Democrats, particularly those from Austin. Indeed, the Texas Constitutional Union Party

---

44. *Official Report of the Proceedings of the Republican State Convention Held at Fort Worth, April 29 and 30 and May 1, 1884* (Austin, Tex., 1884), 18, 106; Rickels, *Thomas Bangs Thorpe*, 91, 169; A. P. Field to Abraham Lincoln, 20 September 1863, Lincoln Papers; S. Belden to Henry Clay Warmoth, 20 February 1866, Henry Clay Warmoth Papers, Southern Historical Collection; James K. Greer, "Louisiana Politics, 1845–1861," *LHQ* 13 (July 1930): 654–56; Oliver Knight, *Fort Worth: Outpost on the Trinity* (Norman, Okla., 1953), 46–47.

of 1860 (actually the remains of Houston's coalition) provided the nucleus for the formation of the Texas Republican Party.[45]

As in Texas, an opposition fusion party in Louisiana ran candidates in the 1859 state election, including two future Republicans, former Whig John Ray, of Monroe for lieutenant governor, and former Democrat Thomas J. Durant of New Orleans for attorney general. Unlike the Houston coalition, however, the Louisiana coalition carried less than 40 percent of the vote and failed to field a ticket in the next presidential election. In 1860, Opposition Party politicians again divided along national party lines—with Whigs backing Bell, and union Democrats declaring for Douglas. As in Alabama, however, some individual Whigs, such as James Madison Wells, supported Douglas.

Several spokesmen for Douglas in New Orleans, such as Durant and Michael Hahn, a member of the Little Giant's state committee, helped found the wartime Louisiana Republican Party. Their presence in the Republican Party was partly a result of their strong nationalistic sentiments and weak ties to the slave system. Even more significant were their opportunities when the Union army occupied lower Louisiana. Because of the roles these Douglas supporters played in Union-controlled New Orleans, most of the state's scalawags have been labeled former Douglas Democrats. But this was not the case. Only about 40 percent have been identified as former Democrats, few of whom backed Breckinridge in 1860; all the other Republicans were former Whigs, about one-half of whom resided in Orleans Parish, with the remainder from parishes throughout the state.[46]

In Arkansas, politicians did not create an Opposition coalition of Whigs and union Democrats during the latter 1850s. There the minority Whigs of-

45. Baggett, "Constitutional Union Party," 236, 240–48; James Alex Baggett, "Origins of Early Texas Republican Party Leadership," *JSH* 40 (August 1974): 445.

46. *New Orleans Weekly Delta,* 17 September 1859; Stabler, "History of the Constitutional Union Party," 184, 616–29; Thomas J. Burke to Stephen A. Douglas, 28 May 1860, Douglas Papers; Walter M. Lowrey, "The Political Career of James Madison Wells," *LHQ* 31 (October 1948): 1003; John Slidell to James Buchanan, 11 November 1860, reprinted in Louis M. Sears, *John Slidell* (Durham, N.C., 1925), 174; *New Orleans Era,* 31 January 1864; Michael Hahn to Abraham Lincoln, 3 July 1863, Lincoln Papers; Donald E. Reynolds, *Editors Make War: Southern Newspapers in the Secession Crisis* (Nashville, 1970), 74; *New York Tribune,* 8 June 1864; Peyton McCrary, *Abraham Lincoln and Reconstruction: The Louisiana Experiment* (Princeton, N.J., 1978), 53n, 251; Robert W. Taliaferro to James G. Taliaferro, 1 June 1864, James G. Taliaferro and Family Papers, Louisiana and Lower Mississippi Valley Collections, Louisiana State University Libraries, Baton Rouge; *Report of the Select Committee on the New Orleans Riots of July 30, 1866* (Washington, D.C., 1866), 467–68.

fered only feeble resistance to Democratic control. Lack of significant differences within or between the parties impeded the rise of a fusion party. Antisecessionists dominated both parties. Although union Democrats lacked a reason to abandon their own party, a small Douglas faction did develop in 1860. Once the Illinois senator had been popular in Arkansas, and he still had supporters (including several future Republican leaders). Whether most of the Democrats who later became Republicans supported Douglas or Breckinridge in 1860 is unknown. The individuals who eventually formed the state's Republican Party had largely known each other on the local level, as friends and kin. For example, in Huntsville a number of relatives, neighbors, and friends filled several state offices during Reconstruction. But these local politicos came together statewide only as a result of the war, when pockets of anti-Confederate sentiment united through Union Leagues and military camaraderie in the Union army.[47]

While many Southwest scalawags were Whigs, most were not. Of those whose prewar partisanship is identified, only in Louisiana did former Whigs outnumber former Democrats (four to three); in Arkansas, the reverse was true, and in Texas, former Democrats outnumbered former Whigs two to one. Among redeemers, former Democrats were even more numerous, exceeding former Whigs nearly three to one (see table 6). The prewar party identification of scalawags as a group resulted largely from the nature of the Opposition Party (1857–59) within each section: totally Whiggish in the Upper South, mostly so in the Lower South, while in the Southwest, at least in Louisiana and Texas, fusion parties developed. Altogether, the greater identification of former Whigs with the Republican Party in the South has more to do with the particular political circumstances in a given state than with the appeal of a particular political philosophy, although stronger unionist sentiment among former Whigs throughout the South was a significant factor.

Still, a substantial majority of scalawags in the Upper South viewed the Republican Party as the Whig Party's successor. Scalawag leaders there had been Whigs, those with the will to resist the Confederacy, mainly those from less affluent mountainous areas, where slavery was weakest. The more unwa-

---

47. Ralph A. Wooster, *The Secession Conventions of the South* (Princeton, N.J., 1962), 155, 170; Luther C. White to Stephen A. Douglas, 14 July 1858, Isaac Murphy to Douglas, 25 November 1858, Robert J. T. White to Douglas, 30 January 1860, Douglas Papers; Granville Davis, "Arkansas and the Little Giant," *WTHSP* 22 (1968): 30–50; William D. Snow to Abraham Lincoln, 16 November 1860, Lincoln Papers.

vering their unionism, the more likely these unionists were to become Republicans. Those individuals saw the Republican Party as the Whig Party's logical successor as a political party in standing for union, nationalism, and improvement through federal action. Joseph E. Segar in 1867 stated it thus: "I am an Old Line Whig of the Henry Clay, Daniel Webster type, or more properly, a Federalist of the olde school. I struggled for the Union in Secession's gloomy hour."[48]

Not all unionists who became Republicans had been Whigs, not even in the Upper South and especially not in the Lower South. More than one unionist political tradition existed. This was reflected in the 1860 election, where Stephen A. Douglas, a strong nationalist on the ballot, represented one wing of the Democratic Party. Although he drew only a small vote in the South, his campaigners were a determined lot and a significant number of them later became Republicans. Within every Confederate state were those who still agreed with Andrew Jackson that the "Federal Union . . . must be preserved." In some cases, their determination to restore the Union led them to join the Republican Party.

48. Alexander, *Reconstruction in Tennessee*, 37.

2

~

Opposing Secession

Whatever their political party allegiance in 1860, future scalawags over-whelmingly opposed secession, even after Lincoln's election in No-vember. Those serving as legislators at the time contested their states' seizures of federal property, the summoning of a secession convention, and the finan-cing of war preparations. As citizens, they created antisecessionist committees, campaigned for unionist candidates for office, and in some cases ran for seats to the state conventions as antisecessionists themselves. Those elected as dele-gates sought to delay their states' separation from the Union. Everywhere, they fought secession, publicly and privately, in the press and on the stump. When secession came, many serving as public officials still refused to take an oath of allegiance to the Confederacy. They hoped that the next election would undo what the secessionists had done.

Even in the Southeast, where secession commenced, over 80 percent of scalawags opposed their state's withdrawal from the Union (see table 4). If one excludes heavily black South Carolina and Mississippi, scalawags against secession in the Southeast varied little from those elsewhere. This is not to say, however, that all equally supported staying in the Union whatever the situation or that all opposed secession with the same intensity. Broadly they fell into two groups, unconditional unionists and conditional unionists. Within the conditional unionists' ranks, variations existed depending upon their convictions, often expressed in constitutional terms, and the circum-stances of their lives. In the weeks following Lincoln's election, most scalawags from the Southeast took their stance as conditional unionists. They joined with others against immediate secession in what was known as the cooperationist movement. Cooperationists opposed secession without having a referendum, and they opposed states seceding singularly. Whatever the final decision, they urged a united front by all, or at least most, southern states. Being a cooperationist meant one not only had a willingness to negotiate with Washington and a willingness to wait for the decision of other southern states but also a willingness to abide by the decision to secede if that became the only honorable option.

Patriotism for most southerners, as David M. Potter states, was "constructed upon faithfulness to a particular place and people and past, not upon some abstract idea such as 'democracy' or 'freedom.'" For southerners being an unconditional unionist entailed more than standing for "the abstraction of national loyalty"; it meant forsaking "dearer concrete loyalties" such as "familiar surroundings, esteem of friends, long associations, and not infrequently, love of family itself." Former senator Henry S. Foote of Nashville, Tennessee, claimed he "held out firmly against the Disunion movement . . . until the war . . . commenced, and . . . all his nearest friends and kindred, including his own sons, had enlisted in the disunion cause." After a given point, being an unconditional unionist meant resisting southern solidarity, subjecting oneself to ridicule as a "coward and submissionist," to intimidation and, possibly, violence.[1]

Because southerners thought they had to legally negate what their states had agreed to in 1788, when each met in convention, they called again for conventions to reverse the agreement. Beginning with South Carolina on December 20, 1860, each state's secession convention (or in the case of Tennessee, its legislature) withdrew the state from the Union. Representatives from seven states formed a provisional government at Montgomery, Alabama, on February 4. The next wave of secession did not occur for two months, after Lincoln's inauguration, the Confederates' firing on Fort Sumter, and Lincoln's call for troops, including quotas from the Upper South states to quell the rebellion. Lincoln's action sealed the secession of four more states. Virginia went out on April 17, Arkansas on May 6, Tennessee a day later, and North Carolina two weeks later. From Lincoln's election in November 1860

---

1. James M. McPherson, *Ordeal by Fire: The Civil War and Reconstruction,* 2d ed. (New York, 1992), 131–32; Don E. Fehrenbacher, ed., *History and American Society: Essays of David M. Potter* (New York, 1973), 89; "Henry S. Foote Autobiographical Sketch," 19, Claiborne Papers.

to the spring of 1861, the battle for and against secession was waged in newspapers, in campaigns for convention seats, in referendums, and in the forming of citizens groups. The struggle also occurred in legislatures over the calling of state conventions, seizure of United States property, and the arming of citizens. For the most part, those who later became scalawags or redeemers were active in these affairs. These events were central in their lives. By them, they would be judged then and later.

Although future scalawags from South Carolina resigned themselves to separation if Lincoln won the 1860 presidential election, until that election most sought to stanch secession. At the state's Democratic Party convention in April 1860, James L. Orr lauded the Union and praised the state's past participation in the national Democratic convention. Even later, some considered Orr a reluctant Rebel, "lugged in awfully against the grain," as Mary Boykin Chesnut expressed it. Orr's course was much like that of his Jewish friend Franklin J. Moses of Sumter, who had read law under the tutelage of well-known unionist James L. Pettigru. Moses fought "nullification as taught by Mr. Calhoun & his followers," and while a young man, "distinguished himself" at the state's 1832 Union convention. During much of the 1850s, as chairman of the state senate's committee on federal-state relations, Moses tried to keep South Carolina in the Union. After John Brown's raid in 1859, however, Moses wavered, and with Lincoln's election and secession, as did Orr, Moses went with his state.[2]

Some future scalawags, however, even in South Carolina, embodied "unconditional Unionism." Such was Lemuel Boozer of Lexington and his friend Manuel S. Corley, both leaders in the state's Lutheran church. From his German family, who had settled in the state a century earlier, Boozer inherited "an undying gratitude" to America for giving its members "a home and freedom." As a popular lawyer and prosperous landowner, Boozer had been involved for years in state and local politics. He acted as a magistrate, served in the legislature, and represented his party as a presidential elector in 1844. In 1860, he became one of two South Carolina delegates to the national Demo-

2. White, "National Democrats," 383–84; Isabella D. Martin and Myrta L. Avery, eds., *A Diary from Dixie, as Written by Mary Boykin Chesnut* . . . (Boston, 1949), 168, 343; Howard K. Beale, ed., *Diary of Gideon Welles, Secretary of the Navy under Lincoln and Johnson* (New York, 1960), 2: 359; Elzas, *Jews of South Carolina*, 197–98; Montgomery Moses to Andrew Johnson, 11 July 1865, Records Relating to the Appointment of Federal Judges, Marshals, and Attorneys. General Records of the Justice Department, RG 60, National Archives; Steven A. Channing, *Crisis of Fear: Secession in South Carolina* (New York, 1970), 97n.

cratic convention at Charleston who refused to join the "sectional stampede" out of the convention. He stayed seated, as did well-known unionist editor Benjamin F. Perry of Greenville. Boozer stood so loyal to the Union during the war that he became one of a select group of southerners the United States government would later pay for goods confiscated by the Union army (in his case, horses, mules, cattle, forage, and provisions).[3]

Corley, a tailor and a temperance newspaper editor, as well as an owner of several hundred acres of woodland, claimed his opposition to the "secession swindle" caused him to be "preached at—sneered at, hated and despised." Earlier in the 1850s, he stood against another secession attempt. Later he claimed he had been the only editor in South Carolina to condemn as "disgraceful" Preston Brooks's assault on Charles Sumner in the United States Senate. Becoming widowed in the mid-1850s, with several children and an aged mother, he had, in his words, "ventured North in search of a wife." He married a woman in Vermont. After secession, he would have left South Carolina if his mother hadn't refused to accompany him. Despite his responsibilities to his mother, his five children, and his new wife, he was "compelled to go into the army." He yielded to conscription into the Confederate army because, as he later observed, being "a live dog was better than [being] a dead lion." Unfortunately, his enemies believed that "the next best thing to killing Yankees" would be to give one's own life for the southern cause.[4]

James M. Rutland of Winnsboro was "one of the few men who proclaimed themselves Unionists" after South Carolina seceded. Although his pro-Union stance was condemned by most of his neighbors, "his boldness and consistency commanded the esteem of his friends." Rutland, a bachelor, always had been determined, if not stubborn. He worked as a farmhand, clerk, and teacher while getting an education. Eventually he graduated with a law degree from the University of Virginia, where he was a classmate of Orr. During the 1850s, he subscribed to Perry's pro-Union *Southern Patriot*. Rutland said he found the newspaper "refreshing" and filled with "solid sense and sound views" on issues "distracting the country and threatening no less than a dissolution of the Union." On more than one occasion, Rutland later resisted Con-

3. Brooks, *Bench and Bar*, 171–76; Williamson, *After Slavery*, 373; *Consolidated Index of Claims Reported by the Commissioners of Claims to the House of Representatives from 1871 to 1880* (Washington, D.C., 1892), 3: 28.

4. Corley to Charles Sumner, 6 December 1866, 26 August 1867, Charles Sumner Papers, Houghton Library, Harvard University, Cambridge, Mass.; *BDAC*, 786.

federate impressment of his property. He would also have his life threatened by mobs. Because he had refused to be a cooperative Confederate, he reported that "two different mobs on two separate occasions visited my house to hang me; I happened to be absent from home on both occasions, and my life was . . . saved by accident."[5]

Even Charleston, the "Cradle of Secession," had some unionists left in 1861, but out of fear, they kept their thoughts to themselves. Albert G. Mackey, a physician and medical school professor, a rare southern Unitarian, and a Masonic lodge leader, still felt his "paramount allegiance" should be to the United States government. He believed that his "fellow-citizens . . . were led [astray] by the abstractions of their political leaders." Schoolmaster Frederick A. Sawyer of the State Normal School for Girls at Charleston, a disciplined New Englander who was proud of his intellect as well as his physique, remained unchanged in his loyalty by secession. The Harvard graduate of 1844 had come south in 1859 to accept the normal school post. Although he liked the school and Charleston, he was "too honest to conceal his convictions." Following "long and persistent efforts" by his friends on the school board, he obtained a pass for his family to cross Confederate lines. Thereafter, during 1864 and 1865, he made patriotic speeches in the North.[6]

When Mississippi seceded, individuals who had campaigned during 1860 to prevent secession, now on the whole, "saw the irresistible tide . . . , accepted the situation, and threw [themselves] into the current." Often unionists-turned-secessionists used the metaphor of rapidly running water—with words such as "the flood," "the tide," or "the current"—to describe themselves or others. Like religious converts in their fervor, some antisecessionists metamorphosed overnight into rabid rebels, at least publicly. When the bell of "secession sounded," for example, William W. Chisolm, the newly elected probate judge of Kemper County, cast his ballot for the secessionist delegates from his county, even though his seven brothers, like himself, were former Whigs and voted for the Union delegates. Chisolm reputedly "leaped lustily

5. Brooks, *Bench and Bar,* 174; Rutland to Benjamin F. Perry, 17 March 1851, Benjamin F. Perry Papers, Southern Historical Collection; Rutland to Andrew Johnson, 6 July 1865, Andrew Johnson Papers, Library of Congress, Washington, D.C.

6. *Proceedings of the Constitutional Convention of South Carolina Held at Charleston, S.C., beginning January 14th and ending March 17th* (Charleston, 1868), 1: 17; William H. Barnes, *The Fortieth Congress of the United States: Historical and Biographical* (New York, 1870), 2: 95–96.

into the madden current . . . outswam the tide, helped to clear its channels, and undike its swelling floods."[7]

Privately some Mississippians, especially former Whigs such as James L. Alcorn of Coahoma County, still questioned the wisdom of secession. Alcorn, a wealthy Delta planter, attorney, and veteran legislator, campaigned throughout his area to get pro-Union delegates to the state's secession convention meeting in Jackson in early January 1861. He was elected as a delegate and nominated as its president but defeated by the large secessionist majority. Although Alcorn and others used the standard delaying tactics of cooperationists elsewhere, insisting on a meeting with representatives from other southern states and insisting on holding a state referendum on secession, they failed. So now fearing more than ever that they would be given "the epithet of coward and submissionist," unionists voted with the secessionists. When Alcorn, always an impressive figure of a man—in attire, stature, and speech—got the floor, he took full advantage of the dramatic situation. He had wanted "a different course . . . and to that end . . . [he had] labored and spoken," he said. But now, he declared, "The die is cast—the Rubicon is crossed—and I enlist myself with the army that marches on Rome." His action, as he later acknowledged, "was one of simple rebellion." That secession would bring war he never doubted. He hoped for a short war, even for a reunion by political means. But even if reunion never came, Alcorn felt he could do nothing other than ally with his state, his people, because his "own honor" was by far "dearer to [him] than country or life itself."[8]

Other scalawags, including some losing candidates for Mississippi's secession convention, continued to be Union men "down to the last and final struggle." The "tyranny of the majority" silenced Vicksburg's future scalawags in 1861. The town's Confederate commander warned townspeople that if they opposed the new government, they would be "imprisoned, Shot or Sent Out of the Country." So they made what adjustments they had to make to the new order. Other Mississippi unionists largely sat out the war because they owned

7. John H. Echols petition, n.d., Thomas T. Swann to Hon. Geo. S. Boutwell, 10 February 1869, Petitions for the Removal of Legal and Political Disabilities Imposed by the Fourteenth Amendment, Records of the Adjutant General's Office, RG 233, National Archives; James D. Lynch, *Kemper County Vindicated, and a Peep at Radical Rule in Mississippi* (New York, 1879), 22.

8. Pereyra, *James Lusk Alcorn*, 39–45, 50.

enough slaves to keep them out of the army, held a minor local office, or they were beyond the conscription age. Joshua S. Morris, of Port Hudson, "doubted the wisdom or necessity of secession," yet he accepted it because he "was devoted to [his] people." But after secession, he used "all of the excuses at his command" to stay out of the Confederate army before obtaining an exemption by being elected "to the very respectable little office of Probate Judge." He considered himself "loyal," and he never saw a time when he "would not . . . have had the Union restored."[9]

Some Mississippi unionists faced painful circumstances that may have later led them to become Republicans. Such was Robert W. Flournoy, a Douglas Democrat and large slaveholder from Pontotoc County, who won a seat in the Mississippi convention as a unionist. But he ultimately agreed to vote for secession because he wanted to "cast his lot with his people." He even organized a local company of troops and led them north to defend Virginia, where he had finished college in 1832 at Charlottesville. But after reflecting on his decision for several weeks, he did a complete turnabout, just as he did in deciding to support secession, but this time it stuck. As an old Confederate said, Flournoy "could not bring himself to bear arms against the United States government." Flournoy explained that his "conscience did not allow . . . [him] to stay in the service, and . . . [he] resigned." Thus he returned to Mississippi, where "on more than one occasion he experienced trouble at the hands of the Confederates."[10]

Young Theodoric C. Lyon of Columbus, Mississippi, was another scalawag who refused to conform. He described himself as having fought secession "by precept and example." Even after his state left the Union, Lyon published an antisecession tract in nearby Tennessee. For more than a year, he avoided serving in the army. Finally, after the adoption of the Conscription Act in the spring of 1862, he reported to the military. That autumn, because of their respect for him, his unit of local lads elected him lieutenant in the Forty-third Mississippi Regiment. But Lyon never accepted secession, and in the summer of 1863 he published "The Thompson Letter," which, according to Confeder-

9. Charles C. Shackleford petition, n.d., Ephraim S. Fisher petition, n.d., RG 233; Lynch, *Bench and Bar,* 357; Peter F. Walker, *Vicksburg: A People at War, 1860–1865* (Chapel Hill, 1960), 103–4; Harold Hyman, *The Era of the Oath: Northern Loyalty Tests during the Civil War and Reconstruction* (Philadelphia, 1954), 77; *KKK Report,* Miss., 298, 315, 319, 324–25; Morris to Thaddeus Stevens, 28 February 1867, Thaddeus Stevens Papers, Library of Congress.

10. *KKK Report,* Miss., 91; William L. Barney, *The Secessionist Impulse: Alabama and Mississippi in 1860* (Princeton, N.J., 1974), 54–79.

ates, advocated "a treasonable reconstruction of the Old Union." For this, Lyon said he was "imprisoned, court-martialed, [and] cashiered." But later, perhaps because of the great need for soldiers, Confederates conscripted him once again and transferred him to the "other end of the Confederacy." Understandably, in a later reference to the Confederacy, Lyon says that he "grieved . . . its inception . . . mourned over its existence, and . . . rejoiced over its fall."[11]

Several studies show that scalawags from Alabama opposed secession in 1861. According to one study identifying more than 300 scalawags whose stance is known, 95 percent opposed immediate separation in January 1861. The study also found only five party candidates and party officeholders out of 266 examined to have been secessionists. And of the twenty-four secession convention delegates who eventually became Republicans, only two voted for immediate secession. Indeed a record of having stood against immediate secession became the hallmark of the state's white Republican leaders. Opposition to secession was almost a requirement for candidacy and officeholding as a Republican.

Among scalawags who opposed secession at the Montgomery convention in January 1861 were two lawyers from Lawrence County in north Alabama, James S. Clarke and David P. Lewis. Clarke, a former legislator and a cooperationist spokesman, argued that secession by Alabama alone would settle virtually nothing. Alabama's secession would not resolve the issue of slavery in the territories or change northern opinion. Rather, secession would leave the Union in Republican hands. If reconciliation between the North and the South could not be met, then Clarke favored secession only by a united South. In any case, if Alabama seceded, Clarke, along with other cooperationists (the group with almost all of the future scalawags), argued that the convention should allow the people to vote on the convention's secession ordinance. Clarke made the case that if any new government failed to respect north Alabama, civil war could come to that section and it could join itself to Tennessee, with which it shared many commonalties. Clarke kept to his law practice until 1863, when he was elected to the legislature as a peace party candidate.[12]

11. Theodoric C. Lyon petition, 20 February 1869, RG 233.
12. Cash, "Alabama Republicans," 130, 265–66; Wiggins, *Scalawag in Alabama Politics,* 131; Malcolm Cook McMillan, *Constitutional Development in Alabama, 1798–1901: A Study in Politics, the Negro, and Sectionalism* (Chapel Hill, 1955), 119–24; Fleming, *Civil War and Reconstruction in Alabama,* 28–35; David L. Darden, "Alabama Secession Convention," *AlaHQ* 3 (fall and winter 1941): 382.

In the months after secession, Lewis's life followed the same course as many who experienced mixed emotions about events occurring around them. Generally, they were moved more by attachments and events than by their ideological convictions. Showing good faith toward cooperationists, the secession convention elected Lewis to the Provisional Confederate Congress, meeting soon after in Montgomery. However, Lewis failed to take an oath to the Confederacy as required, and he resigned in April 1861 after serving only three months. In 1863 he avoided conscription by accepting an appointment as a circuit judge from Governor John G. Shorter. Nevertheless, in November 1864, after Federal troops occupied some of his district, Lewis left north Alabama to settle in Union-occupied Nashville. Lewis, eventually a Republican governor, always argued he was loyal because he served "the rebellion, only so far as prudence, inspired by an honest sense of safety advised; and [that he] sincerely rejoiced at the restoration of the national authority." He felt then, and later, that some had been "forced into rebellion against their votes, & their wishes." He saw a major difference between spokesmen for secession and those forced into the Confederacy "by the circumstances of their lives."[13]

Alabama's youngest 1861 convention delegate, twenty-one-year-old schoolteacher Christopher Sheats, from Winston County in north Alabama, stepped forward as an uncompromising antisecessionist. He voted against secession and refused to sign either the ordinance or the accompanying letter to the public. He wanted, as he said, "to expose [the] fiendish villainy" of secessionists to "the world." Some of his courage came from knowing he was supported by the folks back home who had elected him without opposition to oppose secession. He was a speaker at the pro-Union meeting at Looney's Tavern in Winston County, where more than 2,500 people gathered and threatened to withdraw from Alabama if it seceded from the Union. During early 1861, ultraunionists in Winston and other northern Alabama counties discussed the possibility of joining the counties of East Tennessee to form the state of Nick-a-Jack, a Native American name for the area where the two states join. The two sections had more in common with each other than they did with other sections of their respective states. They also had a shared waterway, the Tennessee River. Consideration of such a plan, however, ceased once Lin-

    13. Sarah Woolfolk Wiggins, "Amnesty and Pardon and Republicanism in Alabama," *AlaHQ* 26 (summer 1964): 240–48; Owen, *History of Alabama*, 4: 1043.

coln issued his proclamation of April 10, 1861, calling troops to quell the rebellion in the South.[14]

Most Georgia scalawags saw secession at the least as economically ill-ad-
vised and at worst as unparalleled madness. Many thought it militarily irre-
sponsible because they believed the South could not win its independence.
Congressman Joshua Hill, a tall, broad-shouldered, rugged-faced planter and
freethinker from Morgan County, noted for his "plain horse sense," foresaw
"a long and bloody war." He took "little comfort in the flippant assurance . . .
that the Yankees could not fight if they would and would not if they could."
When Governor Joseph E. Brown seized Fort Pulaski from the Federals in
January 1861, Hill condemned him from the floor of the United States House
of Representatives. Soon thereafter, Hill refused to exit en masse with the
other Georgia congressmen, because they had tied their resignations to the
right of secession. Although he shortly thereafter resigned and walked out,
he still "denied that the ordinance of secession took . . . [his] State out of the
Union."[15]

Henry P. Farrow, who moved from Cartersville to Atlanta in 1865 and
joined with the Atlanta unionists to help found the Georgia Republican Party,
avoided service to the Confederacy as long as possible. His behavior reflected
his background. He hailed originally from Laurensville in the Uplands of
South Carolina, where his father opposed the nullifiers in the 1830s. In the
mid-1850s Farrow fought with his secessionist roommate at the University of
Virginia. Upon his return to Laurensville, he studied law and engaged in pro-
Union politics. Because secessionists "denounced [him] for supporting the
National Democracy" rather than the "States rights—Southern rights—
Secession party," he fired a parting shot at them in the local press and "left
the State in disgust." He settled in Cartersville, Georgia, just north of Atlanta,
where he championed Stephen A. Douglas in 1860 and served as a delegate
for the Little Giant to the Democratic National Convention in Baltimore.
Once again he found himself "battling in a minority against Sectionalism and

14. Goodspeed, *Northern Alabama, Historical and Biographical* (Birmingham, 1888), 327;
Clarence Phillips Denman, *The Secession Movement in Alabama* (Montgomery, 1933), 166; Durwood Long, "Unanimity and Disloyalty in Secessionist Alabama," *Civil War History* 11 (September 1965): 269; Fleming, *Civil War and Reconstruction in Alabama,* 54.

15. *DAB,* 9: 42–43; Joseph E. Brown to Alexander H. Stephens, 22 August 1863, in *The Correspondence of Robert Toombs, Alexander H. Stephens, and Howell Cobb,* ed. Ulrich B. Phillips, vol.
2, Annual Report of the American Historical Association for the Year 1911 (Washington, D.C.,
1913), 638; Joshua Hill to Andrew Johnson, 10 May 1865, Johnson Papers.

Secession." After Lincoln's election, Farrow continued to oppose secession. "For nearly two years of the rebellion," Farrow said, he stayed "free of any participation." Finally he was "conscribed . . . and sent, under guard . . . to duty in the nitre and mining bureau." But he never "uttered a sentiment in support of the Confederacy," nor did he give it "any voluntary aid."[16]

Atlanta antisecessionists formed a Union Association during 1860. Because most of them hailed from the North and many townspeople had grown antagonistic toward northerners during the presidential campaign, the association of about fifteen professionals and merchants met covertly. Most often they gathered at the real estate office of Dr. Nedom L. Angier, a teacher from New Hampshire turned physician turned businessman. There they "sympathize[d] with each other" and discussed "the best means of preventing secession." The association included several political types who would later serve as Republican officials and public officeholders. A number had already held local offices, including William Markham and Jonathan Norcross, who served as mayors in the 1850s. Angier was elected to the city council in 1860. Most identified with the Whig Party and its successors, but a few, like Angier, were Douglas Democrats. Those who engaged in Reconstruction politics as Republicans—in addition to Angier, Markham, and Norcross—included Atlanta Machine Works owner James Dunning, the most outspoken of the group; attorney Amherst W. Stone; banker Alfred Austell; and schoolmaster Alexander N. Wilson. Most of the northerners had resided in the South for twenty years or more. East Tennessee native Wilson represented one of the few southerners in the Association.[17]

Some other Georgians who later turned Republican claimed to have stood by the Union as long as possible in 1861. Mayor Foster Blodgett of Augusta boasted that he had chaired "the *last* Union meeting held in Georgia." Before yielding to the advice of friends to join the Confederate army in 1861, he claimed himself "threatened time & again . . . with a coat of tar & feathers . . . & even death itself." Although, as appropriate for a man of his standing, he raised a company of troops, his term of service was short, ending in April

16. Henry P. Farrow, *Hon. Henry P. Farrow, United States Senator Elect. What Are His Antecedents?* Pamphlet, Washington, D.C., 1870, 1–2; George L. Jones, "The Political Career of Henry Pattillo Farrow, Georgia Republican, 1865–1904" (Master's thesis, University of Georgia, 1966), 5–11.

17. Thomas G. Dyer, *Secret Yankees: The Union Circle in Confederate Atlanta* (Baltimore, 1999), 36–37, 80.

1862. For months, he lived with his wife's people in South Carolina. As he later told it, "by good management . . . [he] succeeded in keeping out of the Confederate service."[18]

Unionists in Florida soon were cowed into conformity by Confederates. According to William H. Christy of Jacksonville, he was "the Editor of the last 'Union' paper in the State & opposed secession to the last, but in vain." The town's population divided almost equally among northerners, southerners, and blacks. But a few of the town's northerners resisted and paid a price. After John S. Sammis of New York, owner of a huge plantation near Jacksonville, lobbied against secession at Tallahassee in January 1861 and later refused to buy Confederate bonds as a sign of his loyalty, Confederates seized his property worth more than $70,000. Another future officeholder, Otis L. Keene, originally from Maine, managed the Judson House, Florida's best hotel. As long as Keene served only in the Jacksonville Light Infantry, of which he was a charter member in 1859, he preferred to go along to get along. But after the mustering of the infantry into the Confederate army in August 1861, he resigned because, he said, he "could not close [his] hotel." His action, however, caused Confederates to consider him a unionist and ultimately caused him to identify with other loyalists. Only at federally occupied Key West, the state's largest town, did the greatly outnumbered unionists express their loyalist sentiment by spring 1861.[19]

Only a few scalawags from the Southwest supported secession. Scalawags served on antisecession committees, supported Union candidates for the conventions of 1861, and in some instances ran for seats. Some elected to the conventions proved to be dedicated diehards. This contrasted starkly with the backing given separation by the section's redeemers—more than two-thirds of redeemers from the Southwest supported secession (see table 6).

Schoolmaster Isaac Murphy of Washington County, Arkansas, a former legislator and a man of "considerable information but not much cultivation," stood his ground despite demands to yield by fellow delegates at the secession convention in Little Rock. According to his own account, he did not compromise his "Loyalty to the Stars and Stripes in a solitary instance." Speaking to

18. Coleman and Gurr, *Dictionary of Georgia Biography*, 1: 92.
19. Jerrell H. Shofner, *Nor Is It Over Yet: Florida in the Era of Reconstruction, 1863–1877* (Gainesville, Fla., 1974), 4; Richard A. Martin, "Defeat in Victory: Yankee Experience in Early Civil War Jacksonville," *FHQ* 53 (July 1974): 7–9; Christy to Edward McPherson, 22 March 1867, Edward McPherson Papers, Library of Congress.

the other delegates, he declared: "I have cast my vote after mature reflection, and have duly considered the consequences, and I cannot conscientiously change it. I therefore vote 'no.'" His sole moral support came from a female admirer who tossed him a floral bouquet from the gallery. Almost all of the state's scalawags opposed secession—most openly—until the war. Some, including Murphy, given the opportunity, continued their opposition during the war.[20]

Some Louisiana scalawags sought secession convention seats by running under the United Southern Action banner, a coalition endeavoring to delay disunion. Others served as leaders in the organization. Only Wade H. Hough of Caldwell Parish and James G. Taliaferro of Catahoula Parish, well-known attorneys in the northern half of the state, won seats in the convention. There they "opposed and voted against" secession and "refused to sign that Treasonable Ordinance." Taliaferro, "a rugged, straight-forward, old man," had moved from Virginia to Kentucky with his family at age eight and on to Louisiana before returning to Kentucky to attend Transylvania College. Afterward, he stayed for several years in Kentucky, where he married, studied law, and became acquainted with Henry Clay, a fellow Whig. By 1861 he had dwelt in the Delta for four decades, prospering by planting and by practicing law. Along the way, he served as parish judge for fifteen years and published his own newspaper, fittingly called the *Harrisonburg Independent.* Its masthead carried the judge's favorite Cicero quotation: "I defended the republic in my youth; I shall not stop as an old man."[21]

After the death of his wife in 1850, Taliaferro completed the rearing of the two youngest of their ten children, one named after John Quincy Adams and another after Daniel Webster. Even before the January 1861 convention, Taliaferro's unbending unionism so enraged some of his secessionist neighbors that in December they had burned his lumberyard and cotton gin. Once be-

20. Alfred Holt Carrigan, "Reminiscences of the Secession Convention," Publications of the Arkansas Historical Association (Little Rock 1906–17), 1: 312–13; Jesse N. Cypert, "Secession Convention," in Publications of the Arkansas Historical Association, 2: 319; Murphy to Abraham Lincoln, 17 February 1863, Lincoln Papers.

21. Charles B. Dew, "The Long Lost Returns: The Candidates and Their Totals in Louisiana Secession Convention," *LH* 10 (fall 1969): 364–68; Hough to Andrew Johnson, 24 July 1866, Hough to U. S. Grant, 20 August 1871, RG 60; Wynona Gillmore Mills, "James Govan Taliaferro, 1798–1876: Louisiana Unionist and Scalawag" (Master's thesis, Louisiana State University, 1964), 1–9; Robert W. Taliaferro to James G. Taliaferro, 9, 21 December 1860, Taliaferro and Family Papers; Roger W. Shugg, "A Suppressed Co-operationist Protest against Secession," *LHQ* 19 (January 1936): 199–203.

fore, in 1852, he served as his county's constitutional convention delegate, but this time it was different: like Murphy of Arkansas, Taliaferro was soon isolated. When finally allowed to address the convention, he denounced secession as unwise, unnecessary, premature, and illegal, a "right unknown to the Constitution of the United States." He warned the delegates that secession would spawn "anarchy and war" and destruction of property. Because they decided against a ratification referendum, he accused them of violating "the great principle of American government, that the will of the people is supreme."[22]

Several New Orleans scalawags showed their courage by opposing secession. Judge Philip H. Morgan of New Orleans, a veteran of the Mexican War, and later, like Taliaferro, a justice of the state supreme court, told a Canal Street mob he would join them against abolitionists by peaceful means, but he could not fight against the Union. Morgan warned them that if they fired on the "Stars and Stripes," their slaves would become their "political master." Shortly after secession, German-born Maximilian F. Bonzano, assayer at the New Orleans Mint, broadcast his hatred for secession by destroying "all the coining dies" and fleeing to New York City. In August 1861, outspoken unionist Anthony P. Dostie, a Canal Street dentist, was forced to leave the Crescent City. Dostie, a New Yorker of French and German descent, had usually felt quite at home in New Orleans. After establishing himself in the city in the early 1850s, Dostie, an inveterate joiner, became master of a Masonic Lodge. During what he described as "a reign of terror" in 1861, Confederates incarcerated his dental assistant in a "loathsome prison" and exiled Dostie. Writing about his experience, Dostie exclaimed, "I departed from what had been my beautiful and genial home, to come where I could once more see the old banner wave o'er the land of the free and the home of the brave."[23]

Early in the war, John Ray of Monroe refused to contribute funds to the first Confederate company organized in the town, "avowedly for the reason that he feared this might be giving aid to the enemy." But, as a humanitarian, he opened his home to the families of draft dodgers "driven from the country

---

22. Mills, "James Govan Taliaferro," 7–9.

23. *DAB*, 13: 187; W. G. Wyley to Andrew Johnson, 15 July 1865, RG 60; Zenon Labauve petition, n.d., RG 233; R. K. Howell to Benjamin F. Butler, 14 March 1867, Benjamin F. Butler Papers, Library of Congress; Goodspeed, *Biographical and Historical Memoirs of Louisiana . . .* (Chicago, 1892), 1: 303–4; Bonzano to Salmon P. Chase, 5 May 1862, Letters of Application and Recommendation, General Records of the Treasury Department, RG 56, National Archives.

by the conscription laws," as well as to needy families of Confederate soldiers. When Monroe fell to Union troops in 1863, according to Ray's biographer, he "reaffirmed his love and allegiance for the Union."[24]

Future Republicans campaigned to keep Texas in the Union and encouraged friends elsewhere to oppose secession. Rio Grande Valley Judge Edmund J. Davis met with Robert E. Lee, a fellow West Pointer, before Lee's return to Virginia from his assignment in Texas to try to persuade him to remain with the Union. And former congressman Lemuel D. Evans of Marshall warned Texas and the nation in the January 11, 1861, *Washington National Intelligencer* that southern senators were plotting the seizure of federal arsenals in the South. Several newspapermen and legislators who later became Republicans crusaded against secession. Mobs destroyed some of their presses, and most of them fled into exile. After the war, these men published Republican newspapers and became prominent officeholders.[25]

Unionist legislators delivered lengthy speeches to their colleagues in Austin, reviewing the nation's history, emphasizing the shared experiences of the North and the South, and warning of a devastating civil war. On February 6, they joined other unionist legislators and secession convention delegates in signing a broadside entreating Texans to reject secession. Appealing to his Starr County constituents on both patriotic and practical grounds, legislator John L. Haynes of Rio Grande City defended his unpopular stand in a circular. According to his analysis, Texas received from the national government almost twice what its people paid in federal taxes. Haynes cherished a prized newspaper clipping citing a quotation from Shakespeare used by his friend Sam Houston during the secession crisis: "Is there not some chosen curse, some hidden thunder in the stores of heaven" for those "who owe their greatness to their country's ruin?" Haynes, a Civil War refugee and a Union army colonel, later became the first chairman of the Texas Republican Party.[26]

After the secession convention in Austin voted 166 to 8 for withdrawal, the people voted 46,129 for to 14,697 against. Unionist votes mostly came from two areas, north Texas, with a high percentage of small farmers and a low

---

24. Williams, "John Ray," 242.

25. Baggett, "Origins of Early Texas Republican Party Leadership," 446–47.

26. John L. Haynes, "Address to the People of Starr County," imprint, n.d., John L. Haynes Papers, Center for American History, University of Texas at Austin;. The Houston quotation is a slightly altered version of Joseph Addison's *Cato*, 1.1. 21–24, Haynes Scrapbook, p. 36, Haynes Papers. "Address to the People of Texas," imprint, 1861, Haynes Papers.

ratio of slaves, and south central Texas, with a large proportion of Germans owning virtually no slaves. Northern Texas prairie farmers originally from the Upper South, the Border States, and the Midwest still resented such laws as the "planter law" of 1858. The act allowed a slaveholder to preempt 160 acres of the public domain for each three slaves he held. Moreover, they believed planters to be overrepresented in, not sufficiently taxed by, and highly subsidized through the Texas legislature. South central Texas farmers disliked planters for similar reasons. The area also had a high concentration of German natives. Although these Germans condoned slavery, they considered the institution to be morally indefensible. Such factors in northern Texas and in south central Texas caused the two sections to vote against secession. A comparison of counties showing a high percentage of voters against secession with counties where the Republican vote exceeded the adult male black population during Reconstruction shows the effects of earlier antislavery and unionist views.[27]

Scalawags from the Upper South opposed secession as legislators, as secession convention delegates, as members of Union conventions at Wheeling, Knoxville, and Greeneville, and as individuals in numerous gatherings. They repeatedly said during the 1860 campaign that Lincoln's election would not be grounds for secession. Many believed Lincoln would act moderately because his Whig background would make him "a conservative Chief Magistrate." Responding to a Knoxville speech of secessionist William L. Yancey, Parson Brownlow said if the fire-eaters marched on Washington to overthrow the president, they would have to "walk over [his] dead body on their way." Even if Lincoln acted unconstitutionally, Brownlow said, the Congress and the Supreme Court, neither of which the Republicans controlled, would restrain him.[28]

When secession started, Upper South scalawags favored a national compromise to entice the Lower South back into the Union. Conciliatory steps in the United States Senate came from John J. Crittenden of Kentucky and in the House from Alexander R. Boteler of Virginia, a future Republican and chair of the special Committee of Thirty-three, composed of one member from each state. Virginia's legislature also sponsored a February 1861 Peace

---

27. James Alex Baggett, "The Rise and Fall of the Texas Radicals, 1867–1883" (Ph.D. diss., University of North Texas, 1972), 23.

28. Ambler and Summers, *West Virginia*, 187; Ollinger Crenshaw, *The Slave States in the Presidential Election of 1860* (Baltimore, 1945), 180.

Convention in Washington, D.C., attended by representatives of twenty-one states. But compromise failed because the incoming Republican administration rejected any concession threatening its party's raison d'être: opposition to the extension of slavery.[29]

After Lincoln's inauguration, the federal government still functioned in the Upper South. So offices had to be filled. Lincoln foresaw the potential of patronage there to build a Republican Party as well as to win allies who wanted to save the Union. He conferred personally with several future Republicans from Virginia. They discussed the possibility of secession as well as patronage. John M. Botts, a former congressman from Richmond and spokesman for the state's unionists, talked with Lincoln early in April. He hoped he could prevent war between the North and the Confederacy and keep Virginia in the Union. According to him, Lincoln promised to evacuate Fort Sumter if the Virginia secession convention would adjourn immediately.[30]

In Virginia's counties bordering Ohio and Pennsylvania, where commerce flowed back and forth from the Northeast and Midwest and much of the population came from the North, people favored staying in the Union. Individuals in this most industrialized and least slaveholding section of Virginia felt overtaxed and underrepresented. Because of a lack of state-sponsored internal improvement for projects west of the Allegheny Mountains, the people there felt underfunded by Richmond. They agreed with Waitman T. Willey, soon a Republican convert, that secession would place the section at the "tag end" of any southern government, exposing it to devastation by invading Federal forces from across the Ohio River. So in spite of the state's convention voting in April for secession, four-fifths of the delegates from the northwestern counties voted against Virginia's withdrawing. They returned home to rally the section's unionists. After many local rallies, more than four hundred delegates from twenty-seven counties met at Wheeling on May 3. After three days, they decided to delay a decision on separation from Virginia until after the state's secession referendum. After secession passed in the state as a whole, delegates

29. *Journal of the House of Delegates of the State of Virginia for the Extra Session, 1861* (Richmond, 1861), 65–67; *New York Tribune,* 1, 8 February 1861; Allan Nevins, *The Emergence of Lincoln* (New York, 1950), 2: 410–12; Robert G. Gunderson, *Old Gentlemen's Convention: The Washington Peace Conference of 1861* (Madison, Wis., 1961).

30. David M. Potter, *Lincoln and His Party in the Secession Crisis* (New Haven, 1942), 37–38; *New York Times,* 8 March 1861; George S. Boutwell, *Reminiscences of Sixty Years in Public Affairs* (New York, 1902), 2: 62–64; *Report of Joint Committee on Reconstruction* (Washington, D.C., 1866), pt. 2: 114; Botts, *Great Rebellion,* 195–97, 275–77.

reassembled at Wheeling on July 11, protected by Ohio troops and hastily recruited loyalists. Rather than create a new state, however, the delegates established the Restored Government of Virginia, which they claimed to be the legal government of the entire state. Conditions for statehood were completed in April 1863, and West Virginia became a free state on June 20. When this happened, the "restored" government moved to Alexandria, near Washington, D.C.[31]

Meanwhile future scalawags elsewhere in Virginia fought secession. Legislators Lewis McKenzie of Alexandria and Joseph E. Segar of the Eastern Shore opposed every step taken by the state government toward secession. Speaking to the Virginia House of Delegates, Segar objected to "extraordinary resolutions . . . sent us from the Senate, [directing] the Governor to seize and hold, by military force, the property of the United States." Rather than "sustain them," he said he "would so help [him], God—sooner die in [his] seat." John F. Lewis of Rockingham County became, as he later described himself, "the only member of the convention east of the Allegheny Mountains who refused to sign the ordinance of secession."[32]

Several postwar Tennessee Republican congressmen, some of whom served in Congress before the war, courageously attacked disunion in 1861. William Crutchfield, "an eccentric, erratic" Chattanooga hotelier, responded to a secessionist speech by a well-known guest of his hotel, Jefferson Davis. Davis was returning to Mississippi from Washington, D.C., after resigning his seat. Crutchfield condemned the desertion by Davis and other congressmen who "might have prevented . . . hostile legislation to the institutions of the South." Speaking atop his hotel clerk's desk, he rebuked Davis as well "for interfering in the [Tennessee] election . . . by advising the people to vote for a Convention, which was virtually for secession." Horace Maynard of Knoxville labored to stop what he saw would be a "disastrous and deplorable civil war." He campaigned, as he said, among southerners "at home on every hilltop and in

31. Curry, "Reappraisal of Statehood Politics," 412–15; Ambler and Summers, *West Virginia,* 187, 195–303; James C. McGrew, "The Secession Convention," in Hall, *Rending of Virginia,* 216–28, 517–35; *Wheeling Intelligencer,* 10 May 1861; Moore, *Rebellion Record,* vol. 1, pt. 2: 57; Francis H. Pierpont to Mrs. Francis H. Pierpont, 20 June 1861, Francis H. Pierpont Papers, West Virginia and Regional Collection, West Virginia University, Morgantown; Virgil A. Lewis, ed., *How West Virginia Was Made: Proceedings of the First Convention of the People of Northwestern Virginia at Wheeling, May 13, 14, and 15, 1861, and the Journal of the Second Convention of the People of Northwestern Virginia at Wheeling, which Assembled June 11th, 1861* (Charleston, W. Va., 1909), 54–57.

32. Moore, *Rebellion Record,* vol. 2, pt. 2: 214–22; *OR,* 2: 1525–26; OR, 51(2): 318.

every valley . . . imploring them to stay the hands of . . . parricidal men . . .
hurrying [the people] to swift and terrible destruction."[33]

The dilemma faced by Congressman William B. Stokes of DeKalb County,
Tennessee, as well as his response, typifies what happened to many scalawags
during 1861–62. In December 1860, he blamed the South's "red hot fire eat-
ers, and fanatics North" for endangering "the best Government . . . ever
formed by mortal man." Referring to the Union, he pledged to "cling to the
old ship, as long as there is [a] stick left." And in February, the tall, dapper
Stokes, while addressing the United States House of Representatives, condemned those in the South who accused their neighbors who wanted to save
the Union of being submissionists. The "Bald Eagle of the Mountain," as
Stokes was called, campaigned and voted against secession along with more
than four out of ten DeKalb County voters. Once the state seceded, Stokes
supported the movement to create a new state of East Tennessee. In July, he
talked of going to Washington but could not bring himself to do so. Instead
he retired to his farm to become what an enemy called "an anti-war semi-
Union man." For the remainder of the year and during the first few weeks of
1862, he "remained quietly at home." But after the fall of Fort Donelson in
February 1862, Stokes found his enemies had made his part of the "country
. . . too hot," and he "took to the woods." When General Don Carlos Buell
occupied Nashville, Stokes "went to him." After assisting the restoration
movement for a few months, Stokes received a colonel's commission in the
Union army.[34]

Similar meetings to those held in West Virginia convened in East Tennessee
during the spring of 1861. An area rally met at Knoxville May 30–31 to protest
the secession referendum, which had been opposed by almost all of the section's legislators. Delegates denounced the state's newly formed military
league with the Confederacy, and though they opposed the upcoming election, they urged everyone to vote to defeat secession. They agreed to reconvene, if necessary, upon the call of the convention president, Thomas A. R.
Nelson. After separation passed statewide on June 8 but lost by more than
two to one in East Tennessee, which accounted for 70 percent of the state's
antisecession vote, delegates reconvened at Greeneville on July 17. As dele-

33. Temple, *Notable Men of Tennessee*, 109–13; Barnes, *Fortieth Congress*, 2: 286; John Trimble to U. S. Grant, 12 December 1872, RG 60.
34. Marsha Young Darrah, "Political Career of Col. William B. Stokes of Tennessee" (Master's thesis, Tennessee Tech University, 1968), 10–58, 64–73.

gates deliberated at the Greene County Courthouse, troops from the Lower South passed through town by rail to defend Virginia. Louisiana Tigers, stopping over for a meal, amused themselves by threatening delegates and cutting down Old Glory, flying outside the Courthouse. Despite such threats, delegates petitioned the state general assembly to allow East Tennessee to create a state within the "Old Union." After the state rejected the delegates' petition, some of those who attended the Greeneville convention advocated resistance to the Confederacy. Several honored a pledge they had made to secretly recruit and train unionist militia units.[35]

Shared experiences cherished by the Knoxville and the Greeneville delegates later contributed to the association of most with the Republican Party, which they eventually felt had saved the Union. They included politicians from throughout East Tennessee: Governors Brownlow of Knoxville and DeWitt C. Senter of Grainger, administrators of state departments, congressmen, state judges, federal officeholders, and legislators.

Most North Carolina scalawags had longtime antisecession records. As prewar legislators, some resisted secession. Following the election of Lincoln but before his threat of coercion in April 1861, almost all still opposed secession. Former Whigs spearheaded the struggle to stay in the Union. They were joined by Douglas Democrats led by Robert P. Dick, a federal district attorney who had headed Douglas's campaign for president in the state, and even by a few Breckinridge supporters, such as editor William W. Holden, who publicly backed Breckinridge but privately favored Douglas. Holden and other Democratic and former Whig unionists won an initial victory when on February 28 the people defeated a proposal to hold a secession convention. But the drift toward disunion continued. Time and circumstance weighed heavily on the side of secessionists.[36]

Ultimately, most of the state's future scalawags and redeemers took identical paths: both opposed separation before Lincoln's troop requisition for an invasion of the South, and both, with few exceptions, then accepted secession. Unlike the original fire-eaters, however, conditional unionists, later the lead-

35. *Nashville Union*, 3 March 1861; Tennessee *House Journal*, 33d GA, 2d sess. (Nashville, 1861), 32–33; Philip M. Hamer, *Tennessee, A History, 1673–1932* (New York, 1933), 2: 544, 550–51, 558–59; *OR*, 52(1): 148–56, 168–79; Charles F. Bryan, "A Gathering of Tories: The East Tennessee Convention of 1861," *THQ* 39 (spring 1980): 27–48.

36. Noble J. Torbert, ed., *The Papers of John Willis Ellis* (Raleigh, N.C., 1964), 2: 473; Holden, *Memoirs*, 71.

ers of both of the state's postwar parties, did not rejoice over separation but resigned themselves to it. According to Holden, a secession convention delegate, when the ordinance passed, the assembly resembled "a sea partly in storm, partly calm, the secessionists shouting and throwing up their hats and rejoicing, the Conservatives sitting quietly, calm, and depressed." Depressed or not, conservatives astutely protected themselves by forming a new party from the antisecessionist elements of recent months, mostly former Whigs but including Douglas Democrats.[37]

During 1860–61, as always, reactions for the most part depended on changing events and circumstances, especially on President Lincoln's decisions. Already discouraged by his unwillingness to compromise over slavery in the territories, sentiment to support the Union soured overnight when Lincoln called for troops to suppress the rebellion. Now many unionists saw their families and friends rallied in defense of the South. In 1861 young Virginian John S. Mosby, later a well-known Confederate cavalry colonel and a less-known postwar Republican diplomat, stood alone in his community in opposing secession. But, according to Mosby, when Lincoln called for troops and Virginia seceded, reason died and passion prevailed, and he "went along with the flood like everybody else." Mosby mused, "A few individuals here and there attempted to breast the storm of passion, and appeared like Virgil's shipwrecked mariners. . . . All that they did was to serve 'like ocean wrecks to illuminate the storm.' "[38]

Some exceptions existed to the Unionism shown by most scalawags during the secession crisis, but those individuals acting otherwise represent only a small number of those eventually becoming Republican leaders. Some scalawags had edited prosecessionist newspapers. Others as politicians sought the winning side of all issues, and a few bureaucrats wanted to retain their position as well as their standing with "relatives and friends." Several younger scalawags embraced the romantic spirit of southern nationalism. Franklin J. Moses Jr., then serving as private secretary for South Carolina's governor, rushed to fallen Fort Sumter to raise the Rebel flag. But these men proved to be the exception rather than the rule.[39]

37. Holden, *Memoirs*, 15–17; William K. Boyd, "William W. Holden," *Annual Publication of Historical Papers Published by the Historical Society of Trinity College* 3 (1899): 66.
38. "Henry S. Foote Autobiographical Sketch," Claiborne Papers; Mosby, *War Reminiscences*, 6–7.
39. John H. Echols petition, n.d., Thomas T. Swann to Hon. Geo. S. Boutwell, 10 February 1869, RG 233; Lynch, *Kemper County Vindicated*, 22.

A score of scalawags authored works on secession. Their accounts correspond closely to those of historians supporting the "Needless War" theory. Being nationalists, scalawags spurned notions of an "irrepressible conflict" caused by differences in two separate civilizations. As slave owners, they did not see the peculiar institution as causing a "Slaveholders' War." Henry S. Foote, a well-traveled Tennessean, completely rejected the opinion championed by editor Horace Greeley that secession came because of the sections' "heterogeneous institutions." Instead, Foote insisted, it was caused by the "incessant agitation" of fanatics, "North and South," and the "unskillful and blundering management of men in power." Because these scalawags were lawyers and editors often involved in politics, they saw the coming of the conflict, as did Knoxville unionist Oliver P. Temple, in terms of "offices, power, and patronage" and its cause as being the doings "alone of ambitious politicians." The antislavery movement served as "the pretext" for separation, according to Botts of Virginia. But "the perpetuation of power" really lay behind the moves "made on the political chess-board" by the perpetrators of disunion, whom Botts characterized as "demagogues and designing men."[40]

According to this unionist-scalawag scenario, a core of conspirators, centered in the Lower South, had plotted for secession since the 1830s, awaiting the opportune season. Following the South's failure to back South Carolina during the nullification crisis of 1832–33, these secessionists attempted separation again during the early 1850s when a crisis occurred over slavery in the territories. In 1860, as in 1856, according to this version, the conspirators wanted the election of a Republican president as an excuse for secession. Alexander H. Jones of North Carolina contended that these fire-eaters intentionally split the Democratic Party at the 1860 Charleston national convention and then and during the presidential campaign that followed "knowingly, purposely, and premeditatedly, aided in the election of Mr. Lincoln." After Lincoln's victory, according to Temple, "no compromise, no concession, no constitutional guarantees would have satisfied them," since their real goal was "independence—a new government, outside of the Union."[41]

Temple raised the rhetorical question of why he and other loyalist politicians of East Tennessee (most of whom became Republicans) "cling to the Union so tenaciously and so heroically" and then he answers his own query.

40. William C. Harris, "The Southern Unionist Critique of the Civil War," *Civil War History* 31 (March 1985): 39–56.
41. Ibid.

What he had to say could well have been said for most of the future scalawags of the South in 1861. Loyalists believed that the crisis in 1860–61 was not sufficiently adequate "for a dissolution of the government." Moreover, they believed that "secession was no remedy for any existing evil," such as "the insecurity of slave property." Although they admitted "the right of revolution" when wrongs became intolerable, they denied "the constitutional right of secession." They thought that remaining in the Union could not save slavery. They denied the possibility of "peaceable secession." They insisted that the North would fight to save the Union and would if necessary "reduce the people of the seceding states to submission, and that slavery would perish" as a consequence. They knew that a southern Confederacy built on states' rights would repudiate the nationalistic views they had held. They believed that a government based on "the doctrine of states' rights . . . could not permanently endure" because it would "eventuate in anarchy."[42]

For men of these views, the war and its consequences affirmed their position in 1860–61. So, many felt that given the turn of events—secession, war, emancipation, and glorification of the Lost Cause—their best choice was to become Republicans. What Edmund Ruffin of Virginia wrote in his diary about Brownlow and his progression during the war could be said of others in 1864 and later:

> There is a remarkable contrast between the present position of Brownlow & that which he occupied . . . in 1860. He was then one of the most ardent & thorough-going, & efficient defenders of negro slavery in the South, & against the malignant & illegal assaults made on the institution by the North. His strong political feelings, as a Whig, & opposer of southern disunionists, carried him so far in opposition to the southern movement, that he became the devoted partizan of the North, & even the advocate for the destruction of slavery by the process of the illegal general emancipation offered & declared in Lincoln's proclamation.

Ruffin did not live to see that the same allegiances and beliefs would eventually cause Brownlow and others to accept black suffrage and join the Republican Party.[43]

On the whole, the difference between scalawags and redeemers everywhere

42. Ibid.
43. William K. Scarborough, ed., *The Diary of Edmund Ruffin* (Baton Rouge, 1972–89), 3: 380.

in 1860–61, other than for moderate differences in status, was in part beliefs that stemmed from their political affiliation. Such beliefs involved love of Union or, contrariwise, feelings of southern nationalism: on the one hand, a belief in the wisdom of remaining in the Union and, on the other hand, fears of real or imagined threats to "the southern way of life." To future scalawags, the struggle over slavery in the territories seemed unrealistic—nature had already resolved the question by making some areas unsuitable for the peculiar institution. Furthermore, they believed slavery safer in the Union than out of the Union. They despised equally all disunionists: fire-eaters, who they feared would pay the price of secession in hope of saving slavery, and abolitionists, who they felt would disrupt the Union to free the slaves. Eventually many future scalawags became reluctant Confederates, some retired from public life altogether, and a few fled as war refugees, or even resisted the Confederacy.

3

~

Resisting the Rebels

Resistance by large numbers of future Upper South scalawags to the new Confederacy continued throughout the war. In East Tennessee, where many crossed over into Union-occupied areas of Kentucky, and in the northwestern part of Virginia, die-hard unionists raised troops to fight the Confederates. In North Carolina, dissent by future Republicans was expressed in the formation of the secret society Heroes of America and in the protests of the peace party. Initially, Lower South resistance to the war was limited, covert, and passive, but it increased once Federals entered the Appalachian foothills and Confederates began conscription and impressment. For the most part, Southwest unionists bowed to the new order, but some rebelled or fled. A few, notably those beyond conscription age, avoided public life by being "stay-at-homes."

As part of an overall strategy to strangle the Confederacy by blockading its seacoast, Federals held coastal locations in Florida for most of the Civil War. They never abandoned the crucial military bases of Key West, stopover station at the entrance of the Gulf of Mexico, and Fort Pickens on Santa Rosa Island, protecting Pensacola Bay. Fernandina on Amelia Island (an excellent coaling station for ships), Saint Augustine fifty miles farther south, Pensacola, and Apalachicola remained in Federal hands continually after 1862. For much of the war, Union troops occupied Cedar Key, midway between Tallahassee and Tampa. United States warships, at times accompanied by troops, captured Jacksonville on the Saint Johns River on four occasions. Several future scalawags took refuge at these locations. Some sailed to their destination or hailed one of the American vessels searching for refugees and recruits along the Apalachicola and the Saint Johns Rivers. Others, like Lemuel Wilson of Gainesville, a "Hotel Landlord," rode into a Union-held town—in his case, on a stolen horse, to Jacksonville.[1]

As early as fall 1861, Confederate army deserters took refuge at Fort Pickens. When Rebels evacuated the bay area the next spring, Federals stationed themselves at a few strategic points. But other than trade in black market cotton and a few forays into the interior, their stay was rather uneventful until fall 1863, when General Alexander S. Asboth assumed command of the West Florida District. He recruited soldiers by having small vessels pick up draft dodgers and deserters along the rivers and bays to the north. Assisting Asboth was unionist newspaperman Levi J. Gallaway, publisher until early 1861 of the *Columbus (Mississippi) Expositor*. Gallaway had fled with his family to Pensacola, where Asboth authorized him to raise the First Florida Cavalry Regiment. After unionist recruits increased to several hundred, Asboth formed the Second Florida Cavalry, soon stationed down the coast at Cedar Key, from which it later occupied Tampa.[2]

At Tampa, Second Cavalry troops, many from surrounding areas, found closely linked unionist families who had been subjected to "social proscription" and mistreatment by Confederates. Lawyer Ossian B. Hart protected them from pillage by Union soldiers. Hart acted as leader of the unionists when state senator John T. Magbee departed in 1863 after losing his bid for reelection. Hart was well known in Florida. His father, Jacksonville's first storeowner, had planned the streets of Jacksonville in the 1820s, naming several of them for his children. Ossian completed his formal education in Washington, D.C., before beginning a career that took him to much of Florida: briefly to his hometown, then to the Indian River frontier, where he served in

1. William Watson Davis, *The Civil War and Reconstruction in Florida* (New York, 1913), 243–67; George Winston Smith, "Carpetbag Imperialism in Florida, 1862–1868," *FHQ* 27 (October 1948): 99–130; Smith, "Carpetbag Imperialism," 28 (January 1949): 260–99; Richard L. Hume. "Florida Constitutional Convention of 1868," *FHQ* 51 (July 1972): 12n; *KKK Report*, Fla., 177, 195–96.

2. *OR*, 35(1): 356; Levi J. Gallaway to Johnson, 24 March 1865, *PAJ*, 7: 534–35; Homer G. Plantz to Salmon P. Chase, 12 December 1863, Salmon P. Chase Papers, Library of Congress; Plantz to Zachariah Chandler, 8 June 1866, Zachariah Chandler Papers, Library of Congress; Walter C. Maloney, *A Sketch of the History of Key West, Florida* (Gainesville, Fla., 1968), 45–46; Samuel Walker to Abraham Lincoln, 2 April 1864, Lincoln Papers.

the legislature, then to Key West and to Tampa. He "took a firm stand against secession" in 1861. His new friend, pharmacist Claiborne R. Mobley, a recent resident of Tampa, was forced to join a local Confederate company, but Hart avoided conscription by obtaining a physician's certificate of disability. All three men—Hart, Magbee, and Mobley—would someday serve as Republican state judges, and Hart would in 1873 become Florida's governor.[3]

Since Union troops never evacuated Key West, some islanders organized a volunteer company in May 1861, "subject to the commander of the United States Forces at Key West." That same month, the military ordered all residents to take a loyalty oath or leave the island. The military also seized the island's disloyal newspaper *Key of the Gulf* and established *The New Era,* whose managers aimed, they said, "to add our mite toward the spread of true Republicanism." But most islanders avoided the military as well as politics. They came to make money, and few intended to remain for long. They simply wanted to live and let live. One official estimated only about one-third of voters were what he called "unconditional Union men." To conduct business, however, all needed to be considered loyal legally. Few considered themselves antislavery, and the island was excluded from the Emancipation Proclamation. Nonetheless, each season, an increasing number of residents wanted Florida to become a free state. The military started schools for black children, and a few men, mostly newcomers, eventually favored suffrage for the island's blacks.[4]

The island provided a haven for men on the make, on the run, or both. Lyman C. Stickney stayed there during 1861. Vermont-born Stickney had spent much of his life in the South, mostly in Memphis. There he promoted railroad speculation and served as associate editor of the *Memphis Enquirer,* a Whig daily. Stickney sojourned in New Orleans during 1859–60 before moving on in 1861 as an agent of Crescent City capitalists investing in South Florida land. By spring, he abandoned the enterprise near Fort Myers, however, to seek ready cash by operating an old sloop between the mainland and Union-occupied Key West. When the island's commander, distrustful of Stickney, embargoed the sloop, Stickney suggested that fellow islanders send him as a

    3. *National Cyclopaedia of American Biography* (New York, 1892–1906), 11: 380; Canter Brown Jr., *Ossian Bingley Hart: Florida's Loyalist Reconstruction Governor* (Baton Rouge, 1997), 151.
    4. Ovid L. Futch, "Salmon P. Chase and Civil War Politics in Florida," *FHQ* 32 (January 1954): 171–72, 176; John E. Johns, *Florida during the Civil War* (Gainesville, Fla., 1963), 155.

territorial delegate to Congress. But he left posthaste after the commander slapped a quietus on that plan as well. Without paying his hotel bill, Stickney sailed for Washington. There he hawked Florida real estate and wooed politicians. He impressed treasury secretary Salmon P. Chase, who named him one of Florida's three direct tax commissioners.[5]

In Jacksonville, because Confederates threatened them with confiscation or worse, unionists feared that any resistance would bring quick reprisal. Most were northern settlers. Some were prosperous merchants or lawyers, and a few owned slaves. Alarmed about the plights of their families and fortunes, not to mention their own skins, some joined the home guard. But they still refused to take a Confederate oath. Vermonter Calvin L. Robinson hid as much of his property as possible, closed his store, and concentrated on his lumber mill, anticipating that after the war, "Southern pine lumber would bring high prices." In any event, lumber would be "a safer investment" than Confederate currency. Jonathan C. Greeley, another businessman, took a different course of action. As president of the Florida, Atlantic, and Gulf Central Railroad, he had completed the track between Jacksonville and Lake City in March 1860. After refusing a Confederate officer's commission in 1861, Greeley served briefly in a state defense unit, "against [his] conscience," as he told it. He helped others "over & under age to get out of the Rebel Service." With the support of grateful unionists, he won a seat in the state legislature to get himself discharged. In January 1864, he left the town for his "former home" in Maine.[6]

A few Rebel hotheads, foreseeing the capture of Jacksonville in March 1862, torched a hotel and several sawmills, stores, and warehouses of known loyalists, including those of "Robinson and Company." A few days later, following the evacuation of the Confederates, Robinson and Philip Fraser and their families sighted the first Union ships. According to Robinson, "Never did greater joy more suddenly take possession of hearts in great despondency." Under a flag of truce, the two men boarded the gunboat *Isaac Smith*,

5. Johns, *Florida during the Civil War*, 164–72; Smith, "Carpetbag Imperialism," 27: 110–12; Stickney to Chase, 24 February 1864, John Niven, ed., *The Salmon P. Chase Papers* (Kent, Ohio, 1993–98), 4: 305–6.

6. Eighth Census, RG 29; Martin, "Defeat in Victory," 7–17; *New York Times*, 21 March 1862; DuPont to Mrs. DuPont, 15 March 1862, in *Samuel Francis DuPont: A Selection from His Civil War Letters*, ed. John D. Hayes (Ithaca, N.Y., 1969): 1: 366; Horace Greeley to Charles Sumner, 14 March 1867, Sumner Papers.

where they were cordially received with "wine, crakers [sic] and cake." And they, in essence, surrendered the town of Jacksonville to the Union forces.[7]

On March 20, about one hundred people appeared at the Jacksonville courthouse to sign an oath of loyalty to the United States. Afterward they held a meeting supporting the state's restoration to the Union and adopted a resolution that "government is a compact in which protection is the price of allegiance." Four days later, loyalists from throughout the area agreed to hold a convention April 10 to establish a state government. Much to their disappointment, they soon learned that the Federals would evacuate after being there only a few weeks. More than thirty disappointed Jacksonville families embarked on April 2; some sailed only as far as Fernandina, or Saint Augustine, both held by federal forces, but many continued on to New York, including future scalawags such as Robinson and Fraser.[8]

The Florida families joined other exiles like Stickney, entrepreneurial as well as political types, working for an enduring occupation, accompanied by officeholding. Before the close of 1862, they backed Massachusetts congressman Eli Thayer as military governor. He had furthered Yankee immigration to Virginia and had settled free soilers in Kansas. Though Lincoln never felt circumstances warranted appointing a military governor, he saw the naming of other officials as necessary for practical as well as political reasons. Lincoln's outlook mirrored that of Secretary Chase, who felt "that military occupation should immediately be followed by political reconstruction, in order to secure permanent advantage." The federal court at Key West continued to function, and later Lincoln filled judiciary offices for north Florida, headquartered at Saint Augustine. At Chase's urging, Lincoln named three direct tax commissioners, all stationed at Fernandina. Eventually an alliance emerged, composed of newcomers, longtime northern-born residents, and a few southern-born loyalists, foreshadowing the state's leadership during Reconstruction.[9]

While considering his renomination and reelection, Lincoln dispatched his private secretary John Hay to Jacksonville in February 1864 accompanied by an invasion force under General Quincy Gillmore. Hay's mission was to initi-

7. Moore, *Rebellion Record,* vol. 4, pt. 2: 325, 349; *OR,* 6: 251–52; *New York Times,* 2 April 1862.

8. *New York Times,* 2 April 1862.

9. Martin, "Defeat in Victory," 25–31; Citizens of Florida to Lincoln, 30 April, 9, 17 May, 5 December 1862, Lincoln Papers; Shofner, *Nor Is It Over Yet,* 5; Abraham Lincoln to Edward Bates, 27 March 1863, *Collected Works of Abraham Lincoln,* 7: 150; Futch, "Salmon P. Chase and Civil War Politics," 163, 169, 171, 174–80.

ate Reconstruction under Lincoln's plan by having 10 percent of the state's 1860 voters take a loyalty oath to the United States. He received sixty signatures his first day, including those of "men of substance and influence." But Hay soon became discouraged about the loyalists. Many were unwilling to come forward for fear the Rebel army would return. After registering voters at Jacksonville, Saint Augustine, and Fernandina until early March, he knew he could not get "the President's 10th." So he returned to Washington.[10]

Meanwhile, Florida unionists split into two factions: one pro-Chase, controlled by Stickney, and composed mostly of United States Treasury employees supporting their chief; the other pro-Lincoln, backed by most unionists. Both sent delegates to the Republican National Convention of 1864, which seated the pro-Lincoln faction (minus voting rights) and named one of them, Robinson, to the party's national committee. Of scalawags serving as Union officeholders, Florida had the highest percentage of any state in the Southeast—a consequence of its occupied coastal towns. Before the war ended, many of its scalawags identified with the Republicans. Others, such as refugees, deserters, and soldiers of the First and the Second Florida Union Cavalry, became good party prospects.[11]

Up the coast on the Sea Islands of South Carolina, which were occupied by troops under General Benjamin F. Butler in November 1861, a few northerners and blacks organized as Republicans in May 1864. Some northerners and a few black leaders at Beaufort elected a racially mixed delegation to represent the state at the Republican National Convention. At Baltimore, they were accorded convention seats but denied official recognition and voting rights. Some of them saw the action as being racially motivated and accused the Republicans of being "ready to have the negroes fight for the Union, die for it, but were hardly ready to let [them] vote for it." The delegation contained a few men who would become founders of the state's Republican Party in 1867, but no known white southerners. At least one white southerner, Dr. William H. Brisbane, held an important office on the islands at the time. Brisbane, an oddity, a South Carolina planter born to wealth turned "Yankee"

10. John Hay, *Lincoln and the Civil War in the Diaries and Letters of John Hay,* selected and introduction by Tyler Dennett (New York, 1939) 145–46, 155–67; Beale, *Diary of Gideon Welles,* 1: 531–32.

11. Shofner, *Nor Is It Over Yet,* 14; Futch, "Salmon P. Chase and Civil War Politics," 186–87; Smith, "Carpetbag Imperialism," 28: 291–93; Amnesty Papers, Records of the Adjutant General's Office, RG 94, National Archives.

abolitionist, had returned from his self-imposed exile to be one of the three direct tax commissioners.[12]

When Federals entered northernmost Mississippi in spring 1862 shortly after Shiloh and into its southwestern counties in spring 1863, their officers came into contact with unionist collaborators. During the occupation of Tishomingo County, Robert A. Hill, a declared neutral, and others pledged not to aid the Confederacy if the Federals allowed them to keep the local government under their control. Hill, a former attorney general for Tennessee, continued as the county's probate judge with the "consent of both sides." He had already played the angel of mercy during fighting around Corinth and Iuka, attempting to "alleviate the suffering and sorrow" of soldiers on both sides. After the war, Hill served as the area's federal district judge and supported the Republican Party.[13]

After Vicksburg fell to the Federals in July 1863, the town's loyalists offered their assistance. A trio of L. S. Houghton, Armistead Burwell, and Alston Mygatt soon founded a local Union League of America chapter. They became disheartened, however. "The Season of deliverance has Come at Last," wrote Houghton. "But it has found us exhausted! And worst of all Misunderstood! Unfortunately to the Victorious army Now here, all of us appear alike." Scalawags elsewhere in the state, such as Hill, formed better relationships with Union officers. John F. H. Claiborne, congressman turned historian, acted as a spy on the Gulf Coast for General Nathaniel P. Banks. And planter Charles Shackleford, according to General William T. Sherman, provided his "officers and soldiers with kindness and information."[14]

To avoid conscription and to thereby help fellow unionists, some Alabama scalawags sought public office. An observer in Randolph County commented wryly that officeholding became "more sought after than Heaven." Other scalawags engaged in what has been dubbed "the politics of livelihood." Milton J. Saffold of Selma, Alabama, claimed that to avoid being conscripted and be-

12. Willie Lee Rose, *Rehearsal for Reconstruction: The Port Royal Experiment* (Indianapolis, Ind., 1964), 13–22, 202; 316–17; McNulty, "William Henry Brisbane," 119–25; Abraham Lincoln to David Hunter et al., 10 February 1863, *Collected Works of Abraham Lincoln*, 6: 98.

13. John F. H. Claiborne, *Mississippi as a Province, Territory and State, with Biographical Notices of Eminent Citizens* (Jackson, Miss., 1880), 471–72n; Sansing, "Role of the Scalawag in Mississippi," 180; Hill to John Sherman, 13 March 1867, John Sherman Papers, Library of Congress.

14. Burwell to Abraham Lincoln, 28 August 1863, Mississippi Union League to Lincoln, 15, 24 February 1864, Houghton to Lincoln, 29 August 1863, Lincoln Papers; Herbert H. Lang, "J. F. H. Claiborne at 'Laurel Wood' Plantation, 1853–1870," *JMH* 18 (October 1956): 10–11.

cause he was "almost entirely without an income," he had accepted a position as "inspector" (a euphemism for *inquisitor*) of imprisoned Union sympathizers. Saffold later said he managed to release many of the Union sympathizers. Such may have been the case, as he never seemed to have had any complaints from individual loyalists.[15]

Because he was a schoolteacher with many students, Christopher Sheats was able to stay out of the Confederate army. After Federals entered north Alabama following Shiloh, their recruiting parties rode south into the mountains to Davis Gap, where Sheats had been camping with a group of draft dodgers and deserters. When they arrived, Sheats encouraged his fellows to join the Union army. That fall, the legislature, to which Sheats had been elected in 1861, expelled him for treason to the Confederacy and had him arrested and imprisoned in a "loathsome jail" at Mobile. After Sheats was confined for more than a year without trial, Federals at Huntsville retaliated by holding as a hostage General William M. Dowell, "a violent rebel," until Sheats was released.[16]

In north Alabama, a coterie led local resistance movements. In Randolph County, they "sent from 200 to 300 . . . men across the lines into the Union army," according to one witness. There, news of William H. Smith's speech at the county courthouse in 1862 created such a sensation that Confederates dispatched a company of cavalry from Montgomery to Widowee. Before they arrived, however, Smith fled with his father to north Mississippi. There he met Colonel George Spencer and became an army recruiter. Smith enlisted, among others, three of his own brothers. By early fall 1862, Spencer and the Union army had organized the First Alabama Union Cavalry, mostly composed of men from north Alabama but including enlistees from Mississippi, Georgia, and Tennessee.[17]

Many Alabama scalawags had by 1863 associated with secret societies and/

15. James M. K. Guinn, "History of Randolph County," *AlaHQ* 4 (fall 1942): 364; Wager Swayne to Salmon P. Chase, 28 June 1867, Chase Papers; Lawrence N. Powell, "The Politics of Livelihood: Carpetbaggers in the Deep South," in *Region, Race, and Reconstruction*, 315–47; Saffold petition, n.d., Amnesty Papers, RG 94.

16. Goodspeed, *Northern Alabama*, 327.

17. Robert T. Smith to Lewis E. Parsons, 3 August 1865, Governor Lewis E. Parsons Papers, Alabama Department of Archives and History, Montgomery; W. E. Connelly to Commissioners of Claims, 7 January 1873, Records of the Commissioners of Claims, RG 56; Guinn, "Randolph County," 291–413; William Stanley Hoole, *Alabama Tories: The First Alabama Cavalry, U.S.A., 1862–1865* (Tuscaloosa, 1960), 17–19.

or their state's peace party. They worked through legal means such as petitions and the ballot box, as well as through covert activities. Many supporters of the cooperationist party of 1860–61 (which had tried to delay secession) still resented the Confederacy, and their bitterness only increased as the war lingered. Some anti-Confederates won seats in the legislature in August 1863. The next summer, a few of them sought but were denied permission to confer with party leaders at the Democratic National Convention in Chicago about a possible peace plank. Afterward, Lewis E. Parsons of Talladega initiated a lengthy debate in the legislature when he called for negotiations on the basis of the platform approved at Chicago. Although Parsons's resolution in the legislature failed, other scalawags continued to hold peace party meetings in north Alabama. These included David C. Humphreys of Huntsville. "Peace is loudly called for," he informed Governor Thomas H. Watts in January 1865. He urged him to "let a convention now determine what is to be done."[18]

Some unionists in the Southeast formed underground groups to support each other. Such cells existed in Alabama at Mobile and Montgomery, in Georgia at Atlanta and Columbus, and in Florida at Jacksonville and Tampa. Those from Montgomery and Columbus were said to "have never given any more aid & Comfort to the Enemy than they were compelled to do by the tyranny of their neighbors." Wartime Montgomery unionists included at least five prominent future Republicans, including Thomas O. Glasscock, president of Alabama's Union League during Reconstruction. A number of Atlanta unionists met "regularly and secretly." Most, but not all, carefully concealed their true feelings. Because stubborn James Dunning, former owner of Atlanta Machine Works, attempted "no concealment of his views," he was imprisoned for much of the war. Evading conscription became a major concern of his friends. Some avoided serving either by an age or occupational deferment. They tried to help others identified with their cause, including Union army soldiers. They did whatever they could to help those housed near the town with little shelter, including smuggling them food and blankets. When Union armies marched into Atlanta, Dunning "climbed a pole and put up a flag" of the United States.[19]

18. Fleming, *Civil War and Reconstruction in Alabama*, 108, 143–47; Moore, *Rebellion Record*, vol. 8, pt. 1: 52; *OR*, 4(3): 393–98; D. C. Humphreys to Watts, Jan. [?] 1865, Parsons Papers.

19. John G. Winter to Johnson, 4 October 1864, *PAJ*, 7: 211–18; Roberta Steele, "Some Aspects of Reconstruction in Mobile, 1865–1875" (Master's thesis, Auburn University, 1937), 36–37; James Michael Russell, *Atlanta, 1847–1890: City Building in the Old South and the New*

Former congressman Joshua Hill emerged from political retirement in 1863 to head Georgia's peace party. He became the "rallying point" for a growing faction in north Georgia after newspapers in Atlanta and Rome nominated him for governor. The extent of his campaigning was to remind voters of his 1860–61 stand "that the destruction of the Union would be followed by a long and bloody war." He suffered a two-to-one defeat in his bid to unseat popular governor Joseph E. Brown, who simultaneously fought Federals and quarreled with Jefferson Davis. Despite his victory, Brown kept his options open, including the possibility of the Confederacy's defeat. At Brown's private urging, Hill ran for a vacant seat in the state senate. While serving in that post, he spoke with General Sherman in September 1864. Afterward Hill vainly sought legislative support for a separate peace between Georgia and the United States to halt Sherman's march through his state.[20]

A few scalawags resided outside the South when the war erupted. Some from North Carolina resided in the North because of the unpopularity of their antislavery views. A small number attended northern colleges. Frederick G. Bromberg, son of a Mobile merchant, was a wartime student and tutor at Harvard College. One young man settled temporarily in the North because of his recent marriage to an Ohio girl. Another worked for the American Foreign Service in Europe. Others from the Lower South, finding they could neither avoid conscription nor ignore the Confederacy, departed for the North. Most of these scalawags first fled to Union-occupied territory in the South. Some, including deserters and resisters, fled to Middle Tennessee. George W. Ashburn, a Columbus, Georgia, cotton broker, initially took refuge at his summer home on Lookout Mountain before moving north to occupied Murfreesboro. There he raised a regiment of southern loyalists and served as its colonel before receiving a federal appointment in Nashville.[21]

Some scalawags, like lawyer J. R. G. Pitkin of New Orleans, served briefly in the Confederate army or home guard before soldiering in the Union army. Pitkin, a native of New Orleans "educated mainly in Connecticut," his father's

(Baton Rouge, 1988), 94–95; Franklin M. Garrett, *Atlanta and Environs: A Chronicle of Its People and Events* (Athens, Ga., 1969), 1: 628–29; Dyer, *Secret Yankees,* 92–93, 206–7.

20. Avery, *History of the State of Georgia,* 260–61, 304; *American Annual Cyclopaedia, 1863,* 447; Joseph E. Brown to Alexander H. Stephens, 30 September 1864, *Correspondence of Toombs, Stephens, and Cobb,* 653.

21. *OR,* 32(2): 214; John W. DuBose, *Alabama's Tragic Decade: Ten Years of Alabama, 1865–1874,* ed. James K. Greer (Birmingham, 1940), 207, 267, 311; Shadgett, *Republican Party in Georgia,* 30; Owen, *History of Alabama,* 3: 221–22.

home state, reported for Confederate service when the governor called out the local militia "to which he had long been attached." Because Pitkin knew that "suspicious eyes" looked on him because of his past unionism, he "made no protest and went for 90 days service." After that term, however, he "bought" his discharge. He returned to New Orleans once it fell to the Federals, then he sailed north and joined the Union army "to shoulder [his] musket." Other scalawags, such as James Ready, a physician from Tennessee, also enrolled in the federal home guard. He had headed a unionist committee chosen "to hoist the United States Flag over the City Hall." His proudest moment of military service he claimed, occurred in the spring of 1863 when he "raised a regiment . . . of nine hundred of the best Colored citizens" of New Orleans to defend their city and their freedom.[22]

In the western parishes of Louisiana, resisters included members of prominent families such as the Wells of Rapides, the Taliaferros of Catahoula, and the Wrotnowskis of East Baton Rouge. After first persuading his parish to delay for months any military appropriations and after Rebels later destroyed some of his property, James Madison Wells and his sons resorted to violence, raiding and wrecking Confederate supply wagons. They hid in the woods for weeks at a stretch before finally fleeing to Union-held territory. Judge James G. Taliaferro's loyalty to the United States eventually caused the old man's imprisonment. His youngest son, Henry, had dropped out of Louisiana State Seminary in 1861 to follow its superintendent, William T. Sherman, into the Union army. And Henry's older brother Robert soon joined a unionist guerrilla band. Polish immigrant Stanislas Wrotnowski's stand cost him the destruction of his city house and his cattle ranch by Rebel vigilantes. More devastating, he also lost one of his two sons in the Union army. These families became wartime converts to the Republican Party. During the next two decades, they counted among their immediate members a governor, a state chief justice, a state secretary of state, two congressmen-elect, and several federal officeholders.[23]

Unionists throughout the Southwest found their way to Union-occupied New Orleans. In spring 1863, Robert V. Montague of Madison Parish, imme-

22. Benjamin Lynch to Benjamin F. Butler, 25 March 1869, RG 233; Pitkin to Charles Sumner, 26 April 1869, Sumner Papers; *Report of the Select Committee on the New Orleans Riots*, 238–40; *New Orleans Times*, 17, 19 March 1864; *New Orleans Picayune*, 27 March 1864.

23. Lowrey, "Political Career of James Madison Wells," 1007–8; Mills, "James Govan Taliaferro," 42–45; *New Orleans Era*, 14 February 1864.

diately across from Vicksburg, found his plantation in the midst of Ulysses S. Grant's army. He provided "valuable information" to Grant and other Union army officers. He soon refused an offer from a neighbor of "three hundred thousand dollars . . . in cotton for his slaves." Instead he and his slaves sailed together to New Orleans, where he freed them. During 1864, Montague represented Madison Parish in the Louisiana constitutional convention. While serving in that capacity, the state's first Republican convention elected him a delegate to the party's national convention at Baltimore. Shortly after the president's reelection, Lincoln appointed Montague to a position with the Treasury Department.[24]

On the heels of secession, Texas unionists organized secret societies with the hope they could win the August 1861 general election. According to journalist James P. Newcomb, they would have "secession undone [and] the State re-revolutionized through the peaceful means of the ballot box." Some Austin unionists (most eventually Republicans) met regularly upstairs at Hancock's store. They joined with legislators from other areas to form an underground Union Association "to effect a reconstruction of the United States in connection with the Border Slave States." Events, however, paralyzed their plans: the legislature required all public officials to take a loyalty oath to the Confederacy, and following the firing of Confederates on Fort Sumter, Lincoln's call for troops to crush the rebellion, gave Texans, and others, the impression that the South was being invaded.[25]

Other Texas locations also experienced some overt, as well as covert, resistance from future scalawags. By late 1862, a peace society, committed to resist conscription, had formed in the northern counties, whose members were known to each other only through passwords, grips, and signs. In less than a year, however, they were discovered by Confederates, and in Cooke County sixty-five members met their deaths swinging from a tree, twenty-five without benefit of trial. This did not prevent others in the area from fleeing to enlist in the Union army in Arkansas. In counties where Germans represented a majority, those subsequently becoming scalawags led the resistance. German-

24. Lorenzo Thomas to Johnson, 7 April 1863, *PAJ*, 6: 207–8.
25. Mary Starr Barkley, *History of Travis County and Austin, 1839–1899* (Waco, 1963), 88; "Union Association of Texas to Effect a Reconstruction of the United States in Connection with the Border Slave States and an Agreement to Protect and Defend Each Other," R. Niles Graham and Elisha Marshall Pease Collection, Austin History Center, Austin Public Library, Austin; Claude Elliott, "Union Sentiment in Texas, 1861–1865," *SwHQ* 50 (April 1946): 453.

born unionists printed peace pamphlets, circulated anticonscription petitions, and organized Union Leagues, pledging themselves "not to bear arms against the Federal government." They also tampered with the mail and in countless other ways frustrated the state's attempt to commandeer them for the war effort.[26]

Among the Germans was a group of young men from central Texas. Hoping to avoid the draft, they organized a local militia, ostensibly for frontier defense against Indians. When Confederates, suspecting them of unionist sympathies, ordered the units disbanded and conscripted them into the regular army, a group of sixty-three Germans, five Anglos, and a Mexican fled toward Mexico. En route, however, Confederate troops overtook them at the Nueces River. Without offering the youths a chance to surrender, the troops savagely fired on them. Realizing the hopeless circumstance, the militia's commander cried, "*Laszt uns unser Leben so teuer wie moglich verkaufen*" (Let us sell our lives as dear as we can). Outmanned and outarmed, one-half of the Germans were shot, and after their defeat, others were hanged. A handful escaped during the slaughter and crossed the Rio Grande, some of whom eventually joined the Union army. After the war the "bleached bones" of unburied boys, still on the battlefield at the Nueces River, were interred in a mass grave at Comfort, Texas, beneath the simple inscription *Treur der Union*. Several survivors, such as Captain John W. Sansons and Jacob Kuechler, and several relatives of those killed later became Republican leaders—Congressman Edward Degener, for example, lost two sons, Hilmer and Hugo, at the battle—as did other German refugees, resisters, and Union soldiers.[27]

Future Republicans from every part of Texas fled to all parts of the North. Some settled temporarily in Mexico or occupied areas of the Confederacy, and a few went west, including Newcomb, who became a San Francisco newspaperman. Many crossed over into Mexico and sailed from Matamoros to New Orleans in the wake of its capture by Union forces in 1862. And the flow continued throughout the war. Some went unwillingly after they distributed a peace pamphlet, "Common Sense." A slow but steady trickle of attorneys

26. Thomas Barrett, *The Great Hanging at Gainesville, Cooke County, Texas, October, A.D. 1862* (Gainesville, Tex., 1885); Baggett, "Rise and Fall of the Texas Radicals," 20–35.

27. Guido E. Ransleben, *A Hundred Years of Comfort in Texas: A Centennial History* (San Antonio, 1954), 81, 87–99; R. H. Williams and John W. Sanson, *Massacre on the Nueces River* (Grand Prairie, Tex., 1965), 36.

left Austin, including several who later served as state officials. Thomas H. Duval was typical of this strong-willed group. After being told the governor planned to muster the militia, Duval confided in his diary on May 26, 1863: "My mind is deliberately made up to take no part in this revolution on the side of the Confederacy. Before I will be forced to take a gun in my hand to aid in breaking up the Government of my fathers, I will sacrifice all—even life itself."[28]

Andrew J. Hamilton of Austin remained in Washington until his congressional term expired in 1861, after other congressmen had withdrawn. Following his return, to the dismay of secessionists, he was elected to the legislature. Ultimately, he refused to serve because legislators were required to take a loyalty oath to the Confederacy. Instead he took charge of the unionist underground in Travis County and the surrounding areas of the state. After leaving the state to avoid arrest, Hamilton accepted President Lincoln's appointment as military governor of Texas to plan for the state's restoration. In the winter and spring of 1863–64, he had his one chance to act as military governor of Texas, after Union troops occupied Brownsville in November 1863 and fought several skirmishes in the Rio Grande Valley. Among those serving Hamilton's short-lived regime were fellow refugees who would later be leaders in the state's Republican Party.[29]

Rancher Gilbert D. Kingsburg, a New Englander who had served as Brownsville's postmaster in the latter 1850s, remained in Texas until after 1863. He loved his adopted state and considered himself a Texan. Possessing an insatiable desire to learn, he had collected 1,100 books, the largest library in South Texas. Though he accepted secession, he withdrew from public life, having no intention of aiding the Confederacy. When Rebels threatened his arrest and conscription in early 1863, he simply crossed the Rio Grande into Mexico. Writing to a friend, he explained: "It may surprise you that I have fled the State to avoid Conscription. If our countrymen were fighting anything except the flag of our fathers, I should have been in the ranks without waiting for a

28. James P. Newcomb, *Sketch of Secession Times in Texas and Journal of Travels in Mexico* (San Francisco, 1863), 3; 26 May, 14 November 1863, 4 January, 10 February 1864, Thomas H. Duval Diaries, Center for American History.
29. John L. Waller, *Colossal Hamilton of Texas: A Biography of Andrew Jackson Hamilton, Militant Unionist and Reconstruction Governor* (El Paso, 1968), 35–50, 54–55; *OR*, 53: 455; Frank H. Smyrl, "Texans in the Union Army, 1861–1865," *SwHQ* 45 (October 1961): 242–43.

conscript law. But I will die sooner than assail this 'Land of the Free.'" Kingsburg stayed in the North until 1865, when he became a U.S. customs collector at Brownsville.[30]

Judge Edmund J. Davis of Corpus Christi, a tall, blue-eyed Floridian, had resided in the Rio Grande Valley since the Mexican War, serving in a series of offices. Like Hamilton, Davis refused to take a Confederate oath of allegiance, and in May 1862, after explaining his stand in a "Circular to the Citizens of the 12th Judicial District" (a triangle-shaped circuit running from Corpus Christi to Brownsville to Laredo), he rode to Matamoros and sailed to Federal-occupied New Orleans. At General Butler's suggestion, Davis organized some refugees into the First Texas Cavalry. On a return trip to South Texas, Davis recruited most of his soldiers. They numbered about three Mexicans and two Germans for every Anglo. The troops guarded the Crescent City for much of the war and saw action along the Texas Coast, in the western part of Louisiana, and up the Rio Grande as far as Laredo. Several of their officers besides Davis became key Texas Republicans. Colonel John L. Haynes, for example, later served as party chairman.[31]

After Isaac Murphy returned to Huntsville from the secession convention at Little Rock, where he had been the only delegate voting against Arkansas's withdrawal from the Union, he met a hostile reception from Madison County secessionists. They were angry about Lincoln's recent call-up of troops to invade the South. Later, as the threat of Union army occupation grew closer, with General Samuel Curtis's army only thirty miles away in Missouri, "assassination was hinted" against Murphy and Dr. James M. Johnson. They fled to Missouri where they found the tail end of Curtis's army at Keitsville on April 15. Murphy and Johnson joined General Curtis's staff. Johnson was commissioned as a colonel to raise Arkansas soldiers for the First Arkansas Infantry in spring 1863, and Murphy continued with Curtis until Little Rock's occupation in September 1863.[32]

30. Walter L. Buenger, *Secession and the Union in Texas* (Austin, 1984), 179.

31. Ernest W. Winkler, *Check List of Texas Imprints* (Austin, 1949–63), 2: 12; *OR*, 26(2): 68; George S. Denison to Chase, 27 October, 14 November 1862, *Diary and Correspondence of Chase*, 328, 331; H. C. Hunt, "The First Texas Cavalry of U.S. Volunteers—Its History by an Officer of the Regiment," clipping, Haynes Papers; Muster Rolls of the First and Second Texas Cavalry in the Union Army, Texas State Library and Archives Commission, Austin; Buenger, *Secession and the Union in Texas*, 179.

32. Sketch of Governor Isaac Murphy by Mrs. J. R. Berry, Facts and Reminiscences by Hon. James R. Berry, 18, 21–23, Berry Papers; Murphy to Abraham Lincoln, 17 February 1863, Lincoln Papers.

Meanwhile Murphy's son-in-law's path took a very different course. County clerk James R. Berry served briefly in 1861 as receiver of the U.S. Land Office at Huntsville under an appointment from the Lincoln administration. Berry had served in state as well as local posts. The people of Madison County elected him to the state legislature in 1862, but instead of serving, he resigned and worked as deputy treasurer of Arkansas for much of 1862 and 1863. In spring 1863, Berry and his family left Little Rock for Huntsville. In fall 1863, Berry received word from Captain John Worthington of the First Union Arkansas Infantry, who apparently considered Berry a unionist, "that delegates were to soon assemble at Little Rock looking to the establishment of a [loyal] state government." Worthington asked Berry to proceed to Fayetteville to link up with a military escort to Little Rock. Berry arrived there in early January 1864.[33]

Some wartime converts to the Republican Party from Arkansas, such as Judge Elisha Baxter and state attorney Lafayette Gregg, both antisecessionists in 1861, served as officeholders under the Confederacy until the Union army entered their area. Gregg, from Fayetteville, had served a term in the legislature before being elected prosecuting attorney for the fourth district in 1856. After going over to the Federals in the middle of the war, Gregg later commanded the Fourth Arkansas Cavalry, all of whose companies were organized at Little Rock. Baxter, a North Carolina native, settled in Batesville in 1852. He was elected mayor a year later. At the beginning of the war, he tried neutrality. He had no interest in raising a Confederate regiment, and in spring 1862, he refused a Union army officer's commission and "the command of a Regt. of loyal Arkansians." He did not want, he said, "to make war upon the people of the South." Following an attack by the Rebel press accusing him of cowardice, he left Arkansas.[34]

Confederate soldiers found Baxter operating in Missouri, where he had taken his family. The soldiers turned him over to Arkansas authorities, who charged him with "high treason against the Confederacy" and imprisoned him at Little Rock. There he "resolved that if God would grant [him] deliverance [he] would at once enter the Federal Army." God and the wife of another

33. Facts and Reminiscences, 17–23, Berry Papers.

34. Ted R. Worley, ed., "Elisha Baxter's Autobiography," *ArkHQ* 14 (summer 1955): 172–73; Goodspeed, *Biographical and Historical Memoirs of Northwest Arkansas* (Chicago, 1889), 1075; Fay Hempstead, *A Pictorial History of Arkansas, from Earliest Times to the Year 1890 . . .* (St. Louis, 1890), 412–17.

Arkansas scalawag, Mrs. Enoch H. Vance, answered his prayer. Enoch, an antisecessionist editor of the *Pine Bluff Democrat,* had crossed over into Missouri in 1861 to enlist in the Eighth Missouri Cavalry. When his wife visited him, she stole the keys from a guard and liberated Vance and Elisha Baxter. After Baxter escaped and subsisted in the wild "on *raw* corn and berries for eighteen days," according to his own words, he "sought and obtained permission to recruit a regiment of loyal Arkansans for the Federal service." Returning to Batesville in fall 1863, he recruited and served as colonel of the Fourth Arkansas Mounted Infantry until he was elected a judge of the state supreme court of the newly organized state government in spring 1864.[35]

Another Arkansan who joined the Republican Party during the war was Brigadier General Edward W. Gantt of Hempstead County, the highest ranking Rebel military officer switching sides. Gantt, whom some enemies in his own party considered "a facetious little disorganizer," supported saving the Union before Lincoln defeated Breckinridge. In spring 1861, the young, wealthy lawyer joined other party chiefs in stumping northwest Arkansas, the state's unionist stronghold, for secession. Speaking there, Gantt pledged his "best energies, . . . present and future hopes, . . . his life, his all to the Confederacy." Soon after he raised the Twelfth Arkansas Volunteers. Initially he impressed his soldiers and his superiors. His regimental surgeon Roscoe Jennings wrote: "The Colonel is a man of undoubted ability and Genius." But the doctor soon felt disappointment, or perhaps some envy, about Gantt. "As to the women," Jennings wrote, "he is a second Aaron Burr."[36]

Eventually Gantt's morale declined more rapidly than his morals. The war he savored became nightmarish. He was twice captured by Federals, once at Fort Davidson and then at Island Number Ten, after which he was imprisoned for a while at Fort Warren in the Boston Harbor. On one occasion, after being exchanged, he almost lost his life from the bursting of a nearby enemy shell. Feeling he had suffered enough, as had the South, he returned to his Hempstead County home in early 1863, hoping to sit out the rest of the war.[37]

But Gantt remained restless, and in June 1863, perhaps seeking an oppor-

35. Worley, "Elisha Baxter's Autobiography," 172–73; Hempstead, *Pictorial History of Arkansas,* 412–17.

36. Michael B. Dougan, *Confederate Arkansas: The People and Policies of a Frontier State in Wartime* (University, Ala., 1976), 17, 36; Eugene A. Nolte, "Downeasters in Arkansas: Letters of Roscoe G. Jennings to His Brother," *ArkHQ* 58 (spring 1959): 1–25.

37. Dorris, *Pardon and Amnesty,* 36; *OR,* 24(1): 97; OR, 24 (3): 353; Nolte, "Downeasters in Arkansas," 17–23.

tunity from the Federals, he surrendered himself to General Grant (whom Gantt had once met under a flag of truce), who was located above Vicksburg. Gantt told Grant his motive was "to bring the war to a close." In October, after the September fall of Little Rock, Gantt issued a twenty-nine-page paper, "An Address to the People of Arkansas," revealing his rationale for submission. Speaking to Confederates, he said, "Our armies are melting [away] and ruin approaches us." He advised his fellow citizens to oppose the destructive, demoralizing, futile war and to renew their allegiance to the United States government. In early December, Gantt was one of the first individuals pardoned by President Lincoln under the amnesty plan. Afterward, Gantt worked with Murphy and others to reconstruct Arkansas.[38]

East Tennesseans who resisted the Confederacy included many delegates from the Knoxville and Greenville conventions in May and June 1861. Some of them recruited and drilled loyal militias, "keeping the Union spirit up to a high pitch" while awaiting the arrival of Federal troops. Joseph A. Cooper, a farmer and Mexican War veteran from Campbell County, trained more than 500 men a week by August 1861. He plowed during the day and recruited at night, and "on Saturday he met . . . for muster in the old fields, in out-of-the-way places, and gave . . . instruction in military tactics." After voting against the Confederate constitution on August 1, he fled with 150 men and reached Barboursville, Kentucky, two days later. About as many more followed him in a day or two. But a lack of arms and other supplies prevented troop organization until early 1862. Colonel Cooper formed several companies in the spring. Altogether during the next three years he took his regiment "on foot and otherwise" almost ten thousand miles, leading his men into battle in Tennessee and Georgia.[39]

As part of an overall plan to cut Confederate transport through East Tennessee and pave the way for Federals to invade the region, another farmer, Alfred M. Cate of Mouse Creek Valley in McMinn County, helped execute the plot to burn several railroad bridges entering lower East Tennessee. Cate and others torched five of the nine bridges they wanted to destroy. But, as one refugee wrote, the event sparked "the fiery vengeance of the Rebel horde," causing some conspirators to be imprisoned and others to be hanged, a few

38. *OR*, 24 (1): 97; John G. Nicolay and John Hay, *Abraham Lincoln: A History* (New York, 1890) 8: 410.

39. Temple, *Notable Men of Tennessee*, 77–78, 85–87, 104–5, 182–85; Leonidas C. Houk to Johnson, 7 December 1861, *PAJ*, 5: 41, 149n.

of whose bodies, as a lesson to loyalists, dangled for days near the burned bridges. Cate himself fled and hid until he joined Cooper's Sixth Tennessee Volunteer Infantry Regiment in May 1862 as a captain of Company G. Some men eventually arrested for clandestine activities included members of the general assembly. Others escaped certain imprisonment by journeying through the mountain passes into Union-controlled Kentucky, where they helped organize refugees into Union regiments at Camp Dick Robinson near Lexington.[40]

William B. Stokes, a future gubernatorial candidate, had fled to Nashville in early spring 1862 to volunteer for the Union army. For him, it was a costly decision. His citizen-soldiers complained often and returned home whenever they pleased. Without Stokes, according to one Union officer, his soldiers were "a rabble and entirely worthless." Because Stokes became irritated, he ruled with a "spirit of harshness and tyranny." Once, when some of his soldiers entered a home, entertained themselves, and then started to commandeer goods without authorization, the lady of the house finally threatened to tell "the Colonel." That comment, alone, frightened them: they left without the goods, and the grateful woman named her next child "Colonel" in honor of Stokes.

Stokes's iron-fisted style often caused his officers, especially those who considered him incompetent to have "heart-burnings and hatreds." While the former congressman struggled with his regiment, his family suffered because of his loyalty. In 1863, the Rebels, he wrote, "have taken all my stock, have attempted to burn my house, insulted my family, [and] fired on my wife." At times his tribulations seemed too great to bear. He threatened to resign on numerous occasions but ultimately continued in the army until the end of the war. Stokes returned to Congress in 1866 and ran unsuccessfully for governor in 1869. Several of his regimental officers also later served as Republican officeholders.[41]

40. Robert L. Stanford to Johnson, 31 December 1861, *PAJ*, 5: 87; Goodspeed, *History of Tennessee from the Earliest Time to the Present . . .* (Nashville, 1886), 497–507.

41. *OR*, 23(2): 475; *OR*, 52(1): 513; Christine S. Jones, archivist, Tennessee Tech University, interview by author, 17 April 1985; Henry L. Newberry to Johnson, 25 October 1862, *PAJ*, 6: 38–39, 39n; Stokes to Johnson, 5 March 1863, PAJ, 6: 162–63, 163n; Newberry to Johnson, 25 October 1862, PAJ, 6: 38–39, 39n; Stokes to Johnson, 19 January 1863, 5 March 1863, PAJ, 6: 124, 162–63; Tennessee Civil War Centennial Commission, *Tennesseans in the Civil War: A Military History of the Confederate and Union Units with Available Rosters of Personnel* (Nashville, 1964), 1: 329–30.

After Shiloh and the Confederates' retreat from West Tennessee to Mississippi, loyalists recruited troops throughout the Third Grand Division. Enlistments occurred earliest in the two tiers of counties immediately west of the Tennessee River, most of which voted heavily against secession in 1861. The Hawkins family led the way in Carroll County by organizing three companies and by getting one of their own, attorney Isaac Hawkins, a Mexican War veteran, elected colonel of the Second West Tennessee Cavalry Regiment. During December 1862, the Second West Tennessee Cavalry engaged in several skirmishes along the route of the Mobile and Ohio railway around Jackson, Tennessee. Remnants of the Second Cavalry continued to see action during 1863, as they guarded West Tennessee rail lines and assisted scouting expeditions into north Mississippi. When Forrest's Confederates attacked Union City in northwest Tennessee in March 1864, Hawkins surrendered to what he thought to be superior numbers. After being exchanged, he and his soldiers served at Paducah, Kentucky.[42]

By 1861, Fielding Hurst, another Union colonel, and his brothers and their "clannish, close-knit family" were McNairy County, Tennessee's, largest landowners, holding a long neck of land from the central to the northwestern part of the county. Hurst, a fifty-one-year-old man with a two-year-old son named Napoleon and the owner of several slave families, was his family's acknowledged leader as well as ruler of the so-called Hurst Nation. He was one of almost 600 voters (many of whom would later join the Union army) of more than 1,900 overall who cast ballots against secession in McNairy County on June 8, 1861.[43]

At the county seat of Purdy, where Hurst voted, county officials insisted on voice voting that day. When his turn came, without hesitation, Hurst said, "against secession." But a man who ruled a clan and named his only son Napoleon would do more than that: the former county surveyor then gave a speech denouncing the secessionists. Hurst was immediately arrested and put on the next train to Nashville's penitentiary, to lie on "the cold stone floors" for a few weeks. But Hurst, a stubborn sort, had not learned his lesson. After

42. Civil War Commission, *Tennesseans in the Civil War,* 1: 333–37; Peggy Scott Holley, "The Seventh Tennessee Volunteer Cavalry: West Tennessee Unionists in Andersonville Prison," *WTHSP* 42 (1988): 39–51; Charles L. Lufkin, "West Tennessee Unionists in the Civil War: A Hawkins Family Letter," *THQ* 46 (spring 1987): 33–42.

43. Gary Blankinship, "Colonel Fielding Hurst and the Hurst Nation," *WTHSP* 34 (1980): 71–87.

his release and return to Purdy, he formed a secret militia of kinfolk and friends. So when the Federals invaded West Tennessee in spring 1862, Hurst and his men went to General Grenville M. Dodge at Trenton, Tennessee. Wearing "a tall silk hat, a long coat with brass buttons, baggy jean pantaloons, and an old sword," Hurst offered his recruits as scouts for the Union army.[44]

After Shiloh, Hurst's farmer-soldiers scouted for General Grant's army as far south as Corinth, Mississippi, where Grant allowed them to return home. Hurst then recruited and organized six companies of troops from McNairy County at Bethel in August and September. He marched his men to be mustered in at Trenton, where companies from other counties joined his First West Tennessee Cavalry Regiment. As their regiment's motto, Hurst's soldiers chose "I give my head and my heart to God and our country—one country, one language, one flag," a sentiment that reflected Hurst's Whiggish and nativistic political beliefs. During the next three years, in an area often crisscrossed by Forrest's Rebels, Hurst made life miserable for many Confederates. Hurst may not have been as daring as Forrest, but he was every bit as elusive, partly because, as one observer put it, Hurst knew "every pig path in the area."[45]

After the war, many of West Tennessee's Union army officers became Republican officeholders. Most held local offices, where unionists represented a majority or where, after spring 1867, a combination of white and black Republicans created a majority. Others served in the legislature. After serving briefly in the state senate, Fielding Hurst became judge of the so-called saddlebag circuit straddling the Tennessee River, covering counties on both sides. Hurst's second in rank, Colonel William J. Smith of Grand Junction (who went on to become a general under another command), also held a seat in the postwar legislature before moving on to bigger plums. Isaac Hawkins became a postwar congressman. His son, Lieutenant Samuel W. Hawkins, went on to achieve, among other honors, the gubernatorial nomination in 1888, hoping (albeit unsuccessfully) to follow in the footsteps of his second cousin, Governor Alvin Hawkins.[46]

Some Tennesseans went north during 1861. Ohio-born Joseph S. Fowler, president of Howard Female College in Gallatin, took advantage of Jefferson

44. Ibid.

45. Ibid.

46. Ibid., 85–86; *BDTGA,* 2: 444–45, 651–52; Lufkin, "West Tennessee Unionists," 33, 41n, 42n.

Davis's "forty day" free period. "Leaving friends and home and property," Fowler "sought a refuge where the Stars and Stripes could still float over him." He settled briefly in Springfield, Illinois, before returning in 1862 to join Military Governor Andrew Johnson's cabinet as secretary of state. Another refugee, Andrew J. Fletcher of Greene County, foresaw that the war would be settled "like the crusades of old . . . through seas of blood." By June 1861, he worried more about his own blood. He purchased a pistol for protection, but when Confederate soldiers came to his house, Fletcher could not bring himself to fire it; instead he fled. He soon settled in Evansville, Indiana, where he fought the anti-Republican copperheads, and in 1864, he campaigned for Lincoln's reelection.[47]

Some Tennesseans went to Washington after winning one of many Union congressional races that transpired in the Confederacy. Both Confederate and unionist candidates ran for Congress at the same polls in the first four congressional districts of East Tennessee in August 1861. Three of the unionists who claimed victory—all of whom eventually became Republicans—made it to Washington: Horace Maynard of Knoxville, George W. Bridges of Athens, and Andrew J. Clements of Lafayette. Joining this group of congressmen in Washington was Emerson Etheridge, a former congressman from Dresden in West Tennessee. He served as clerk of the House for several months before breaking with the administration over the issue of emancipation.[48]

Several unionist editors left Tennessee for safer lands during the first year of the war. Before editor-publisher William G. Brownlow of Knoxville left the Confederacy, he folded Old Glory, which had been seen floating over his home for weeks after secession. He announced he was "not a candidate for martyrdom or imprisonment." Yet he refused to take a loyalty oath to the Confederacy, and rather than print pro-South battle accounts, he stopped publishing in October 1861. Still Brownlow remained a "thorn in the flesh" to the Confederacy. After being imprisoned in December, Brownlow requested his own deportation from officials, including Confederate Secretary of War Judah P. Benjamin, who granted the request. During spring 1862,

47. Walter T. Durham, "How Say You, Senator Fowler?" *THQ* 42 (spring 1983): 39–44; James H. Embry to Johnson, 11 March 1862, *PAJ*, 5: 196; Thomas B. Alexander, *Thomas A. R. Nelson of East Tennessee* (Nashville, 1956), 69–70; Temple, *Notable Men of Tennessee*, 123–25; Fletcher to Oliver P. Temple, 26 July, 15 October 1861, [?] June 1864, Oliver P. Temple Papers, University Archives and Special Collections, University of Tennessee, Knoxville.

48. Robert E. Corlew, *Tennessee: A Short History*, 2d ed. (Knoxville, 1981), 299.

Brownlow spoke to northern audiences about the tribulations of East Tennesseans and played the martyr's role for crowds in Cincinnati, New York, and Philadelphia. That same season, he finished *Sketches of the Rise, Progress, and Decline of Secession,* a 450-plus-page book, a compilation of articles from his *Knoxville Whig.* Soon his publisher had printed 75,000 copies to satisfy public demand. By 1863 Brownlow was back in Tennessee at Nashville, serving as an assistant special agent of the Treasury Department.[49]

Meanwhile in Richmond, several future Republicans, along with other unionists, were imprisoned because of suspected loyalty to the "old Flag." After being warned of a Union army attack from the east, President Jefferson Davis declared martial law in the Confederate capital on March 1, 1862. Because he considered local unionists an internal threat, he ordered the arrest of more than fifty of them. Those imprisoned included former congressman John M. Botts; his friend Franklin Sterns, a wealthy whiskey distiller; and Burnham Wardwell, an ice merchant, all postwar scalawags. Confederates kept them in McDaniel's Negro Jail, a four-story brick building in an area of bawdy houses and livery stables, until almost May of 1862. Some, such as Sterns, whose pragmatism often outweighed his principles, went home after taking an oath of allegiance to the Confederacy. Botts was released after agreeing to leave Richmond. Confederates transferred others, including Wardwell, to the military prison at Salisbury, North Carolina, where they were imprisoned until late September, when Lincoln offered in exchange to free some Fredericksburg citizens held as hostages because of the Richmond unionists. Meanwhile, Botts moved to his Culpeper County plantation, soon to be in the midst of the Union army. His manor filled with officers offering Botts the "flattering attention of a hero." He had little to give in return, however, but shelter, information, and fenceposts, which during 1863 decreased from "25 or 30 miles of fencing" to only three posts.[50]

During 1864, members of Richmond's unionist underground, most of whom were born outside the South, made contact with General Butler and his army to the east and with General Grant and his army to the north. They helped some prisoners of war escape and slip through the Confederate lines.

---

49. Moore, *Rebellion Record,* vol. 2, pt. 1: 71, vol. 3, pt. 1: 58, vol. 4, pt. 1: 77; *Knoxville Whig,* 7 September 1861; *OR,* 2(1): 902–31; *OR,* 23(2): 524.

50. Botts to John B. Fry, 22 January 1864, John B. Fry to Abraham Lincoln, 12 April 1864, Lincoln Papers.

They also provided intelligence, especially about the size and movement of Lee's Army of Northern Virginia. Some underground members eventually became postwar officeholders, including Wardwell, an anti-Confederate spy, and Superintendent Samuel Ruth of the Richmond, Fredericksburg, and Potomac Railroad, who had "forwarded information, agents, and refugees to Washington."[51]

Others who later became Republicans voiced sentiments for peace during the war, including friends of Botts such as William C. Wickham and Alexander Rives. Wickham, one of the last of the state's secession convention delegates to yield to the majority, became a Confederate general but eventually abandoned all hope for victory. He was elected to the Confederate Congress on the pledge to, in his words, "at once and assiduously . . . work to bring about the termination of the blood strife that was being waged." Such sentiments became widespread in parts of Virginia toward the end of the war. Rives, of Albemarle County, wrote a friend in early 1865 that it was "now time to ordain State Conventions, and thus enable the people in each State to dispose of themselves in their own way."[52]

Some scalawags from North Carolina avoided serving the Confederacy every way possible. Foreseeing "the outbreak of the rebellion," Israel G. Lash, a Salem banker, invested heavily in northern and western land, purchasing more than 200,000 acres. After North Carolina seceded, he "promptly declined" an offer to serve in the Treasury Department at Richmond, and despite a requirement that magistrates do so, he never took "an oath to support the Confederate Government." For many months he also refused to accept Confederate money in his bank until he was "compelled by the authorities." Others served the Confederacy only to the degree necessary to keep out the army or to aid fellow unionists. Solicitor David M. Furches of Davie County said that he held office "for the purpose of keeping himself out of the *army*," and that he was "known and treated as a peace man." The state's chief justice Richmond M. Pearson stayed on the bench "to maintain the right of [his]

---

51. Meriwether Stuart, "Colonel Ulric Dahlgren and Richmond's Union Underground, April 1864," *VMHB* 72 (April 1964): 152–204; Angus J. Johnston II, "Disloyalty on Confederate Railroads in Virginia," *VMHB* 63 (October 1955): 420–25.

52. William C. Wickham petition, n.d., Amnesty Papers, RG 94; Alexander Rives to William A. Graham, 18 January 1865, William A. Graham Papers, North Carolina Division of Archives and History, Raleigh.

fellow citizens." Although he became obnoxious to the Richmond government, Pearson did not deny a single writ of habeas corpus releasing anyone accused of disloyalty to the Confederacy.[53]

Some crossed over the mountains into Kentucky to join the Union army. Alexander H. Jones raged against rich planters, whom he referred to as "bombastic, high faluten, aristocratic fools." He said they had "been in the habit of driving negroes and poor helpless white people" until they thought they could "control the world of mankind." He refused to accept *their* Confederacy. After organizing Union Leagues in western North Carolina and into East Tennessee, he enlisted in the Union army in 1863. While raising a regiment of loyalists, he was captured in Tennessee and imprisoned for months before being drafted into the Confederate army. But he promptly deserted to rejoin the Federals. Apparently Jones had a following in western North Carolina, because in 1865 he was elected to Congress.[54]

Soon after the war started, the state's former Whigs started criticizing Jefferson Davis and his administration for engaging in the "exclusion of all once termed anti-secessionists from office" because they were "slow to leave the old Government." They accused him of elevating only Democrats to high office. Of the first twenty-one brigadier generals Davis appointed, they said, only one had been a Whig. And, as the war lingered—with the loss of Hatteras Inlet in the summer of 1861 and the occupation of Roanoke Island, Elizabeth City, and New Bern during the first quarter of 1862—increasingly Whigs condemned Davis's policies as oppressive and unfair, especially those suspending the writ of habeas corpus and exempting planters from conscription.[55]

In North Carolina during 1863, some individuals in the state's Conservative Party formed a peace faction championed by William W. Holden, publisher of the *North Carolina Standard.* Holden had raised the cry of a "rich man's war and a poor man's fight" because Confederate laws and regulations favored the planter class. The peace party, as the faction came to be called, demanded a state convention to sue for peace, with the cooperation of other Confederate states if possible, if not, without it. Edwin G. Reade suggested privately what later became a peace party hallmark: that the state name com-

53. Barnes, *Fortieth Congress,* 2: 229–30; *DNCB,* 1: 305; D. M. Furches petition, n.d., Amnesty Papers, RG 233; Richmond M. Pearson petition, n.d., Amnesty Papers, RG 94.

54. Jones, *Knocking at the Door,* 8.

55. Holden, *Memoirs,* 23; *OR,* 51(1): 831–32; Edgar E. Folk and Bynum Shaw, *W. W. Holden: A Political Biography* (Winston-Salem, N.C., 1984), 146.

missioners to negotiate peace between North Carolina and the United States. During summer 1863, more than one hundred peace party meetings adopted resolutions, all urging Governor Zebulon Vance to convene the legislature, which would, in turn, call a convention to arrange a negotiated peace.[56]

Holden's peace party garnered many followers, especially in western North Carolina from the ten thousand–member, antiaristocratic Heroes of America. The Heroes was one of several such secret unionist societies operating in the South. Some existed in only one or two counties and had brief existences, others encompassed entire sections, and a few expanded into adjoining states. The Heroes, widely known as the Red Strings, was named for the group's lapel emblem. The emblem, as well as the passwords, "Three" and "Days," came from the story of Rahab in Joshua, chapter 2. Rahab concealed Israelite spies in exchange for the sparing of her family after the fall of Jericho. The Heroes applied the story to their hiding of draft dodgers, deserters, and escaped prisoners of war. Influential Heroes included several merchants (a number of stores in western North Carolina were the focus of antiwar activities) and George W. Logan, an attorney elected as a peace candidate to the Confederate Congress in 1863, "for the two-fold purpose of opposing tyranny and keeping *out* of the rebel army."[57]

The peace party failed to win statewide elections in North Carolina largely because it represented "peace-at-any-price men," while Conservatives pursued a conciliatory course, and won the votes of original secessionists. In the race for governor in 1864, Zebulon Vance won by a vote of 43,579 to Holden's 28,982. The victory margin came mostly from the army camps, where Vance won 13,209 to 1,824. But peace party candidates for the legislature, such as Robert P. Dick and John Pool, emerged from political retirement to embarrass their enemies. Pool offered a resolution in the state senate, which failed by only 4 votes, to appoint "five commissioners . . . to act with commissioners from other Confederate states, in negotiating a peace with the United States." A similar appeal in the house failed by only 2 votes. A host of lesser-known Whigs joined some Douglas Democrats, including surviving 1860 Douglas electors, to support the peace movement. Of the peace party men who re-

56. Folk and Shaw, *W. W. Holden*, 146; E. G. Reade to William A. Graham, 4 February 1862, Graham Papers.
57. William T. Auman and David D. Scarboro, "The Heroes of America in Civil War North Carolina," *NCHR* 58 (autumn 1981): 327, 336, 342, 346–48; George W. Logan petition, n.d., Amnesty Papers, RG 94.

mained politically active during Reconstruction, most became Republicans. One historian goes so far as to conclude that the "peace movement of 1863–64 . . . was the principal catalyst in making Republicans of native Whites."[58]

During the 1870s, many scalawags who claimed wartime loyalty filed with the federally funded Southern Claims Commission for losses of livestock, wagons, forage, and provisions confiscated by the northern troops. Each was asked, along with his neighbors, a lengthy battery of questions, including: "Which side did you take . . . in 1860 and 1861 . . .? Were you in any service, business, or employment for the Confederacy . . .? Did you take any oath to the . . . Confederate States . . .? Did you ever sell or furnish any supplies to the . . . Confederate States . . .? And did you ever subscribe to any loan of the . . . Confederate States?" Nearly two-thirds of scalawag claimants received some of their claim, compared with less than one-third of the claimants as a whole, whereas redeemer claimants were nonexistent.[59]

Frank W. Klingberg says the strictness of the procedure guaranteed that only loyal individuals were compensated. As with others filing claims, some scalawags (about one-third) were denied compensation, signifying the strictness, and at times unfairness, of the policy. For instance, Georgia's peace party leader Joshua Hill, claiming he had supplied more than $25,000 to the Union army in "horses, mules, cotton, houses, farming implements, commissary and quartermaster stores," was denied his petition because he served in the wartime state senate.[60]

Although a large majority of scalawags had fought secession and some opposed the rebel government, most rendered some sort of service to the Confederacy. When secession came, most Union men fell into the current. They justified their changed position then and later in terms of accepting the will of their people or of going along with their section or state. Many believed secession a *fait accompli*, and after Lincoln's call for troops, they considered the defense of the South urgent. Several scalawags received recognition for their courage on behalf of the Confederacy. These former Confederate army

---

58. Horace W. Raper, *William W. Holden: North Carolina Political Enigma* (Chapel Hill, 1985), 54–56, 57; *(Raleigh) North Carolina Standard*, 29 November 1864; *American Annual Cyclopaedia, 1864*, 589; Lancaster, "Scalawags of North Carolina," 50, 418.

59. *Consolidated Index of Claims.*

60. Frank W. Klingberg, *The Southern Claims Commission* (Berkeley, Calif., 1955), 213–19; *Index of Claims;* Hill to Andrew Johnson, 10 May 1865, Johnson Papers.

officers accepted the war's results, including Congressional Reconstruction, with the same finality they had exhibited toward secession. Still there were far fewer scalawags than redeemers in the Confederate army. In the Southeast, twice as many redeemers as scalawags fought for the Lost Cause, two-thirds as against one-third. About one-fifth of the redeemers and the scalawags served in a Confederate civilian capacity. Of the South as a whole, William B. Hesseltine's study *Confederate Leaders in the New South* found that "of 585 prominent Confederates, only 22 at one time or another joined the Republicans." Another study, Jon L. Wakelyn's *Biographical Dictionary of the Confederacy*, identified only 27 of 651 Confederate leaders as Republicans during Reconstruction.[61]

Individuals who proved disloyal to the Confederacy and who later became Republicans were motivated by many factors. In most cases, a connection existed between two factors: "disloyalty" and becoming a Republican. It existed partly because it represented a natural progression, that is, to join the party that saved the Union they loved. But perhaps equally important, the Fourteenth Amendment and the Reconstruction Acts caused these men to be in demand since Confederates who had been antebellum officeholders were temporarily barred from holding office. Individuals with anti-Confederate backgrounds composed most of the early white Republican state officeholders. They could do this better than others who were not disfranchised because of their political experience. They also recommended others who supported their cause for congressional pardon under the provisions of the Fourteenth Amendment, especially original unionists who reluctantly or unwillingly supported the Confederacy.

In most cases, the decision to become a Republican was not so much an individual decision as it was a decision to keep moving with a group of former associates, be they Union friends, compatriots in blue, loyalist refugees, or peace party members. Some scalawags seemingly operated in isolation in deciding to rebel against the Confederacy and later to join the Republican Party, but they were exceedingly rare. Most operated with the advice and encouragement of like-minded individuals. The loyalty of Confederate resisters was, as has been said, "imperfect, rarely unconditional, and often influenced by circumstance." Concessions were made to survive and to please family and

---

61. *OR*, 2: 520; OR, 16(1): 891; OR, 17(1): 683; OR, 24(2): 404; OR, 25(1): 982; *KKK Report*, Miss., 22; William B. Hesseltine, *Confederate Leaders in the New South* (Baton Rouge, 1950), 103–15; Wakelyn, *Biographical Dictionary of the Confederacy*, 553–70.

friends. But some did resist, and they later associated that resistance with their joining the Republican Party. In the 1870s at hearings throughout the South before representatives of the Southern Claims Commission, even conservative neighbors on the whole testified that loyalists reported truthfully about their claims of resisting the Confederacy.

4

~

Wartime Reconstruction

After Union armies descended into parts of Virginia and Tennessee, unionists in the occupied areas recruited soldiers, established loyal governments, and formed political factions. Along with others from sections of Arkansas, Florida, and Louisiana, these loyalists enlisted home guards, sponsored elections, and sent delegates to the 1864 Republican National Convention. When the Union army occupied south Louisiana and north Arkansas, unionists created loyal state governments. Serious attempts at Reconstruction took place in three states—Arkansas, Louisiana, and Virginia—and to a lesser degree in Tennessee. Unionists also created West Virginia. Issues faced later during Congressional Reconstruction concerning loyalty and race were confronted or avoided during wartime Reconstruction in these states. Many individuals who participated in the wartime Reconstruction governments became Republicans during the war and helped lay the groundwork for the party in their state.[1]

Unionists from the northwestern part of Virginia engaged in the series of meetings and elections leading to statehood for West Virginia. The events in-

1. Frederick W. Moore, "Representation in the National Congress from the Seceding States, 1861–1865," *American Historical Review* 2 (January 1897): 279–93, 461–71; *Proceedings of the First Three Republican National Conventions,* 193, 203; James G. Randall and Richard N. Current, *Last Full Measure,* vol. 4 of *Lincoln the President* (New York, 1955), 1–31; Richard N. Current, *Lincoln's Loyalists: Union Soldiers from the Confederacy* (Boston, 1992), 159–94; Herman Belz, *Reconstructing the Union: Theory and Policy during the Civil War* (Ithaca, N.Y., 1969), 159–64.

cluded the fall 1861 constitutional convention at Wheeling creating the Restored Government of Virginia and the spring 1862 ratification referendum in Union-controlled counties. This was followed by the consent of the Restored Government's legislature to separate West Virginia from Virginia and Lincoln's endorsement of Congress's condition of gradual emancipation to achieve statehood. Then in 1863, a constitutional convention met to approve emancipation, voters approved the action, and finally West Virginia was admitted to the Union by Congress. With rare exceptions, future Republican politicians supported statehood as approved by Congress, that is, with emancipation and many pro-Confederate counties included, while opponents of the same became Democrats.

While some postwar Democrats from West Virginia served as loyal wartime officials, they numbered far fewer than postwar Republicans, about one-fourth, compared with three-fourths. Because of their prior affiliation with the Republican Party, some unionists from Virginia's Panhandle received federal appointments. Others who eventually became Republicans won seats in the United States Congress.[2]

After United States forces evacuated the naval yard at Norfolk on April 20, 1861, Federals still held a toehold at Fortress Monroe. Then during autumn 1861, Virginia's Eastern Shore fell to Federals, who attacked from Maryland. Much of the Tidewater area remained in Union hands throughout the war, including the counties of the Eastern Shore and four others and the towns of Norfolk and Portsmouth.

Unionists gathered at Oxford Hall in Portsmouth on May 22, 1862. After hearing an army brass band from Michigan "enliven the occasion," the unionists petitioned Washington to require local officials to take a loyalty oath to the United States. They elected Daniel Collins, an original Virginia Republican, and James H. Clement, a naval yard worker, to convey the petition to Lincoln. Others soon involved in Tidewater politics included several lawyers, physicians, and merchants, along with a few naval yard craftsmen. Attorney Lemuel J. Bowden of Williamsburg, a former legislator and Bell elector in 1860, and other members of his family supported a movement to restore Virginia to the Union. Merchant Lewis W. Webb and Dr. Warren W. Wing, along

2. State Committee of the Republican Party of Virginia to Abraham Lincoln, 4 February 1861, Lincoln Papers; Harry J. Carman and Reinhard H. Luthin, *Lincoln and the Patronage* (New York, 1943), 222; *Proceedings of the First Three Republican National Conventions*, 172–73 ; Barnes, *Fortieth Congress*, 1: 59–64.

with others, soon created the Norfolk Union Association and published the *Daily Union*, a pro-Lincoln sheet.[3]

On May 22, the same day as the initial Portsmouth meeting, loyalists met at the courthouse at Alexandria. They heard from two of the area's Yankee settlers: Charles H. Upton, a onetime local official, and Virginia's best-known Republican John C. Underwood. Afterward the group adopted resolutions thanking Lincoln for his "sagacity and wisdom" and asked Governor Francis H. Pierpont of the Restored Government to call for county elections in the occupied areas. Alexandria, which replaced Wheeling as the Restored Government's capital in 1863, and Norfolk became centers of political activity. Most of the Alexandria-area activists, as well as those from the Tidewater, held offices during the war and became Republicans.[4]

United States congressional elections occurred in the first and second districts of the Eastern Shore and the Tidewater, as well as in the seventh, consisting of Fairfax and other counties along the Maryland border. On the heels of secession, Upton claimed the seventh district's seat after an unauthorized election by a handful of voters. The House allowed him to sit as a Republican until February 1862, when it decided against him. Because of low turnout in the three districts during 1862, Congress refused to seat any of the claimants. After Joseph E. Segar won with a larger vote weeks later in the first district, Congress seated him. Almost all of the congressional candidates from the occupied portion of the eastern half of Virginia identified with the Republican Party during the war.[5]

Once Governor Pierpont moved the Restored Government from Wheeling (which became West Virginia's capital) to Alexandria in spring 1863, unionist politics quickened in towns on the south bank of the Potomac and in the Tidewater. Twenty delegates representing the occupied districts met for a state political convention at Alexandria on May 14. The group included mostly former Whigs along with a few of Virginia's original Republicans. As anticipated, the delegates nominated Pierpont for governor before adding other solid loyalists to the ticket. Two weeks later, Pierpont's ticket, along with candidates

3. Moore, *Rebellion Record*, vol. 4. pt. 1: 66, vol. 5, pt. 2: 340; J. E. Bouch to Charles Sumner, 1 January 1867, Sumner Papers.

4. Report of the Joint Committee on Reconstruction, pt. 2: 6–20; Moore, "Representation in the National Congress," 291–93; Undersigned Democrats to Justice Department, 9 March 1863, RG 60; Lemuel J. Bowden to Abraham Lincoln, 7 March 1863, John C. Underwood to John G. Nicolay, 9 March 1863, Lincoln Papers.

5. Moore, "Representation in the National Congress," 281, 470–71; *BDAC*, 1172–42.

for a legislature representing the occupied counties, won against token opposition. For the most part, those chosen were southern-born former Whigs and
middle-class attorneys and farmers. Because a majority of the officeholders
eventually became Republicans, some scholars have concluded "for all practical purposes the unionists of Virginia were Republicans."[6]

During the remainder of the war, loyal governments existed at all levels
in occupied Virginia. According to an analysis by Underwood, the legislature
represented twenty-four of the 1860 legislative districts, eight senatorial districts, at least one-half of three congressional districts, and more than a dozen
counties with a population exceeding 190,000. For the first time, in December
1863, the tiny assembly met in Alexandria's town council chambers. The legislature filled several offices, elected as United States senators Underwood and
Segar (to replace Bowden, who died in January 1864), and called an election
for a constitutional convention. A year later, the legislature ratified the Thirteenth Amendment. Constitutional convention delegates, whose characteristics mirrored those of the legislators, met from February to April 1864. The
delegates abolished slavery, democratized voting, and disfranchised Confederate officials. Without submitting the document to the people in occupied Virginia, they announced its adoption.[7]

Shortly after the Restored Government arrived in Alexandria, it clashed
with General Benjamin F. Butler, who lacked respect for Pierpont's "Lillipu-
tian regime." He had returned from New Orleans to Norfolk–Hampton
Roads, site of some of his earlier military experience, to command Federals in
the Tidewater area. Because he felt he was in a war zone, with his back to the
Atlantic, he commanded as he saw fit. He insisted on trying civilians in the
military court, and he went so far as to arrest the loyal district judge and district attorney. Finally, in August 1864, Lincoln reprimanded Butler for interfering with Virginia officials in Norfolk and Portsmouth. While Lincoln
acknowledged to Butler the "somewhat farcical air of Pierpont's regime," he
defended its legitimacy as well as its usefulness "as a nucleus to add to."[8]

    6. Hamilton James Eckenrode, *The Political History of Virginia during the Reconstruction* (Bal-
timore, 1904), 17–25; Nan Netherton et al., *Fairfax County, Virginia: A History* (Fairfax, Va.,
1978), 364–69; *Report of the Joint Committee on Reconstruction*, pt. 2: 14, 36, 38; Charles H. Ambler, *Francis H. Pierpont, Union War Governor of Virginia and Father of West Virginia* (Chapel
Hill, 1937), 220–21; *Journal of the Constitutional Convention which Convened at Alexandria on the
13th Day of February, 1864* (Alexandria, Va., 1864).
    7. *Journal of the Constitutional Convention, Alexandria, 1864.*
    8. Thomas R. Bowden to Abraham Lincoln, 17 October 1863, Francis H. Pierpont to Lincoln,
4 August 1864, Lincoln to Benjamin F. Butler, 9 August 1864, Lincoln Papers; Ambler, *Francis
H. Pierpont*, 222–23; Eckenrode, *Political History of Virginia during Reconstruction*, 22–23.

Early in March 1864, politicians organized a Union Central Committee representing all of the occupied areas. In May, the committee chose five delegates to represent Virginia at the Republican National Convention at Baltimore in June. Although seated by the convention, they were not allowed to vote (another reflection of the attitude of Republicans toward the Restored Government). Others in the state established Lincoln clubs, and Pierpont campaigned for Lincoln in the North. On election day in Alexandria, Republicans even attempted to set up polls, but the military would not allow it.[9]

When Federals moved into Middle and West Tennessee in early 1862, they established outposts along the way. Most of the area's Confederate troops evacuated south into north Mississippi. Shortly after the Stars and Stripes flew over Nashville in February, President Lincoln named Senator Andrew Johnson of Greeneville military governor. Governor Johnson issued an Appeal to the People of Tennessee, soliciting help from his "fellow-citizens." He promised to honor those who had "maintained their allegiance to the Federal government" and welcomed the "erring and misguided" back into the Union fold. He offered "complete amnesty" to most, while allowing it might "become necessary . . . to punish . . . treason in high places."[10]

Johnson failed to win over the masses or to persuade them that the Confederate army would not return. When he required loyalty oaths to govern or to trade and silenced Rebel presses, he lost more friends than he gained. He did find a few spokesmen, however, brave enough to urge reunion, and for a while he felt he could convert others. So in May 1862, he and his followers held a series of meetings in Nashville and nearby garrisoned towns reachable by rail to consolidate fearful unionists and win over reluctant Confederates. Within a month, the governor spoke to gatherings in Nashville, Murfreesboro, Columbia, and Shelbyville. Several well-known loyalists signed the call for the Nashville meeting summoned to restore "the former relations of [the] State to the Federal Union," some of whom had given limited support to the Confederacy.[11]

9. Eckenrode, *Political History of Virginia during Reconstruction,* 18–22; Netherton, *Fairfax County,* 364–67 ; Underwood to Charles Sumner, 21 February 1865, Sumner Papers.

10. Peter Maslowski, *Treason Must Be Made Odious: Military Occupation and Wartime Reconstruction in Nashville, Tennessee, 1862–1865* (Millwood, N.Y., 1978), 89–90; Clifton R. Hall, *Andrew Johnson, Military Governor of Tennessee* (Princeton, N.J., 1916), 32–33; *PAJ,* 5: xxix, xxxii; Appeal to the People of Tennessee, 18 March 1862, PAJ, 209–12.

11. *PAJ,* 5: xliv–liii; James W. Smith to Johnson, 18 September 1861, PAJ, 5: 9–10; Speech at Nashville, 12 May 1862, PAJ 5: 379–85, 385n; Maslowski, *Treason Must Be Made Odious,* 76; Hall, *Andrew Johnson,* 47–48.

On Saturday, May 24, Johnson spoke at Murfreesboro in Rutherford County, which was known as "the hot-bed of secession." His audience included "a queer mixture of blue coats and butternuts" (Confederate partisans). As was often his practice, he spoke for more than three hours, painting, as usual, a broad canvas of time and geography. Johnson urged "deluded and erring Union men . . . to return to the allegiance" of the Union. A week later, Monday, June 2, he left Nashville by train, with thirteen carloads of soldiers and supporters, to speak at Columbia in Maury County. The gathering met at a marketplace, with a "butcher's block [of] the stump of a huge oak tree" serving as a platform. As at Murfreesboro, most listeners had arrived from the surrounding countryside. Some had stayed away, however, because of roaming bands of Rebels.[12]

Five days later, the governor journeyed to Shelbyville, seat of Bedford County, where more than three thousand individuals, including many women, turned out to hear him at the county fairground. Bedford was among the strongest antisecessionist counties in Middle Tennessee. According to one report, when Federals entered Shelbyville, citizens welcomed them with "Union Flags displayed and shouts & waving of handkerchiefs from every quarter—." The county eventually raised eleven Federal companies. When Johnson returned by train via Murfreesboro, he saw the corpses of several Union men left there by Rebel guerrilla bands. After a brief stopover, the governor's party reached Nashville at nine o'clock that night, only shortly before guerrillas tore up much of the tracks over which he had ridden.[13]

Only a few Murfreesboro and Columbia citizens sought restoration to the Union. Murfreesboro had some merchants and bankers, such as William Y. Elliott and his business partner Edward L. Jordan, who later became active in the Nashville Union League. Those from the Columbia area included planter Joshua B. Frierson, along with some of his relatives, such as leather manufacturer Samuel M. Arnell. Arnell rallied the county's "scattered . . . Unionists," only to see Rebels seize his leather when they reoccupied the county.[14]

12. Speech at Murfreesboro, 24 May 1862, *PAJ*, 5: 416–17; George W. Blackburn to Johnson, 8 September 1862, PAJ, 6: 7–8; John Savage, *The Life and Public Services of Andrew Johnson: Including His State Papers, Speeches, and Addresses* (New York, 1866), 263–68; Jill K. Garrett and Marise P. Lightfoot, eds., *The Civil War in Maury County, Tennessee* (Columbia, Tenn., 1966), 157.

13. Ormsby M. Mitchel to Johnson, 30 March 1862, *PAJ*, 5: 257, 257n; Moore, *Rebellion Record;* vol. 5, pt. 1: 24; Savage, *Life and Public Services of Andrew Johnson*, 266–67.

14. Johnson to William Y. Elliott et al., 25 April 1862, *PAJ*, 3: 333–34, 334n, 377n; 443n; PAJ, 6: 481n; Blackburn to Johnson, 8 September 1862, PAJ, 6: 7–8, 8n; BDTGA, 1: 79; BDTGA, 2:

Outside of Nashville, Shelbyville and surrounding Bedford County contained the most prominent area unionists. Loyalists there divided about equally into what became conservative unionists and radicals (later Republicans). Conservatives included the Cooper brothers, Edmund and Henry. Radicals were represented by such individuals as former Speaker of the Tennessee General Assembly William H. Wisener and circuit court clerk Lewis H. Tillman, soon a Union army officer. Tillman serves as a good example that there could be family rewards for converting to the Republican Party. Of his eleven children, several reaped the benefits of political influence: Samuel became a professor of chemistry at West Point Military Academy; Edwin, an officer in the United States Navy; and Abram, an official of the Internal Revenue Service.[15]

To help protect unionists in the outlying areas, Governor Johnson in June authorized former congressman William B. Stokes of Alexandria to raise a cavalry regiment at Nashville. Stokes was an attorney, an owner of a "herd of fine blooded stock" that included "the celebrated racer 'Ariel,'" and the father of thirteen children. Most of the colonel's recruits that summer for his First Middle Tennessee Cavalry Regiment were refugees from DeKalb, his home county, and Bedford County. They arrived in the state capital just as Confederates were retaking their communities. Many of the recruits had traveled in "squads, making their way generally by night through a country infested by guerrillas and rebels."[16]

On June 6, 1862, the Stars and Stripes flew over Memphis. The next month, loyalists organized the Washington Union Club of Memphis, which soon numbed sixteen hundred members and had branches as far away as Jackson, Tennessee, eighty miles northeast. Unionists gathered around Andrew Jackson's statue on the courthouse square on August 15. There the speaker pointed out Old Hickory's words inscribed upon the statue's base: "The Federal Union Must and Shall Be Preserved." The crowd included southern-born as well as northern-born merchants and lawyers, Democrats

19–20, 493–94; Garrett and Lightfoot, *Civil War in Maury County,* 157–59; Barnes, *Fortieth Congress,* 2: 285–86.

15. Charles R. Gunter Jr., "Bedford County during the Civil War" (Master's thesis, University of Tennessee, 1963), 21, 28; *BDTGA,* 1: 164–65, 767, 813–14; Alexander, *Reconstruction in Tennessee,* 123; Goodspeed, *History of Tennessee,* 180–81.

16. Civil War Commission, *Tennesseans in the Civil War,* 1: 329–30; *Report of the Adjutant General of the State of Tennessee on the Military Forces of the State from 1861 to 1866* (Nashville, 1866), 441; Goodspeed, *History of Tennessee,* 72–98.

and Whigs, mostly men who opposed secession yet later out of self-interest and fear aided the Confederacy. Now reverting to their forsaken allegiance, they sponsored Union meetings, formed home guards, and sought public office.[17]

In April 1863, James B. Bingham, a Virginian who with a partner had purchased the *Memphis Bulletin* in 1861–62, became the newspaper's editor. After visiting Nashville, he soon became a confidant of the governor. Bingham mailed Johnson the *Bulletin* daily, so Johnson could "learn all that is politic to make public." He also kept Johnson informed about private matters through letters. During early 1864, Bingham mailed voter registration commissions to a unionist in each West Tennessee county. Some already held local offices. Several would take office later as Republicans.[18]

One of the youngest Tennessee unionists, thirty-one-year-old David A. Nunn of Brownsville, a planter who owned forty-six slaves, went on to hold several high-ranking offices as a Republican. Brownsville had a core of unionists, including the two Smith brothers, attorneys Thomas G. Smith and William M. Smith, Virginia-born sons of a Methodist minister. William, a former legislator and state judge, fled to Memphis in 1862. There he became the spokesman for Haywood County refugees and for those who remained at home. Before the end of the war, he became judge of the Common Law and Chancery Court of Memphis, and when that court was divided in 1865, his brother Thomas became judge of the city's Law Court. The apex of William's career came in 1881 when he became speaker of the state senate and lieutenant governor of Tennessee.[19]

Loyalist leaders in Memphis who identified with the Republican Party during the war and served the party then and later as officeholders included several attorneys, merchants, and railroad executives, men representative of the

17. Joseph H. Parks, "Memphis under Military Rule, 1862 to 1865," *ETHSP* 14 (1942): 32–42; *PAJ,* 6: 27n; Washington Union Club of Memphis to Johnson, 19 December 1862, PAJ, 6: 102–3; Thomas L. Sullivan to Johnson, 16 February 1863, PAJ, 6: 144–45; Ernest W. Hooper, "Memphis, Tennessee: Federal Occupation and Reconstruction, 1862–1870" (Ph.D. diss., University of North Carolina, 1957), 64.

18. Bingham to Johnson, 11 August 1863, *PAJ,* 6: 324–25; PAJ, 326–27n; James M. Tomeny and Bingham to Johnson, 17 September 1863, PAJ, 6: 371–75, 75n; Bingham to Johnson, 4 November 1863; PAJ, 6: 453–54, 454–55n; 15 November 1863, PAJ, 6: 477–78; 2 January 1864, PAJ, 6: 533–36, 536–37n.

19. Russell Fowler, "Chancellor William Macon Smith and Judicial Reconstruction: A Study of Tyranny and Integrity," *WTHSP* 48 (1994): 35–59; James A. Rogers to Brownlow, 15 May 1865, Governor William G. Brownlow Papers, Tennessee State Library and Archives, Nashville.

town's antebellum business class. Many served in the town's more than 3,000 strong loyal militia. They represented a mixture of nativity and politics (although most had been Whigs), not at all unusual for Memphis. Attorneys included Henry G. Smith, a wealthy and witty man who returned to the city council in 1864 after serving before the war. He later served on the state's supreme court. Merchants included William R. Moore, an Alabamian reared in Rutherford County, Tennessee. Moore reputedly enjoyed a good credit rating in New York City because of his "known loyalty and business experience."[20]

United States congressional elections occurred in West Tennessee during winter 1862–63. Lincoln authorized southern visitors to the White House and Union generals in occupied districts to arrange such elections. The president appealed as well to Governor Johnson. Johnson also heard from others claiming to represent county conventions. At these meetings, loyalists had chosen delegates to congressional district conventions, for the ninth at Trenton on December 1 and for the tenth at Bolivar on December 15. Delegates at Trenton nominated Alvin Hawkins of Huntingdon, cousin of Colonel Isaac Hawkins of the U.S. Fifth Tennessee Cavalry. Those attending the Bolivar meeting desired "reconstruction of the union on the old terms of the Constitution." They instructed their nominee, Thomas G. Smith of Brownsville, to oppose the Emancipation Proclamation.[21]

Despite Johnson's misgivings about turnout, he issued a writ authorizing an election on December 29, stipulating that each voter "give satisfactory evidence . . . of his loyalty to . . . the United States." Because of General Nathan Bedford Forrest's raid into some counties, only about one-tenth of voters cast ballots in the ninth district and the election had to be postponed in the tenth district. Congress refused to seat Hawkins, and when another attempt occurred on January 20 in the tenth district, turnout was insignificant and the victor unclear. Despite confusion, low voter turnout, and the two districts'

20. *PAJ*, 5: 454n, 455n, 536n, 537n; PAJ 6: 616n; John M. Keating, *History of the City of Memphis* (Syracuse, N.Y., 1888), 2: 46–47, 71; *BDTGA*, 2: 792–93, 914; Enrolling Officers Report, Charles W. Dustan Papers, Alabama Department of Archives and History.

21. Moore, "Representation in the National Congress," 290–91; Abraham Lincoln to Major General Grant and Governor Johnson & All Having Military, Naval, and Civil Authority under the United States within the State of Tennessee, 21 October 1862, *PAJ*, 6: 33–34, 34n; Isaac Hawkins to Johnson, 29 November 1862, PAJ, 76–77; William F. Bradford to Johnson, 15 December 1862, PAJ, 6: 99–100, 100n; Writ of Election for Congressional Districts, 8 December 1862, PAJ, 6: 91–93; Mason Brayman to Johnson, 17 December 1862, PAJ, 6: 101, 101–2n.

failure to gain seats, hundreds of voters declared their political allegiances, a step toward eventually bringing some into the Republican Party.[22]

Meanwhile in Middle Tennessee, Nashville's Union Club, founded in January 1863, counted seven hundred members by spring. The club represented the radical unionist position and opposed officeholding by all disloyal since secession. Members included some Union army officers and unionists from nearby towns. Nashville's Germans formed a second club in August 1863. Others created councils in nearby towns. In November, the first Tennessee Grand Council met in Nashville and endorsed Johnson and Lincoln's "war measures," including the Emancipation Proclamation. Altogether, by the end of 1863, Tennessee had seven councils with more than four thousand members, many who considered themselves Republicans.[23]

Forerunners of the league existed in East Tennessee as early as 1861, when loyalists formed secret militias. Secret societies emerged in the Midwest during 1862, when Lincoln's administration felt threatened by the subversion of antiwar copperheads. From the Midwest, where thousands joined, the Union League spread swiftly to eastern cities such as Philadelphia, New York, and Boston. Everywhere the league became the right arm of the Republican Party. As soon as the Union army and its camp followers moved south, northerners joined with natives to establish Union Leagues. By December 1863, in addition to Tennessee, West Virginia had ten councils with eight hundred members, and Virginia's occupied areas had four with four hundred members.[24]

During 1863, Tennessee unionists divided into two factions, one backing Johnson and his policies, including some, such as league leaders, pushing him to the left; and a conservative wing seeking to restore the Union as it was, without emancipation or disfranchisement. The proadministration men who favored a more radical agenda than most Johnson supporters desired immediate emancipation (Tennessee had been excluded from the Emancipation Proc-

22. Calvin S. Ezell to Johnson, 10 January 1863, PAJ, 6: 112, 112–13n; Moore, "Representation in the National Congress," 290–91.

23. Nashville Union Club to Johnson, 31 January 1863, *PAJ*, 6: 131–32, 132n; Memorial from Union League Councils to Johnson, 10 November 1863, PAJ, 6: 466–67, 467–68n, 551n; Maslowski, *Treason Must Be Made Odious*, 81–84; Tennessee Grand Council to Abraham Lincoln, 2 November 1863, Lincoln Papers.

24. *Proceedings of the Annual Meeting of the Grand National Council, Union League of America, 1863* (Washington, D.C., 1863), 17–19; *Proceedings of the Annual Meeting of the Grand National Council, Union League of America, 1869* (Washington, D.C., 1869), 7–8; Allan Nevins, *The War for the Union* (New York, 1959–60), 1: 162–65.

lamation), disfranchisement of the disloyal, and the recruitment of black soldiers. Johnson modified his more moderate opinions and his policy, partly because Tennesseans failed to rally to his cause.[25]

When unionists from forty counties rallied at Nashville for their first state-wide meeting on July 1, 1863, anti-Johnson delegates appeared numerous, but in a minority. Pro-Johnson men took control of the podium, the committees, and the convention itself. Brownlow, back from his exile of speech making and bookselling and now serving as a United States Treasury official at Nashville, chaired the opening session. He oversaw questions of credentials, representation, and organization, and he appointed proadministration majorities on the committees. Johnson's opponents wanted to be conciliatory toward Confederates and to have a general election to replace the military government; pro-Johnson men defended the proscription of Confederates as being essential to protect unionist gains, and they opposed holding an election until Federals occupied East Tennessee. Before the convention adjourned, it elected a unionist state executive committee composed of Johnson's handpicked politicians.[26]

Federal advances in autumn 1863 allowed thousands of East Tennessee unionists to enlist in the Union army and their leaders to resume public lives. Some received political appointments and others won local offices in March 1864. Samuel Milligan of Greeneville, soon to join the ranks of officeholders, wrote to his old friend Andrew Johnson that though "broken in [his] profession" and with "little means" left, he remained "*an unyielding Union man.*" He had spent his time for the "last two years . . . reading and studying . . . Law-books, and tracing up the history of slavery." Although some of his ideas had changed, he was uncertain whether it came "from unbiased convictions, or the stress of circumstances." One thing of which he said he was convinced was that the nation could "no longer hope for a permanent and prosperous peace, while . . . slavery exist[ed] in a single state of the Federal Union."[27]

Brownlow now transferred his Treasury office to Knoxville, along with a printing press and a $1,500 federal subsidy to revive his *Knoxville Whig.* He had promised to "publish a vigorous war sheet, sustaining the [Lincoln] Administration without ifs or buts." Brownlow's *Whig and Rebel Ventilator* expressed his "lowest contempt" for Confederate leaders. Although he initially

25. Maslowski, *Treason Must Be Made Odious,* 80–81.
26. Hall, *Andrew Johnson,* 96–98; Hamer, *Tennessee,* 1: 576–77.
27. Milligan to Johnson, 21 October 1863, *PAJ,* 6: 428–29.

supported exempting Tennessee from the Emancipation Proclamation, he now favored it because he believed slavery was doomed by the war. His tone pleased most East Tennesseans. Beginning in spring 1864, Brownlow's *Whig,* as well as the *Nashville Times,* edited by S. C. Mercer, a Kentucky unionist, and Bingham's *Memphis Bulletin* received funds from Washington for publishing the laws of the United States.[28]

Some of Chattanooga's best-known unionists returned home during 1863–64. William Crutchfield, who had gained notoriety by verbally attacking Jefferson Davis in 1861, had stayed in town for months before fleeing behind Federal lines into Middle Tennessee. In 1863, he accompanied the Union army into Chattanooga. His service proved invaluable because of his insights about the terrain. Despite his assistance, Federals commandeered some of Crutchfield's farm property, "horses, cattle, forage, fuel, . . . etc.," for which he eventually received a claim of $2,400. Editor James R. Hood, Brownlow's Chattanooga counterpart, returned to reestablish the *Chattanooga Gazette,* a sheet similar in tone to the *Whig.* Hood returned, as he put it, "to that place where the traitors whom I know have been humbled."[29]

To advance the course of restoring individuals and states to the Union, Lincoln issued the Proclamation of Amnesty and Reconstruction on December 8, 1863, outlining his future policy toward Confederates and their governments. Lincoln offered amnesty to those engaged in the rebellion except for high-ranking civil and military officials. His conditions required the individual to take an oath of allegiance to the United States, promising to accept all federal laws and proclamations concerning slavery. For this pledge, the president would grant a full pardon and restore all property "except as to slaves." When the number of such persons in any one state counted 10 percent of the total number voting there in the 1860 presidential election, wartime loyalists and pardoned former Confederates could establish a state government—when they provided for the freedom and education of blacks.[30]

28. Horace Maynard to Johnson, 28 September 1863, *PAJ,* 6: 387, 388n; Johnson to William H. Seward, 5 March 1864, PAJ, 6: 637; Coulter, *William G. Brownlow,* 246–51; Charles F. Bryan, "The Civil War in East Tennessee: A Social, Political, and Economic Study" (Ph.D. diss., University of Tennessee, 1978), 122–26; Brownlow to Abraham Lincoln, 27 March 1863, Lincoln Papers; OR, 24(2): 524.

29. Gilbert E. Govan and James W. Livingood, "Chattanooga under Military Occupation, 1863–1865," *JSH* 15 (February 1951): 28, 37–44; Salmon W. Wilder to Johnson, 27 December 1861, PAJ, 5: 80; BDAC, 809; *Consolidated Claims Index,* 3: 61.

30. Basler, *Collected Works of Abraham Lincoln,* 7: 53–56.

Lincoln's proclamation raised questions for Tennessee unionists. For unconditional unionists, it meant that if large numbers of Confederates took Lincoln's oath, former rebel votes, plus conservative unionist votes, would turn them out of office. To prevent this from occurring, Lincoln allowed Johnson to write his own oath for use in upcoming state elections. Called the "damnesty oath" by conservatives, it required each individual to swear that he "ardently desire[d] the suppression of the present rebellion" and that he would assist in accomplishing it. Making matters worse for conservative unionists after many decided to swallow Johnson's oath was State Attorney General Maynard's ruling in February 1863 that former Confederates were ineligible to vote until they had established six months of residency after taking the oath.[31]

In support of Lincoln's Reconstruction plan, unionists met on January 21, 1864, at Nashville. Their resolutions favored a constitutional convention of loyalists to restore Tennessee to the Union once all parts of the state could be represented. The first step toward full restoration was choosing loyal local officials in an upcoming March election. In spite of all the care Johnson and Maynard took to guarantee good results, turnout was small and in many cases, officeholders elected were conservative unionists. Short of the severe proscription of Confederates or bringing blacks into the franchise, ultraunionists could not win elections, not even local ones, outside of East Tennessee and a few counties in West Tennessee.[32]

During 1863 and 1864, conservative unionists in all the South's occupied areas parted with Lincoln over issues such as emancipation, confiscation, and disfranchisement and over his failure to pursue a negotiated peace settlement. In Tennessee, former governor William B. Campbell and former congressmen Thomas A. R. Nelson and Emerson Etheridge (their Washington connection with antiadministration men, who served for a while as clerk of the House) formed the Union Peace Party in 1864. They declared for Democratic presidential nominee George B. McClellan. Since 1862 they had been distancing themselves from more determined but less affluent loyalists. Basically they wanted to restore the Union as it was in 1860. But they were confronted with the tide of events and, as Oliver P. Temple put it, by "a new set of men who to a large extent belonged to the army, and who had imbibed by suffering and

31. Hall, *Andrew Johnson,* 114–18.

32. Speech on Restoration of State Government, 21 January 1864, *PAJ,* 6: 574–88, 589–90n; Maslowski, *Treason Must Be Made Odious,* 88–89.

persecution, feelings quite unlike those of the men who had neither suffered nor entered the army."[33]

Conservative unionists in East Tennessee saw an opportunity to further their position by reconvening the convention of 1861, which had met initially at Knoxville and later at Greeneville. So they summoned the convention to meet at the Knoxville courthouse on April 14, 1864. Conservative delegates consumed much of the four days seeking to embarrass Andrew Johnson, an old political enemy. Johnson, who always liked a good fight, traveled from Nashville to confront his detractors. Ultimately, with the help of some old allies as well as new wartime friends, Johnson deadlocked the convention, which adjourned. The governor's supporters then reconvened nearby and passed resolutions endorsing the military governor's stewardship.[34]

The state's Union Executive Committee, controlled by pro-Johnson men, hoping to see Tennessee represented at the Republican National Convention at Baltimore on June 7, 1864, asked loyalists in the three grand divisions to select a specified number of delegates. Unconditional unionists from throughout the South supported Lincoln's administration, his renomination, and his reelection. Lincoln, in turn, as Pennsylvania politico Alexander K. McClure observed, "encouraged these southern allies—to assure his nomination and his election." Some southern states, including Tennessee, Virginia, South Carolina, Florida, Louisiana, and Arkansas, sent delegates to the 1864 Republican National Convention at Baltimore. At the convention, Brownlow condemned the copperhead party of Campbell and Etheridge in Tennessee and nominated his old enemy Andrew Johnson for vice president of the United States. Lincoln's managers, who had control of the convention, already had word that Johnson was to be chosen. Delegates selected him to broaden the party's appeal to war Democrats and southern loyalists, whose votes might be needed in the Border States.[35]

33. Curry, *Radicalism, Racism, and Party Realignment*, 42–43, 91–92; Abraham Lincoln to William B. Campbell et al., 22 October 1864, *Collected Works of Abraham Lincoln*, 8: 58–65.

34. Edwin T. Hardison, "In the Toils of War: Andrew Johnson and the Federal Occupation of Tennessee, 1862–1865" (Ph.D. diss., University of Tennessee, 1981), 318–20; Temple, *Notable Men of Tennessee*, 407.

35. Temple, *Notable Men of Tennessee*, 407; *Nashville Union*, 17 April 1864, Hardison, "In the Toils of War," 317–20; *New York Times*, 21 March 1864; Moore, *Rebellion Record*, vol. 8, pt. 1: 63–64; Hall, *Andrew Johnson*, 126–27, 764–65, 788; Alexander K. McClure, *Abraham Lincoln and Men of War-Times* (Philadelphia, 1892), 107–9; James G. Smart, ed., *A Radical View: The "Agate" Dispatches of Whitelaw Reid, 1861–1865* (Memphis, 1976), 2: 163, 167–68; *Proceedings of the First*

On August 4, the Union Executive Committee issued a call for a state political convention at Nashville on September 25 to consider holding a presidential election in Tennessee. Delegates from more than fifty counties attended,
most chosen irregularly or coming of their own accord. They endorsed holding a presidential election in Tennessee. Voters would have to take an oath to
defend the Union and "oppose . . . negotiations with rebels in arms." Conservative unionists responded by selecting delegates to attend the Democratic
National Convention that month at Chicago. Their delegation, headed by
Campbell (mentioned as a possible vice presidential nominee), included those
who gave their movement birth in 1862. They voted for the party's nominee,
General McClellan, and after they returned home, they and their followers
named an electoral ticket.[36]

Afterward they established a Constitutional Union Club in Nashville and
started holding meetings. In mid-October, they sent a delegation to President
Lincoln to protest several outrages, including the recent loyalty oath issued
by Governor Johnson. John Lellyett of Nashville presented a petition from
Tennessee's McClellan electors to Lincoln. The president merely saw it as one
more step to deprive him of a second term. He asked Lellyett "how long it
took [him] and New York politicians to concoct that paper." Then after Lellyett's denial, Lincoln said he expected "to let the friends of George B. McClellan manage their side of this contest in their own way," and that he would
manage his in his way. A few days later, the conservative unionists announced
that their ticket had been withdrawn from the presidential contest.[37]

Meanwhile Republicans continued to campaign for Lincoln. Brownlow,
hardly an unbiased witness, thought that McClellan's supporters in East Tennessee were a "mere *faction* led . . . by . . . sore-headed Union men . . . [with]
a bad Union record." Actually, as later events and elections would prove, conservative unionists there represented a sizeable following, and some, but not
most, of their leaders had records of loyalty equal to that of Brownlow. Two-
thirds of the votes for president came from East Tennessee, yielding a total of
about 12,000 total voters. One-half of Middle Tennessee's vote came from the

Three Republican National Conventions, 193, 203; Eric Foner, *Reconstruction: America's Unfinished
Revolution, 1863–1877* (New York, 1988), 44.

    36. Hall, *Andrew Johnson,* 140–42.

    37. Basler, *Collected Works of Abraham Lincoln,* 8: 58–62; Hamer, *Tennessee,* 1: 590; *Nashville
Union,* 1 September 1864.

Nashville area. In West Tennessee, only Shelby County, with 1,600 votes, reported having an election.[38]

After Lincoln's election, more than five hundred loyalists from sixty counties, many wearing their blue army uniforms, rallied on January 9, 1865, at Nashville. Many "men of the mountains," headed by Brownlow, arrived from Knoxville after a long, cold, dreary boxcar ride. Middle Tennessee was also well represented, but West Tennessee mustered fewer than fifty delegates. Politically, three-fourths of the delegates were former Whigs, but few had been prominent in politics. Three days into the convention, Governor Johnson and Milligan convinced delegates they should assume the role of a constitutional convention. As a constitutional convention, the delegates nullified all acts of the Confederacy and freed the state's slaves. Then, as a political convention— considered their only proper role by many—they nominated Brownlow for governor, along with a slate of other candidates, including those for the legislature.[39]

At that time, as Brownlow saw it, Tennesseans divided into three political camps, "the Radical Union party," which favored "Lincoln and Johnson and controlled the January convention," and the "Conservative-Constitutional-Peace party," which was ready to welcome the third group, returning Rebels. Nonetheless, with the war still waging, the state constitutional amendments passed, and the entire slate, all running unopposed on a single yes-or-no ballot, won almost unanimously. Because Confederates and conservatives boycotted the balloting, the total vote of 26,865 indicated areas of unconditional unionist strength. Holding in his hands the government and its patronage, Brownlow appointed only "hard shell" unionists. Most of his appointees eventually identified with the Republican Party.[40]

More than 90 percent of Tennessee's scalawags served either in the Union army or as loyal officeholders in occupied areas during the war, as did about 20 percent of the state's redeemers (see table 2). Though equally animated by patriotism, redeemers regarded the Republican policy as too radical. The

38. Hamer, *Tennessee*, 1: 588–89; Brownlow to Johnson, 5 November 1864, *PAJ*, 7: 267; *Knoxville Whig*, 9 November 1864.

39. Hamer, *Tennessee*, 1: 592; Alexander, *Reconstruction in Tennessee*, 26; *Nashville Dispatch*, 10 January 1865.

40. Hamer, *Tennessee*, 1: 594–96; Wilson D. Miscamble, "Andrew Johnson and the Election of William G. ('Parson') Brownlow as Governor of Tennessee," *THQ* 37 (fall 1978): 318–20; Queener, "Origin of the Republican Party in East Tennessee," 82–83; Hall, *Andrew Johnson*, 140–41.

redeemers, of course, eventually included President Andrew Johnson, who returned in 1869 to participate in the state's redemption, as well as some of his wartime colleagues. Redeemers also counted among their number Union army officers and wartime federal appointees. But many more redeemers, over 70 percent, served the Confederacy.

Wartime Reconstruction started in Louisiana during General Butler's stormy stay in New Orleans, from May to December 1862. Occupation began when Tennessee-born David G. Farragut's Gulf Expeditionary Force of twenty-four ships and Butler's 15,000 Federals captured the city on April 29. Two longtime New Orleans residents landed with General Butler, railroad executive Benjamin F. Flanders and journalist Thomas B. Thorpe; other returning refugees soon followed. Flanders had been driven into exile for showing sympathy for Union prisoners of war by providing them with clothing and blankets. Flanders's friend Thorpe, a noted folktale writer, had been a local newspaperman and politician before he returned to the North in the mid-1850s. Within a few weeks, the general named Flanders city treasurer and Thorpe city surveyor.[41]

Secretary of the Treasury Salmon P. Chase's special agents Dr. Maximilian F. Bonzano and George S. Denison, both refugees from the Confederacy, landed in June 1862. Bonzano, returned as the mint's acting superintendent. Chase's nephew, Denison, had been a wealthy San Antonio attorney. Because of "confidence" in Denison's "blood," Chase said, he appointed him as special agent and acting collector of customs. As was expected, he always kept his uncle abreast of affairs. Soon after arriving, Denison wrote atop his list of priorities—ahead of "to suppress smuggling" and clean up the "notorious Custom House"—his goal "to appoint . . . men of such political opinion, that the Government (through its officials) can present here a strong nucleus for a Republican Party."[42]

41. McPherson, *Ordeal by Fire*, 231–32; Randall and Donald, *Civil War and Reconstruction*, 445–46; *DAB*, 6: 286–91; *Boston Journal*, 15 December 1862, clipping, Benjamin F. Flanders Papers, Louisiana and Lower Mississippi Valley Collections; *New York Tribune*, n.d., clipping, Flanders Papers; Rickels, *Thomas Bangs Thorpe*, 91, 117, 169, 195, 214; J. Madison Wells to Abraham Lincoln, 28 October 1864, Lincoln Papers.

42. Denison to Chase, 28 June 1862, *Diary and Correspondence of Chase*, 307–8; McCrary, *Lincoln and Reconstruction*, 106; Special Order 246, 7 August 1862, Jessie Ames Marshall, ed., *Private and Official Correspondence of Gen. Benjamin F. Butler during the Period of the Civil War* (Norwood, Mass., 1917), 2: 162–63; James A. Padgett, ed., "Some Letters of George Stanton Denison, 1854–1866," *LHQ* 23 (October 1940): 1134–37.

Anthony P. Dostie, a dentist and Masonic Lodge leader, also returned that summer. He reopened his practice on Canal Street "to remove . . . teeth without pain." Otherwise he busied himself at "Union meetings, Associations and Leagues" supporting "the cause of his country." In 1863, the military appointed Dostie, along with Flanders, a former school principal, and German-born Michael Hahn, a former school board member, to replace the city's pro-Confederate board of education.[43]

Lincoln named General George F. Shepley, like Butler a New England Democrat, military governor of Louisiana. Shepley and Butler ruled New Orleans together the last part of 1862, with Butler, by the force of his will, being more powerful. They established bureaus for public works and for relief. They also formed militias and encouraged the organization of local loyalists seeking Louisiana's restoration to the Union. Along these lines, the two men tried to separate the sheep from the goats by ordering all residents to take an oath of allegiance to the United States or to register as its enemies by September 24. The city's merchants and professionals took the oath to avoid the confiscation of their property and to legally engage in their business. The number voting in Union-sponsored elections and joining militias better indicated the strength of committed loyalists.[44] Men from other areas increased the number of loyalists in New Orleans. Attorneys James K. Belden and his son, Simeon, of nearby Saint Martin Parish, resided in the city for most of the war. Because of his loyalty, the elder Belden fled to New Orleans "for protection six times in seven months, before [being] arrested and . . . forced to leave the Confederate lines." He served as judge of the state's third district during 1864 and 1865 while his son Simeon presided over the lower house of the legislature.[45]

When General Banks invaded the Red River Valley in 1863, James Madison Wells of Rapides Parish, who spent 1861–62 opposing Confederates, went to him for protection. The general provided a temporary guard for Wells's plantation and wrote him a pass to use whenever he felt threatened. In November

43. Emily Hazen Reed, *The Life of A. P. Dostie; or, The Conflict of New Orleans* (New York, 1868), 15–19; *Report of the Select Committee on the New Orleans Riots*, 22–26; Fred Harvey Harrington, *Fighting Politician: Major General N. P. Banks* (Philadelphia, 1948), 95.

44. James Parton, *General Butler in New Orleans: History of the Administration of the Department of the Gulf . . .* (Boston, 1864), 119–20; Moore, *Rebellion Record*, vol. 5, pt. 1: 33, 85; Benjamin F. Butler to Edwin M. Stanton, 16, 25, May 1862, *Correspondence of Gen. Benjamin F. Butler*, 1: 494, 519, 2: 162–63; Special Order 246, 7 August 1862, *Correspondence of Gen. Benjamin F. Butler*, 164; Taylor, *Louisiana Reconstructed*, 4–5.

45. *Report of the Select Committee on the New Orleans Riots*, 147–49, 424–25, 468.

1863, Wells used his pass. When he reached the mouth of the Red River, he found Union gunboats, on one of which he sailed to New Orleans. In December, he visited Washington, D.C., to talk with Secretary Chase about getting his cotton out of Alexandria. Chase referred him to Flanders, who in turn had Wells accompany Union troops on their next incursion into central Louisiana. Because of Wells's wealth and prestige, only two months later he was nominated on two different political party tickets for lieutenant governor of Louisiana, one headed by Flanders and the other by Hahn, who won.[46]

During summer 1862, Butler named several unionists to manage municipal affairs. Attorney Edward H. Durell, a former member of the city council who had written the present city charter, chaired the Bureau of Finance, and auctioneer Julian Neville chaired the Bureau of Streets and Landings. Neville, a longtime conservative Whig, hoped that at worst Reconstruction would mean "compensated emancipation." With Butler's approval, some future Republicans, such as some of the judges who opposed secession, retained offices they held before the war. Several scalawags received federal appointments in 1863 and 1864, primarily in the judiciary or in the Treasury Department, especially in the Customs Service. In 1860, the port of New Orleans had provided more high-paying federal jobs than any other place in the South.[47]

"Soon after the capture of the City," Denison wrote, "a few noble men undertook to arouse and organize the Union sentiment." According to Denison, "They persevered—called meetings, made speeches—organized Union associations—Union home guards, etc." The first rally on May 31 created the Union Association of New Orleans. A few days later, unionists in the city's four districts elected delegates to the association's first convention.[48] Unionists' efforts for 1862 culminated in a rally at the Saint Charles Theater on November 15, with General Butler, Governor Shepley, and Admiral Farragut as honored guests. Mrs. Butler, who resided with her husband at the Saint Charles Hotel, wrote to a friend that "the theater was crammed [and] thousands [stood] outside" and that she heard a speech by Thomas J. Durant, "an orator" some felt worthy "of mention . . . with Wendell Phillips." In his "fin-

46. Lowrey, "Political Career of James Madison Wells," 995–1123.

47. Billings, *Struggle*; *Harper's Weekly*, 6 June 1868, 363–65; *Report of the Select Committee on the New Orleans Riots*, 99–102, 261; Gerald M. Capers, *Occupied City: New Orleans under the Federals, 1862–1865* (Lexington, Ky., 1965), 125.

48. McCrary, *Lincoln and Reconstruction*, 95–96; Denison to Chase, 29 November 1862, *Diary and Correspondence of Chase*, 334–35.

ished, classical speech," Durant contended that the founding fathers looked toward the eventual abolition of slavery. He had recently visited the North, where he found a movement for emancipation underway. After his return, he quickly gained the confidence of some loyalists. In February 1863, he declared for a free state government, and soon thereafter freed his own family of domestic slaves.[49]

Lincoln suggested to loyalists in fall 1862 that they hold congressional elections as soon as feasible. In Louisiana, he entrusted the task to military governor Shepley and former congressman John Bouligny of New Orleans, a recent White House visitor who in 1861 had refused to participate in a walkout from Congress. In November 1862, the Union Association nominated Flanders for the first district and Durell for the second district. Others also ran independently in the December election, including Bouligny, who was decisively beaten by Flanders. Hahn defeated Durell, who was unpopular because of his close association with Butler. Some, including the winners, favored Louisiana's becoming a free state, while others wanted to continue slave-state status. Within a few weeks, Hahn and Flanders were seated in the United States House.[50]

During February 1863, conservative planters, mostly former Whigs opposed to the free-state movement, organized. Lincoln had pleased them recently by excluding the occupied parishes from his Emancipation Proclamation and replacing General Butler, whom they distrusted, with General Nathaniel Banks. But Banks proved a disappointment as well, giving the planters less control over labor than they desired: a one-year contract between individual planters and their slaves. After Banks explained the plan to forty planters at the Saint Charles Hotel on February 5, planters soon organized to oppose the Union Association.[51]

Later in the month, the Union Association considered the issue of free-state status. Within a few weeks, it approved a statement declaring that seces-

49. Mrs. B. F. Butler to Harriet Heard, 18 November 1862, *Correspondence of Gen. Benjamin F. Butler*, 2: 489; Reid, *After the War*, 232; *New Orleans True Delta*, 25 December 1860.

50. Lincoln to Benjamin F. Butler, 14 October, 6 November 1862, *Collected Works of Abraham Lincoln*, 6: 350; Lincoln to George F. Shepley, 21 November 1862, Collected Works of Abraham Lincoln, 5: 504–5; Cox, *Union—Disunion—Reunion*, 94; Butler to Abraham Lincoln, 28 November 1862, Lincoln Papers; George S. Denison to Chase, 29 November, 4 December 1862, 30 April 1863, *Diary and Correspondence of Chase*, 334–35; McCrary, *Lincoln and Reconstruction*, 105.

51. McCrary, *Lincoln and Reconstruction*, 176–77.

sion destroyed the state's proslavery constitution of 1853. It recommended a new document that included emancipation. The association replaced itself in May by creating the Free State General Committee, which had five members from each of the city's districts. The committee soon called for the registration of loyal voters to elect delegates to a constitutional convention. Then, in early June, Shepley named the committee's chairman, Durant, state attorney (a post he held in the 1850s) and state commissioner of voter registration. Meanwhile, Free State Committee members took their message to the North and to Washington and to a receptive president, who wanted an example for other Confederate states to emulate. Some committee members mounted a letter-writing campaign. Others spoke at patriotic rallies, and a few raised funds in the North.[52]

In September, the planters, or conservative unionists, established an executive committee of two members from each occupied legislative district. They also agreed to proceed with an election to fill the seats of Hahn and Flanders, whose terms ended, as well as to elect a congressman-at-large. On November 2, the usual scheduled election date, conservatives held an election in a number of rural parishes. They announced as winners Alexander P. Field, from the first district, Thomas Cottman from the second, and Joshua Baker from the state at large. As expected, Congress refused to seat the three.[53]

During 1863, Durant delayed voter registration because he, Shepley, and others wanted to wait until Federals controlled "a considerable territory." But in November, Lincoln, growing impatient, ordered General Banks to seize control of the situation, to have Durant register voters without delay, and to create a "tangible nucleus which the remainder of the state [might] rally around." Banks had complained to Lincoln about his own lack of authority because New Orleans had no fewer "than four distinct govts . . . exercising original and independent powers." Now having full authority from Lincoln, Banks and Hahn overshadowed Shepley and Durant, and during 1864 they exercised almost complete control of elections in occupied Louisiana.[54]

Hahn spoke for moderates when he addressed the Free State Committee in November 1863. He said he was a "friend of [the] Negro and emancipation

52. Ibid., 129–32; David H. Donald, ed., *Inside Lincoln's Cabinet: The Civil War Diaries of Salmon P. Chase* (New York, 1954), 186.

53. McCrary, *Lincoln and Reconstruction,* 167–68.

54. Lincoln to Banks, 5 November 1863, *Collected Works of Abraham Lincoln,* 7: 1; Hay, *Lincoln and the Civil War,* 140–41.

but oppose[d] [to] civil rights for blacks" and that he favored a "new labor
system" for blacks. The division between moderates and radicals became apparent at the mid-December 1863 state convention called to elect delegates to
the Friends of Freedom Convention of the Border States, meeting in Louisville. After Durant successfully seated a few blacks, moderate delegates became
incensed. Now two factions clearly existed within the free-state movement,
radicals and moderates. The Durant-Flanders, or radical, faction favored
Congressional Reconstruction, accompanied by black suffrage, the sole route
it saw to sustain power. The Lincoln-backed Banks-Hahn, or moderate, faction desired immediate restoration for Louisiana to the Union without black
suffrage, avoiding what it foresaw as a complete alienation of the whites.[55]

All of these unionist factions contained future scalawags. No one group
gained much of a political foothold from spring 1862 to spring 1864 because
of the divided city governance. But patronage was abundant, and those who
owed their job to the federal government identified with the Republican Party.
Although only two of the congressmen-elect, Flanders and Hahn, were ever
seated, the congressional elections aided the party-building process, as candidates and voters chose labels and identified with factions. The unseated victors
were, for the most part, caught up in the struggle over who would control
Reconstruction, the president or Congress. Nine of the eleven Louisiana congressmen-elect were Republicans throughout Congressional Reconstruction.

Some notable figures from these factions won congressional elections during 1862–65. Four congressmen-elect—Field, Hahn, Flanders, and Bonzano—could have held office during any era; in fact, they did off and on for
thirty years. Others proved to be a mixed lot. Thomas M. Wells and Robert
W. Taliaferro, sons of prominent politicians, proved their manhood on the
battlefield, but they drank too much and lived in the shadow of their fathers.
Others were mediocre men, such as senators-elect R. King Cutler, an attorney
and accused horse thief from the Midwest who briefly sided with the Confederates and organized and served as captain of "King Cutler's Guards," and
Charles Smith, former sheriff of Saint Mary Parish and president of the state
senate in 1864.[56]

55. Michael Hahn, *What Is Unconditional Unionism?* (New Orleans, 1863), 4–6; McCrary,
Lincoln and Reconstruction, 195–97.

56. McCrary, *Lincoln and Reconstruction,* 79, 218, 250–52; 269–70, 298; James A. Payne to
Mrs. Kate F. Sterrett, 18 September 1864, in John D. Barnard, ed., "Reconstruction on the Lower
Mississippi," *Mississippi Valley Historical Review,* 21 (December 1934): 389. George S. Denison to

Field, a tough, hard-drinking old chameleon with wide political experience, had served as Illinois secretary of state for more than a decade. Though often an opportunist, Field did have principles, but they changed periodically. On occasion, he would defend his convictions, especially if he was inebriated. While in Washington claiming his congressional seat, he got roaring drunk, drew his pocketknife in a hotel dining room, and slashed the arm of Congressman William D. "Pig Iron" Kelley, who opposed seating Louisiana's delegation. Eventually Field's desire to endure, albeit interspersed with moments of courage and conviction, moved him in five years from Confederate to conservative, to moderate, and finally to radical, where he appeared to remain, his last political plum being elected state attorney general in 1872.[57]

After receiving Banks's backing, Hahn, a spokesman for the German working class, headed the moderate ticket. Although "short and lame," he was otherwise a commanding figure with broad shoulders, "dark, curly hair, and a brown complexion." He had served on Stephen A. Douglas's state committee in 1860 and later on the state's "co-operation" committee that sought to delay secession. He was also one of a small group who met at Polar Star Hall on Saint Louis Street shortly after Farragut's landing to show support for Louisiana's reunion. Hahn won the 1864 election by appealing to white urban laborers.[58]

In March, again with the general's help, moderates captured most of the seats for the constitutional convention. Meeting from April until July, delegates drafted a document reflecting the desires of their blue-collar constituency: fair labor laws, abolition of slavery, legislative reapportionment, free but segregated schools, and a franchise limited to white men only. Lincoln endorsed the new constitution, although he had suggested privately to Hahn that "intelligent" blacks be given the vote. Banks acquired an almost unanimous vote for ratification. During early June, some of the lawmakers, along with others, represented the state at the Republican National Convention.[59]

Chase, 25 November 1864, *Diary and Correspondence of Chase*, 453–54; Stephen A. Douglas, *Letters*, ed. Robert W. Johannsen (Urbana, Ill., 1961), 446n.

57. Pease, Collections of the Illinois State Historical Library, 18: 504–5; *Report from the Select Committee to Investigate the Assault upon the Hon. W. D. Kelley*, 38th Cong., 2d sess., No. 10; Field to Abraham Lincoln, 10 September 1863, Lincoln Papers.

58. Amos Simpson and Vaughan Baker, "Michael Hahn: Steady Patriot," *LH* 13 (summer 1972): 229–52; Cox, *Union—Disunion—Reunion*, 427–28.

59. N. P. Banks to Abraham Lincoln, 6 March 1864, Lincoln Papers; Roger W. Shugg, *Origins of Class Struggle in Louisiana: A Social History of White Farmers and Laborers during Slavery and*

By mid-1863 it became clear that much of Arkansas had to be occupied by the Union army before large numbers of its people would support the Union. Once the conquest of all territory north of the Arkansas River moved forward, several mass meetings in the northwestern section of the state passed resolutions supporting creation of a loyal state government. At least one meeting south of the Arkansas River occurred, at Benton in Saline County, attended and controlled by Arkansas Union soldiers. At some point, these meetings and unionist clubs sponsored by them began electing delegates to attend a constitutional convention in Little Rock in January 1864, a convention announced by the *Little Rock Unconditional Union* and the *Fort Smith New Era*.[60]

When Federal troops occupied Fort Smith in September 1863, Valentine Dell, principal of a local academy, took the lead there in seeking to restore Arkansas to the Union. Dell, a German native, served in the United States Army from 1849 to 1854 in Indian campaigns from Florida to Kansas. After farming a while in Kansas, where he supported the antislavery party, the young bachelor settled in Fort Smith, Arkansas. There he began teaching, his family's profession for three hundred years. Dell formed a unionist club the first day the Federals arrived, and days later published his first issue of the *New Era*, calling for a convention at Fort Smith "to open political connections with the Federal government." More than one thousand loyalists from twenty counties in western Arkansas met there on October 30. They recommended that delegates be elected to a state convention at Little Rock to reorganize the state government. Later in 1863, Dell organized a branch of the national Union League.[61]

Following its occupation by Federals in September 1863, Little Rock served as a hub for unionist operations. Unionists soon published a newspaper and started a local club they hoped would be the precursor of "Union clubs all over the State." Men like Isaac Murphy and Elisha Baxter mingled with returning refugees and recent Confederate converts to unionism. They joined with others, such as William D. Snow, fleeing from behind Confederate lines to the south. He had continued his telegraph business until 1862, when Rebels

after, 1840–1875 (Baton Rouge, 1939), 155, 198–99; Lincoln to Hahn, 13 March 1864, *Collected Works of Abraham Lincoln,* 7: 243.

60. Thomas S. Staples, *Reconstruction in Arkansas, 1862–1874* (New York, 1923), 13; *OR,* 24(1): 97; OR, 3: 353; Dougan, *Confederate Arkansas,* 17, 36; Dorris, *Pardon and Amnesty,* 36, 67–68; Nolte, "Downeasters in Arkansas," 17–23.

61. *Encyclopedia of the New West,* 56–57.

confiscated his line because he refused to take a loyalty oath to the Confederacy.[62] Elsewhere in Arkansas, members of newly founded Union Leagues called for a constitutional convention to restore the state to the Union. Eventually the convention was scheduled for January 1864. Some delegates were chosen by local caucuses, others by the state's Union army soldiers, and some, reportedly, by citizens in the streets of Little Rock. Only a few delegates had ever served in a legislative body. Most came from recently captured counties south of the Arkansas River, where loyalists had just begun to organize. More than one-half were farmers, mostly nonslaveholding; others included a sprinkling of attorneys, physicians, merchants, ministers, and tradesmen. A few were southern born and bred, and all but fourteen had lived in Arkansas for more than a decade. Politically, they divided evenly between former Whigs and Democrats.[63]

Once the convention opened, delegates quickly declared secession "null and void" and slavery dead, but they left the state's black codes intact. To protect themselves and other loyalists, they made "guerrillaing [sic], jayhawking and bushwaching [sic] . . . a felony punishable by hanging." Then they established a provisional government headed by former state senator Isaac Murphy. Murphy and other candidates also were nominated to run in a general election. Lincoln encouraged Murphy "to get out the largest vote possible; and, of course, as much of it as possible on the right side." Murphy later reported to the president that "the entire vote [would] exceed ten thousand," a total he considered good considering that guerrillas had "threatened to hang everyone that went to the polls."[64]

In the March election, voters approved the constitution by more than 12,000 votes out of 12,400 total and elected Murphy's ticket by about the same margin. During the following year, the loyal legislature held three sessions. The first session elected as United States senators Elisha Baxter and William

62. William D. Snow to Abraham Lincoln, 29 February 1864, Isaac Murphy to Lincoln, 23 January 1864, E. Baxter, W. M. Fishback, J. M. Jacks, N. M. Johnson, and A. C. C. Rogers to Lincoln, 23 June 1864, Lincoln Papers; Moore, *Rebellion Record*, vol. 8, pt. 1: 11; *Report of the Joint Committee on Reconstruction*, pt. 3: 128; Christopher C. Andrews to Johnson, 23 October 1863, *PAJ*, 6: 434–35.

63. Moore, *Rebellion Record*, vol. 7, pt. 1: 67, vol. 8, pt. 2: 324–26; *Journal of the Convention of Delegates of the People of Arkansas. Assembled at the Capitol January 4, 1864* (Little Rock, 1870); *Journals of the House of Representatives of the Sessions of 1864, 1864–65 and 1865* (Little Rock, 1870), 3–4; *Little Rock Unconditional Union*, 23 January 1864.

64. Lincoln to Murphy, 12 March 1864, *Collected Works of Abraham Lincoln*, 7: 240; Murphy to Lincoln, 27 March 1864, 7: 240n.

Fishback, neither of whom was ever seated, and enacted militia laws and revenue acts, neither of which was successful during the war. The second established an oath for voting, which included the voter's promise to support the
United States. The third witnessed the unanimous passage of the Thirteenth
Amendment.[65]

Those elected for state offices in March 1864, along with those elected to
Congress, most of whom both later became Republicans, typified wartime Arkansas unionist leaders. Before the war, some were Douglas Democrats and
others Whigs. A few had served in the Union army. Some of these had been
refugees. Some simply tried to stay at home. The only really gung-ho Confederate had been Senator-elect Fishback, a sort of Joseph E. Brown of Arkansas
politics who was, like Brown, first in war, first in Reconstruction, and first in
redemption (and who, like Brown, could tell you why). The convention and
the legislature following it were significant party builders. Most of the convention's delegates and those elected in the March 1864 state election eventually
became Republicans. A majority first identified with the Republican Party
when they attended conventions in May 1864 that endorsed Lincoln's reelection. On April 8, the *Little Rock Unconditional Union* endorsed Lincoln for
president and Andrew Johnson of Tennessee for vice president. The newspaper called for a state convention to meet in Little Rock on May 2 to nominate
a Union electoral ticket and to elect delegates to the Republican National
Convention. At the national convention, Colonel James M. Johnson of Arkansas was named to the Republican National Executive Committee.[66]

Fully one-half of Arkansas and Louisiana scalawags held office under a
loyal wartime government (see table 6). Their opportunity came after north
Arkansas and south Louisiana fell to Union forces in 1862 and 1863, allowing
New Orleans and Little Rock to become cities of refuge. Although federal patronage was less significant in Arkansas than in Louisiana, a few Ozark scalawags received Treasury or Justice Department appointments. Governor
Murphy requested that Lincoln delay federal appointments "until the fate of
our . . . efforts to restore our State to the Union is determined and the undoubted union men have time to be heard from." So Lincoln waited several

---

65. Staples, *Reconstruction in Arkansas,* 60–73.
66. *Little Rock Unconditional Union,* clipping, n.d., in Christopher C. Andrews to Abraham
Lincoln, 8 April 1864, Lincoln Papers; *New York Tribune,* 6 June 1864; Edward McPherson, *The
Political History of the United States during the Great Rebellion . . . ,* 2d ed. (Washington, D.C.,
1865), 798–99; *Proceedings of the First Three Republican National Conventions,* 242.

weeks after the March 1864 election, until he had heard from Arkansas's congressmen-elect and from Murphy again, before he made federal appointments for the state.[67]

From 1863 to 1865, about one-third of Arkansas scalawags joined the Union army, mostly as officers of regiments they recruited, as was the case with Baxter, Johnson, and Lafayette Gregg. Later their troops merged into trans-Mississippi companies under officers from the Midwest, foreshadowing the later influence of men such as Powell Clayton from Kansas. After the regiments disbanded, the war years' camaraderie continued. Some veterans became officeholders. Many later attended Republican conventions and served on the state party's committees. They also organized branches of the Grand Army of the Republic and held GAR meetings well into the 1880s. Nearly an equal number of scalawag officeholders from the Southwest served in the Union and Confederate armies, about 15 percent. This differs drastically from the military experience of the redeemers: over three-fourths served in the Confederate army, and none served in the Union army. The postwar Democratic conventions in Arkansas, Texas, and Louisiana to a large degree consisted of high-ranking Confederate veterans.[68]

Arkansas unionists divided along lines similar to those in other states undergoing wartime Reconstruction. Josiah Snow, whose son William was defeated for one of the United States Senate seats by Fishback, accused the speaker of the Arkansas House, Horace B. Allis of Pine Bluff, of being a copperhead. According to Snow, Allis controlled "seven belonging to his side in the House" and was expelled "for facetiousness and attempts to disorganize." Allis represented Anthony A. C. Rogers, also of Pine Bluff, and his faction. Colonel Christopher C. Andrews, the commander at Little Rock, believed that Rogers was among those "who pretend to acquiesce in the proclamation setting slaves free [who] still cling to their slaves and to the hope that they will sometime again hold them as slaves." Rogers and Fishback would later be two of the founders of the Conservative (Democratic) Party in their state.[69]

In addition to wartime Reconstruction in Louisiana, Arkansas, Virginia, and Tennessee, unsuccessful efforts at restoration occurred elsewhere on the

67. Murphy to Lincoln, 27 March 1864, *Collected Works of Abraham Lincoln,* 7: 240.

68. *Report of the Adjutant General of Arkansas for the Period of the Late Rebellion and to November 1, 1866* (Washington, D.C., 1867).

69. Staples, *Reconstruction in Arkansas,* 39, 62; Andrews to Abraham Lincoln, 8 April 1864, William Snow to William Seward, 10 May 1864, Lincoln Papers.

fringes of the Confederacy. Ill-fated attempts were made on the North Carolina coast, at Jacksonville, Florida, and at Brownsville, Texas. Short-lived occupation resulted in failed efforts in Florida and Texas. Lincoln's plan to reconstruct Florida collapsed when his private secretary John Hay could not persuade the required one-tenth of the state's 1860 voters to sign a loyalty oath and Union forces abandoned the Jacksonville area before a loyal state convention could be held. Plans to reconstruct Texas by way of Brownsville from October 1863 to July 1864 involved establishing a loyal state government initially at Brownsville and recruiting troops in the Rio Grande Valley. Federals fought a number of skirmishes, but the overall mission failed because not enough troops could be recruited.

In North Carolina, after Hatteras Island fell in 1861, more than 250 individuals took a loyalty oath to the United States government. Charles Henry Foster, a Maine native who arrived in the state in 1859 and edited a Murfreesboro newspaper, rallied some of them. At a poorly attended convention at Hatteras on November 18, a provisional government was established under his leadership, which received recognition from practically no one. Afterward Foster ran for Congress but received only four hundred votes as the sole candidate in Hyde County, the only county participating. Seeing his usefulness, Lincoln appointed Foster as the occupied area's army recruiter. In 1862, Federals seized several points on the mainland, where Foster and others established recruiting stations. They enlisted enough men for the First and Second North Carolina Union Volunteers. A second attempt at reconstructing the state got underway when Lincoln appointed Beaufort County native Edward Stanly, a former congressman who was then living in California, as North Carolina's military governor. Stanly did his best, but because he disapproved of Lincoln's emancipation policy, he resigned in January 1863 after serving only eight months. Lincoln did not replace him. These abortive attempts at wartime Reconstruction in Texas, Florida, and North Carolina included the activities of several individuals, such as Foster, who later became Republican politicos in their state.[70]

Throughout the South, several types welcomed occupying Federals:

---

70. William C. Harris, "Lincoln and Wartime Reconstruction in North Carolina, 1861–1863," *NCHR* 63 (April 1986): 149–68; Current, *Lincoln's Loyalists*, 61–68; Wayne K. Durrill, *War of Another Kind: A Southern Community in the Great Rebellion* (New York, 1990), 43–56; Norman C. Delaney, "Charles Henry Foster and the Unionists of Eastern North Carolina," *NCHR* 37 (July 1960): 344–66; Hamilton, *Reconstruction in North Carolina*, 81–95.

northern-born citizens still responding positively to Yankee ideas, ultraunionists viewing Confederates as the enemy, poor whites hating the southern aristocracy, and blacks seeking a liberator. Some hoped to cooperate with the Federals in reuniting their state to the Union. Because of their record and feelings, they believed they, rather than outsiders or secessionists turned unionists, should lead such a restoration. To reconstruct, they needed protection from the possible, if not likely, return of Confederate forces and from Confederate supporters at home. Many problems, however, made wartime Reconstruction difficult. Unionist numbers remained small compared with the number of Confederates in the occupied areas, mostly because of fear of retaliation, and unionists divided over Lincoln's war aims, such as emancipation. Some unionists were disillusioned or insulted by the behavior of the Federals and confused by conflicting civilian and military authorities.[71]

Nonetheless, in garrisoned towns Federals provided unionists with employment, local public offices, protection from harassment, public education for their children, and because of Lincoln's support, an opportunity to reconstruct their state governments. Unionists connected with failed attempts to reconstruct, along with those in states undergoing wartime Reconstruction, formed relationships that caused many of them to become Republicans. Out of the wartime constitutional conventions, a connection with the Republican Party occurred in 1864 when members of these conventions chose delegates to the Republican National Convention. Such support made them good candidates for federal posts, which connected them with the Republican administration. The division between radicals and conservatives in states undergoing Reconstruction continued into 1865 and 1866. Radicals generally became Republicans and conservatives joined with former rebels to create conservative (Democratic) state parties.

71. Stephen V. Ash, *When the Yankees Came: Conflict and Chaos in the Occupied South, 1861–1865* (Chapel Hill, 1995), 108–48.

5

~

Postwar Disillusionment

Unionists from the occupied areas of the Confederacy generally supported Lincoln's administration. In 1864 they sent delegates to the Republican National Convention, where one of their own, Andrew Johnson, became the president's running mate. Wartime loyalists continued to be a tiny cadre, however. That they could create a broad-based constituency was highly doubtful. Then during 1865–66 they experienced several shocks, including the assassination of Lincoln, sponsor of their regimes in the Virginias, Tennessee, Arkansas, and Louisiana; the presidency of Johnson, who turned from his wartime goal in Tennessee that "treason must be made odious" to an objective of marshaling allies against congressional radicals; and after a brief acquiescence, the return of secessionists to office, seeking to salvage the past. Meanwhile unionists recruited candidates, proposed policies, and lobbied Washington. But it was not until the beginning of Congressional Reconstruction in 1867 that they formed political parties in most of the former Confederate states.

Eventually most wartime unionists broke with Johnson because he allowed former Confederates to hold office and because he lacked support in the North, as the 1866 congressional elections demonstrated. These loyalists, who felt abandoned by the president, had a powerful ally in the Republican Party—a party, as Parson Brownlow said, that commanded "*two-thirds* in both houses of Congress . . . backed by the loyal masses North." Yet such an alliance became a mixed blessing for loyalists because it consolidated their enemies, that is, Democrats, north and south. Democrats saw they could regain national supremacy only by restoring their southern wing, now dominated by former Confederates. They quickly realized this could best be done with the backing of Johnson, still a Jacksonian Democrat at heart.[1]

Already in the minority, wartime unionists faced the tough question of just who would be pure enough to enter their ranks. If they defined loyalty too strictly, thousands would be disfranchised and they would find it difficult to rule or to build a base of support. If, on the other hand, they defined loyalty too liberally, their enemies would overwhelm them at the first election. If past loyalty rather than current loyalty counted, when did it need to commence? Should there be a national standard, such as December 1863 when Lincoln issued his amnesty proclamation? Or should unionists from each southern state establish a date to their political advantage? Also there was the question of what proved patriotism. Did devotion to the United States need to be absolute or, given the circumstances, only relatively consistent?

Most of the wartime unionists counted three classes as being loyal: the "truly loyal," active supporters of the Union during the war; draft dodgers, deserters, and all other anti-Confederates; and so-called stay-at-homes, who contributed as little as possible to the Confederacy. But they were confronted on every hand by "original Unionists," men opposed to secession who joined prosecessionists to fight invading Federals, now desiring loyalty status while still condemning the other three classes as traitors to their communities.[2]

Southern political party lines stayed unclear during 1865–66, partly because office seekers eschewed prewar labels, due to a sort of blame game. For example, northern newspaperman Sidney Andrews reported that in North Carolina, "The Democratic party, one class affirms . . . , made secession . . . , and brought the State to the verge of ruin. . . . The Whig party, the other class retorts . . . , was half disloyal to the State, and caused disaster by its . . . coldness in behalf of the war." Loyalists preferred the term *unionist,* and all others liked the word *conservative;* the latter worked well for former Whigs who refused to rally with their former enemies under the banner of Democrat. Each saw the other as illegitimate: to conservatives, unionists equaled radicals seeking to overturn traditional authority; to unionists, conservative meant Con-

---

1. Brownlow to Oliver P. Temple, 25 January 1866, Temple Papers; Eric L. McKitrick, *Andrew Johnson and Reconstruction* (Chicago, 1960), 72–74; LaWanda F. Cox and John H. Cox, *Politics, Principle, and Prejudice, 1865–1866: Dilemma of Reconstruction America* (New York, 1969), 50–67.
2. Fleming, *Civil War and Reconstruction in Alabama,* 317–18.

federate by a name that smelled no sweeter. Actually, factions during 1865–66 are best understood divided into four groups: loyalists, original unionists, former secessionists, and die-hard secessionists. Loyalists, forerunners of the earliest scalawags, accounted for about one-fifth of whites centered in larger towns and hilly areas. Original unionists accounted for about one-third of whites, and when combined with former secessionists, they commanded a majority. Die-hard secessionists, like the loyalists, represented a weak minority.[3]

Initially, loyalists trusted Johnson as president. He recognized the wartime governments established by Lincoln in Tennessee, which he himself had headed, and those in Virginia, Louisiana, and Arkansas, all with governors elected during the war. Also his provisional governors seemed loyal enough: refugees such as Andrew J. Hamilton of Texas, peace advocates such as William W. Holden of North Carolina, and stay-at-homes such as James Johnson of Georgia. Only Benjamin F. Perry of South Carolina, an original unionist, had consistently supported the Confederacy throughout the war. Although President Johnson granted amnesty to most Confederates, he reserved fourteen classes of exceptions whereby pardon could only be given by him, which included ranking officeholders, military officers, and men with estates exceeding $20,000 in 1860, whom Johnson believed bore greater guilt for the war. Also with his blessing, restoration progressed in Tennessee.[4]

Only hours after the fall of Richmond on April 3, the so-called Brownlow Assembly in Tennessee, whose term would continue into 1867, ratified the Thirteenth Amendment, freeing the slaves. According to one observer, "The Legislature convened amid the thunders of Artillery—fired in honor of the deathblow that had Just been given to a gigantic Conspiracy"—and the main city streets were "literally covered with Stars & Stripes" celebrating the occasion. Brownlow took the oath of office two days later before a large crowd, which included "three hundred ladies." But by mid-May, Brownlow worried he would lose control of the lower house of the legislature. Loyalists had a solid majority in the state senate, but he feared the house would "allow all rebels to vote." He felt some members were being motivated by the fact that

3. Thomas B. Alexander, "Persistent Whiggery in the Confederate South, 1860–1877," JSH 27 (August 1950): 313–15; Andrews, *South since the War*, 136.

4. Michael Perman, *Reunion without Compromise: The South and Reconstruction, 1865–1868*, 57–67.

they "had rebel kin in trouble [and] that others wanted to make a record upon which they could get back to the Legislature on, or into Congress."

Despite Brownlow's pessimism, if he properly managed the situation, he had the votes to protect the state's unionist minority. Before adjourning in June 1865, the assembly approved the bulk of Brownlow's request, much of which proscribed Confederates and protected loyalists.[5]

Assemblymen from mountainous areas of the state believed, as did Brownlow, that only disfranchisement could keep East Tennessee from becoming an "appendage to a rebel state." Others thought that if loyalists could guarantee to Congress that loyalists would control Tennessee, they might gain congressional representation. And some shared the bitterness of the disfranchisement bill's sponsor, Representative Samuel M. Arnell of Maury County. While describing secession's toll of desolation, despair, and death, Arnell yelled, "I represent . . . no rebel . . . I represent Union men alone . . . I want protection for them." In the upper house, with only one senator dissenting and others abstaining, the bill—disfranchising the mass of Confederates for five years and high-ranking ones for fifteen years—passed quickly. In the lower house, legislators from the east and west grand divisions favored the bill by almost two to one. But most from Middle Tennessee opposed it. Almost all of the bill's supporters later became Republicans, many high-ranking officeholders. But this bill alone did not fix political party lines, even in the legislature.[6]

Individuals sorted out more along party lines during the congressional election of August 1865, when more than twenty candidates, mostly Whigs, sought eight seats. One-half of them backed Brownlow's administration as being, in the words of Horace Maynard, "a legal, constitutional, rightful government." Others joined with wartime conservative unionists in denying the legality of its existence and/or its acts. Four radicals and four conservatives (the latter all wartime conservative unionists) won. Statewide, voters for scalawag candidates accounted for about one-half of the total; in East Tennessee, they accounted for more than two-thirds. But overall, twice as many people voted as in March, showing a decline for Brownlowism.

5. James W. Scully to Johnson, 6 April 1865, *PAJ*, 2: 548–49; Brownlow to Johnson, 19 May, 8 June 1865, PAJ, 2: 91–92, 199–200.

6. James Welch Patton, *Unionism and Reconstruction in Tennessee, 1860–1869* (Chapel Hill, 1934), 90–102; S. R. Rogers to Oliver P. Temple, 13 May 1865; Temple Papers; Robert H. White, *Messages of the Governors of Tennessee, 1796–1907* 8 vols. (Nashville, 1952–72), 4: 432–38; Brownlow to Andrew Johnson, 8 June 1865, Johnson Papers; Queener, "Origin of the Republican Party in East Tennessee," 87.

To slow the upswing of conservative voters, the governor required county clerks to file reports on their enforcement of the Franchise Act. The results showed that clerks generally understood the act, that many did their best to enforce it, and that others had violated it. When in March 1866, a conservative-Confederate coalition won county elections in Middle and West Tennessee (with Johnson's blessing, according to Brownlow), the governor backed a bill scrapping the previous registration and allowing him to appoint commissioners of registration in each county. A series of struggles commenced: a conservative filibuster in the general assembly, followed by resignations to break the quorum; elections to fill those seats; seating of the winners to provide a quorum; and finally on April 12, adoption of the bill.[7]

Meanwhile, the governor broke openly with President Johnson in a speech he delivered to Knoxville's German Union League in March. Brownlow announced that "If Andy Johnson [led] the way in reconstruction with the Democratic Party at his back," he would "go the other way . . . with the Congress of the United States, the so-called radicals." Still many loyalists in Tennessee stayed on cordial terms with the president until the summer of 1866. On occasion, they applauded his policy and appealed to him for patronage. Some lauded him for his veto of the Freedmen's Bureau Bill. But after Johnson aided their enemies inside and outside the state and lost control of Reconstruction to a Congress friendly to them, loyalists distanced themselves from him.[8]

The showdown came for Tennessee radicals when the general assembly considered the Fourteenth Amendment. Radicals had been slow to support civil rights for blacks. The tide for black suffrage turned during the summer when congressional Republicans promised to readmit Tennessee to the Union if the state legislature ratified the Fourteenth Amendment. After Governor Brownlow called the legislature into a special session on July 4, 1866, to ratify the amendment, conservatives once again tried to prevent a quorum. But after rounding up enough legislators, the Brownlow Assembly on July 19 approved the Fourteenth Amendment. The amendment declared blacks to be citizens under "equal protection of the laws," allowed reduction of congressional representation for states forbidding blacks to vote, denied office to antebellum

7. Alexander, *Reconstruction in Tennessee,* 79–97; Proclamation of 11 August 1865 and responding letters, Brownlow Papers.

8. Brownlow to Oliver P. Temple, 8 March 1866, Temple Papers; Curry, *Radicalism, Racism, and Party Realignment,* 55; Brownlow to Salmon P. Chase, 20 June 1866, Chase Papers.

officials who had aided the rebellion, and prohibited the government from paying Confederate debts or remunerating individuals for the loss of slaves.[9]

Political party lines now solidified in Tennessee: supporters of the amendment identified with Republicans and opponents with Democrats. While the struggle over the Fourteenth Amendment waged in Tennessee, conservatives organized their followers to attend the pro-Johnson National Union convention scheduled in August at Philadelphia. Radicals rallied their supporters to attend the Southern Loyalist Convention in the same city in September. The vote on the Fourteenth Amendment and the subsequent requests for individuals to commit themselves for or against Brownlow's program by supporting one of the two national conventions became a watershed in Tennessee politics. As far as scalawags are concerned, the events of 1865–66 thinned their ranks only to a limited degree. Conservatives, however, increased in the number of their followers (not necessarily their voters) as former Confederates joined with wartime conservative unionists and a few radicals dissatisfied with Brownlow's proscriptive policies.[10]

At this time in East Tennessee, radicals (Republicans), largely former Whigs, outnumbered conservatives (Democrats) by more than three to one. West Tennessee Republicans could hardly be found at all outside of Memphis and a few of the Tennessee River counties where anti-Confederate sentiment had existed during the war, mainly among former Whigs. General Alvan C. Gillem, who held a seat in the general assembly in 1865, believed the radicals in Middle Tennessee represented only "one *fifth* of the voters under the 'Franchise law.'" They were composed of three groups of individuals, residing mostly in the towns. The first class, according to Gillem, was "Northern men, who came in *rear* of the army to make money or have settled here because of their failure elsewhere," of which he listed several examples of Nashville businessmen, some of whom held local offices. The second class Gillem saw as men "who have been thrown to the service of political affairs by the waves of the revolution." The third group, although "small in number," did, he admitted, contain "a few men of some ability who forgot to be patriots to remember they were Whigs. Such as [Horace H.] Harrison and [John] Trimble" of Nashville.[11]

9. Brownlow to M. E. W. Dunnaway, 5 July 1866, Brownlow Papers; Patton, *Unionism and Reconstruction,* 217–25.

10. Patton, *Unionism and Reconstruction,* 217–25.

11. Gillem to Johnson, 30 September 1866, *PAJ,* 11: 287–88, 289n; Queener, "Origin of the Republican Party in East Tennessee," 89–90.

In Virginia, after the Alexandria government moved to Richmond, unionists split into moderates, mostly former Whigs such as Governor Pierpont, and into radicals, with assorted antecedents. John M. Botts, recognized for his integrity and intelligence despite his "well-fed bullfrog" appearance, was the main moderate spokesman. He was among a few wealthy former Whigs who became Republicans in 1865–66. Others included his friends John F. Lewis, a livestock breeder from Rockingham County, and William C. Wickham, a railroad president who served as a Confederate general and congressman and who after 1863 had backed the peace bloc in the Confederate Congress. Pierpont and other moderates considered proscription unacceptable. Despite misgivings even among some allies, the governor endorsed appeals for presidential pardons and the removal of voter restrictions imposed by the wartime Alexandria government.[12]

Ultraunionists saw Pierpont's policy as a sellout. In June 1865, they formed the Union Association of Alexandria and endorsed suffrage to "loyal male citizens without regard to color." The association was the first of several such groups—most soon identified with the Union League of America—that entered the state's occupied areas during the war. Richmond's customs collector J. R. S. Van Fleet, president of the city's league, reported in August 1865 that, in addition to his council, others functioned in Alexandria, Petersburg, and Norfolk and that local black organizations cooperated with the white councils. Black leaders did not make important moves, he said, without the "advice, consent or direction of the League."[13]

Chief among Virginia's radicals stood James W. Hunnicutt, a clergyman and publisher from Fredericksburg who fled early in the war to Washington, D.C. Back in Fredericksburg a year later under the Army of the Potomac's protection, he briefly resurrected his *Christian Banner* to attack secessionists. In Washington during December 1863, he established the Union League Association of Virginia. After he issued his first edition of the *Richmond New Na-*

12. Richard Lowe, "Another Look at Reconstruction in Virginia," *Civil War History* 32 (March 1986), 57–58; Richard Lowe, "Francis Harrison Pierpont: Wartime Unionist, Reconstruction Moderates," in *The Governors of Virginia, 1860–1978*, ed. Edward Younger (Charlottesville, 1982), 39–40; Charles H. Lewis to Andrew Johnson, 3 July 1865, Johnson Papers.

13. Richard Lowe, *Republicans and Reconstruction in Virginia, 1856–1870* (Charlottesville, 1991), 34–44; *Alexandria Gazette*, 12, 13, 23, June, 8 July 1865; Van Fleet to Benjamin F. Butler, 1 August 1865, Butler Papers; Squires, *Unleashed at Long Last*, 70–71; Joseph P. Harahan, "Politics, Political Parties, and Voter Participation in Tidewater Virginia during Reconstruction, 1865–1900" (Ph.D. diss., Michigan State University, 1973), 76.

tion in October 1865, Hunnicutt toured New England to raise capital before he resumed publishing the newspaper in March 1866. For months he toiled, ate, and slept in one "dimly lit room." Ostracized by his white brethren, Hunnicutt preached to black congregations. Hunnicutt's closest ally was Burnham Wardwell, who had suffered imprisonment during the war.[14]

Virginia unionists of all shades were disappointed by the fall 1865 election returns in which less than one-fourth of voters favored candidates who had opposed the Confederacy. Original unionist Whigs won by "combining their credentials as [prewar] Union men and as Confederates." Only three loyalists won seats in the legislature and one in the Congress, able and outgoing federal district attorney Lucius H. Chandler, who was accused of being chummy with Confederates. Now out in the cold altogether, wartime unionists complained of former Rebels being elected on their military records. Governor Pierpont's moderates despaired as legislators, led by Speaker John B. Baldwin, a former Confederate congressman, tried to nullify the war's results. They deposed unionist state officeholders and even petitioned the president to replace Pierpont with Robert E. Lee.[15]

Southern loyalists, mostly from nearby Virginia, represented about one-half of 145 witnesses who appeared before the Congressional Joint Committee on Reconstruction in early 1866. Some were already visiting Washington for one reason or another: as congressmen-elect hoping to be seated, such as those testifying from Arkansas and Tennessee; as attorneys acting as pardon brokers and seekers of war claims; or as politicians sampling the waters and looking for "fishes and loaves." Other witnesses included a few well-known Confederates—the highest ranking being Alexander H. Stephens and Robert E. Lee—seven freedmen, and an array of northerners. The northerners included federal employees recently or presently stationed in the South, including army officers, travelers (especially journalists and presidential advisers), and recent settlers below the Mason-Dixon Line. Virginia loyalists of both

14. *Report of the Joint Committee on Reconstruction*, pt. 2: 150; John Thomas O'Brien Jr., "From Bondage to Citizenship: The Richmond Black Community, 1865–1867" (Ph.D. diss., University of Rochester, 1974), 415–17; Richard G. Lowe, "Virginia Reconstruction Convention: General Schofield Rates the Delegates," *VMHB* 80 (July 1972): 346; Michael B. Chesson, *Richmond after the War, 1865–1890* (Richmond, 1981), 111.

15. Lowe, *Republicans and Reconstruction in Virginia*, 42–44; Jack P. Maddex Jr., "Virginia: The Persistence of Centrist Hegemony," in *Reconstruction and Redemption in the South*, ed. Otto H. Olsen (Baton Rouge, 1980), 116–17; John C. Underwood to Andrew Johnson, 10 July 1865, Thomas Bowden to Johnson, 26 July 1865, Johnson Papers.

factions testified. George S. Smith's testimony was typical. When asked about the president's "liberal policy" toward restoring the South, Smith said, "It has brought forward the original leaders of the rebellion," who otherwise would not have sought office, and has "left Union men in despair."[16]

Seeking to remedy their situation, Virginia unionists of both factions met in May 1866 at Alexandria to form the Union Republican Party of Virginia. The delegates battled bitterly over a platform calling for exclusion of former Confederates "from suffrage and holding office" and the "enfranchisement of all Union men, without distinction of color." They eventually adopted it and elected an executive committee composed mostly of radicals.[17]

In North Carolina during 1865–66, wartime factions continued, as clashes continued between groups who "cherished different recollection[s] of the past." In a carryover from 1864, conservatives opposed peace party followers of publisher William W. Holden, whom President Johnson, himself a Raleigh native, named provisional governor in May 1865. Both had overcome difficult beginnings and the disdain of their "betters" to become champions of the common man and leaders in their state Democratic Party. Holden's duty, like that of other provisional governors, was to direct the restoration of his state to the Union. In doing so, he hoped to further his own ambition as well as that of President Johnson. Holden viewed politics and policy as parts of an inseparable whole. In consultation with friends throughout North Carolina, especially peace party men, Holden ascertained "the antecedents and . . . disposition of every man appointed." Altogether, directly or indirectly, Holden made more than four thousand appointments, and most of his appointees would remain his followers.[18]

Holden avoided building his party, however, solely on the foundation of favors granted or denied. Not all appointees were cronies or even former allies. A few appointees held positions in the Vance administration. Holden wanted to prevent some individuals from holding office altogether. He refused to endorse pardons for those prolonging the war after all hope of victory had vanished. He denounced former governors William A. Graham and Zebulon B. Vance for wanting "to unite enough . . . old Whigs to the Secessionists" to pay off "the Rebel debt and destroy the Union party." As an editor as

16. *Report of the Joint Committee on Reconstruction*, pt. 2: 6–51.
17. Lowe, *Republicans and Reconstruction in Virginia*, 37–38, *New York Tribune*, 19 May 1866.
18. Cox, *Union—Disunion—Reunion*, 386–87; *OR*, 5: 37–39; Raper, *William W. Holden*, 61–69.

well as a politician, Holden always stood for something. He believed that ideology was indispensable in holding a political party together.[19]

Holden found the constitutional convention election returns in September 1865 "gratifying." He believed the returns pointed toward "a short and harmonious session" filled with "ultra union . . . sentiment." Two-thirds of the delegates elected had opposed secession. The delegates declared secession "repealed, rescinded, and abrogated" and slavery "forever prohibited." Then they provided for the restoration of state and local government. Most hoped to leave the state war debts issue to the forthcoming legislature, thereby, at least for the time being, evading an unsightly struggle that would be witnessed by the North. But Thomas Settle, the broad-shouldered, black-bearded former speaker of the general assembly, whose path paralleled Holden's since 1860, rallied those opposed to assumption. So after a lengthy debate, delegates agreed to cancel the debt. Although not strictly a partisan issue, Holden's followers generally desired repudiation.[20]

At the time of the constitutional convention's first session, a four-day freedmen's convention met at Raleigh's nearby African Methodist Church. The homespun-clad delegates petitioned the white men's meeting to fund education for all children, abolish discriminatory laws, and to protect workers from cruel employers. The delegates avoided the thorny issue of black suffrage. At the last minute, they formed a chapter of the Equal Rights League, an organization dedicated to black suffrage. Some in North Carolina, as elsewhere, saw black suffrage as unavoidable. The Barringer brothers, for example, insisted that the North would impose suffrage if the South did not apply voting requirements equally to whites and blacks. While a prisoner of war in the North, where he talked with many northerners, Rufus Barringer saw the inevitability of suffrage. He probably influenced his brother, for in the summer of 1865 Victor Barringer penned a series of unsigned articles for the *Raleigh Sentinel* favoring qualified black suffrage.[21]

19. Raper, *William W. Holden*, 63–66; Holden to Andrew Johnson, 24 July 1865, Johnson Papers; *(Raleigh) North Carolina Standard*, 29 January 1866.

20. Holden to Andrew Johnson, 21 September 1865, Johnson Papers; Andrews, *South since the War*, 132–33, 136–39, 169–73; Dan T. Carter, *When the War Was Over: The Failure of Self-Reconstruction in the South, 1865–1867* (Baton Rouge, 1985), 48, 55; John Richard Dennett, *The South as It Is: 1865–1866*, ed. Henry M. Christman (New York, 1965), 157–58; Hamilton, *Reconstruction in North Carolina* (New York, 1914), 56, 121–22; Raper, *William W. Holden*, 74–77, 88; *Journal of the North Carolina Constitutional Convention* (Raleigh, 1865), 92.

21. Dennett, *South as It Is*, 148–54; Andrews, *South since the War*, 119–31, 161; W. McKee Evans, *Ballots and Fence Rails: Reconstruction on the Lower Cape Fear* (Chapel Hill, 1966), 89–93; Leon F. Litwack, *Been in the Storm So Long: The Aftermath of Slavery* (New York, 1979), 502–7; Hamilton, *Reconstruction in North Carolina*, 150–51; Victor Barringer to Andrew Johnson, 23

Before the session in 1865 adjourned, fifty-plus delegates petitioned Holden to be a gubernatorial candidate in the November election—a request, as anticipated, he accepted as his nomination. Expecting this, conservatives— "the rebellious element aided by the aristocracy," as Holden called them— searched for an opponent. At the eleventh hour, they persuaded state treasurer Jonathan Worth, "a small man of moderate abilities," to run. Worth differed from Holden primarily over the pardoning of noted conservatives. One observer saw Worth as more honest and Holden as more able. Both candidates left campaigning to the newspaper editors. Several factors caused Holden's defeat by 6,000 votes in what amounted to a carryover from 1864. But much of it was personal. Many voters saw in Holden nothing more than opportunism. Holdenites actually won four of the seven seats for Congress, but they won fewer seats in the legislature than in the 1865 convention.[22]

Other than organizing itself, ratifying the Thirteenth Amendment, and approving appointments, the general assembly accomplished little during 1865. Early in 1866, it approved a special Freedmen's Code Commission's recommendations for a black code, whose most liberal feature was the granting of the right to testify in court. The assembly consumed much of the time thereafter on debtor relief, state debt and taxation, and railroad development. According to one legislator, "The disposition of members" was to "meddle as little as possible with National politiks [sic]."

Still Holdenite lawmakers of 1865–66 constituted more of a party bloc than did loyalist legislators elsewhere. Only in the conventions of Alabama, Tennessee, and Texas and in the legislatures of Tennessee and Alabama did blocs exist that later helped forge state Republican parties. Earlier, such blocs existed in the wartime loyal assemblies of Arkansas, Louisiana, and the Virginias. Of the 1865–66 North Carolina lawmakers who stayed in politics, most convention delegates and many legislators became Republicans. Initially united by previous common interests, especially support of the peace movement, Holdenites agreed on other causes also, for example, opposition to paying off the war debt and support of counting whites only for legislative

December 1865, Johnson Papers; *DNCB*, 1: 102; V. C. Barringer to Daniel Barringer, 20 December 1866, Daniel M. Barringer Papers, Southern Historical Collection.

22. Holden, *Memoirs*, 64–65, 68; Worth to John Pool and Lewis Thompson, 16 October 1865, in *The Correspondence of Jonathan Worth*, ed. J. G. de Roulhac Hamilton (Raleigh, 1909), 1: 429–31; Carter, *When the War Was Over*, 55; Jennie Brin to Johnson, 1 December 1865, Johnson Papers.

apportionment. They agreed to a lesser degree about the Fourteenth Amendment, which in instances penalized them. Throughout, they held that the state had to do whatever was needed for readmission to the Union.[23]

During 1866, ultraunionists revived the Heroes of America, an anti-Confederate secret society; other loyalists, along with newcomers, formed Union Leagues. Albion W. Tourgée of Ohio organized an independent Loyal Reconstruction League at Greensboro in early 1866. While failing at a nursery business in Greensboro, he used his training as an attorney to defend harassed unionists and freedmen and his talents as a writer to issue weekly newspapers, the *Red String* for the Heroes of America and the *Union Register* for a more moderate reader. Union Leagues also existed elsewhere in the state during 1865–66. Leaguers at Wilmington participated in a Lincoln Memorial Procession in April 1865, and in the local election a few months later, the "Loyal League" ticket received a few votes. Before 1867, the few councils that existed were scattered, small, and totally white.[24]

Following calls from the "straitest-sects" at Guilford and New Bern, Holdenites from a handful of counties met at the state's capital on September 20, 1866. Under Holden's prompting, they endorsed the Fourteenth Amendment, nominated Alfred Dockery of Richmond County to oppose Worth in the October election and approved a fourteen-man party steering committee, which included an array of future Republican governors, congressmen, and judges. By now, the faction exceeded being "the germ" of the state's Republican Party, as J. G. de Roulhac Hamilton called it. It was "an embryo" of a full-blown political party. Although former congressman Dockery declined the nomination, he still announced his support for the Fourteenth Amendment. Holden and his *North Carolina Standard* still campaigned for Dockery. Conservatives won the governor's race nearly three to one. They also elected a solid majority in the legislature.[25]

After rejecting the Fourteenth Amendment, the newly elected legislature

23. Otto Olsen and Ellen Z. McGrew, eds., "Prelude to Reconstruction: The Correspondence of State Senator Leander Sams Gash 1866–1867," *NCHR* 60 (January 1983): 47–48, 52–55; Olsen and McGrew, "Prelude to Reconstruction," *NCHR* 60 (April 1983): 214, 221; Lancaster, "Scalawags of North Carolina," 91, 124, 161, 201–2.

24. Otto H. Olsen, "Albion W. Tourgée: Carpetbagger," *NCHR* 40 (autumn 1963): 437–39; Olsen and McGrew, "Prelude to Reconstruction," NCHR 60 (April 1983: 224, 238; Evans, *Ballots and Fence Rails*, 86; Hamilton, *Reconstruction in North Carolina*, 327–37.

25. Hamilton, *Reconstruction in North Carolina*, 181; Raper, *William W. Holden*, 88–89; *(Raleigh) North Carolina Standard*, 22 September 1866.

deposed some leading Holdenites: Settle, speaker of the senate; Curtis H. Brogden, state auditor; and senator-elect John Pool, whose short term expired. Unlike most legislators, Pool believed President Johnson faced a losing fight in which "his policy" would be "modified . . . until nothing [would] be left of it—but a mere outline." Pool thought legislators should adjust accordingly.[26]

On the national scene, once it became apparent President Johnson was losing his struggle with the Congress over Reconstruction, conservatives closely identified with Johnson's administration tried to create a new political coalition. They sought to unite Douglas Democrats and conservative Republicans of the North and the original unionists of the South. In the spring of 1866, they initiated the National Union movement. In late June, they issued a convention call for August 14 in Philadelphia. For the most part, southerners attending the convention had opposed secession before following their state's lead in 1861. After the opening session witnessed South Carolina delegates walking arm in arm with Massachusetts delegates into the hall, well-orchestrated sessions continued for three days. Even the band carefully interspersed the playing of "Dixie" with "Yankee Doodle." An adoption of the Declaration of Principles endorsing President Johnson highlighted the final day.[27]

Southern delegates to the National Union Convention generally thereafter supported the Democratic Party. But exceptions existed, mostly men who eventually gave up on Johnson and accepted a belief that salvation lay with congressional Republicans. Referring to his former position, Joshua Morse of Alabama said, "We made an active, forward movement. It was not enough, and we failed to reconstruct." Others supporting the National Union movement at the state level included most South Carolina and Mississippi scalawags, many of whom did not join the Republican Party until 1868. Some of these politicians sought to guide Congressional Reconstruction once it came, men such as James L. Orr of South Carolina. A few later accepted the appeal of President Grant in 1869 for peace, such as Lewis E. Parsons of Alabama. Others, though very few, joined the Republican Party in the 1870s only after they found life among the Democrats unrewarding.[28]

26. *Journal of the Senate of North Carolina, 1866–67* (Raleigh, 1867), 37–39, 45–49, 106–9; Pool to Thomas Settle, 4 February 1866, Thomas Settle Papers, Southern Historical Collection.

27. Raper, *William W. Holden*, 90; McPherson, *Political Reconstruction*, 124; Patrick W. Riddleberger, *1866: The Critical Year Revisited* (Carbondale, Ill., 1979), 203; Perman, *Reunion without Compromise*, 209–21.

28. McPherson, *Political Reconstruction*, 240; Riddleberger, *1866*, 203–12; Perman, *Reunion without Compromise*, 209–21; Morse to Wager Swayne, 17 August 1867, Governor Wager Swayne Papers, Alabama Department of Archives and History; Edward J. Cashin, *The Story of Augusta*

Hoping to rally their own and win support in the North, more than fifty southern radicals met in Washington, D.C., on July 4, and signed an address, To the Loyal Unionists of the South. They condemned current state governments in the South and the policies of President Johnson. They called upon loyalists to meet at Independence Square in Philadelphia on September 3 to join with "true friends of republican government in the North." Since they placed no limits on the number of delegates, the representation from each state depended upon a combination of factors, including the distance to Philadelphia and the climate of opinion at home. The decision to invite delegates from nearby Maryland and West Virginia as well as from Kentucky would later have a conservative impact, because those states would contribute about one-third of the total southern delegates.[29]

Most delegates came from the Border States and the Upper South. Brownlow, already ill and further weakened by his journey, headed a delegation of eighty, including an array of officeholders and former Union army officers. The West Virginia delegation was similarly composed. Old Dominion delegates, mostly from counties along the Potomac River, included prewar Republicans, politicos once associated with the Alexandria government, and some carpetbaggers. Although North Carolina Holdenites stayed away because they were not quite ready to break with President Johnson, the state had a small but diverse delegation: three native North Carolinians, two prewar settlers, and four carpetbaggers. Louisiana and Texas each had more than fifteen delegates, several of whom figured prominently in the proceedings, including Thomas J. Durant, who now resided in Philadelphia. Arkansas reportedly was "represented by some of her loyal sons of the North." Alabama delegates from such towns as Mobile, Montgomery, and Moulton included two carpetbaggers. George W. Ashburn of Columbus led the Georgia group of mostly Atlanta scalawags and Augusta carpetbaggers. Ossian B. Hart headed the six-man Florida delegation from Jacksonville. Of Mississippi's four delegates, only one would later be significant, Joseph W. Field of Columbus, Mississippi. South Carolina was the sole southern state unrepresented.[30]

(Augusta, Ga., 1980), 132–33; John R. deTreville, "Reconstruction in Augusta, Georgia, 1865–1868" (Master's thesis, University of North Carolina, 1979), 45.

29. *The Reporter: A Periodical Devoted to Religion, Law, Legislation, and Public Events,* 3 September 1866.

30. *Convention of Southern Unionists* (Washington, D.C., n.d.); *Harper's Weekly,* 22 September 1866, p. 598; *Reporter,* 30 October 1866, 5 November 1866; *New York Tribune,* 3 September 1866; Hamilton, *Reconstruction in North Carolina,* 179–80; *New York Tribune,* 3 September 1866;

Northerners at the convention, designated as honorary delegates, included several governors, congressmen, mayors, and journalists. They saw themselves as being there to counteract the recent National Union Convention and to encourage the four hundred "fire-tried Southern Unionists." But they would not necessarily applaud all the ideas of the southerners, especially those that might be costly during an election year. Only one black appeared among the northerners, Frederick Douglass, a former Maryland slave and longtime abolitionist leader currently publishing the *Rochester North Star*. Douglass knew that most Republicans wanted him to act, as he said, like the "ugly and deformed child of the family, and to be kept out of sight as much as possible while there was company in the house." But he refused to hide, even for the sake of harmony, because he symbolized suffrage for his people.[31]

On Monday morning, September 3, delegates rallied in Independence Square. With 100,000 spectators waiting at eleven o'clock, a thousand local Union League members led a parade, followed by the conventioneers, then by hundreds of Union veterans in uniform. Once the procession arrived at Union League House, northern delegates stayed there for their meetings. Southerners "remarshaled, and took up the line of march" to National Hall on Market Street. Entering the hall, they saw bright decorations everywhere, a huge portrait of Lincoln, and a banner reading:

WELCOME, PATRIOTS OF THE SOUTH!

> Ye bore as Freedom's hope forlorn
> The private hate, the rebel scorn;
> Yet held through all the paths ye trod
> Your faith in man and trust in God.

The next day southerners granted Henry Clay Warmoth of Louisiana a request that a member from each unreconstructed state be appointed to a committee to write a report on conditions in their states. Speaking to northern delegates that afternoon, General Butler unsuccessfully sought to have a committee confer with the Resolutions Committee of the southerners. North-

---

Eric Foner, *Reconstruction*, 270; Richard N. Current, *Those Terrible Carpetbaggers* (New York, 1988), 109.

31. Current, *Those Terrible Carpetbaggers*, 55–56; Benjamin Quarles, *Frederick Douglass* (New York, 1968), 229–32; Frederick Douglass, *Life and Times of Frederick Douglass Written by Himself*, rev. ed. (Boston, 1892), 387–90.

erners listened politely to Douglass speak about black suffrage on Tuesday morning, but they played it safe politically. Only the New York delegation was willing to endorse black suffrage.[32]

On Wednesday, committees developed reports. Then on Thursday, the convention adopted the Resolutions Committee report, which claimed that "the political status of the States lately in rebellion . . . [are] clearly within the control of Congress." Although the convention stopped short of explicitly supporting black suffrage, because of northern and Border State opposition, some speakers favored it, including the irrepressible Brownlow. The "thin and emaciated" governor mentioned Tennessee's need for "one more law." Loyalists, he said, required "a law enfranchising the negroes . . . to weight down the balance against rebelism."[33]

When the convention assembled on Friday, Chairman Joseph H. Speed declared the work of the convention completed and he withdrew. Whereupon, as prearranged, First Vice President John M. Botts of Virginia seized the gavel and called to order a so-called adjourned session. Warmoth gave his committee's report. He spoke at length about the New Orleans "massacre." Then he read a list of resolutions, including one that stated "impartial suffrage" was the "one all-sufficient remedy" for southern loyalists. Immediately, Chairman Botts countered with resolutions denying congressional authority to regulate the franchise. He was supported by Daniel R. Goodloe, who favored qualified manhood suffrage given by the states. When delegates denied Botts the right to have his resolutions recorded, he left in a huff.[34] P. B. Randolph of Louisiana spoke "as the only representative of four million blacks in the South." He urged the delegates and the Republican Party to seize the day by meting out justice to his race and thereby acquiring black voters. After a call for the vote, the count was sixty-six to eleven in favor of the resolutions.[35]

Despite divisions over black suffrage, the Philadelphia meeting awakened

32. *Harper's Weekly*, 22 September 1866, p. 598; Henry Clay Warmoth Diary, 3–7 September 1866, Warmoth Papers; *New York Times*, 3, 4, 5, September 1866; Ellis P. Oberholtzer, *A History of the United States since the Civil War* (New York, 1917–37), 1: 392–94.

33. Oberholtzer, *A History of the United States since the Civil War*, 1: 392–94; Quarles, *Frederick Douglass*, 231.

34. *Harper's Weekly*, 22 September 1866, p. 598; Current, *Those Terrible Carpetbaggers*, 56–57.

35. *Harper's Weekly*, 22 September 1866, p. 598; McPherson, *Political Reconstruction*, 242; Current, *Those Terrible Carpetbaggers*, 57–59; Quarles, *Frederick Douglass*, 233–34; Douglass, *Life and Times of Frederick Douglass*, 396.

the loyalist element in the South. It showed clusters of loyalists in each state that they had counterparts elsewhere in the South and that they had supporters in the North. It convinced loyalists that they had found a home in the national Republican Party, that they should consider universal manhood suffrage, and that they could effect change, given favorable election results in the North. By coming to Philadelphia, southerners also showed northern Republicans their plight and that there was hope for building a Republican Party in the South.

Following each of the Philadelphia conventions, some of the southern delegates campaigned with northern politicians in the North. President Johnson also hit the campaign trail, severely damaging his own cause by allowing "the excitement of the movement to draw from [him] extemporaneous speeches." In the so-called adjourned session, delegates chose speakers to campaign in the North for congressional candidates who endorsed the vote for blacks. More than a score of speakers, including several Tennesseans, made a pilgrimage to Lincoln's grave in Springfield, Illinois. Afterward the Tennesseans spoke in cities including Indianapolis, Toledo, Boston, and New York before returning to Philadelphia and then home. Everywhere, they supported Negro suffrage to offset "rebel votes."[36]

Meanwhile in Louisiana, following Governor Hahn's move to the United States Senate in March 1865, his successor James Madison Wells sought to win over conservative unionists and former Confederates to his administration. Other than resisting the Confederacy, Wells had a nebulous record on wartime issues. As time eventually proved, his views paralleled those he once opposed, the status quo conservative unionist views. Because the governor by background belonged to "the planting interests," he wanted partisans who would "consolidate his power—." He cared little for the moderates' pro-white labor platform, which would shift political power to urban New Orleans, and even less for the pro-black agenda of radicals. Because they stood in his way, Wells purged key moderates, such as state auditor Anthony P. Dostie. When Dostie ignored an order to step down, the governor dispatched policemen to remove him bodily from his office, on the grounds that Dostie had not provided a "sufficient bond."[37]

36. *New York Times,* 8 September 1866.

37. Reid, *After the War,* 237; George S. Denison to Hugh McCulloch, 6 May 1865, George S. Denison Papers, Library of Congress; McCrary, *Lincoln and Reconstruction,* 308; Lowrey, "Political Career of James Madison Wells," 1008–14; Wells to Andrew Johnson, 5 May, 3, 29 July, 23 September, 20 October 1865, Loyal Citizens of Louisiana to Johnson, 12 July 1865, Johnson Pa-

Radicals believed Wells betrayed the unionist cause. Led by towering, ca-
daverous Durant, they formed the biracial Friends of Universal Suffrage. The
group included Benjamin F. Flanders, who somehow survived as a special
agent of the Treasury Department despite his radicalism; other scalawags; and
a few carpetbaggers, some from the moderate camp. Drawing upon theories
of congressional radicals, with whom they connected, the Friends of Universal
Suffrage held that Louisiana, along with other seceded states, reverted to territorial status. Consequently, the state government and the constitution of 1864
that created it were illegitimate. Reconstruction, they argued, should come
through a biracial elected convention of delegates who would draft a constitution acceptable to Congress. In June 1865, the group created a Central Executive Committee, which was chaired by Durant and composed mostly of
scalawags but included a few carpetbaggers and blacks. The committee kept
allies in Washington informed and supervised the politicization of blacks beyond New Orleans. They sponsored "voluntary elections" in which blacks
(along with white radicals) chose delegates to the group's convention and
elected a territorial delegate to Congress.[38]

Influential blacks such as Louis Roudanez, publisher of the *New Orleans
Tribune*, and Captain James H. Ingraham, president of the state chapter of the
National Equal Rights League, worked closely with the committee. Ingraham
extended his organization into neighboring parishes. Thomas W. Conway, a
former Baptist preacher who managed the Bureau of Free Labor under Banks
and now headed the state's Freedmen's Bureau, also aided their cause. Shortly
after its creation, the committee asked Wells to allow loyal males to be registered as voters "without distinction of race or origin." In rejecting their request, he said, among other things, that "nine out of ten" freedmen would
only "support their former masters."[39]

---

pers; Gilles Vandal, *The New Orleans Riot of 1866: Anatomy of a Tragedy* (Lafayette, La., 1983),
62–63.

38. Reid, *After the War*, 232–33, 268; *New Orleans Tribune*, 2 May 1865; Jean-Charles
Houzeau, *My Passage at the New Orleans "Tribune": A Memoir of the Civil War Era*, ed. David C.
Rankin (Baton Rouge, 1984), 38; Garner, "Thomas Bangs Thorpe," 43; *Proceedings of the Conven-
tion of the Republican Party of Louisiana Held at Economy Hall, New Orleans, September 25, 1865;
and the Central Executive Committee of the Friends of the Universal Suffrage of Louisiana, now the
Central Executive Committee of the Republican Party of Louisiana* (n.p., n.d.).

39. *Proceedings of the Convention of the Republican Party of Louisiana in 1865*, 2–3, 10;
Thomas W. Conway to Salmon P. Chase, 8 August 1865, Chase Papers; Taylor, *Louisiana Recon-
structed*, 74–75; Houzeau, *My Passage*, 96–97; William S. McFeely, *Yankee Stepfather: General
O. O. Howard and the Freedmen* (New Haven, 1968), 68, 170, 177; Charles Vincent, *Black Legisla-*

Commenting on the orderly mid-September election of delegates to the Friends of Universal Suffrage Convention, the *New Orleans Tribune* observed that blacks could be "safely trusted with the right of suffrage." Those elected, mostly white professionals and educated mulattos, met only days later, September 25 to 28. They changed their title to the National Republican Party of Louisiana, chose the *New Orleans Tribune* as the party's official organ, and called upon Congress to enfranchise the freedmen. As a territorial delegate to Congress, they nominated twenty-three-year-old Henry Clay Warmoth, a Union veteran "with a genius for politics" who had served during 1864 as a local provost court judge. Defending black suffrage to the converted, Rufus Waples, a longtime New Orleans attorney originally from Delaware, contended that suffrage would be in the interest of the nation, of local loyalists, and of blacks, cultivating in them "self-respect and laudable ambition."[40]

Moderates rallied for the July 4 celebration at the customhouse, which was bedecked with flowers and flags, to hear General Banks berate Governor Wells. Beyond their support of President Johnson, however, moderates were disoriented, divided, and for months inactive. They failed to field a ticket in the state's November election. Only after the decisive victory of the Democrats did any of them go over to the radicals. Moderates devised their own plan to enfranchise blacks by changing the state constitution through reconvening the convention of 1864. In the spring of 1866, they organized the National Union Republican Club under the leadership of Hahn, Dostie, Warmoth (who was ambitious enough to be identified with both factions), and a few black elite.[41]

The Conservative Union Party occupied the middle ground. It avoided what Wells felt was the "usurpation of both rebels and yankees." Its members accepted the 1864 constitution and opposed, along with radicals and moderates, assumption of the state's Confederate debts. Besides Wells, party leaders included future conservative Republicans such as the state supreme court jus-

---

tors in Louisiana during Reconstruction (Baton Rouge, 1976), 29–39; New Orleans Union Suffrage Committee to Andrew Johnson, 13 July 1865, Johnson Papers.

40. *New Orleans Tribune,* 12 July, 8, 13, 16, 19 September 1865; *Proceedings of the Convention of the Republican Party of Louisiana,* 11–27; Vandal, *New Orleans Riot,* 77–79; David C. Rankin, "The Origins of Black Leadership in New Orleans during Reconstruction," *JSH* 40 (August 1974): 435–40; Lonn, *Reconstruction in Louisiana,* 7n; *Chicago Tribune,* 7 October 1865, clipping, Henry Clay Warmoth Scrapbook, Warmoth Papers.

41. McCrary, *Lincoln and Reconstruction,* 320; Howard A. White, *The Freedmen's Bureau in Louisiana* (Baton Rouge, 1970), 17; Taylor, *Louisiana Reconstructed,* 74–77; Philip D. Uzee, "The Beginnings of the Louisiana Republican Party," *LH* 12 (summer 1971): 207–8.

tices. Some disliked Wells's appointment of former secessionists and his fail-ure to prevent them from registering to vote. But being dependent upon Wells, party members faced a dilemma as he edged toward the Democratic camp. So they nominated him (he was already the candidate of the National Democrats) to head their ticket; without him, they had little hope. Many of the party's candidates were veterans of the wartime pro-Union government. Although some other party nominees had aided the Confederacy after oppos-ing secession, the party avoided prominent Confederates. They chose James G. Taliaferro for lieutenant governor, and as congressional candidates they selected men of ability and experience, such as party chairman Alexander P. Field of New Orleans and John Ray of Monroe.[42]

National Democrats, on the right of the political spectrum, were almost all former Confederates. Other than accepting emancipation, they acted as though the war had never happened. These former rebels recognized the state government as merely de facto. They really wanted Louisiana to follow those states under Johnson's plan, that is, hold a convention and salvage as much from the past as possible. Beyond that, they wanted federal compensation for former slaveholders, state assumption of Confederate debts, black codes, res-toration of confiscated property, and a general amnesty. Meeting in August 1865 for the first time since 1860, Louisiana Democrats declared that govern-ment was for the "exclusive political benefit of the white race." And other than nominating Wells for governor—because of his influence with the presi-dent—they chose candidates with antebellum as well as Confederate creden-tials.[43]

To the right of the National Democrats stood Conservative Democrats, an antiblack, antiurban, anti-Catholic element composed mostly of small farmers from the Red River Valley counties. As their candidate, they chose former Confederate governor Henry W. Allen, who was still exiled in Mexico City. Because of the challenge from the far right, at Wells's advice the president removed Freedmen's Bureau chief Conway, an "agitator for negro suffrage and equality" who allowed "the negroes to go where they please[d] and to

42. James Madison Wells to his wife, 23 May 1865, James Madison Wells Papers, Louisiana State Museum Historical Center, New Orleans; Donald H. Breese, "Politics in the Lower South during Presidential Reconstruction, April to November, 1865" (Ph.D. diss., University of Califor-nia, 1964), 340–50, 363–67; Vandal, New Orleans Riot, 85–90.

43. New York Times, 5 October 1865; John Rose Ficklen, History of Reconstruction in Louisi-ana through 1868 (Baltimore, 1910), 109, 111n; Breese, "Politics in the Lower South," 332–40; Wells to Andrew Johnson, 6 October 1865, Johnson Papers.

work for whom they please[d]." Johnson replaced him with General James S. Fullerton, soon a favorite with whites because he enforced antivagrancy laws, closed Freedmen's Bureau courts, restored confiscated property, and abolished taxes for freedmen schools.[44]

National Democrats won the election on November 6 by a wide margin. Wells defeated Allen 22,312 to 5,497. Most of the National Democrats' other nominees won by even wider margins. The only Conservative Union Party bright spot was John Ray's election to Congress. Radicals held a "voluntary election" at special polls. Warmoth received 19,000 votes, equally divided between New Orleans and a few select parishes. He received 2,500 white votes (an indication of white Republican numbers).

Soon after having to deal with former Confederate legislators, even Wells became disillusioned with the Democrats. In December, he vetoed an act deferring wartime taxes for formerly unoccupied parishes because such a distinction rewarded rebellion. And in January 1866 when legislators rescheduled local elections from June to March, which threatened his appointees, Wells vetoed the bills. After the legislature overrode the veto, Wells appealed to the president, but it was in vain. Then he realized his worst fear when New Orleans returned Confederate Mayor John T. Monroe to office.[45]

Some Conservative Union Party members, including Chairman Field, now crossed over to the Republicans. They had hoped to steer a middle course, but Democrats had grasped the helm. Field, Flanders, and Dostie tried to merge radical and moderate factions in early 1866. Radicals had shown that blacks could be mobilized by having them vote in an unofficial election, and moderates now accepted black suffrage as a way to reverse the policies of former Confederates. But most loyalists opposed radical leadership, radicals' state-suicide-by-secession theory, and their civil rights commitment. Instead, with the connivance of Governor Wells, back in his anti-Confederate mode, and with perceived congressional encouragement, they planned a coup d'etat. They would have the constitutional convention of 1864 reconvened by a call from its chairman. First they would fill any vacant seats in a special biracial

44. Willie Malvin Caskey, *Secession and Restoration in Louisiana* (Baton Rouge, 1938), 176–77; McFeely, *Yankee Stepfather,* 177–80; White, *Freedmen's Bureau in Louisiana,* 19–21; Wells to Andrew Johnson, 29 July 1865, Johnson Papers.

45. Ficklen, *History of Reconstruction in Louisiana,* 112–14; Sworn document of Warmoth's election to Congress, diary entry, 18 November 1865, Warmoth Papers; *New Orleans Tribune,* 15 November 1865; Vandal, *New Orleans Riot,* 92–93; Henry Clay Warmoth, *War, Politics and Reconstruction: Stormy Days in Louisiana* (New York, 1930), 45.

election. Then, through the convention, they would change the constitution to enfranchise blacks and disfranchise "rebels."[46]

But the 1864 convention president, federal district judge Edward H. Durell, doubted both the plan's legality and its prudence. He believed the long-forgotten provision for reassembling the convention had long since transpired. Still, out of respect for the conventioneers, he consulted General Philip H. Sheridan and he wired a trio of congressmen inquiring about their supposed support. Sheridan said his small army could safeguard delegates but not shield black voters, and because of preelection jitters, the congressmen remained mute. Choosing discretion as the better part of valor, Judge Durell began an extended northern vacation. Undeterred, some delegates from 1864 replaced Durell with state supreme court justice R. K. Howell, whom Durell had defeated for the position of convention president in 1864. Shortly thereafter, Howell issued a call for delegates to meet July 30 at the Mechanics' Institute. Then he left to get congressional support. The best he could muster, however, was Thaddeus Stevens's statement that "if your people adopt a constitution . . . we will entertain it as favorably as we can as individual members of Congress." Howell chose to interpret that as "encouragement."[47]

Officials other than Governor Wells saw reconvening as illegal, dangerous, and threatening. Despite opinions by the military that the convention should be protected but otherwise ignored, Mayor Monroe was determined to arrest the conventioneers. When radicals spoke to blacks on Friday night, July 27, none advocated violence or urged blacks to arm themselves. Nor did the meeting resolutions. Outside the building after the meeting, however, matters changed. At Dostie's urging, torch-bearing blacks marched to city hall. There Dostie made some provocative remarks, including that if any whites "strike you, kill them."[48]

46. C. W. Stauffer to Henry Clay Warmoth, 6 February 1866, Bernard Soulie to Warmoth, 12 February 1866, Flanders to Warmoth, 23 November 1865, Warmoth Papers; Breese, "Politics in the Lower South," 372, 375; Taylor, *Louisiana Reconstructed*, 82; Tunnell, *Crucible of Reconstruction*, 101–2, 109–14; Lowrey, "Political Career of James Madison Wells," 1076–77; *Report of the Select Committee on the New Orleans Riots*, 29, 409; Taylor, *Louisiana Reconstructed*, 109–14.

47. *Report of the Select Committee on the New Orleans Riots*, 46, 60, 262–63; Houzeau, *My Passage*, 124–26; Ficklen, *History of Reconstruction in Louisiana*, 157–65; Albert Voorhies and Andrew J. Herron to Andrew Johnson, 27 July 1866, A. Baird to Edwin M. Stanton, 28 July 1866, Johnson to Voorhies, 28 July 1866, Johnson Papers.

48. *Report of the Select Committee on the New Orleans Riots*, 2–3, 28–39, 64–67, 102, 239, 409, 422, 466; Lowrey, "Political Career of James Madison Wells," 1081; Reed, *Life of A. P. Dostie*, 292–97; Donald E. Reynolds, "The New Orleans Riot of 1866, Reconsidered," *LH* 5 (winter 1964): 10–13; Houzeau, *My Passage*, 131.

Because conventioneers expected to be arrested, some prearranged bond. Others became too frightened to attend the opening session July 30. At noon, when only 27 delegates gathered at the Mechanics' Institute, they adjourned for an hour to muster a quorum. Outside, 200 to 300 blacks, accompanied by an American flag and a drum, marched down Burgundy Street. When someone fired a shot, a fight erupted. Frightened blacks barricaded themselves inside the Mechanics' Institute, where delegates awaited the session's resumption. Momentarily, a general alarm "of twelve taps" sounded, bringing the police force, as well as a posse of former Confederate soldiers, with Mayor Monroe's order to arrest the delegates. The police charged the building, firing their guns, shattering windows, and demolishing doors. Once they gained entrance, a bloody slaughter started. Although delegates wildly waved their white handkerchiefs in surrender, a policeman shouted, "We have the . . . damned Yankee sons of bitches . . . and will kill them all, damn them." In what turned into a riot, police killed 34 blacks and wounded 119, all there to witness the opening session. They also murdered three whites and wounded eight others. Dostie was stabbed in the stomach and shot in the spine as he rushed to aid the bleeding, lame Hahn. Not a single policeman died in the melee; ten received wounds.[49]

Almost all of the conventioneers were moderates and conservative unionists. Fewer than 20 of the 166 individuals identified as delegates and supporters had affiliated with the radicals, and of these, only a handful, including Warmoth and Waples, were leaders. Most of the 44 original delegates who cooperated with the 1866 movement—either by attending the preliminary rally or the reconvened session—had held office until recently, more than 25 of whom served as legislators during 1864–65. Black leaders favored Congressional Reconstruction rather than the Reconstruction proposed by the conventioneers. Of the more than two hundred local blacks who were leaders between 1863 and 1866, fewer than thirty-five appeared at the riot. Because of the riot, some scalawags fled and others retired from public life. One loyalist estimated that their number in New Orleans now counted fewer than three hundred. Durant, who witnessed the slaughter of blacks in the streets from his office window, sold his "recently purchased house" and sailed with his furniture and books to his birthplace of Philadelphia.[50]

49. Houzeau, *My Passage*, 131; Ficklen, *History of Reconstruction in Louisiana*, 169–70; *Report of the Select Committee on the New Orleans Riots*, 351.

50. Vandal, *New Orleans Riot*, 195–99; Houzeau, *My Passage*, 129; *Report of the Select Committee on the New Orleans Riots*, 7–9, 34; State Central Committee, Republican Party of Louisiana,

In Arkansas as elsewhere after Appomattox, unionists differed about the role of former Confederates. Some wanted to require loyalty oaths and adopt a go-slow policy toward appeals for presidential pardons. For example, former Confederate general turned loyalist Edward W. Gantt favored "as few pardons as possible before the character of each [was] sifted." He urged the president to lean heavily on the advice of General Joseph J. Reynolds of Kentucky, commander of the Department of Arkansas. Isaac Murphy's behavior often proved inexplicable: one minute he would exclaim that secessionists "ought to be hung" for rebelling against the "best government the world ever saw"; the next minute he would endorse an application for pardon. Still the governor was not about to turn over his administration to former Confederates, whatever their capabilities. He appointed mostly state unionists but named northerners as well. Murphy originally was from Pennsylvania.[51]

For a while, a carryover of wartime camaraderie continued among unionists and newcomers. Once mustered out, many northern veterans chose to stay. This was the case not only at Little Rock but in other areas as well. Most newcomers had brought their politics with them; a few had held office elsewhere, some as Republicans and others as Democrats. Benjamin F. Rice, later state Republican chairman, had been a Kentucky legislator and an 1856 Fremont elector, and his counterpart, 1867 Democratic chairman Robert A. Howard, had served as the United States attorney in the Nebraska Territory before joining General Frederick Steele's staff.[52]

Several northerners met with Little Rock loyalists August 29, 1865, for a rally of the National Union Men of Arkansas, as they called themselves. They endorsed a former Tennessee senate member Gayle H. Kyle for Congress and adopted resolutions favoring free schools, immigration, and industrial development. Finally the group called for the recognition of blacks as "entitled to

---

to Andrew Johnson, 8 August 1866, Johnson Papers; Thomas J. Durant to Henry Clay Warmoth, 5 June 1867, Warmoth Papers; Milton J. Saffold, *Address to Native White Republicans, October 1870* (n.p., n.d.).

51. Gantt to Andrew Johnson, 29 June, 4 July 1865, T. M. Jack to Johnson, 18 July 1865, Murphy to Johnson, 19 July 1865, Johnson Papers; James E. Sefton, *The United States Army and Reconstruction, 1865–1877* (Baton Rouge, 1967), 29; John M. Harrell, *The Brooks and Baxter War: A History of the Reconstruction Period in Arkansas* (Saint Louis, 1893), 5, 10–11, 21–22, 27, 44; John I. Smith, *The Courage of a Southern Unionist: A Biography of Isaac Murphy, Governor of Arkansas, 1864–1868* (Little Rock, 1979), 65, 75; Martha Ann Ellenburg, "Reconstruction in Arkansas" (Ph.D. diss., University of Missouri, 1967), 38–39.

52. Ellenburg, "Reconstruction in Arkansas," 38–39; Benjamin C. Truman to Johnson, 9 April 1866, *PAJ*, 10: 382; *Report of the Joint Committee on Reconstruction*, pt. 3: 97–98.

the 'absolute rights' of a citizen." A few weeks later, some members cooperated in founding the Arkansas Immigration Aid Society.[53]

Former Confederates pursued two different courses. Some tried toppling Murphy's administration by persuading the president to establish a provisional government like those elsewhere. Others patiently waited until the next election, planning to capture the government and modify or abolish the 1864 constitution. The first group convened in Little Rock on December 12, 1865, to organize a "People's Party." The group protested "disfranchisement" as a form of "taxation without representation." But after the state supreme court in an act of reconciliation declared the loyalty oath unconstitutional, former Confederates united and set their sights on the August 1866 election.

In the August 1866 election, conservatives threw unionists off guard by running as candidates members from their small wartime unionist contingency. They also raised race and class issues, warning of the dangers of black equality and labeling white Union Leaguers the "scum of society." Finally, they attacked Governor Murphy, who was not up for election, calling him a "lump of stupidity and imbecility." Thrown on the defensive, loyalists responded, albeit unconvincingly, that many former Confederates wanted to renew the Civil War. Being a minority, Unionists lost all congressional seats, almost all the legislative ones, and several state races. The governor's son-inlaw, state auditor James R. Berry, a declared Republican, received only 6,476 votes, fewer than one-fifth of the total vote in his reelection run.[54]

The newly elected legislature, composed mostly of former Confederates, elected as United States senators a former Confederate senator, Augustus H. Garland, and another Lost Cause supporter, John T. Jones. In the same spirit, members of the legislature memorialized Jefferson Davis for his "noble and patriotic manner" as president of the Confederacy. They overrode Murphy's veto of an act pardoning all crimes committed during the war except that of rape and overwhelmingly rejected the Fourteenth Amendment. They also impeached two loyalist judges of adjoining northwest Arkansas districts.[55]

---

53. Beverly Watkins, "Efforts to Encourage Immigration to Arkansas, 1865–1874," *ArkHQ* 38 (spring 1979): 32–35; *Report of the Joint Committee on Reconstruction,* pt. 3: 97–98.

54. Staples, *Reconstruction in Arkansas,* 102–4, 108–9; B. F. Rice et al. petition, RG 233.

55. Smith, *Courage of a Southern Unionist,* 88–91; Hallum, *Arkansas,* 435; Staples, *Reconstruction in Arkansas,* 109–14; Goodspeed, *Biographical and Historical Memoirs of Northwest Arkansas,* 1093–94; Paige E. Mulhollan, "The Arkansas General Assembly of 1866 and Its Effect on Reconstruction," *ArkHQ* 20 (winter 1961): 331–44; John Whitcock to John Sherman, 21 December 1866, Sherman Papers.

By 1867, those supporting Congressional Reconstruction formed two factions. Radicals, led by scalawags James M. Johnson and Valentine Dell, met at the Fort Smith Courthouse on December 13, 1866. They adopted anti–Andrew Johnson resolutions and selected a three-man committee to convey their message to Congress. Moderates, with more newcomers and fewer loyalist leaders, convened in February 1867 in a meeting chaired by Thomas M. Bowen, a former Iowa legislator who had arrived in Arkansas with the Union army. They criticized the radicals and called for "security for the future rather than indemnity for the past." They endorsed the constitution of 1864, which would with "slight amendment" guarantee control by "loyal men." Despite the differences between the two groups, once the Reconstruction Acts passed in March, moderates accepted the radicals' views and united with them.[56]

Meanwhile, events in Texas showed that many Texans had been far from being unstintingly loyal to the Confederacy. Hundreds of refugees returned, including troops of the First Texas Volunteer Cavalry (Union army), who sailed home from New Orleans to aid in the state's restoration. Recently appointed provisional governor Andrew J. Hamilton disembarked at Galveston with his family and more than forty of his refugee friends in July 1865. He immediately issued a proclamation stating that "suitable persons" would be appointed to county offices, that a constitutional convention would be held as soon as "practicable," and that blacks were "not only free" but would be protected "in their freedom."[57]

Many loyalists, including office seekers, accepted the governor's invitation to visit Austin and apprise him of conditions in their areas. He also received a massive amount of correspondence concerning patronage; some, in the form of petitions, requested appointment of individuals to office on the basis of a prior pro-Union record. Almost all loyalists contended that secessionists should not be armed with authority. Hamilton agreed that to appoint the nation's enemies would be a disavowal of his war record as well as political sui-

56. Staples, *Reconstruction in Arkansas*, 115–20; Albert H. Allen, *Arkansas Imprints, 1821– 1876* (New York, 1947), 124; V. Dell to Edward McPherson, 5 March 1867, McPherson Papers; *Encyclopedia of New West*, 56–57.

57. *OR*, 48 (2): 1031–33; "Address of Colonel Hayes to 1st Regiment Texas Cavalry Vol., October 31, 1865," newspaper clipping, n.d., Haynes Papers; Proclamation By A. J. Hamilton, Provisional Governor, To the People of Texas, Executive Record Book 281, 25 July 1865, Texas State Library and Archives Commission, Austin. Much of the next few pages from James Alex Baggett, "Birth of the Texas Republican Party," *SwHQ* 78 (July 1974): 1–20.

cide. He appointed loyalists where available, and elsewhere he named former Confederates who reputedly "accepted the situation honestly."[58]

Hamilton was helped in his selection of appointees by former governor Elisha M. Pease, who had remained in Austin during the war and who had "had opportunities for communication with the union men from all parts of the state." Hamilton's earliest appointments included his cabinet, filled almost completely with Austin loyalists. Hamilton made a clean sweep of all office-holders in some counties. After consulting with loyalist leaders, he issued a series of proclamations. In mid-November, the governor set the constitutional convention election date as January 8, 1866.[59]

Soon the fledgling unionist group was dubbed the Hamilton-Pease party. For the first few months of Reconstruction, many Texans, who were either reluctant to approach Hamilton directly or were better acquainted with Pease, sought patronage, endorsements for presidential pardons, or other behests through Pease. Hamilton himself favored Pease as the gubernatorial candidate in the next election. After Pease's defeat, their friendship continued, and upon Pease's 1867 appointment by the military as provisional governor, he named Hamilton to the Texas supreme court. Although Pease seemed less subject to outbursts of radicalism than Hamilton, their positions at any given time differed very little. Other neighbors aided the twosome. Included in this "Austin clique" were Amos Morrill, Hamilton's onetime law partner and fellow refugee in New Orleans; William Alexander, another attorney and refugee; and Morgan C. Hamilton, Andrew's merchant brother.[60]

In the January 1866 election for delegates to a state constitutional convention, Texans refused to repudiate their wartime leaders. According to Hamilton, the delegates elected were "about two thirds original secessionists to one

58. *Austin Southern Intelligencer,* July, August, September 1865; Charles W. Ramsdell, *Reconstruction in Texas* (New York, 1910), 58–59, 62–63; Waller, *Colossal Hamilton,* 65–66.

59. Frank Brown, "Annals of Travis County and of the City of Austin from the Earliest Times to the Close of 1875," 24: 47, Frank Brown Collection, Center for American History; Hamilton to Pease, 7 August 1865, Graham-Pease Collection. See lists of Hamilton appointees, *Austin Southern Intelligencer,* 11 August, 11 September 1865, and list of 1864 county officers, *Texas Almanac, 1865* (Austin, 1865), 45–47.

60. For examples of petitions addressed to Pease, see the Graham-Pease Collection for 1865–66; Webb, *Handbook of Texas,* 1: 27, 760; Webb, *Handbook of Texas,* 2: 88; Brown, "Annals of Travis County," 4: 22, Brown Collection; A. J. Hamilton to M. C. Hamilton, 19 October 1865, Executive Record Book 283, p. 36, Texas State Library and Archives Commission; Barkley, *History of Travis County and Austin,* 304; Elisha M. Pease to General Charles Griffin, 22 July 1867, Pease to Carrie Pease, 3 August 1867, Graham-Pease Collection.

third original Union men." Governor Hamilton told the delegates what he considered the minimal requirements for restoration: affirmation of the illegality of secession and state debt incurred in supporting the rebellion and the legality of the abolishment of slavery. He advised them to grant full civil rights to blacks and to establish voter qualification by "rules of universal application."[61]

The convention's loyalist minority hailed mostly from the state's southwest and from the Red River area. By bringing the loyalists together, the meeting proved useful to the Hamilton-Pease faction. The loyalists included many future officeholders: a governor, Edmund J. Davis; a United States senator, J. W. Flanagan; a congressman, Edward Degener; and several state judges, federal appointees, and state legislators. Loyalists rallied around three issues: the ab initio ordinance declaring secession void from the beginning, civil rights for freedmen, and the division of Texas into two states to protect unionists in the southwest. Seven delegates, including three Germans, favored qualified black suffrage. Before adjournment, the loyalists nominated Hamilton for governor and after he declined, named a slate headed by former governor Pease (who knew he lacked the remotest chance of being elected). They adopted a platform condemning all who would "pursue such a course in the future as [would] justify what [had] been done in the past." The Conservative Party, controlled by secessionists but containing some so-called soft unionists, nominated constitutional convention president James W. Throckmorton. The party also commended President Johnson and condemned those favoring "elevation of the negro to political equality."[62]

Although the election results seemed certain, the campaign aired some issues—such as qualified black suffrage and education of black children, financed by the state's school fund—and cemented the two factions. To woo voters, Pease moderated his comments. Nonetheless, he announced that if it were required for the readmission of Texas, he would favor suffrage for literate blacks and said that he supported state-funded schools for *all* children. Throckmorton attacked black suffrage, "qualified or otherwise," and opposed

61. A. J. Hamilton, Message to the Constitutional Convention, 10 February 1866, Executive Record Book 281, pp. 161–69; *American Annual Cyclopaedia, 1866,* 741; *Austin Southern Intelligencer,* 3 May 1866.

62. Charles W. Ramsdell, *Reconstruction in Texas* (New York, 1910), 106–8; Winkler, *Platforms,* 95–98; Claude Elliott, *Leathercoat: The Life History of a Texas Patriot* (San Antonio, 1938), 119–20; Elisha M. Pease to Carrie Pease, 8 May 1866, Graham-Pease Collection; Benjamin C. Truman to Johnson, 9 April 1866, *PAJ,* 10: 381–83.

sharing school funds with black children. He voiced the feelings of the majority of Texans, and he won the June election easily, 49,277 votes to 12,168 for
Pease. The state's political alignment had changed little since 1861: fewer than
1,000 votes marked the difference between the number against secession and
the total received by Pease in 1866. Conservatives also captured almost all the
seats in the legislature. Those elected were mostly former Confederates, including many former secessionists. Even conservatives in the know conceded
that under Throckmorton's administration, "Confederates exercised . . . political control as they had done of old."[63]

With mounting trepidation, Texas radicals saw the spiraling events: political defeat, persecution (real and imagined), and patronage to the rebels. General Edmund J. Davis, recently defeated for the state senate and denied a
regular army appointment by Johnson because his politics "stood in the way
with that gentleman," advocated an immediate movement for a division of the
state. Davis urged Pease, visiting at the time in Hartford, Connecticut, to attend the next session of Congress convening in December 1866 and reminded
him "that a very qualified right of suffrage for the negroes will not be of much
service to them or to us." Other Texas radicals, while "prejudiced in favor of
the white race," either considered black suffrage essential to circumvent the
reenslavement or serfdom of blacks or, in the case of most, they simply accepted the condition that loyalists and blacks were "natural allies . . . so long
as the passions and prejudices aroused by the rebellion lingers in the hearts of
the secessionists."[64]

Meanwhile, Texas legislators, in session from August to November 1866,
elected two former Confederates to the United States Senate. Other than providing blacks minimal rights, the legislature accorded them little. Blacks, who
owned little or no property, could operate their schools with only those taxes
"collected from . . . persons of African descent." A renewed public plea by

63. Diary, 10 May 1866, Eugene C. Bartholomew Papers, Austin History Center, Austin Public Library; *Austin Southern Intelligencer* (extra), 1 May 1866; Elliott, *Leathercoat*, 129; *Dallas Herald,* 16 June 1866; Ramsdell, *Reconstruction in Texas,* 112–14; *American Annual Cyclopaedia, 1866,*
742; Robert W. Shook, "Federal Occupation of Texas, 1865–1870" (Ph.D. diss., University of
North Texas, 1970), 193, 195, 198–99; M. C. Hamilton to Andrew Hamilton, 8 January 1867,
Andrew Jackson Hamilton Papers, Center for American History.

64. Davis to Elisha M. Pease, 14 July, 24 November 1866, Pease to Carrie Pease, 30 March
1866, Graham-Pease Collection; *Speech Delivered by Hon. E. M. Pease at Turner Hall, Galveston,
Texas, July 12th, 1880* (Galveston, 1880), 23; Dale A. Somers, "James P. Newcomb: The Making
of a Radical," *SwHQ* 72 (April 1969), 464; *Flake's Galveston Bulletin,* 17 April 1867.

former Confederate Postmaster General John H. Reagan that limited black suffrage be permitted fell on deaf ears. Members of the Texas legislature gerry-mandered unsympathetic loyalist judges out of office. All the while, they ignored cries that such steps would unleash the wrath of a militant Congress.[65]

The years 1865–66 were a bitter disappointment to loyalists who expected to be given posts in government. They were further disillusioned because their political enemies received positions of power. Such a circumstance made them willing to consider the use of black suffrage to gain authority and protection. Many feared a condition approaching those during secession and war when the majority persecuted them because of their allegiance to the Union. Despite their disillusionment, loyalists never became entirely inactive in politics during 1865–66. In some states—those that underwent wartime Reconstruction—they controlled one or more branches of state government. In others, they witnessed some short-term success before being deposed. In all, loyalists created a Union party.

65. Ramsdell, *Reconstruction in Texas*, 116; Joseph B. James, "Southern Reaction to the Proposal of the Fourteenth Amendment," *JSH* 22 (November 1956): 483–85; *The Laws of Texas, 1822–1897* (Austin, 1898), 5: 863–1185.

Governor William W. Holden of North Carolina

Courtesy North Carolina Division of Archives and History, Raleigh

Governor William G. Brownlow of Tennessee

Courtesy Tennessee State Museum Collection

Governor Ossian B. Hart of Florida
Courtesy Florida State Archives

Chief Justice Joseph E. Brown of the Georgia Supreme Court
Courtesy Georgia Department of Archives and History

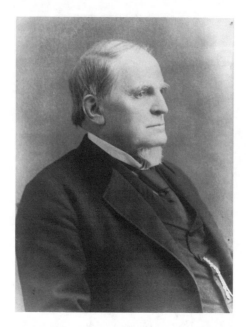

Provisional Governor Lewis E. Parsons of Alabama
Courtesy Alabama Department of Archives and History, Montgomery

Governor James L. Alcorn of Mississippi
Courtesy Mississippi Department of Archives and History

Governor Michael Hahn of Louisiana
Courtesy Louisiana State Library

Governor Elisha Baxter of Arkansas
Courtesy Arkansas History Commission

Provisional Governor Andrew J. Hamilton of Texas
Courtesy Texas State Library and Archives Commission

6

~

Only One Remedy

Loyalists residing in the Southeast—Alabama, Florida, Georgia, Mississippi, and South Carolina—were less prepared to establish state Republican parties than those in the Upper South and the Southwest. Unlike those sections, the Southeast had not initiated any wartime Reconstruction governments. Nor had it mustered peace parties with anything resembling the strength of the Holden-led movement, which laid the foundation for the birth of the Republican Party in North Carolina. Loyalists in the Southeast had also shown less inclination to join the Union army when it occupied their section than had individuals elsewhere, especially in Tennessee, Virginia, and Arkansas. They also had a much smaller membership in the postwar Union League in 1865–66. Without the Reconstruction Acts, it is doubtful the Republican Party would have become even a minor party in the Southeast.

Other than newcomers in the semicircle of states from South Carolina to Mississippi, about the only Republicans resided along the east coast of Florida. Some federal officeholders, especially those in Fernandina, Jacksonville, and Key West, had affiliated with the party during the war. Other Republicans included deserters from the Confederate army and wartime refugees. In spring 1865, hoping to influence President Johnson to appoint a strong unionist as provisional governor, these Republicans and others who claimed loyalty to the Union sent Calvin L. Robinson of Jacksonville, Lemuel Wilson of Alachua County, recently indicted for having commandeered a horse in 1862 to escape to the Federal lines, and Dr. Samuel T. Day of Key West to lobby the president. But before they arrived, the president named former federal judge of the South Florida district William Marvin provisional governor.[1]

Marvin seemed acceptable enough to Florida loyalists until he ignored them as an insignificant faction. Their disappointment worsened when only a small number elected as constitutional convention delegates and legislators qualified as unionists even by Marvin's measurement. Nonetheless loyalist ranks rose as Yankees, mostly Republicans, came to plant, buy lumber, practice their professions, fill federal positions, and to recuperate in a state already known as the "grand national sanatorium." Some newcomers as well as loyalists favored black suffrage. A petite Frenchman named Adolphus Mott, a longtime resident who was chosen mayor of Fernandina by a unionist-black coalition in an irregular election during spring 1865, felt blacks should not be "left at the hands of prejudiced Southern men." Mott's friend Lyman C. Stickney, who boarded the ship of his mentor Salmon P. Chase on Chase's southern tour at Jacksonville and sailed with him to Key West, advocated black suffrage. Newspaperman Whitelaw Reid, traveling with Chase, reported that Key West was divided between "old citizens" wanting blacks "put under State control" and newcomers "willing for negro suffrage" to be tried.[2]

By 1866, onetime Whig legislator Ossian B. Hart emerged as Florida's leading Republican. Hart had returned in 1865 from Tampa to his birthplace of Jacksonville. Because of his unionist record, Hart in February 1866 was appointed Freedmen's Bureau agent for Duval County. That month, a loyalist group, which included Hart, Jonathan C. Greeley, and Robinson, took over editorial management of the *Florida Times*. Along with that group and others elsewhere, Hart decided to support the creation of a Union party, one that would give "preference to men who, during the rebellion, have been known to sympathize with the Government of the United States." On March 15, 1866, at a meeting in Tampa where a majority of South Florida counties were represented, the party was founded. The convention appointed a central committee, which included Hart, Claiborne R. Mobley, one of the three Tampa members, Levi J. Gallaway of Pensacola, and others residing in Key West. In

1. *Official Register of the United States, Containing a List of the Officers and Employees in the Civil, Military, and Naval Services* (Washington, D.C., 1861–80); *KKK Report*, Fla., 195–96; Calvin L. Robinson, Lemuel Wilson, and Samuel T. Day to Andrew Johnson, 19 July 1865, Johnson Papers; *Report of the Joint Committee on Reconstruction*, pt. 2: 6–7.

2. Reid, *After the War*, 161, 163, 179, 187; Mott to Salmon P. Chase, 30 June 1865, Stickney to Chase, 3 November 1865, Chase Papers; George R. Bentley, "The Political Activity of the Freedmen's Bureau in Florida," *FHQ* 28 (July 1949): 29–37.

August 1866, Hart chaired a Tallahassee meeting called to elect delegates for the Southern Loyalists Convention in Philadelphia. Although the handful attending at Tallahassee were disrupted by "rough and bitterest traitors," they reconvened and elected delegates.[3]

In Alabama during spring 1865, Democrats in the northern counties put forward some 1860 Douglas supporters for provisional governor, including David C. Humphreys of Madison County, Thomas M. Peters of Lawrence County, and William H. Smith of Randolph County. All had been anti-Confederate activists: Humphreys as a peace party advocate, Peters as a leader of the unionist underground, and Smith as a recruiter and adviser for the Union army. Pro-Smith petitions emphasized that he was "the poor man's friend and champion." Smith received some of the staunchest backing from Colonel George E. Spencer, a twenty-eight-year-old Union army veteran from Iowa. Spencer had known Smith ever since Smith arrived in occupied Corinth, Mississippi, while fleeing from Confederates. During 1863, Smith and Spencer together recruited enough unionist malcontents from Memphis to Huntsville to form the First Alabama Cavalry, commanded by Spencer. The Iowan had already met with President Johnson to endorse Smith for the appointment; now by holding rallies in north Alabama and gathering petitions, he wanted to prove to the president that Smith had popular support.[4]

Spencer warned Johnson about a delegation of rich Rebels heading his way with other nominations for provisional governor. The delegation to which Spencer referred actually consisted of antisecessionists from the northern part of the state who later supported the Confederacy before reverting to unionism and backing the peace party of 1864. Despite Spencer's warning, the former peace party members returned to Alabama "well pleased" with the president and "confident" that he was doing everything he could for "the people of these unfortunate States." Soon thereafter, on June 21, President Johnson named the delegation's choice for provisional governor, Lewis E. Parsons, a talented Talladega attorney with widespread commercial connections.

3. *National Cyclopaedia of American Biography,* 11: 380; *New York Tribune,* 3 September 1866; Shofner, *Nor Is It Over Yet,* 93; C. L. Robinson to Benjamin F. Butler, 3 March 1867, Butler Papers.

4. John J. Seibels to Johnson, 31 [30] June 1865, *PAJ,* 8: 322–24, 324n; Petition from the citizens of Pikesville, Alabama, to Johnson, 6 May 1865, D. P. Lewis to Johnson, 16 May 1865, Loyal Citizens of Alabama to Johnson, 1 June, Alabama Citizens' Petition to Johnson, 2 June 1865, Petition from Alabama Citizens to Johnson, 8 June 1865, Johnson Papers; Guinn, "Randolph County," 399; Wiggins, *Scalawag in Alabama Politics,* 9.

Parsons, a descendant of Puritan theologian Jonathan Edwards and an Alabama resident since the 1840s, had headed the wartime peace party. But he had worked through the system as a judge and legislator and had ties to disillusioned Rebels as well as to unionists. His approach to restoration was conciliatory. In his initial proclamation, for example, he said, "The appeal to arms has been made and decided against us, but not until our sons and brothers . . . exhibited a degree of courage and endurance which commands the respect and admiration of the world."[5]

Parsons's approach, however, soon caused ultraunionists to complain about his checkered wartime record and his willingness to retain Confederate officeholders. Unionists typically thought along the lines of William H. Smith: "If there are only half a dozen true men in a county, they should be appointed to office in preference to the secessionists." Mobile unionists accused the governor of once again turning over the city to their "tormentors." The *Huntsville Advocate* editorially castigated Parsons for his wholesale appointment of former Confederates. Smith, briefly a district judge during 1865, said that in a conversation he had with Parsons, he told the governor about this concern. "If these men are rewarded for their treason against the government," said Smith, "the plain simpleminded men will say the government must be satisfied that they have not done wrong or it would not reward them." Smith said the governor responded, "I agree to that; but let us wait until we get the state reconstructed." "Do you mean, wait until these men are all in power?" Smith replied. "That would be too late. We Union men will then all be driven out of the country."[6]

Of the delegates elected to the constitutional convention in August, Douglas Democrats won in north Alabama, while Whigs won elsewhere. Original unionists, who had supported the war in one way or another, composed the majority of delegates, loyalists only about one-third. Anthony W. Dillard of Livingston lost to former governor John A. Winston. Dillard claimed Winston favored secession and now opposed emancipation. Humphreys was defeated

5. Current, *Those Terrible Carpetbaggers,* 30–31; John J. Giers to Johnson, 30 May 1865, *PAJ,* 8: 145–46, 146n; Sidney C. Posey to Johnson, 30 May 1865, PAJ, 8: 146; John J. Seibels to Johnson, 31 [30] June 1865, PAJ, 8: 322–24, 324n; Proclamation of Governor Lewis E. Parsons, 20 July 1865, Parsons Papers.

6. D. H. Bingham and J. H. Larcombe to Andrew Johnson, 27 June 1865, copy, Joseph C. Bradley to Parsons, 25 July, 9, 17 August 1865, George W. Horton to Parsons, 1 August 1865, W. H. Smith to Parsons, 4 August 1865, Parsons Papers; *Report of the Joint Committee on Reconstruction,* pt. 3: 12.

by another candidate "who took decided grounds against amending the Constitution of the United States abolishing slavery." Still the convention's delegates were hardly pro-Confederate. For instance, they unanimously voided secession, abolished slavery by a vote of 89 to 3, overwhelmingly repudiated the state's Confederate debt, and approved legislative apportionment based on counting whites only (a measure that effectively destroyed the dominance of the plantation counties).[7]

Loyalists and original secessionists failed to field a gubernatorial candidate for the November election. Seeing no hope of winning, they left the race to three "original Unionists," all from north Alabama. Robert M. Patton, a Florence merchant who had been president of the state senate in 1861, won the contest. Before the war, Patton claimed, he had been "always an ardent and faithful supporter of the Union." He served in 1860 as a Douglas delegate to the Democratic National Convention at Charleston, and during the months after the election, as president of the state senate he "exercised all his influence to prevent" secession. Once the war came, however, he "in common with nearly all the union men in Alabama . . . fell into the current, and sided with the Rebellion." After 1862, when Federals invaded his area of the state, he sought to sit out the war "quietly." Patton resembled Holden of North Carolina in his willingness to do whatever was necessary to get his state back into the Union, and he, like Holden, later joined the Republican Party. Patton opposed the Fourteenth Amendment in November 1866 as being too punitive, too proscriptive, and detrimental to good government because of the lost leadership of talented individuals. By the first week in December, however, after seeing the election results in the North, he completely changed course and recommended that the Fourteenth Amendment be ratified by the legislature purely on the pragmatic grounds of getting Alabama back into the Union.[8]

In the election following the convention, loyalists won only one congressional seat, with Burwell T. Pope carrying the fifth district over his rival by only 31 votes. Several defeated 1865–66 congressional candidates joined the Republican Party within the next two years. In the legislative races, one close

7. Fleming, *Civil War and Reconstruction in Alabama,* 358–65, 378–83; Anthony W. Dillard to Johnson, 14 August 1865, *PAJ,* 8: 582–83, 583n; Joseph C. Bradley to Johnson, 8 September 1865, PAJ, 9: 44–46, 46n.

8. Fleming, *Civil War and Reconstruction in Alabama,* 395–97; Robert M. Patton to Johnson, ca. 1 July 1865, *PAJ,* 8: 337.

observer of Alabama politics wrote that the legislature elected was "composed
³/₄ of officers & privates from the Confederate Army." Still some future Republicans, mostly original unionists, won seats. About one-third of the combined membership of the constitutional convention and the legislature after
it eventually became Republicans. Most other scalawag leaders were also politically active during 1865–66. Some won offices, and others continued in ones
they already held. For example, scalawags captured eight of twelve circuit
judgeships. Many also received federal appointments after being recommended by their fellow citizens. These officeholders seemed acceptable
enough to thousands of white Alabamians in 1865.[9]

Opposition to the Johnson administration in Alabama as elsewhere came
mostly from outspoken anti-Confederate, out-of-office politicians. Some of
them attacked Johnson and provisional governor Parsons before the Joint
Committee on Reconstruction in early 1866. Others met later, in July 1866,
in the nation's capital to call for the Southern Loyalists Convention. And after
the 1866 congressional elections repudiated the president's policy, they called
for ratification of the Fourteenth Amendment.

Several organizations prepared the way for the founding of the Alabama
Republican Party. Two Republican newspapers appeared soon after the war,
the *Huntsville Advocate,* a voice for north Alabama unionists, edited by scalawag William B. Figures, and the *Mobile Nationalist,* the organ for blacks in
south Alabama, started by and for blacks. As in other states, the Union League
was a forerunner of the Republican Party. The league initially had been established during the war among Union army officers and camp followers in such
towns as Huntsville, Athens, and Florence. After Appomattox, some newcomers and members of the wartime peace society supported the league. Many
lodges, as they were called, existed in counties north of the Black Belt, with a
total of about three thousand members before 1866.[10]

Ministers of the Methodist Episcopal Church North, such as the Reverend
Aram S. Lakin of Ohio, sent by his denomination to take charge of missionary
work in Alabama, encouraged members to join the league. Lakin resided in

9. Cash, "Alabama Republicans," 246; *Journal of the Proceedings of the Convention of the
State of Alabama, Held in the City of Montgomery, on Tuesday, September 12, 1865* (Montgomery,
1865), 627–31; Joseph C. Bradley to Johnson, 15 November 1865, *PAJ,* 9: 383–90.

10. *Report of the Joint Committee on Reconstruction,* pt. 3: 10–14, 63–64; McPherson, *Political
Reconstruction,* 124; Michael W. Fitzgerald, *The Union League Movement in the Deep South: Poli-
tics and Agricultural Change during Reconstruction* (Baton Rouge, 1989), 34–36; Fleming, *Civil
War and Reconstruction in Alabama,* 556–57.

Huntsville but recruited throughout the state for religious converts and entire churches, as well as for league members. After two years, he shepherded a flock of more than nine thousand and supervised forty ministers, who rode as many circuits. As "emissaries of Christ and the Radical party," the circuit riders combined preaching and politics. Most white members resided in the hills and to a lesser degree in the pine barrens of the southeast counties. Walker, Winston, and Blount Counties, centers of disaffection during the war, had several white M. E. North churches. Some congregations, even integrated ones, existed elsewhere. Former Confederate general Josiah Gorgas of Bibb County said that on July 4, 1867, there was "a barbecue at the little Methodist Church . . . to which the country people and the negroes flocked," and that "it was a congregation of the 'Union League' . . . organized . . . out of those who skulked during the War, and are now rampant for the Union."

Several Freedmen's Bureau agents also assisted in laying the foundation for the Republican Party in Alabama. Agents were well represented among radicals meeting in north Alabama at Moulton in January 1867. Those attending endorsed the Fourteenth Amendment and stipulated that a distinction should be made between "precipitators" of secession and those "coerced" into rebellion. Among those present was Christopher Sheats, one of the state's nine southern-born agents.[11]

In Georgia, as in Alabama, President Johnson bypassed radical loyalists in naming a provisional governor. Most people anticipated Johnson would appoint Joshua Hill, the sole Georgia congressman who refused to walk out of Congress with his state's delegation in 1861. Unionist Democrats, a group close to Johnson's heart, however, strongly opposed Hill's appointment. One told the president he feared if Hill became provisional governor, that Democrats would be "kept on the back shelves" and that he would "play Brownlow," because Hill, like Brownlow, believed that "the Democracy destroyed the country." As for himself, the writer said he believed that in Georgia there were "as many good Union men democrats as among the opposition [former Whigs]."

In May, several Georgians talked with President Johnson about political conditions in the state. Three future Atlanta Republicans met with the president on May 19. They found that Johnson blamed the disloyalty of Georgians

---

11. Fleming, *Civil War and Reconstruction in Alabama*, 637–39; Rhoda Coleman Ellison, *Bibb County, Alabama: The First Hundred Years, 1818–1918* (University, Ala., 1984), 150; *New York Times*, 23 January 1867.

on the "cunning of artful and unscrupulous leaders." Once the people accepted the fact that "slavery was dead forever," Johnson said, he would consider the state's restoration. Two days later, the president met with Georgia's wartime governor Joseph E. Brown (another future Republican), who was brought to the White House from his cell at nearby Carroll Prison. Brown promised to support Johnson's policy any way he could.[12]

In mid-June, two different Georgia delegations visited Washington, one led by Hill and state district judge Osborne A. Lochrane, the other by former congressman James Johnson of Columbus. Both delegations contained several future Republicans. Lochrane, an outspoken Irishman from Macon, was a defender of civil liberties during the war, "having decided against conscription, the impressment of property in any shape and against putting Foreigners into the Confederate service." To offer a united front, the delegations met and jointly elected Lochrane as their chairman. Then they agreed on a list of applicants for specific offices, including James Johnson, a Whig who had once "shared mess privileges" in Washington with Congressman Andrew Johnson, for provisional governor. The president soon appointed James Johnson provisional governor and several others from the list to federal offices.[13]

James Johnson's "pleasantly inexpressive face" belied intelligence sharp enough for him to tie for top honors with Alexander H. Stephens in the University of Georgia 1832 graduating class. Like Andrew Johnson, James had an independent spirit that caused him to ally himself with "the unpopular side of agitated questions." Although he held thirty-seven slaves, he hated secession and contributed as little as possible to the Confederacy. On at least one occasion during the war, he stood accused of covert peace activities. Some former Confederates thought him "thoroughly radical." But if he was radical, his official responsibilities, at least as he viewed them, limited his actions. Unlike William W. Holden in North Carolina, Andrew J. Hamilton in Texas, and the wartime Reconstruction governors, Johnson never sought to be a party builder. He began his term in office determined enough, denouncing those who had led the state into secession and war, declaring that slavery was dead, and insisting the state's Confederate debt was void. But beyond bringing con-

12. William J. Northen, ed., *Men of Mark in Georgia: A Complete and Elaborate History of the State from Its Settlement to the Present Time* (Atlanta, 1907–12), 3: 71–76; Alexander N. Wilson to Andrew Johnson, 16 June 1865, Johnson Papers; Brown to Johnson, May 20, 1865, *PAJ*, 8: 92.
    13. Alfred Austell to Johnson, 16 June 1865, *PAJ*, 8: 246.

stitutional change the president had recommended, he did little to influence the course of events.[14]

James M. Johnson stood "in the shadow of a giant," former governor Brown, who was back from imprisonment and now championing the president's policy. Despite Brown's prosecessionist stand in 1861, he had an ongoing dispute with Jefferson Davis. Brown championed states' rights and civil liberties. The governor had also protected a number of unionist friends from persecution. Brown, "the leader of the lobby," as one reporter called him, "still occupie[d] the Executive Mansion"; Governor Johnson, the reporter continued, "simply [had] rooms there." Most of the state's politicians considered Johnson merely a necessary evil. With Brown's backing and the president's support, Johnson convinced the state's constitutional convention to declare secession illegal and to void the state's Confederate debt. But his victory cost him the loss of any possible popularity with the people.[15]

Of the three hundred constitutional convention delegates, only about one in four were wartime unionists. Most of those were from the "mountainous and wire-grass regions." One observer believed "a majority of the Delegates . . . from the up Country [were] good men" but the "low Country" delegates were "Gasbags or toads generally." Loyalist spokesmen included Hill, Charles H. Hopkins, and Josiah R. Parrott. Hill ranked "second in influence" in the convention to Charles J. Jenkins, an original unionist. But Hill's sphere was largely the loyalist minority. As that faction's spokesman, he urged a condemnation of secession, opposed a recommendation to pardon Jefferson Davis, and denounced repayment of the state's Confederate debt.

To no avail, Hopkins, a McIntosh County planter, former legislator, and wartime refugee on the Sea Islands, opposed the petition to pardon Davis. Referring to the secessionists, he said, "They told us there would be no war, no blockade, no bloodshed; that twenty men could whip a hundred." "Now let the leader of all these so-called statesmen be tried," he shouted. Parrott, a Cartersville attorney and once judge of his district, announced he "would resist . . . all efforts to tax the poor" to repay the war debt. Although he had

---

14. *National Cyclopaedia of American Biography*, 1: 227; Michael Perman, *Reunion without Compromise*, 120, 163.

15. Andrews, *South since the War*, 241; Brown to Johnson, 15 July, 30 August 1865, *PAJ*, 8: 409, 672; John Erskine to Johnson, 28 August 1865, PAJ, 8: 663–64; Alexander Wilson to Johnson, 25 October, 25 November 1865, PAJ, 9: 286, 431–32.

served as a Confederate general of the home guard, he claimed to have been "an unchanging union man."[16]

Only one week later, Hopkins stood among the loyalists who were losing races for office. In his case, he lost a bid for the state's first congressional district seat to Solomon Cohen of Savannah, a secessionist and the city's Confederate postmaster. Winners everywhere were original unionists who supported the Confederacy, men such as Judge Jenkins of Augusta, elected governor without opposition. Legislators elected, said one observer, were "generally . . . of more ability, but also of less original unionism than those in the Convention." Loyalist candidates for the United States Senate won about one-fifth of the legislature's vote, which was said by Hill to represent "the true and full strength of the serious Union men." Oversimplifying, Hill claimed he had anticipated defeat because Alexander H. Stephens had been "imprisoned for the Confederacy." A pragmatic politician, Brown thought that Hill and James Johnson ought to have been elected merely "on the grounds of expediency and propriety." But the Confederate veterans dominating the chambers cared not a whit for expediency or propriety.[17]

In 1865, the Union League moved into Georgia, where it existed mostly among newcomers and blacks, who met in separate chapters. In May, some newcomers in Savannah calling themselves the Georgia Union Club adopted resolutions supporting "appointment of a military Governor" and opposing as officeholders "sympathizers with secession." They soon joined scalawags such as recent refugees Amherst W. Stone and Alexander N. Wilson. In July, James Simms, a black preacher who had sojourned in Boston during the war, led a march of black Union League members to the center of the city for a speech. Meanwhile in Augusta, a petition signed by several individuals announced formation of a club "similar to that now active in Savannah." One of the individuals issuing the petition, Freedmen's Bureau agent John E. Bryant, later claimed he had received the Georgia Union League's initial charter.[18]

16. A. St. Clair Abrams, *Manual and Biographical Register of the State of Georgia for 1871–1872* (Atlanta, 1872), 22–23, 70–71; Goodspeed, *Biographical Souvenir of the States of Georgia and Florida . . .* (Chicago, 1889), 556; Andrews, *South since the War,* 248–49; Avery, *History of the State of Georgia,* 52–53.

17. Andrews, *South since the War,* 250, 269, 330; Elizabeth Studley Nathans, *Losing the Peace: Georgia Republicans and Reconstruction, 1865–1871* (Baton Rouge, 1968), 13–14.

18. Louis T. Griffith and John E. Talmadge, *Georgia Journalism, 1763–1950* (Athens, Ga., 1951), 33–34; Ruth Currie-McDaniel, *Carpetbagger of Conscience: A Biography of John Emory Bryant* (Athens, Ga., 1987), 60–61.

Bryant's chapter purchased the *Colored American* and published it during the winter of 1865–66. According to Bryant, the newspaper was not only read *by* some blacks but was also read aloud *to* hundreds of blacks at meetings throughout Georgia. Such newspapers represented another important step in the emergence of Georgia's Republican Party. Several started by early 1866. When General Sherman reached the sea in the fall of 1864, he seized the *Savannah Republican* and turned it over to *New York Tribune* correspondent John E. Hayes, who continued it until his death in 1868. Another Freedmen's Bureau agent, J. Clarke Swayze, and his friend Alexander G. Murray, a poor, but deserving "original Union man" capable of taking the ironclad oath with a "clear conscience," revived the *Griffin American Union.* Murray had published the sheet before its suppression "during the rebellion" by a mob and his subsequent imprisonment. According to a friend of Murray, his "type ink and paper are rather muddy but his principles are clear and his speech is elegant."[19]

Other events in Georgia during 1865–66 exemplified those elsewhere in the Southeast. Wartime loyalists joined with outsiders, sustained by federal or religious employment, to lay the groundwork for Congressional Reconstruction. Freedmen's Bureau agents, such as Bryant and Henry M. Turner, established chapters of the Georgia Equal Rights Association (GERA). The GERA sponsored 120 schools in fifty-three counties before merging into the league during 1867. Bryant was a young, idealistic, ambitious former Union army captain. As he claimed, he may have been seeking "a milder climate than Maine . . . because of suffering exposure in the army." But he soon developed an affinity for politics. He believed, as he told Turner, a black preacher, that soon the "day would . . . come when they would have the right to vote."[20]

During 1866, scalawags in north Georgia, such as P. M. Sheibley of Rome, a professor who turned planter during the war to avoid the draft, Dr. L. P. Gudger of Dalton, and attorney Henry P. Farrow of Atlanta, founded white councils of the Union League throughout the area. Gudger felt that there was a "Loyal Element in Cherokee Georgia of about the whites & all the colored,

19. Nathans, *Losing the Peace,* 20, 23–25; J. E. Bryant to Edward McPherson, 4 March 1867, A. G. Murray to McPherson, 2 March 1867, McPherson Papers.

20. Nathans, *Losing the Peace,* 18–31; Speech delivered by Henry M. Turner, 20 August 1874, John Emory Bryant Papers, Rare Book, Manuscript, and Special Collections Library, Duke University; Bryant to L. M. Morrill, 9 December 1876, Bryant Papers; *Proceedings of the Freedmen's Convention of Georgia, Assembled at Augusta, January 10, 1866* (Augusta, Ga., 1866).

making about ¹/₂ the entire population." Bryant, James L. Dunning, and others established black league councils in Augusta, Atlanta, Savannah, and Macon. And black preachers, such as Turner—who later boasted he "put more men in the field, made more speeches, and organized more Union Leagues . . . than any other man in the state"—carried the Union League into the interior of rural south Georgia. Soon after Appomattox, Farrow took the oath of allegiance to the United States and became a Republican because he considered the party "the only hope of the country." Starting in early June 1865, he addressed rallies in Cassville and Dawson in north Georgia and as far south as Fort Valley. Everywhere, he said, in "candor and truth," the "Negro is free, [the] doctrine of secession is extinct," and the people's "allegiance is to the United States." During the summer and fall of 1866, he organized Union Leagues throughout north Georgia. He served initially as the league's state secretary and then as its president.

Ministers of the northern-based denominations—dubbed by some conservatives "politico-ecclesiastical propagandists"—often also bore credentials as bureau agents and league and GERA organizers. Such men included Turner, a self-described "minister of the gospel and a kind of politician"; black planter-preacher Tunis G. Campbell of McIntosh County; and scalawag John H. Caldwell, a longtime Methodist minister from Georgia.[21]

After publishing two sermons on the abuses of slavery in the summer of 1865, Caldwell had been removed from his Newnan church by the presiding elder, a decision sustained in the fall by the state's Annual Conference of Methodists. Undismayed, Caldwell toured the North, speaking and listening to "both secular and religious" groups, engaging in what he termed "a sort of post-graduate course . . . both in religion and politics." Shortly thereafter in Atlanta, along with six other ministers—"all Southern men, and all, but one, members of the M.E. Church, South"—Caldwell organized the Georgia and Alabama Mission District of the Methodist Episcopal Church. By October 1867, the church had "forty traveling preachers" and some "sixty-six local preachers" ministering to 10,617 members. The church's greatest success, Caldwell said, was helping black "poor people . . . in need of schools and churches for their enlightenment and salvation." Only one-fifth of its mem-

21. *KKK Report*, Ga., 43, 48; Roberta F. Cason, "The Loyal League in Georgia," *GHQ* (20 June 1936): 137; Allen C. Smith, "The Republican Party in Georgia, 1867–1871" (Master's thesis, Duke University, 1937), 4, 6; Nathans, *Losing the Peace*, 37; Farrow, *Hon. Henry P. Farrow*, 5. Several pledges to the Union League during 1866 and 1867 are found in the Bryant Papers.

bers were whites, almost all in segregated churches, and all, according to Bryant, "were antislavery people" who had "supported the Union cause."[22]

Some Atlanta entrepreneurs who turned Republican before 1867 fitted a single mold: they came originally from the North, operated well-established local businesses before 1860, opposed secession, and were embittered by their wartime treatment. Atlanta's 1850s Whig mayors William Markham and Jonathan Norcross, industrialist James L. Dunning, and pharmacist David Young typified such unionists. Markham, a rolling mill operator, builder, and realtor, served on the committee surrendering the city in 1864. After visiting the North for a while, he became Georgia's first Union League president. Norcross was often called the Father of Atlanta because he once operated a sawmill and a general store at what became Five Points. Later he branched out into banking, publishing, and railroading. He went north in 1863 and upon his return, became the city's postmaster. These men became spokesmen for Atlanta's blacks. One Atlantan described the Fourth of July in 1866: "The occasion was observed only by the Negro population," who listened to speeches by "Dunning, Markham, and . . . 'Free Dave.'"[23]

Unlike most Atlanta scalawags, several from Augusta continued to support President Johnson until spring 1867. They included Foster Blodgett, Rufus Bullock, and Benjamin Conley. In 1865, Johnson had appointed Blodgett as city postmaster, because he had as mayor in 1861 opposed secession. Despite his less than glorious war record as a Confederate captain, Blodgett, the city's "worthy postmaster" (as a local conservative newspaper dubbed him), was defeated by fewer than 200 votes in April 1866.[24]

Bullock, "a large, handsome" man, had settled in Augusta two years before

22. Edmund L. Drago, *Black Politicians and Reconstruction in Georgia: A Splendid Failure* (Baton Rouge, 1982), 24–27; John H. Caldwell, *Slavery and Southern Methodism: Two Sermons Preached in the Methodist Church in Newnan, Georgia* (Newnan, Ga., 1865); John H. Caldwell, *Reminiscences of the Reconstruction of Church and State in Georgia* (Wilmington, Del., 1895), 2–8; 7–11; Jacqueline Jones, *Soldiers of Light and Love: Northern Teachers and Georgia Blacks, 1865–1873* (Chapel Hill, 1980), 54, 78; "The South," written by John E. Bryant, newspaper clipping, n.d., Bryant Papers.

23. Coleman and Gurr, *Dictionary of Georgia Biography*, 1: 684–85; Arthur R. Taylor, "From the Ashes: Atlanta during Reconstruction, 1865–1876" (Ph.D. diss., Emory University, 1973), 16, 20, 74, 81, 158, 211, 317, 325; Avery, *History of the State of Georgia*, 375, 519; Andrews, *South since the War*, 328; Alfred Austell to Andrew Johnson, 16 June 1865, Johnson Papers; *An Appeal to Republican Senators by Wealthy and Influential Republican Leaders of Georgia* (Washington, D.C., 1870); Thompson, *Reconstruction in Georgia*, 132.

24. Cashin, *Story of Augusta*, 133–34.

the war as superintendent of the Southern Express Company. Although opposed to secession, he later supervised construction of military telegraph lines and shipments of Confederate supplies. Yet many questioned the New Yorker's devotion to the southern cause, and according to one account, Bullock was "always regarded with suspicion by the rebels." Perhaps with reason. Only days after being paroled at Appomattox, he was summoned before Secretary of War Edwin M. Stanton, who entrusted him with a special mission, and soon after returning to Augusta, Bullock hung a picture of Abraham Lincoln in his parlor.[25]

Conley returned from his deceased brother's Alabama plantation in 1865, where he had lived quietly during the war. According to him, he never contributed to or supported the Confederate cause in any way except to pay taxes on that property. Conley, Bullock, and Blodgett, along with other former Whig Augusta businessmen, supported the pro-Johnson National Union Convention. In December 1866, the conservative press still sang the praises of Bullock, calling him a first-class man of business who combined "suavity and energy" with "administrative talent."[26]

In early 1867, Bullock became president of the Macon and Augusta Railway, a company, like others in the South, strapped for capital. So, he went north to seek financial backing from "moneyed friends." They informed him that if he brought Georgia back into the Union, he could "have all the money" he needed for his railroad. This, he said, led to his "embarking on the sea of politics." Bullock and others in Augusta saw the connection between reunion and the revival of trade and business. In early March 1867, Bullock wrote former congressman Hill that the "general disposition among [Augusta] businessmen [was] to cut loose from old wartime political leaders & act at once for a full & final settlement of our political troubles by hearty acquiescence in & action under the Sherman bill."[27]

By fall 1866, former Georgia governor Brown, a close observer of the national scene, saw that President Johnson's Reconstruction policy was doomed. He and his friend Dawson A. Walker of Dalton, a state supreme court justice

25. *DAB*, 3: 258–59; Russell Duncan, *Entrepreneur for Equality: Governor Rufus Bullock, Commerce, and Race in Post–Civil War Georgia* (Athens, Ga., 1994), 19–20; *OR*, 40(3): 435; Shadgett, *Republican Party in Georgia*, 9.

26. Coleman and Gurr, *Dictionary of Georgia Biography*, 1: 91–93; *National Cyclopaedia of American Biography* 1: 229.

27. Duncan, *Entrepreneur for Equality*, 19–20.

and, like Brown, a "self-made man . . . of uncommon ability,"went to Washington in February 1867. They conferred with politicians of all stripes, including Senator John Sherman, author of the bill that became the Reconstruction Act. Brown and the senator, whose brother, William, had devastated Georgia, got along. When the former governor returned home, he released a comprehensive letter to the press declaring his support for Congressional Reconstruction and his reasons for backing a plan opposed by most Georgians. Walker also stepped out in support of Brown's position, addressing a meeting in north Georgia and writing to the state's leading newspapers, advising individuals to register to vote and to cast their ballots for holding a constitutional convention.[28]

Brown's position grew out of his assessment of national political conditions. He saw that the Republican Congress had reached a consensus after the South repudiated the Fourteenth Amendment: that black suffrage would be forced upon the South, that some former Confederates would be temporarily barred from voting and holding office, and that for a while loyalists and their allies would control southern state governments. Brown believed the South would not get better terms. It was better to have one-tenth of the people disfranchised for a while, he reasoned, than to have "the property of the whole people confiscated." Brown urged a state convention to amend its constitution to include universal manhood suffrage. To his political enemies, his motivation was as before, to control the state's government; to his friends, it was to restore the state's overall conditions. Both were correct.[29]

In South Carolina, few anti-Confederates existed with whom to build a Republican Party or to even institute a state government acceptable to that party nationally. President Johnson appointed former congressman William W. Boyce, of Fairfield District, who had joined the peace bloc in the Confederate Congress, to be the lead man in drumming up support for reunion in the state. Because of Boyce's efforts, public rallies were held in almost all of the Upland districts, and recommendations from those meetings were passed on to the president. The proposed reforms included some taken for granted by

28. *Harper's Weekly*, 23 March 1867, p. 179; *Atlanta New Era*, 26 February 1867; Shadgett, *Republican Party in Georgia*, 40.

29. Alexander H. Stephens, *A Constitutional View of the Late War Between the States: Its Causes, Character, Conduct, and Results, Presented in a Series of Colloquies at Liberty Hall* (Philadelphia, 1868–70), 2: 654; Derrell C. Roberts, *Joseph E. Brown and the Politics of Reconstruction* (University, Ala., 1973), 51; Parks, *Joseph E. Brown*, 408, 467; Avery, *History of the State of Georgia*, 377.

citizens of other states: having the people elect the governor and presidential electors and giving the governor authority to veto bills passed by the legislature and to make appointments subject to the legislature's approval. Only with such reforms, according to Boyce, could he and others, including James L. Orr, another former Confederate congressman in the peace bloc, build a political party.[30]

Orr was the ideal candidate for provisional governor: as former Speaker of the House, he was nationally known; as a politician, he was as much a unionist as South Carolina produced before the war. Despite his Confederate service, he worked for peace during the war, and he had fought as much as Benjamin F. Perry, if not more, for the democratic reforms favored by the president. But after the president met with a delegation from Charleston, composed of secessionists and "unexceptional" unionists led by Judge Edward Frost, a "gentleman of high character," Johnson appointed Perry, a man he knew only by reputation. As provisional governor, Perry ignored past allegiances, political or otherwise. He claimed the entire state did not contain "a dozen prominently active and decided Union men." Instead of making distinctions in his power to appoint and to recommend pardons to the president, Perry simply claimed "confidence in the loyalty and fidelity of all." He almost immediately restored all Confederates who had held office at the end of the war, stating he saw this as a way to "harmonize the people."[31]

Some, however, saw Perry's actions as an encouragement to former secessionists and as a lost opportunity to build a unionist party within the state. According to Boyce, "two classes of opinion" existed, one that accepted "the new order of things cheerfully" and the other "sullenly without a willing spirit." By not building on the first class, composed more of former unionists who opposed secession until Lincoln's election, Perry lost the opportunity to build a state party capable of cooperating with the majority Republican Party in the North. Instead, wrote Boyce, Perry had "put upon their legs a set of men, who have been cursing the Government since they could articulate, and who like the Bourbons have learnt nothing & forgotten nothing." Another prominent citizen, Albert G. Mackey of Charleston, a consistent unionist, believed Perry should have made distinctions among disunionists. He felt for-

30. Boyce to Johnson, 23 June 1865, *PAJ,* 8: 274–76, 276n; Boyce to Johnson, 5 July 1865, PAJ, 8: 352–53.

31. John F. Poppenheim to Johnson, 18 June 1865, *PAJ,* 8: 256; Levy T. Moses to Johnson, 23 June 1865, PAJ, 8: 277.

mer fire-eaters "ought in all decency to retire from the scene." Instead of stepping down, Mackey said, secessionists "seem with their loyalty to have lost their modesty." Although he thought there would be "great security" for the government and the people if the amnesty oath were more severe, the "iron clad oath . . . would exclude honest converts."[32]

Settlers on the Sea Islands since 1861 and blacks represented South Carolina's known Republican contingent, and they functioned independently of one another. Before 1867, the color line in politics, as elsewhere, was strictly drawn. Islanders had sent a group that included four blacks to the 1864 Republican National Convention, where the delegation received seats but were denied votes. A year later, islanders chose one of those delegates, James C. Thompson, editor of the *Beaufort Free South,* to represent their district at the 1865 constitutional convention. He was seated by a narrow vote, after Orr argued for it "as an earnest of the . . . good disposition" of South Carolina in its "relation to the Union." A few newcomers also organized a Republican Association of Charleston, whose candidates ran unsuccessfully for the 1865 convention.[33]

Only a few of the state's 1865–66 lawmakers were original unionists, possibly one in four at the 1865 constitutional convention and at most one member in six in the legislature that followed. Thirty-six of the 1865 convention delegates voted for unionist attorney Christopher W. Dudley of the Marlboro District near North Carolina as convention president after Orr nominated him. Dudley was a tall, homely man with a "round-shouldered, slab-sided" physique, whose stature was "ungainly," whose movements were awkward, and whose gait was "shambling in his step." But when he spoke, others listened because of his "ability and rare good sense," his consistent public record, and his "sterling integrity." He had opposed secession since the nullification crisis of the 1830s and was "pre-eminently the advocate of the strictest economy in public affairs" (as he would continue to be through Reconstruction). Dudley had served in both houses of the state legislature, and he was a longtime friend of both Perry and Orr. While serving in the house, he shared a desk with Perry. During the war, in what was a rarity for South Carolina, Dudley "more than once . . . proposed that some effort should be made to stop the war by negotiation." His only service to the Confederacy was serving on a state-appointed board to feed "the wives & children of the absent

32. Boyce to Johnson, 23 June, 5 July 1865, PAJ, 8: 276, Boyce to Johnson, 5 July 1865, PAJ, 8: 352–53; Mackey to Carl Schurz, 23 July 1865, Johnson Papers.
33. Andrews, *South since the War,* 79–80; Rose, *Rehearsal for Reconstruction,* 316–17.

soldiers." He and several who voted for him as convention president later became high-ranking Republican state officeholders, including Orr, Lemuel Boozer, Franklin J. Moses, and Thomas J. Robertson.[34]

Blacks organized quickly in South Carolina, and they continued to hold meetings throughout 1865 and 1866. Hundreds came to Charleston's Zion Church in April 1865 to hear Chief Justice Chase urge them to build their lives on "morality, industry, education, and above all, religion." He promised them the vote some day. Six months later, a state convention of black leaders met at the same church and endorsed suffrage for their race. As elsewhere, such a convention attracted future politicos. In South Carolina, significant ones included a lieutenant governor, a secretary of state, a Supreme Court justice, and some congressmen, as well as a number of legislators. Some Republican newspapers appeared in South Carolina during 1865. Charleston's blacks started the *Charleston South Carolina Leader,* a newspaper dedicated to "equal rights to all," which was published under a succession of editors until 1867. Through attending bureau schools (which taught students of all ages), worshiping in the newly organized black churches, and attending black conventions, blacks became, as Joel Williamson says, "associated in such a way that when they were enfranchised, the establishment of the [Republican] party amounted to little more than formalizing a pattern which already existed."[35]

Nearly as many Mississippi as Alabama scalawags ran as candidates and served as officeholders during 1865–66. With the war's end, most resumed or continued their careers in public office. Some, such as James L. Alcorn, Jehu A. Orr, brother of James L. Orr, and Jason Niles, were seasoned public servants. Although most had opposed secession, few claimed to have been wartime loyalists. More than a dozen served in the 1865 constitutional convention, one of whom, E. S. Fisher, was nominated by that body for governor. Another, Alcorn, was elected by the next legislature to the United States Senate. Three others were elected as congressmen, and several were chosen as state judges. Some also received federal appointments, making their eventual affiliation with the party more likely.[36]

34. Andrews, *South since the War,* 51, 55, 65; Perry and Dudley to Johnson, 31 July 1865, *PAJ,* 8: 509–10, 510n.

35. Reid, *After the War,* 79–83, 584–85; Litwack, *Been in the Storm So Long,* 509; Robert H. Woody, *Republican Newspapers of South Carolina* (Charlottesville, 1936), 6–19; Williamson, *After Slavery,* 365.

36. "Reminiscences of J. A. Orr," Jehu A. Orr Papers, Southern Historical Collection; *Journal of the Proceedings and Debates in the Constitutional Convention of the State of Mississippi, August 1865* (Jackson, Miss., 1865), six unnumbered pages at the end.

But before 1867, only a handful of Mississippians expressed any willingness to identify with the Republican Party. A few ultraunionists who would soon identify with the Republican Party foresaw the danger of Mississippi's being too quickly readmitted into the Union. Former congressman John F. H. Claiborne of Hancock County, who had conducted "confidential relations" with several Union generals since Benjamin F. Butler occupied nearby Ship Island in December 1861, believed the people of his "native State" were unready to administer their "own affairs." He thought that they did "not yet sufficiently comprehend the force of events, and the duty of accepting them in good faith." He believed that for the next "12 months to come, they would be better under the immediate eye of the Executive and controlled by military rule." Other future scalawags were more optimistic. On April 18, Armistead Burwell called upon Mississippians to send "men of well known loyalty" to an informal meeting at Vicksburg on June 5 to consider holding an official convention at Jackson "to amend the State constitution abolishing slavery at once."[37]

Robert A. Hill, named a federal judge by President Johnson, was another likely Mississippi Republican. Hill had known Johnson in Tennessee, where Hill once served as state attorney general. Hill had other friends in high places, including Union generals George H. Thomas and Granville M. Dodge, who commanded at Corinth, and Ulysses S. Grant, who "learned of [his] standing whilst in command" in Mississippi. He also knew Chief Justice Chase, who applauded Hill for setting aside state legislation in conflict with the Civil Rights Act of 1866. Although Hill had been overly optimistic in letters to Chase at one point—for example, predicting the passage of the Fourteenth Amendment if the Congress offered it as its final demand—by March 1867, he was telling Senator John Sherman that there would be "no permanent peace until the people become convinced of the necessity of abandoning the leadership of those who have led them to the verge of extinction." As for himself, Hill gradually moved into the Republican Party during 1867.[38]

During 1866, the most significant individual to the eventual growth of the Mississippi Republican Party, Alcorn, showed that he was, as an enemy said,

37. Sansing, "Role of the Scalawag in Mississippi," 2, 55–58; Harris, "Reconsideration of the Mississippi Scalawag," 9–11, 15–19; William C. Harris, *Presidential Reconstruction in Mississippi* (Baton Rouge, 1967), 243; Wharton, *Negro in Mississippi,* 157.

38. Hill to Salmon P. Chase, 14 November 1866, 20 February 1867, Chase Papers; Hill to John Sherman, 13 March 1867, Sherman Papers; Hill to Edward McPherson, 18 April 1867, McPherson Papers; Hill to Johnson, 15 August 1865, *PAJ,* 8: 599.

"open and above board, frank and independent." He had visited Washington twice during 1865, once seeking a presidential pardon and again seeking a Senate seat. During his first tour, Alcorn talked with "acquaintances" in several government departments. After surveying the political landscape, he saw it would be wise for the South to grant blacks suffrage based upon literacy and/or property. Writing to his wife, Amelia, Alcorn said that southerners "must make the negro a friend," because to do otherwise would risk his becoming "our enemy under the prompting of the Yankee." He denied that allowing blacks to "approach the witness stand & the ballot box" meant "social equality," saying such had never been the case among different classes of whites. Following Alcorn's return to Mississippi, he was elected to the legislature, which in turn elected him to the United States Senate. He went to the nation's capital during December only to be refused his seat along with others, a fate he had foreseen.[39]

For the first few months of 1866, Alcorn devoted himself to his plantations and his law practice. But he could not remain quiet for long. In a July speech, he warned the state delegates to the National Union Convention to avoid "entanglements of party." He told them to concentrate on Mississippi's "right of representation," which he considered hopeless without the "hearty cooperation of the Conservative Republicans." In October, he again spoke out. During a break in circuit court proceedings in Bolivar County, he questioned the legislature's wisdom in rejecting the Fourteenth Amendment, which was soon to be adopted nationally. He characterized the legislature's action as a short-sighted, "childish display of spite," which would usher in harsher measures. Later, in early 1867 while addressing the legislature, he said the amendment should have been adopted as a matter of "expediency." Alcorn blamed what he called the "Jackson clique" for flinging the state "into the arms of a foregone failure." After studying "the temper of the Northern people," he said, he was "determined to yield to the inevitable." Alcorn edged ever closer to the Republican Party during 1867 and the following year entered the fold.[40]

Some original unionists in Mississippi, such as Alcorn, eventually saw President Johnson's program as another "lost cause" and understood that restoration would only follow cooperation with the dominant Republican Party. Others supported Reconstruction only after they had been squeezed out by former

39. Charles J. Swift Jr., "James Lusk Alcorn," Alcorn to his wife, Amelia, 16 August 1865, both in James Lusk Alcorn Papers, Mississippi Department of Archives and History, Jackson.

40. Perman, *Reunion without Compromise,* 216–17; *New York Times,* 2 September 1867; Pereyra, *James Lusk Alcorn,* 90–96; *Reporter,* 27 August 1866.

Confederates who had gained the better offices as well as the president's ear. Many delayed becoming Republicans until after the 1868 presidential election, not so much by design as by circumstances peculiar to Mississippi.

Loyalists in all the southeastern states sent representatives to the Southern Loyalists Convention in Philadelphia in September 1866, which was an important preliminary step toward allying them with the Republican Party in the North. Finally they acquired in that party an advocate who had a large majority in Congress and who won a major electoral victory in November 1866. During these years, loyalists discovered that only by two means could they gain position, power, and protection: Confederate proscription and black enfranchisement. Most came to believe black suffrage was the wiser course. Loyalists and their allies among newcomers and blacks laid the groundwork for the building of state Republican parties. They did this through the founding of Union Leagues, which would be expanded in 1867 into the black community; through a few newspapers; and through the spread of northern denominations in the South, especially among blacks. Most awaited military protection, black suffrage, and the possibility of controlling their state and local government before they became Republicans.

Scalawags felt the Southern Loyalists Convention of September 1866 "had much to do with preparing the minds of the people for manhood suffrage" and with "inducing Congress to pass that just and necessary measure" called the Reconstruction Act. By December, the Southern Republican Association, created as a result of the convention, had relocated from New York to Washington, D.C. Association president Thomas J. Durant soon spent his time lobbying key congressmen, coordinating the visits of loyalists, and creating what one Washington editor called a southern political "network, extending . . . to the remotest hamlets." Durant's chief goal was to replace the Johnson-backed governments and extend the life of new loyalist governments by allowing all men to vote, including blacks but excluding "rebels." According to one scalawag, Milton J. Saffold of Selma, Alabama, who resided in the nation's capital at the time, Durant drafted a bill, "the main features of which were incorporated into the Reconstruction Measure of Congress." Saffold, an insightful man, saw "one great object which Native Republicans had in view was to divide the control of the reconstr. Govts with the conquest-men," that is, northern newcomers.[41]

41. John Hawxhurst to Henry Clay Warmoth, 6 November 1867, Warmoth Papers; Saffold, *Address to Native White Republicans*; Richard H. Abbott, *The Republican Party and the South, 1855–1877: The First Southern Strategy* (Chapel Hill, 1986), 73, 75.

7

~

Not So Sweet a Victory

In the Upper South states of Virginia, North Carolina, and Tennessee and in the Southwest states of Louisiana, Arkansas, and Texas, political foundations, however sandy, had been laid during 1860–66 for building state Republican parties. Four states had undergone wartime Reconstruction—Virginia, Tennessee, Louisiana, and Arkansas—and Union forces occupied much of the latter three by 1864. On a small scale, the Republican Party existed in all four before 1867—in Virginia as early as the mid-1850s. North Carolina had a strong peace party that continued as the Union Party during 1865–66. And in Texas, the unionist coalition of 1861, representing about 20 percent of voters, was revived as the Union Party during 1865–66.

Shortly after the Southern Loyalists Convention, Governor Pierpont of Virginia, who had not attended, broke with President Johnson and, like Brownlow earlier, endorsed the Fourteenth Amendment. Speaking to the legislature, he downplayed the amendment's severity: "The disabilities . . . are not to be perpetual," he said, and "the person of the citizen is safe; his property is not threatened with confiscation." His appeal, however, fell on deaf ears. Virginians along with other southerners felt acceptance of the Fourteenth Amendment dishonored their dead and divided their allies in the North. At best, they reasoned, ratification would be a gamble because the amendment might not represent the final demands of Republicans. By February 1867, legislatures of other former Confederate states, except for Tennessee, rejected the amendment by sizable majorities. Only thirty-three legislators in ten states, mostly in Alabama and North Carolina, approved it. Almost all of them soon became Republicans.[1]

After the Tennessee General Assembly reconvened in November 1866, Brownlow defended his about-face on black suffrage from 1865. Now he argued that a more favorable climate existed nationally for civil rights legislation. Moreover unionists needed black ballots to offset former Confederates' votes. Some within his own radical party from East Tennessee, however, opposed the measure. In early January 1867, radicals introduced the measure in the house. Conservatives opposed the bill on the grounds that to enfranchise blacks without restoring votes to whites would turn society on its head. They offered as a compromise a bill for universal manhood suffrage, which radicals rejected. In February, radicals adopted black suffrage, with many East Tennesseans abstaining. Despite giving blacks the ballot, Tennessee scalawags never intended to share political power with blacks. Some who voted for black suffrage helped to defeat a bill allowing blacks to be jurors and officeholders. Such ambivalence created an opportunity for conservatives to appeal to blacks.[2]

In December 1866, some North Carolina politicians, including Holden and John Pool, went to Washington to consult with congressional radicals about the state's readmission and an alliance linking Holdenites to the national Republican Party. Working through Congressman Thaddeus Stevens, they framed the North Carolina Enabling Bill, providing suffrage for all men who could read or write, regardless of race, or who possessed at least one hundred dollars in real estate. The bill restricted seats in southern state constitutional conventions to those loyal to the Union since March 4, 1864 (when Holden became the peace party candidate for governor). It died in committee following the formulation of more severe Reconstruction measures. Stevens later wrote another bill much more preferable to North Carolina radicals to the left of Holden.[3]

By the time Congress met in December 1866, Republicans had scored a

1. Francis H. Pierpont to A. W. Randall and I. R. Doolittle, 21 July 1866, Pierpont Papers; *Harper's Weekly*, 22 December 1866, p. 803; Perman, *Reunion without Compromise*, 252; McPherson, *Political Reconstruction*, 194.

2. Tennessee *Senate Journal*, Brownlow Assembly, 2d adj. sess. (Nashville), 10–22. Coulter, *William G. Brownlow*, 328–30.

3. Hamilton, *Reconstruction in North Carolina*, 187–88; William C. Harris, *William Woods Holden: Firebrand of North Carolina Politics* (Baton Rouge, 1987), 210–12; Alexander H. Jones to Thaddeus Stevens, 4 January 1867, Stevens Papers.

landslide in congressional elections, the South had rejected the Fourteenth Amendment, and moderate Republicans had become convinced that without the ballot, freedmen could not protect their civil rights. When the moderate and the radical wings of the Republican Party in Congress reached a compromise, the Military Reconstruction Act passed in March 1867. The law's provisions derived from three separate plans: a radical one to depose the states' traditional leaders and replace them with white loyalists, a moderate proposal to simply admit individual states as they approved the Fourteenth Amendment, and another calling for the creation of a temporary military government to protect loyalists and blacks.[4]

The patchwork bill that passed rested on a two-fold premise: lawful governments did not exist in the former Confederate states, and Congress could govern them until they were restored. The law divided the states into five military districts (excluding Tennessee, which had approved the Fourteenth Amendment). A major general named by the president would command each district. Each state had to approve a constitutional convention and elect delegates by a vote of registered voters without regard to "race, color, or previous condition" (excluding as voters and delegates only prewar officeholders who supported the Confederacy). Each convention had to draft a constitution including black suffrage. Each constitution had to be palatable to a majority of the state's voters and to members of Congress. Once a legislature elected under the new constitution approved the Fourteenth Amendment, the state would be readmitted to the Union.[5]

Three weeks later, a second act, also passed over a presidential veto, added procedural details. The new constitutions would need to be approved by "a majority of all . . . registered voters," a provision that worked against Reconstruction and that was changed a year later to read, "a majority of votes actually cast." After voter registration was underway, controversies arose over the interpretation of the Reconstruction Acts. Still unclear to many, including those in the military, was exactly who could register to vote and who qualified to register them. The status of existing state governments and officials and who was disqualified from holding office also remained uncertain. So in July, Congress passed the third Reconstruction Act, declaring the unreconstructed

4. Herman Belz, *Emancipation and Equal Rights: Politics and Constitutionalism in the Civil War* (New York, 1978), 102–3; W. R. Brock, *An American Crisis: Congress and Reconstruction, 1865–1867* (New York, 1963), 188–98.

5. Fleming, *Documentary History of Reconstruction,* 1: 401–4.

states "subject in all respects to the military commanders," including removal and appointment of state and local officials. Moreover, registrars had the power and duty to reject those disfranchised under the law (broadly defined to include all offices created by state law).[6]

On March 11, President Johnson announced the officers responsible for enforcing the Reconstruction Acts. These generals eventually were replaced by others who, like the original commanders, made an impact on the state governments. Beyond that, they also directly and indirectly influenced the growth or lack of growth of the Republican Party in the states under their control. Often they determined whether the leadership of that party would be composed mostly of scalawags or carpetbaggers and what role, if any, would be left to the black leaders. They also played a role in deciding whether moderate or radical Republicans reigned.[7]

The Reconstruction Acts gave birth to the Republican Party in most of the South. Locally the party began when cooperating white and black leaders met to endorse Congressional Reconstruction. Occasionally the partisan nature of a rally was revealed only after it began, when an opportunity arrived for citizens to overtly identify with the Republican Party rather than, as some had covertly done, through the Union League. Many conservatives believed they had to cooperate with the Congress to have their state accepted back into the Union. At the time, they mistakenly believed blacks would just as likely side with them as with the radicals. When the assumption of black support vanished during summer 1867, especially as conservatives saw blacks vote solidly for Brownlow in Tennessee that August, most who earlier backed the congressional plan now either avoided participation in Reconstruction or became outright opponents.[8]

Because the Reconstruction Acts enfranchised blacks, Republican activists organized them as voters, especially through Union Leagues. According to one organizer, councils operated as "night schools," instructing blacks in "the duties they owed to the party which had made them free and given them . . . suffrage." Occasionally councils established earlier for whites now admitted blacks. Organizers included white loyalists, Freedmen's Bureau agents (including some southerners), and black preachers, many sponsored by large northern urban councils. The councils employed religious symbols, the Stars

6. Ibid., 407–18.
7. Sefton, *United States Army and Reconstruction,* 109, 113–15.
8. Foner, *Reconstruction,* 292–94.

and Stripes, a copy of the Declaration of Independence and a copy of the Constitution, a gavel, a ballot, and a sickle. These items respectively represented faith, loyalty, freedom, law, democracy, and labor.[9]

Rapid growth of black leagues in Tidewater Virginia inspired radicals to hold a Republican convention at Richmond's African Church on April 17. Most delegates were blacks residing in eastern Virginia. Whites included wartime unionists, such as veterans of the Alexandria government and of Richmond's loyalist underground, recent party converts from southwestern Virginia, and a few carpetbaggers. The platform combined planks for black rights and Whiggish traditions—such as "encouragement to internal improvements." Other planks threatened the political power and economic holding of Virginia's ruling class, such as taxes on land. Delegates elected a party executive committee composed of James W. Hunnicutt's followers. John M. Botts and his moderates accused the convention of being "imperfectly organized," a reference to its composition, and "exclusively led," referring to Hunnicutt and his cohorts.[10]

During the next two months, Virginia moderates received support from a number of quarters. Some former Union army officers residing in the state, led by General Henry H. Wells of Alexandria, met in convention and adopted a platform they hoped would attract former Confederates. The *Richmond Whig* favored Reconstruction by "the better class of Union men . . . , those who upheld the southern cause, and the better class of [the] colored population." Alarmed by radicalism in Virginia, northern Republicans appealed for moderation to attract southern whites. Senator Henry Wilson of Massachusetts marched in the forefront of those encouraging unity through moderation. Speaking at Richmond, Wilson appealed for the creation of an inclusive biracial Republican Party that would include whites "reluctantly dragged into the rebellion."[11]

Some three hundred men, mostly wealthy Whigs not yet aligned with the Republican Party, announced a pro-Reconstruction convention to meet in

9. Ibid., 283–91; Fleming, *Documentary History of Reconstruction*, 1: 7–19; Eckenrode, *Political History of Virginia during Reconstruction*, 61.

10. Virginius Dabney, *Virginia, The New Dominion* (New York, 1971), 365; James W. Hunnicutt to Charles Sumner, 2 July 1867, McPherson Papers; Lester J. Cappon, *Virginia Newspapers, 1821–1935: A Bibliography with Historical Introduction and Notes* (New York, 1936), 179; Lowe, "Another Look at Reconstruction," 64–65; Squires, *Unleashed at Long Last*, 243–49.

11. *New York Tribune*, 22, 23, 25, 26 April 1867; Abbott, *Republican Party and the South*, 114–17, 122–23; Eckenrode, *Political History of Virginia during Reconstruction*, 70–73.

Charlottesville on July 4. This convention received the backing of Botts and the moderates. Disturbed by the possibility of Virginia having a divided Republican Party at presidential election time in 1868, national party leaders intervened through the Union League clubs of Boston, New York, and Philadelphia. Led by Senator Wilson of the Boston league and John Jay of the New York league, members from the three cities—mostly businessmen, professionals, and a handful of politicians—met with leaders of the two factions on June 16, 1867, in the drawing rooms of the governor's mansion in Richmond.[12]

Spokesmen from both factions addressed the group of about fifty visitors. Botts attacked the April convention as having been racially narrow and geographically limited. He also presented the three hundred signatures, claiming that they mostly represented landholders and old-line Whigs. Although Hunnicutt refused to sanction the Charlottesville meeting, he welcomed all who would endorse the party's platform. After debating all night, the two factions reached an agreement. Another convention would meet to bring about the "perfecting and enlarging" of Virginia's Republican Party. Both wings of the party and the three hundred petitioners would issue the convention call. The convention, however, would be held in Richmond, as Hunnicutt had insisted.[13]

Despite their disappointment, Botts and his followers hoped to win enough blacks and former Whigs to control the upcoming convention. Former Confederates met in at least ten counties, mostly in the central part of the state, to select delegates to the state Republican convention. On July 31, the day before the convention, Botts persuaded a caucus of moderates to declare secession treasonable and the state's Confederate debt void and to endorse manhood suffrage except for high-ranking Confederates. But Hunnicutt's ability to pack the convention doomed the Whiggish "cooperation" movement. When the convention officially opened, pews of the African Church were already packed. Eventually delegates assembled at Capitol Square and endorsed their earlier platform.[14]

12. Abbott, *Republican Party and the South*, 123–24; *Report of Proceedings of Conference in Richmond*, 3–13; *New York Tribune*, 15 June 1867; Eckenrode, *Political History of Virginia during Reconstruction*, 73–74.

13. Eckenrode, *Political History of Virginia during Reconstruction*, 73–74.

14. Alexander Rives to B. J. Barbour, 10 July 1867, B. J. Barbour Papers, Tracy W. McGregor Library, Albert H. Smalls Special Collections Library, University of Virginia, Charlottesville; Eckenrode, *Political History of Virginia during Reconstruction*, 74–78.

Feeling their voices had not been heard, most cooperationists returned to the conservatives. Some later supported the readjusters (who wanted to pay off the state's debt at a reduced rate) and at times backed fusion with the Republicans. Their rejection of Republicans in 1867 diminished the party's chance of having strong native leadership. Many newcomers received appointments from General John M. Schofield, who preferred them to those he considered unqualified scalawags.[15]

In October 1867, close to 60 percent of registered voters approved a constitutional convention. Republicans won easily because of white apathy and heavy black turnout. Supporters included about one-fifth of whites who voted, or 15,000 voters, a good indication of the number of white Republicans. The white vote came from thirty-one voting districts forming three clusters, one along Chesapeake Bay and the Potomac River from Northumberland County south to Norfolk, including the Eastern Shore; a second of Alexandria and five nearby counties; and a third of seventeen counties located at the state's southwestern tip. The clusters had been politically diverse before 1861; whites mostly populated the southwestern cluster and racially mixed groups occupied the others. The common factor for all three had been their anti-Confederate activity.[16]

Virginia Republicans elected more than 70 delegates to the constitutional convention, about equally divided among scalawags, carpetbaggers, and blacks. General Schofield, district commander, labeled 51 of the delegates as "Radicals," including most of the blacks and carpetbaggers; 22 as "Republicans," his term for moderate Republicans; 12 as "Conservatives"; and 19 as "unreconstructed." Working from December 1867 to April 1868 under Chairman John C. Underwood, delegates included in the constitution provisions for an income tax, free schools, and the election of local officials (formerly appointed). Especially galling to most, as well as to Schofield, was the delegates' proscription of Confederates who held office before 1861.[17]

Meanwhile Governor Pierpont's term expired on January 1, 1868. After offering the post to Judge Alexander Rives, General Schofield appointed his

15. Eckenrode, *Political History of Virginia during Reconstruction*, 74–78; Foner, *Reconstruction*, 353.

16. Martin E. Mantell, *Johnson, Grant, and the Politics of Reconstruction* (New York, 1973), 48.

17. Lowe, "Virginia's Reconstruction Convention," 341–60; Eckenrode, *Political History of Virginia during Reconstruction*, 74–79.

friend Henry H. Wells, an "agreeable" New Yorker with "aspiration" to be elected governor. He saw in Wells an unaligned moderate who could unite state Republicans. By May 1868, the general had appointed more than five hundred officeholders, always, he wrote, naming Republicans "where respectable and competent persons . . . could be found." Some natives claimed he placed carpetbaggers "in all the important offices." His appointments accelerated an already increasing hostility between the party's prewar residents and the carpetbaggers.[18]

Capable scalawags minimized carpetbag officeholding in North Carolina. More than anyone else, Holden kept control in the hands of natives. He possessed a much stronger leadership base on which to build, one having roots in reform efforts before and after the war and in the peace party.

When news reached Raleigh about the first Reconstruction Act, overjoyed Holdenites asked legislators to pass a resolution accepting the act "in good faith." Instead, conservatives went on a roaring drunk at a "treat on the East Portico of the Capitol." They jammed the senate chamber, holding an unofficial impromptu session, making "one fool motion after another." Holdenites left to caucus at Holden's newspaper office to plan a convention for those supporting Congressional Reconstruction.[19]

Holdenites reconvened later to invite a list of loyalists for a convention on March 27. Holden named many personally. He held that a majority opposed the Confederacy. He orchestrated the planning to prevent a carpetbagger-black takeover. Holdenites invited only five carpetbaggers, all closely associated with the Union League. They included Albion W. Tourgée of Guilford and David Heaton of New Bern. Unlike Tourgée, who opposed Holden because of his mixed record, Heaton, a longtime politician, stood ready to cooperate with the editor. Holdenites left the convention door ajar for blacks by agreeing to seek their cooperation—eventually inviting them to send one-third of the total delegates.[20]

Delegates from more than fifty counties met for a party convention in the capitol under a banner reading, "Union, Liberty, Equality." There, Holden

18. James L. McDonough, "John Schofield as Military Director of Reconstruction in Virginia," *Civil War History* 15 (September 1969): 237–56.

19. Olsen and McGrew, "Prelude to Reconstruction," NCHR 60 (July 1983): 360; Lancaster, "Scalawags of North Carolina," 206, 210; Raper, *William W. Holden,* 93–94.

20. Lancaster, "Scalawags of North Carolina," 202; *(Raleigh) North Carolina Standard,* 13, 20 March 1867.

concluded, "the former master met his former slave as his equal in all that pertains to . . . the rights of self-government." Most scalawag delegates were former Whigs and peace party men, generally with graying hair, connected in one way or another with Holden during 1865–66. They would represent a majority of the Republican Party's leaders and high-ranking officeholders for many years.[21]

Robert P. Dick recommended that they declare themselves to be the "Republican Party of North Carolina." But two longtime Republicans who had resided in the North for almost a decade, Daniel R. Goodloe and Benjamin S. Hedrick, opposed the resolution. They said that the words *Republican* and *Holden* would fire a double-barreled volley at conservatives, summoning them to a political call to arms. Instead they recommended the title National Union Party. But most delegates believed the party should be called the Republican Party. The title guaranteed the votes of blacks, who saw the party as their emancipator and friend. It also attracted newcomers already identified with that party and linked Holdenites to a powerful congressional ally. So, by an almost unanimous vote, delegates approved the term *Republican*.[22]

Some who accepted the title criticized Holden as unworthy of running under that banner. Holden, already attacked from the right, found himself denounced by the left. Tourgée's partner in publishing, Dr. A. B. Chapin of Greensboro, one of a few carpetbaggers there, condemned Holden and his friends as political opportunists who were soiled by their support of the rebellion. After being booed, however, Chapin staged a one-man walkout.[23]

Thomas Settle delivered the crowning speech, a passionate rationale of why many of the Holdenites had become Republicans. Settle defended his rationale for joining the "party of progress, of education and development." He talked of a "new era . . . where one month flings a greater flood of light . . . than fifty years ordinarily." The party offered "a new start" for the South, and he urged the delegates to help hasten change. Regarding blacks, he said that the notion that southerners were the best friends Negroes ever had was pure "foolishness" and that the "colored man" knew it. He said that white fears of "social equality" were unfounded because even among whites of different

---

21. Lancaster, "Scalawags of North Carolina," 362; Harris, *William Woods Holden,* 220–21.

22. Harris, *William Woods Holden,* 221; Joseph F. Steelman, "Daniel Reaves Goodloe: A Perplexed Abolitionist during Reconstruction," in *Essays in Southern Biography,* East Carolina College Publications in History (Greenville, N.C., 1965), 2: 82–85.

23. Lancaster, "Scalawags of North Carolina," 207–10.

classes, social equality did not exist. He welcomed Yankees, along with "their capital . . . their intelligence, their energy and enterprise." Although Settle did not like the disfranchisement of Confederates who had been victims of circumstances in their lives, he said, "Let me tell you that if I live till grief kills me because of disfranchisement, history will record one older man than Methuselah."[24]

Afterward delegates adopted a platform containing little of substance other than an endorsement of Congressional Reconstruction. Finally, they approved the state's Republican Executive Committee, with Holden as chairman and twenty-three scalawags, including Goodloe (an act of reconciliation on Holden's part), seventeen blacks, and one lone carpetbagger, Heaton. Commenting on the convention, Governor Jonathan Worth pointed out that most of the white delegates were followers of Holden who endorsed the Fourteenth Amendment during the summer of 1866. On the whole, Worth believed the whites to be less conservative than the black delegates, neither of whom had any "kind words for President Johnson."[25]

The convention showed not only who were Holden's enemies but who were his friends as well. His friends consisted of three major groups: members of the Heroes of America; former reform-minded Union Democrats, like Dick and Settle; and former Whigs, such as Alfred Dockery and John Pool. In addition, as president of the Union League, Holden held the reins of that organization, although he needed the cooperation of influential carpetbaggers.

The Heroes of America, an anti-Confederate secret society, witnessed resurgence in early 1867 before going public in May. Its members solidly supported Dockery for governor in October 1866, and soon thereafter they endorsed Congressional Reconstruction. The Heroes of America appealed to whites who did not care to join the Union League, which they associated with blacks although they eventually recognized the significance of black voters. The society demanded confiscation and disfranchisement both as a punishment and as means of redistributing wealth and political influence. It also favored debtor relief and introduced several schemes to accomplish it in the 1866–67 legislature and in the constitutional convention of 1867.[26]

24. Jeffrey J. Crow, "Thomas Settle Jr., Reconstruction, and the Memory of the Civil War," *JSH* 62 (October 1996), 701–2; *(Raleigh) North Carolina Standard*, 3 April 1867; Olsen, "Reconsidering the Scalawags," 315.
25. Lancaster, "Scalawags of North Carolina," 210.
26. Ibid., 214–17.

Former Whigs represented a majority of the state's Republican leaders. One distressed conservative found that most Republican officeholders turned out to be his "old Whig friends." Another estimated that two-thirds of former Whig politicos entered the Republican Party. The attraction for former Whigs rested on a view of the past rather than of the future. The chief spokesman of the Whigs-turned-Republicans, Pool, the Constitutional Union Party candidate for governor in 1860, defined their position in his "Address to the People of North Carolina," published in spring 1867. Self-appointed men who claimed "guardianship of Southern honor and interest" deceived the people into rebelling, said Pool. Then those men and their allies coerced the people into continuing "a bloody and disastrous civil war" far beyond the point of any "hope of success." Afterward they made "past treason a test of honor" and glorified "the most notorious actors in the rebellion." Such intransigence called for stronger measures than those enacted by President Johnson.[27]

Pool now urged North Carolinians, especially the "Peace men and Conservatives of 1864–1865," to retire those "whose past councils [sic] caused so much evil." And, in keeping with the Reconstruction Acts, to respect the rights of blacks. Then and later, Pool disagreed with parts of the Reconstruction Acts, but he believed they "had been adopted by Congress and announced as necessary for the future peace and security of the country." He fully believed, from "all the indications . . . that Congress [meant] to carry the policy out," and he preferred those means "easiest to [his] people." For a while Pool's views stood a chance of convincing conservatives such as David F. Caldwell of Guilford and David M. Carter of Beaufort, both former peace party men, and Bartholomew F. Moore, ever an independent sort, but conservatives ultimately rejected Republicanism as being too radical. [28]

During fall 1867, Republicans elected 107 of the 120 delegates for the 1868 constitutional convention. They received a majority of the white vote in western North Carolina. Scalawags elected outnumbered others two to one. Most resided in the western one-third of North Carolina, had been prewar Whigs and Douglas Democrats, had opposed secession, had supported the peace movement, and favored democratic and progressive reforms.

Delegates met in convention at Raleigh on January 14, 1868, and elected as convention president Calvin J. Cowles, a well-to-do merchant who served

27. *Winston Sentinel*, 1 October 1867.
28. Ibid.

as postmaster at Wilkesboro until 1863 without taking the Confederate loyalty oath. By all accounts, this was the least controversial of the black-and-tan conventions, partly because little effort was made to disfranchise former rebels. Voters approved the constitution overwhelmingly and elected Holden governor by a comfortable margin over Samuel Ashe, a former Confederate running as the conservative candidate. Republicans won almost 30 percent of the white vote, or about 35,000 votes. [29]

Meanwhile in Tennessee, radicals, now calling themselves the Union Republican Party, met at Nashville on February 22, 1867. Brownlow announced that "even in [his] feeble state of health," if nominated, he "would not feel at liberty to decline the nomination." Delegates responded quickly by nominating him. After his acceptance speech and a round of speeches by others, delegates, foreseeing Johnson's impeachment, asked Congress to "legitimately deprive the President of his powers to disturb the peace of the country."[30]

Because they had already lost the battle over black suffrage and now needed black votes, conservatives declared at their state convention in mid-April 1867 that their "colored fellow-citizens [were] entitled to all rights and privileges." Former Democrats took a back seat at the convention as former Whigs dominated the proceedings. Emerson Etheridge, who broke with Lincoln over emancipation, won the nomination. His longtime record of negrophobia, along with the Union League's control over black voters, however, discouraged black support for the conservatives.[31]

Radicals received assistance in organizing blacks from Freedmen's Bureau agents. Some agents used the Union League to organize black voters as Republicans. Of Gallatin's Union League Brownlow Council Number Four's ten officers, seven were black and three were white, a bureau agent, a bureau schoolteacher, and a United States Army officer. By May 1867, one bureau agent reported that he thought the politicization of blacks had been effective, even in the countryside, that they understood "how they ought to vote and who are their friends." He felt all blacks desired now was "protection" and that they would "do their duty to themselves and their country," certainly a correct prognosis by the August election. Of black voters at Columbia, Congressman Samuel M. Arnell reported: "A thousand men assembled adjacent

29. Hamilton, *Reconstruction in North Carolina*, 254–86.
30. Hamer, *Tennessee*, 1: 620–21.
31. Ibid., 621–24.

to one of the main streets . . . in a quiet place in order to obtain and distribute tickets [ballots] . . . to march in columns to the polls."[32]

With such solid black support, Brownlow defeated Etheridge. Although the governor, recently in poor health, had felt too ill to campaign, others had taken to the hustings on his behalf. In addition to winning the governor's race, all of the Republican candidates for Congress and almost all of the party's nominees for the general assembly won. Brownlow had 74,034 votes and Etheridge 22,550, largely the votes of wartime conservative unionists. Most of the white Republican votes came from East Tennessee, where Brownlow defeated Etheridge by 25,789 to 4,155. Elsewhere most Republican voters were black. The conservative *Paris Intelligencer* summed up the results: "The untutored and illiterate fanatics of East Tennessee and the ignorant and superstitious Africans of Middle and West Tennessee have united and elected Brownlow governor for the next two years."[33]

Although scalawags clearly controlled the government from 1865 to 1867, dissatisfaction among them surfaced during 1867–68 because of the number of offices held by carpetbaggers. Tennessee Secretary of State Andrew J. Fletcher, who broke with Brownlow over carpetbagger influence (as well as other issues), often complained of their "pursuit of office." Speaking before the Republican State Convention in Nashville on January 22, 1868, Fletcher, an exile in the North during the war, said he "gladly welcome[d] the Northern man who comes . . . to make a home . . . , but for the adventurer and office-seeker who comes among us with one dirty shirt and a pair of dirty socks, in an old rusty carpetbag, and before his washing is done becomes a candidate for office, [he had] no welcome." Still, Tennessee had fewer carpetbaggers in important state and federal offices than any state besides Georgia, both of which had about 15 percent. Actually, few penniless newcomers of the ilk described by Fletcher came to Tennessee. Most arrived with more than dirty laundry. They often brought intelligence as well as money and frequently mixed idealism with industry. Chattanooga's carpetbaggers got along reasonably well with locals and became some of that city's more successful capitalists.[34]

By early 1867, most former Union soldiers in the Southwest had aban-

---

32. Paul D. Phillips, "The Freedmen's Bureau in Tennessee" (Ph.D. diss., Vanderbilt University, 1964), 29, 50–51, 60; Alexander, *Reconstruction in Tennessee,* 155.

33. Hamer, *Tennessee,* 1: 628–30; Patton, *Unionism and Reconstruction,* 139–40.

34. Temple, *Notable Men of Tennessee,* 123–25.

doned President Johnson to advance their own agenda through the Grand
Army of the Republic, a veterans organization founded in 1866. Beyond its
patriotic theme, the GAR championed the "defense of the late soldiery of the
United States, morally, socially and politically." Like the Union League, the
GAR served as an adjunct of the Republican Party. The strongest state GAR
in the South existed in Louisiana. There former Federals started forming local
GAR posts in early 1867. Henry Clay Warmoth, who recruited over five thousand GAR members, was elected Louisiana's grand commander at the state's
first GAR encampment on the night of January 11, 1868 (held at the time of
the Republican state convention). Before 1867, the party politics of GAR
members had spanned the spectrum, but now almost all resolved to "support
the plan of Reconstruction proposed by the Congress of the United States."
Because of Congressional Reconstruction, Warmoth wrote that northerners
found themselves "up to [their] eyes in politics, made so by conditions" at
hand.[35]

Warmoth, with a group of partners, established an official GAR newspaper,
the *New Orleans Republican.* The first edition contained a joint endorsement
from Benjamin F. Butler and Nathaniel P. Banks. With friends in high places,
the journal was selected almost immediately as an official newspaper to print
U.S. laws and regulations. Two other Louisiana newspapers, the *New Orleans
Tribune,* and the *Homer Iliad,* also received this political plum.[36]

GAR members and blacks such as James H. Ingraham, head of the state's
National Equal Rights League, founded Republican clubs and mobilized more
than 50,000 black voters. Some New Orleans carpetbaggers soon found themselves politically empowered when General Philip H. Sheridan sent them "up
from New Orleans [as registrars] to register the voters." He named almost
two hundred registrars without appointing a single black. Because scalawags
were involved only to a limited degree in organizing black voters or in making

35. *Dictionary of American History,* rev. ed. (New York: Scribner, 1976), 3: 207–8; F. Wayne
Binning, "Carpetbaggers' Triumph: The Louisiana Election of 1868," *LH* 14 (winter 1973): 26;
Warmoth diary, 27 February 1867; Warmoth, *War, Politics, and Reconstruction,* 30, 51; William
Kellogg to William E. Chandler, 17 December 1866, William E. Chandler Papers, Library of Con-
gress; Ted Tunnell, ed., *Carpetbagger from Vermont: The Autobiography of Marshall Harvey
Twitchell* (Baton Rouge, 1989), 109–10.

36. Fayette Copeland, "The New Orleans Press and the Reconstruction," *LHQ* 30 (January
1947): 161–62; Benjamin F. Butler, William D. Kelley, Nathaniel P. Banks et al. to Edward Mc-
Pherson, 23 February 1867, McPherson Papers; Durant to Henry Clay Warmoth, 2 February
1866, Warmoth Papers.

alliances across racial lines, they would eventually pay a heavy cost by having the carpetbaggers seize political control of Louisiana.[37]

By spring 1867, scalawags had taken different paths into the Republican Party. Some, such as the Wellses and the Taliaferros, backed the reelection of Lincoln in 1864 and now returned to that party. A larger group, Congressional Reconstruction supporters since 1863, such as Benjamin F. Flanders and Rufus Waples, founded the state's party in September 1865 and later backed the Southern Loyalists Convention. Others, such as Michael Hahn and R. K. Howell, had favored recalling the 1864 constitutional convention until that resulted in the New Orleans riot of July 1866, and the only road left led to the Republicans. Still others backed Johnson and his National Union Party movement until their cause was overwhelmed in the fall 1866 congressional election, leaving former Whigs like John Ray and Wade H. Hough more comfortable with the Republicans than with the Democrats. Finally there were those such as James Longstreet who believed that the Lost Cause was indeed lost. They concluded they could best help the nation, as well as themselves, by serving the party whose policies had triumphed, the Republican Party.[38]

Only a few scalawags entered the Louisiana Republican Party after 1866, mostly former Whigs from outside New Orleans. North Louisiana converts included former conservative unionists such as congressman-elect Ray of Monroe and former state senator Hough of Caldwell Parish. Ray, who was in and out of trouble with the Confederacy throughout the war, went on to be elected to Congress in 1865. Hough, while representing his district in the secession convention, "voted against the measure and . . . was one of the 'very few' who refused to sign that Treasonable Ordinance," yet later he "took an unwilling part in the Rebellion" as a Confederate officer. Ray and Hough attended the pro-Johnson national convention in 1866 but joined the Republican Party soon after passage of the Reconstruction acts. John T. Ludeling of Monroe, whom Warmoth appointed as the state's chief justice on Ray's recommendation, also became a Republican in 1867. Other Whigs who turned Republican in 1867–68 included the Breda brothers, physician Alexander P.

37. Uzee, "Beginnings of the Louisiana Republican Party," 209; Eric Foner, ed., *Freedom's Lawmakers: A Directory of Black Officeholders during Reconstruction* (Baton Rouge, 1996), 62, 113–14.

38. "Grand Ratification Meeting," newspaper clipping, n.p., n.d., "National Union Club," with "List of the Members of the Club," Warmoth Papers; *Proceedings of the Convention of the Republican Party of Louisiana*, 10–13, 37–38; Vandal, *New Orleans Riot*; *Reporter*, 30 October 1866.

Breda and attorney J. Earnest Breda of Natchitoches. Unlike most who became Republicans, they did not claim to have been antisecessionists or anti-Confederates.[39]

Robert E. Lee's "Old War Horse," General Longstreet, a postwar resident of New Orleans engaged in cotton brokerage, became a prized Republican convert in the summer of 1867. In no aspect did Longstreet fit the public's image of a scalawag. Although he initially opposed secession, following the fall of Fort Sumter he resigned his commission in the United States Army. Longstreet, like many former Confederates in early 1867, counseled cooperation to effect reunion through Congressional Reconstruction. Soon after, Longstreet heard an address by Senator Henry Wilson, who was touring the South. Longstreet said he was "agreeably surprised to hear such fairness and frankness from a politician whom [he] had been taught to believe harsh in his feelings toward the people of the South."[40]

In early June, Longstreet went over to the Republicans. He denounced the national Democratic Party for impeding Reconstruction. Shortly after he wrote to Robert E. Lee, enclosing newspaper clippings of his published letters: "Either those who have conquered or those who have been conquered must make concessions." Longstreet hoped Lee would follow his course; as for himself, he had reached a fork in the road and taken the path less traveled by fellow southerners. His wife, Helen, considered this decision "the noblest act of her husband's life." Writing to fellow Louisiana Republican Robert H. Taliaferro, Longstreet explained his rationale. His purpose was to "save the little that is left" of the South. Further resistance, he believed, would only lead to "confiscation & expatriation." Since the black man had been given the vote, Longstreet believed southerners "should exercise such influence over that vote, as to prevent its being injurious." He saw that as being possible "only ... as Republicans." [41]

During 1867, struggles erupted between the combined forces of Warmoth's

39. Hough to Andrew Johnson, 24 July 1866, J. Madison Wells to Andrew Johnson, 7 August 1865, Hough to U. S. Grant, 20 August 1871, RG 60; Williams, "John Ray," 241–61; John Ray to Henry Clay Warmoth, 30 May 1868, Warmoth Papers; *Biographical and Historical Memoirs of Northwest Louisiana* (Chicago, 1890), 325–26.

40. William L. Richter, "James Longstreet: From Rebel to Scalawag," *LH* 11 (summer 1970): 216–17; Piston, *Lee's Tarnished Lieutenant,* 104–5.

41. Longstreet to Robert E. Lee, 8 June 1867, and newspaper clipping, n.d., James Longstreet Papers, Rare Book, Manuscript, and Special Collections Library, Duke University; Longstreet to R. H. Taliaferro, 4 July 1867, cited in Piston, *Lee's Tarnished Lieutenant,* 106.

GAR and the conventioneers on one side (the two having fused) and the pure radicals of educated blacks and white radicals on the other side. Because the GAR and its allies were less radical than their opponents, their enemies labeled them the "Compromisers." With Durant in Washington managing the Southern Republican Association and practicing law and Flanders guarding his lucrative Treasury Department position, pure radical leadership fell to Louis Roudanez, a leader in the free black community and publisher of the *New Orleans Tribune.* Both factions vied for the freedmen, now a voting majority. Because free blacks generally were more educated and owned property, they considered themselves the freedman's natural leaders. Carpetbaggers, on the other hand, saw themselves as representatives of a superior society, saviors of the Union, and emancipators of the freedmen.[42]

General Sheridan used both factions to reconstruct Louisiana. He removed a number of state and local officials, including Governor James Madison Wells, whose conduct he felt had been "as sinuous as a mark left in dust by the movement of a snake." He filled these offices with northern-born scalawags associated with the pure radicals, including former congressman Flanders as governor. Sheridan also worked with Warmoth's camp by allowing the GAR to politicize blacks. After Thomas W. Conway, a Warmoth supporter, returned from a swing through the South addressing "hundreds of thousands of poor and ignorant freedmen and poor whites," Conway and Warmoth went "into the parishes" to urge the registration of blacks. [43]

At the state's convention in June 1867, each wing of Louisiana's Republican Party won partial victories. Pure radicals pushed through resolutions requiring nominees to the upcoming constitutional convention include equal numbers of blacks and whites and naming the *New Orleans Tribune* the party's official organ. But the compromisers scored a greater and more enduring victory by using clever parliamentary manipulations to pack the party's executive committee with their own, an indication they possessed most of the political experience. Because most scalawags feared black power and had never identified with Durant's radicals, a majority eventually gravitated to the compromisers.[44]

42. Uzee, "Beginnings of the Louisiana Republican Party," 209; Binning, "Carpetbaggers' Triumph," 21–22, 26; Thomas J. Durant to Warmoth, 28 March 1867, Warmoth Papers.
43. Ficklen, *History of Reconstruction in Louisiana,* 187–90; Fifth Military District Headquarters to *New Orleans Tribune,* 6 June 1867, clipping, Flanders Papers; Binning, "Carpetbaggers' Triumph," 27.
44. Binning, "Carpetbaggers' Triumph," 27.

Blacks and carpetbaggers filled two-thirds of the seats in the constitutional convention that met at the Mechanics' Institute, scene of the 1866 race riot. Delegates chose James G. Taliaferro as convention president. Because they gave a few party leaders floor privileges, Warmoth and Conway could direct the strategy of the compromisers. Wartime unionists led the less-well-organized pure radicals. Typically, pure radical whites had been brought up in the North, had settled in antebellum New Orleans as young professionals, had been Andrew Jackson Democrats before the war, and had taken the oath of allegiance shortly after the fall of New Orleans in 1862. They opposed the "convention of 1864, and the Government it had created," the recalling of "that *dead* 1864 Convention" in 1866, and "H. C. Warmoth and his Carpet[-bag] followers." [45]

Voting followed factional lines on bread-and-butter issues but otherwise fluctuated along different lines. Carpetbaggers voted consistently radical, conservatives consistently reactionary, but blacks and scalawags voted according to whether or not they represented a New Orleans district. By a narrow vote of 46 to 45, pure radicals secured black allegiance to the *New Orleans Tribune,* making it the state's official printer. But beyond that, Warmoth's men took command. They defined office-holding qualifications as having citizenship and two years state residency and set the gubernatorial age requirement at twenty-five, making Warmoth eligible. They also created a voter registration board to supervise registration and elections.[46]

During the convention, the state Republican Party convened in January 1868. Delegates nominated Warmoth for governor by a small margin, 45 to 43, over Francis E. Dumas, a wealthy free man of color, who was backed by the pure radicals and the *New Orleans Tribune.* Dumas refused to accept the nomination for lieutenant governor, and delegates chose Oscar J. Dunn, a freeborn mulatto, who served briefly as a Union army captain.[47]

Tribune publisher Louis Roudanez circulated a petition to convention delegates to nominate Taliaferro to head another ticket, with Dumas as his running mate. Warmoth's faction quickly retaliated by replacing the *Tribune* as

45. Binning, "Carpetbaggers' Triumph," 31–32; Ficklen, *History of Reconstruction in Louisiana,* 193–94; Thomas Conway to Charles Sumner, 6 January 1868, Sumner Papers.

46. Richard L. Hume, "The 'Black and Tan' Constitutional Conventions of 1867–1870 in Ten Former Confederate States: A Study of Their Membership" (Ph.D. diss., University of Washington, 1969), 104–27.

47. Binning, "Carpetbaggers' Triumph," 32–34.

the official organ with the GAR's *New Orleans Republican*. The faction also expelled nine "disorganizers" from the party, including those who had signed the petition nominating Taliaferro. Shortly after, Conway went to Washington and persuaded Edward McPherson, clerk of the House of Representatives, to divest the United States government's printing business from the *Tribune* and award it to the *Opelousas Saint Landry Progress*, edited by one of Warmoth's convention floor leaders, Michel Vidal.[48]

Although poles apart politically, Taliaferro and the pure radicals received the support of Democrats. Democrats had little chance and chose to concentrate on winning seats in the legislature. The election became a contest between outsiders and insiders. It pitted carpetbaggers and their freedmen allies against free men of color and white radicals, who were aided by Democratic voters. The pro-Taliaferro press referred to Warmoth as "an adventurer" and Taliaferro as "an old citizen . . . [and] man of character and intelligence." Pro-Warmoth newspapers pointed out that both Taliaferro and Dumas had been slaveholders in 1860 and that Taliaferro originally opposed the Emancipation Proclamation. They also accused Dumas and his sponsor Roudanez of being more pro-French than pro-American.[49]

Many scalawags failed to support Taliaferro because his candidacy divided their party. Writing to Taliaferro, Ray affirmed his willingness to help establish the "Republican Party and [its] policy firmly in the State." He believed Louisiana's "peace and prosperity depend[ed] on it." But Ray refused to campaign for his friend because his candidacy divided the party. Even Roudanez's editor Jean-Charles Houzeau, said he could not "logically reject" the verdict of the party's "nominating convention." He understood "Franco-African" feeling toward "Yankee adventurers" like Warmoth, men who "regarded the colored race" merely as a means for their "profit and advancement." Still he found "the war cry against the Yankees, in the mouth of men of color [to be] illogical, misplaced, and unfortunate."[50]

Despite solid white support for Taliaferro and Dumas, Warmoth and Dunn

---

48. Ibid., 35; Current, *Those Terrible Carpetbaggers*, 77.

49. Binning, "Carpetbaggers' Triumph," 37–38.

50. Ibid., 34–35; William P. Kellogg to William E. Chandler, 13 January 1868, William E. Chandler Papers; J. R. G. Pitkin, Letter of JRG. Pitkin of New Orleans, La. to Hon. B. F. Butler, pamphlet (n.p., n.d.); Ray to James G. Taliaferro, 21 March 1868, Taliaferro and Family Papers; Houzeau, *My Passage*, 150–51.

trounced them 64,941 to 38,046 in the April 1868 election. Carpetbagger William P. Kellogg explained that "there were too many Northern politicians [there] to lose [the] Election." Voters also ratified the constitution. Almost 58 percent of voters cast their ballot in favor; of those, only about 5 percent outside of New Orleans were white. Although Orleans Parish did not record its votes by race, it is unlikely the percentage of whites voting exceeded the percentage of favorable white votes in adjoining Jefferson Parish (4.5). So, if 5 percent of the whites voted for the constitution there, then New Orleans Parish contained about 750 white Republicans compared with about 1,500 outside of the parish. Of the 2,250 or so white voters, many may have been carpetbaggers. Whatever the case, it appears only a few hundred scalawags existed in Louisiana.[51]

One study of Louisiana's scalawags found them often to be educated professionals—such as businessmen, journalists, lawyers, and physicians—who were no strangers to politics and officeholding. Most were strong unionists, dedicated to the American national government despite the wartime and postwar hostility of their neighbors. They wielded their greatest impact during the early phases of Reconstruction by providing officeholders and by representing their party at the 1864 Republican National Convention and the Southern Loyalists Convention of 1866, as well as by reconvening the 1864 constitutional convention in 1866, which caused the New Orleans riot. By 1867 all of them accepted political rights for blacks. But they never supported social equality for blacks, not even for the educated free blacks of New Orleans. Unfortunately, some were typical "Louisiana spoilsmen engaging in corrupt business deals and shady political maneuvers."[52]

In Arkansas, the Reconstruction Acts united unionists of all stripes into the Republican Party. Along with only three blacks, loyalists met at Little Rock in April 1867. Following a round of speeches, they adopted resolutions urging black enfranchisement and Confederate disfranchisement, elected a central committee chaired by Minnesota carpetbagger Benjamin F. Rice, and selected James M. Johnson, Albert Bishop, and Elisha Baxter to represent Arkansas's

51. Binning, "Carpetbaggers' Triumph," 38; Kellogg to William E. Chandler, 26 April 1868, William E. Chandler Papers; Francis J. Wetta, "The Louisiana Scalawags" (Ph.D. diss., Louisiana State University, 1977), 276–81; Donald W. Davis, "Ratification of the Constitution of 1868— Record of Voters," *LH* 6 (summer 1965): 301–5.

52. Wetta, "Louisiana Scalawags," 368–76.

"loyal men" before Congress. According to one account, carpetbaggers "dominated the proceedings," and scalawags calmly yielded leadership to the "newcomers."[53]

By 1868, as in Louisiana, carpetbaggers (mostly Midwesterners) controlled the Arkansas Republican Party. Most newcomers had arrived as Union army officers during the war. General Powell Clayton of Kansas, with his graceful but haughty bearing and enormous mustache, had served as a cavalry commander and commandant at Pine Bluff. He purchased a nearby plantation and married Adaline McGraw of Helena. According to Clayton, he lived peacefully "until ill treatment by his former Confederate neighbors became so pronounced." He felt he had "to take a political stand for the preservation of life and property." So he worked with the "leading Union men . . . [in] organizing a party in harmony with the General Government."[54]

While scalawags accepted black suffrage, mostly Freedmen's Bureau agents and black preachers organized blacks into Union Leagues. According to one observer, "the prospect of voting filled [blacks] with pleasure," and voting became their "principal topic of conversation." This helped Republicans win the November 1867 election to hold a constitutional convention by a two-to-one majority and for them to elect most delegates. They garnered more than 7,000 white votes, mostly from the same scalawags who voted for Republican James R. Berry as state auditor in 1866. Most scalawags elected had been wartime unionists who resided in the westernmost part of the state, while the seventeen carpetbaggers and eight blacks came from predominantly black-populated districts elsewhere, especially from those along larger river valleys flowing into the Mississippi. [55]

A few scalawags were former Confederates who went on to become significant Republican officeholders. George M. McCown of Columbia County, like his older West Point–educated brother, John P. McCown, served as a

53. Harrell, *Brooks and Baxter War,* 33–34; Staples, *Reconstruction in Arkansas,* 166.

54. Ellenburg, "Reconstruction in Arkansas," 35–37; Powell Clayton, *The Aftermath of the Civil War in Arkansas* (New York, 1915), 35–36; Randy Finley, *From Slavery to Uncertain Freedom: The Freedmen's Bureau in Arkansas, 1865–1869* (Fayetteville, 1996), 54–55; *Encyclopedia of the New West,* 56.

55. Harrell, *Brooks and Baxter War,* 39–40; *Debates and Proceedings of the Convention which Assembled at Little Rock, January 7th, 1868* . . . (Little Rock, 1868), 49; Foner, *Freedom's Lawmakers,* 227–28; Richard L. Hume, "Membership of the Arkansas Constitutional Convention of 1868: A Case Study of Republican Factionalism in the Reconstruction South," *JSH* 39 (May 1973): 185, 199–200.

Confederate officer. But afterward he "vibrated to the opposite extreme" and served as a Republican circuit judge. John M. Bradley, a big man, served as a minister in Methodist churches before he raised a company of Confederate troops. After Appomattox, he practiced law. Although he referred to himself as a "back-slidden" preacher, he still spiced his speech with a sprinkling of scripture. Bradley waged an unsuccessful fight in the convention using scripture to try to outlaw miscegenation. Colonel James T. Elliott of Ouachita County claimed to be a "truly and thoroughly 'reconstructed rebel.'" Before the war, the railroad promoter had fought secession. Now he was "glad to see the Union restored." He felt he showed "evidence . . . of the sincerity of [his] repentance" by joining the party that "vanquished secession." [56]

Although scalawags outnumbered carpetbaggers in the 1868 Arkansas constitutional convention, the latter dominated the proceedings by chairing most of the committees and by having one of their own, Thomas M. Bowen of Crawford County, serve as convention president. Both groups backed political rights for blacks, but scalawags split over extending social rights to freedmen. Many scalawags voted with conservatives for antimiscegenation measures, an issue ultimately left to the legislature to resolve. Despite these differences, Arkansas Republicans united to adopt the constitution by a vote of 46 to 20, and in the March 13 referendum boycotted by conservatives, voters ratified it almost unanimously. [57]

In Texas during spring 1867, Union League councils—whose members ranged from a handful to hundreds—mushroomed from the eastern Texas piney woods to the Uvalde County frontier. "The meetings [were] held with closed doors," commented one shocked conservative, and both races met at "the same time in the same room." Wartime refugees, some of whom founded the Texas Loyal League of New Orleans in 1864, organized some of the councils. Other organizers included black preachers and Freedmen's Bureau officers. The state council's executive committee, headed by John L. Haynes of Austin, included six loyalists and three blacks. While Texas scalawags, with rare exception, rejected the idea of racial equality, their attitude differed from

---

56. John Hallum, *The Diary of an Old Lawyer; or, Scenes behind the Curtain* (Nashville, 1895), 437–41; Paul C. Palmer, "Miscegenation as an Issue in the Arkansas Constitutional Convention of 1868," *ArkHQ* 24 (summer 1965): 100–1; David Y. Thomas, *Arkansas in War and Reconstruction, 1861–1874* (Little Rock, 1926), 407; *BDAC*, 908, 1127; Goodspeed, *Biographical and Historical Memoirs of Eastern Arkansas . . .* (Chicago, 1889), 416–18.

57. Hume, "Membership of the Arkansas Constitutional Convention," 191–202.

that of conservatives. They believed in the freedman's ability to progress as well as to labor. They were willing to join hands with him for mutual protection. [58]

Texas Republicans were helped tremendously by General Philip H. Sheridan's subordinate for Texas, General Charles Griffin. Griffin interpreted the first two Reconstruction Acts similarly to his chief: state and local governments were provisional only and "subject to be abolished, modified, controlled, or superseded." Griffin could not find a single state officeholder "whose antecedents [would] justify" trusting him with "assisting in [voter] registration." At his instructions, Freedmen's Bureau agents surveyed seventy-six counties during April 1867 to compile a list of potential officeholders. They catalogued such information as prior federal service, race, occupation, and war record. Of the 846 mentioned, 104 saw service in the Union army, 38 had fled the state as refugees during the war, and 74 were literate freedmen.[59]

In April 1867, the Texas executive committee, residing in Austin and created by the 1866 legislative caucus of radicals, joined with some "colored fellow citizens" to lay the groundwork for organizing the state's Republican Party. They convened in the capitol on May 27 and issued a call for a convention in Houston on July 4, 1867, at the Harris County Courthouse. The meeting, branded the "Radico Congo" by the conservative press, attracted about 600 delegates from twenty-seven counties, a majority of whom were blacks. Convention chairman Elisha M. Pease thought that "the proceedings were conducted in good order" and that the speeches were "fully equal to those . . . heard in any Convention [he had] ever attended in the state." The delegates adopted resolutions favoring Congressional Reconstruction and elected an executive committee dominated by scalawags.[60]

58. George T. Ruby to James P. Newcomb, 1 July 1869; Thomas H. Stribling to Whom It May Concern, 18 April 1867, Joseph Welch to Newcomb, 11 September 1869, James Pearson Newcomb Jr. Papers, Center for American History; *Constitution of Union League of the State of Texas* (Austin, 1867), 1–24; *New Orleans Times,* 19, 24, 28 February 1864; William A. Russ Jr., "Radical Disfranchisement in Texas, 1867–1870," *SwHQ* 38 (July 1934): 43–46; Pease to Carrie Pease, 3 August 1867, Graham-Pease Collection.

59. William L. Richter, "Tyrant and Reformer: General Griffin Reconstructs Texas, 1865–1866," *Prologue* 10 (winter 1978): 232–34; Russ, "Radical Disfranchisement in Texas," 40–44; Robert Shook, "Toward a List of Reconstruction Loyalists," *SwHQ* 76 (January 1973): 315–20; W. C. Phillips to J. P. Newcomb, 6 September 1867, Newcomb Papers.

60. Diary, 15 May 1867, Bartholomew Papers; *Flake's Galveston Bulletin,* 25 May 1867; *Austin Southern Intelligencer,* 18 April 1867; Pease to Carrie Pease, 11 July 1867, Graham-Pease Collection; Carl H. Moneyhon, *Republicanism in Reconstruction Texas* (Austin, 1980), 65.

Pease had been in Hartford, Connecticut, during the fall and winter since attending the Southern Loyalists Convention in early September 1866, except for two visits to Washington in February and June. Secretary of the Navy Gideon Welles, who had known Pease since childhood, believed that his "old friend had been summoned home to replace Governor James W. Throckmorton," as part of "a conspiracy" by congressional radicals and General Sheridan. In July, shortly after Congress adopted the third Reconstruction Act, empowering commanders to remove and appoint officeholders, General Griffin, aided by Pease, who was now back in Austin, compiled a list of potential officials to ranking state posts. On August 3, Pease received a telegram from General Sheridan in New Orleans announcing Pease's appointment as Throckmorton's replacement.[61]

Some loyalists "would have preferred Genl. [Edmund J.] Davis, or someone whom they considered harsher or sterner than Pease." Pease's supporters, however, believed his opponents within the Republican Party to be "impractical." General Griffin soon replaced other state officials with Austin Republicans and named others from throughout the state as justices to the state supreme court. For other district and local offices, of which Texas had about 2,500, Griffin and Pease received recommendations from individual Republicans, league members, bureau agents, and army post commanders.[62]

During September 1867, a yellow fever epidemic, which had swept across coastal Texas and advanced into the state's interior, claimed Griffin as one of its victims. His replacement was General Joseph J. Reynolds, a former classmate of Grant at West Point. Reynolds had been recently stationed on the Rio Grande and before then in Arkansas, where he had become familiar with Reconstruction politics. Reynolds removed as many anti-reconstructionist conservatives as possible from office in the state's one hundred–plus counties before General Winfield S. Hancock, President Johnson's replacement for Sheridan as commander of the Fifth Military District, arrived. Altogether Reynolds replaced several hundred officeholders in more than one-half of the

61. Pease Speech, 1880, p. 4, Pease to Charles Griffin, 22 July 1867, Pease to Carrie Pease, 3 August 1867, Graham-Pease Collection; *Flake's Galveston Bulletin,* 26 June 1867; Beale, *Diary of Gideon Welles,* 2: 641; 3: 105–6, 146–47; Fleming, *Documentary History of Reconstruction,* 1: 415–18.

62. Shook, "Federal Occupation and Administration of Texas," 314–20, 348, 374–76; Executive Record Book 283, pp. 16–30, 66; John P. Carrier, "A Political History of Texas during the Reconstruction, 1863–1874" (Ph.D. diss., Vanderbilt University, 1971), 202–3; *Flake's Galveston Bulletin,* 15 June 1867.

counties before the end of 1867. Pease believed Johnson had appointed Hancock "to fritter away and destroy the effects" of the Reconstruction laws. Hancock most likely would have turned out of office the last-minute appointees of Reynolds except that Grant advised against it. Feeling hamstrung, Hancock requested a transfer. His tenure lasted only three months.[63]

Since Texas Republicans, like most Republicans in the South, were not linked by longtime party allegiance, class, or even race, success frequently caused factionalism. Spreading schisms appeared within the party over ab initio (declaring all state legislation adopted since March 1, 1861, null and void), division of Texas into two or more states, and the disfranchisement of former Rebels. Moderate Republicans, led by Pease and Andrew J. Hamilton, opposed these issues because of their possible economic and political consequences, whereas radical Republicans, under the leadership of former judge and former general Davis, favored them. Judge Davis of Corpus Christi was aided and abetted by two Austin bachelors in Pease's cabinet, comptroller Morgan C. Hamilton and attorney general William Alexander (referred to by an opposition newspaper as "the misty Attorney General and the pious Comptroller").[64]

The constitutional convention election, held February 10 to 14, amounted to a clean sweep for Republicans. Fewer than 5,000 voters cast their ballots against the holding of a convention. Some 83 elected delegates were Republicans. Of these, 74 were whites, mostly native southerners or longtime residents. At least 15 delegates had soldiered in the Union army. Some had at one time held a state office in Texas, including nine former legislators, six judges, two former congressmen, and two former congressmen of the Republic of Texas. Others had held local offices since the war. Unlike some black-and-tan conventions, this one offered the state's best Republican talent.[65]

When the convention met in Austin on June 1, 1868, schism within the state Republican Party surfaced immediately when Davis, backed by Hamilton

63. Ramsdell, *Reconstruction in Texas,* 174–75; Shook, "Federal Occupation and Administration of Texas," 348–49; Pease Speech, 1880, pp. 4, 10, Pease to Carrie Pease, 25 January 1868, Graham-Pease Collection; Diary, 15 October 1867, Bartholomew Papers.

64. *Austin Daily Republican,* 12 December 1868; Ramsdell, *Reconstruction in Texas,* 176–80; Brown, "Annals of Travis County," 23, Brown Collection; Hamilton to Pease, 28 October 1867, Graham-Pease Collection; William L. Richter, *The Army in Texas during Reconstruction* (College Station, Tex., 1991), 123; W. C. Phillips to August Siemering, 29 November 1867, Newcomb Papers.

65. William Alexander to Charles Sumner, 24 March 1868, Sumner Papers; Waller, *Colossal Hamilton,* 112–13; Moneyhon, *Republicanism in Reconstruction Texas,* 236–47.

and other ab initio supporters, was elected president of the convention. Some may have simply voted for Davis because of admiration for the man's courage. Republicans held a convention in Austin on August 12 to endorse the national party's candidates and platform. Harmony ended, however, when the party platform committee failed to endorse ab initio, and about fifteen of its supporters walked out of the convention. Less than a week later, the constitutional convention once again considered ab initio, and in keeping with the Republican Party's stand, defeated the issue 45 to 28. A closing chaotic convention scene witnessed walkouts, fistfights, and further radical defeat, as they were unable to prevent the convention's setting a July date for the general election. Twenty-two protesting members of the Davis faction, which by now appeared to be a coalition of divisionists, ab initio defenders, blacks, carpetbaggers, and Germans, refused to sign the constitution.[66]

Although the convention election of February 1868 swept blacks and carpetbaggers—who were previously spectators—into the political arena, the impact was not as great as in other states undergoing Reconstruction. Statewide, blacks generally voted for longtime unionists. Still, in heavily black-populated areas between the Brazos and Trinity Rivers, many cast ballots for blacks and carpetbaggers associated with the Union League. Most carpetbag politicians were former army officers stationed in Texas after the war, primarily with the Freedmen's Bureau. Texas attracted fewer settlers from the North during Reconstruction than many other southern states. Of the high-level positions treated in this study, carpetbaggers held fewer than one-fifth and blacks never held any.[67]

In the Texas Republican Party, blacks and carpetbaggers played supporting roles. Carpetbaggers collaborated with scalawags rather than controlled them, as came to be the case in Arkansas and Louisiana. During 1867–68 in Texas, about two hundred Republicans represented the party at the constitutional convention, at state and national political meetings, on the party's state executive committee, as executive department chiefs, and in the state courts. Most participated in the party's formation and with few exceptions identified with

66. *Austin Daily Republican,* 13 August 1868; E. M. Pease to Carrie Pease, 24 June 1868, Graham-Pease Collection; *Proceedings of the Texas Republican State Convention Assembled at Austin, August 12, 1868* (Austin, 1868), 9–10.

67. Baggett, "Rise and Fall of the Texas Radicals," 83–87; *American Annual Cyclopaedia, 1868,* 729; J. Mason Brewer, *Negro Legislators of Texas and Their Descendants: A History of the Negro in Texas Politics from Reconstruction to Disfranchisement* (Dallas, 1935), 64–72.

it for more than a decade. From information included in the 1867 Texas Voter Registration List, it is possible to classify some 177 of these Republicans: 133 (75 percent) were scalawags, 31 (18 percent) were blacks, while carpetbaggers numbered only 13 (7 percent).[68]

For scalawags everywhere, the decision to join the Republican Party in 1867 came suddenly for some and slowly for others. Such a choice often involved, as Carl N. Degler says, "several reasons . . . primary and secondary," some which they were "not entirely aware of" themselves. For most, the choice did not represent an abrupt break with the past but simply the taking of the last of several steps. Many as former Whigs disliked the Democratic Party, identifying it with demagoguery and disunion; during the war, the majority were anti-Confederates. Consequently, most were willing to see Confederates punished, if necessary, to restore the Union; and ultimately, as they beheld the peace being lost, they agreed to accept black suffrage—as "a weapon, not a cause"—rather than let their enemies rule over them.[69]

In the Upper South and Southwest, most scalawags had been part of some groups that caused them to become Republicans. They were not acting in isolation. Some joined others in opposing secession and resisting the Confederacy as refugees, soldiers and peace party members. Unless those individuals despised the policies of the Lincoln administration, they became predisposed toward eventually accepting black suffrage and becoming Republicans. In all these states during 1865–66, they formed unionist parties opposing coalitions of conservatives and former Confederates. They generally met defeat in elections for public office, with which they, to a degree, felt they should be rewarded. They also felt they needed public office to protect themselves as a group. Failing to win the white man's vote, they reluctantly accepted the black man's vote to gain power and protection. In the process, they became Republicans.

68. *Texas Republican Convention 1868*, 220–23; Hume, " 'Black and Tan' Constitutional Conventions," 637–53; Texas Voter Registration List, 1867, Texas State Library and Archives Commission; Eighth Census, Schedule I, RG 29.
    69. Degler, *Other South*, 202.

8

~

The Birth of a Party

General John D. Pope, a native Kentuckian, assumed command of the Third Military District—Georgia, Alabama, and Florida—at Atlanta in April 1867. He appointed Edward Hulbert, recently of Atlanta, to supervise the registration of the state's voters. Hulbert, an official with the Southern Express Company headquartered in Augusta, came to the South from Connecticut in 1854. During 1860–61 and 1865–66 he had worked closely with another executive named Rufus Bullock, who had recently, along with other Augusta businessmen, embraced the Republican Party. General Pope directed that one of the three registrars in each district be a black. Bureau agents recommended many of the whites, and they in turn recommended black registrars. Many former Union soldiers, as well as some scalawags, received appointments. In all, slightly more whites than blacks were registered, 102,411 to 98,507.[1]

Hand in hand with voter registration, Union League activity hastened the formation of local Republican parties. Local councils "assumed," as Henry P. Farrow said, "the character of political agencies," recruiting members, sponsoring rallies, passing platforms, and enlisting and endorsing candidates. They also developed election strategies, such as selecting black "captains" to lead

1. Nathans, *Losing the Peace*, 33–34; Thompson, *Reconstruction in Georgia*, 186; Alan Conway, *The Reconstruction of Georgia* (Minneapolis, 1966), 142, 144; *Atlanta New Era*, 25 May 1867; Paul A. Cimbala, *Under the Guardianship of the Nation: The Freedmen's Bureau and the Reconstruction of Georgia, 1865–1870* (Athens, 1997), 44, 68–70.

their people to the polls. Outside of urban areas, black leaders, especially African Methodist Episcopal preachers employed by the Republican Congressional Committee, turned blacks into voting Republicans. By November 1867, Republicans had organized leagues in all but 15 of Georgia's 132 counties, with memberships of about 28,000 whites, mostly in North Georgia, and 60,000 blacks.[2]

White Republicans put most of their effort into holding public rallies in the towns protected by federal troops. In Augusta on Saturday, April 13, at the parade ground, speakers of both races addressed about 1,000 people, the majority of whom were blacks. Herschel V. Johnson, Stephen A. Douglas's running mate in 1860, initially thought the meeting's purpose was to consider "calmly the interest and duty of white and black people in view of their new and altered relation." He was unaware until he arrived that "radical leaders had packed the meeting and prepared a set of resolutions to form a radical party." Still, Johnson and another spokesman hoped they could avert the calamity "of the two races being arrayed in hostile political organizations." Johnson appealed to blacks on the basis of a shared culture with whites. He told them their former master could be trusted to be their best friend. But such talk failed to rule the day. Lewis Carter, a black Congregational minister, who followed Johnson as a speaker, questioned the wisdom of Johnson's words: "That old ship, the institution of slaves is dead . . . Shall I employ its captain . . . to bear it through the ocean again?" The crowd responded with a resounding "No! No!" Johnson and his friends had little hope to offer blacks other than a well-ordered, deferential society—too little, too late for dreamers of equality.[3]

Augusta, along with Atlanta, was the cradle of the Georgia Republican Party. There an alliance emerged between the forces of John E. Bryant, including the Georgia Educational Association, and former supporters of President Johnson, including Benjamin Conley and Foster Blodgett, former mayors of the city who allied themselves with Bullock, superintendent of the Southern Express Company and president of the Macon and Augusta Railway. In March 1867, Bryant, Conley, and Blodgett crossed over to the Republicans.

2. Drago, *Black Politicians*, 31–34; *Harper's Weekly*, 13 April 1867, p. 227; Robert E. Perdue, *The Negro in Savannah, 1865–1900* (New York, 1973), 42; *Atlanta New Era*, 10 May 1867; Jones, "Political Career of Henry Pattillo Farrow," 18–19.

3. Percy S. Flippin, contributor, "From the Autobiography of Herschel V. Johnson, 1856–1867," *American Historical Review* 30 (January 1925): 335; *Atlanta New Era*, 14 April 1867.

That spring, the influence of the new political alliance extended widely through Bullock and Conley's railroad interests, Conley and Blodgett's previous Whig connections, Bryant's influence among blacks, and Bullock's Southern Express Company.[4]

The foundation for the Augusta Ring, as it came to be called, developed when General Pope replaced the mayor and city council members, who were all soon up for reelection, installing Blodgett as mayor and others including Conley and Bullock as councilmen. This circumvented a possible takeover of the city government by carpetbaggers backed by blacks. Soon thereafter, Bryant welcomed Mayor Blodgett into the party before a freedmen's rally at city hall. Within days, the mayor hosted several party rallies, such as one on May 8, which was attended by 5,000 people, including hundreds of whites, who gathered to hear Senator Henry Wilson of Massachusetts. Blodgett hoped to unite his old working-class support with that of poor black men without offending the former. By midsummer segregated Republican clubs claimed 400 whites and 1,600 blacks. [5]

The Republican Party's first state convention occurred July 4 in Atlanta with black attendees in the majority. Urban county delegations were racially mixed. Atlanta's divided about equally between the two races. But almost totally white delegations came from the small towns of north Georgia and almost totally black from rural south Georgia. The delegates, most with Union League connections, adopted the name Union Republican Party of Georgia, approved a platform of five guiding principles—Congressional Reconstruction, equal rights, relief measures, free schools, and homestead laws—and elected a state executive committee chaired by Blodgett.[6]

Some scalawags, especially those from north Georgia, followed Joseph E. Brown's counsel to support Congressional Reconstruction. Hundreds preceded him into the Republican Party. Some, almost all of whom backed relief for Georgia debtors, ran for seats in the 1867 constitutional convention. For example, in Greene County and Oglethorpe County, east of Atlanta, the McWhorter brothers—James H., William H., and Robert L.—all former legislators, joined the pro-Reconstruction camp headed by former governor Brown. Their decision to ultimately become Republicans grew out of several factors: their original opposition to secession, their lack of "confidence that the South

4. Nathans, *Losing the Peace,* 57–58.
5. deTreville, "Reconstruction in Augusta," 54, 60–61, 64; *New York Herald,* 29 July 1867.
6. Nathans, *Losing the Peace,* 41–42.

would achieve her independence," their advocacy for an act "relieving people from debts," and their support to elect loyalists to the U. S. Senate in 1865.[7]

The military recruited loyalist candidates for seats in the constitutional convention as part of its responsibility to make certain the convention occurred. Such was the case with Charles H. Hopkins of Savannah, who qualified to take the 1862 loyalty oath because of his resistance to the Confederacy. With the help of black leaders, Hopkins reported his "district [had] gone for reconstruction by 15,000 maj," despite the efforts of Savannah's Democratic mayor and other enemies, all as "savage as rattlesnakes." Union Leagues also persuaded others to run for seats in the constitutional convention. In Atlanta, a Loyal League Committee solicited Dr. Nedom L. Angier of Atlanta to run for the convention because he had gone north during the war and now approved the Reconstruction Acts as "the most speedy road to peace."[8]

Most Georgia Democrats did not bother to vote, leaving the field to the Republicans. One source reported that proconvention votes represented 32,000 whites. The more than seventy scalawags elected had taken several different paths into the Republican Party. Some as hard-line unionists opposed not only secession but the Confederacy as well, demonstrating their unionism by fleeing from the state, sitting out all or most of the war, and by supporting the peace party candidate for governor, Joshua Hill. Shortly after the war, many of them joined the Union League and later supported the Southern Loyalists Convention in 1866. But most had supported, albeit in many cases halfheartedly, the Confederacy. Although some became Republicans before the beginning of Congressional Reconstruction, most did not.

Most originally opposed secession but backed the Confederacy; indeed, some had been Rebel officers, including convention president Josiah R. Parrott of Cartersville. Although he had attended the pro-Johnson National Union Convention in August 1866, Parrott now believed Congressional Reconstruction was the state's only way out of the dilemma. Such was also the case with Major Madison Bell of Homer, who, like Parrott, was an antisecessionist in 1861 before being called upon to defend the South. Bell, a farmer turned lawyer, raised a company of Confederate troops. When the war ended, he "accepted the defeat of . . . the South as the final solution of those great

7. *Manual of Georgia*, 22–23, 70–71; *Souvenir of Georgia and Florida*, 556.
8. Avery, *History of the State of Georgia*, 57, 119; Hopkins to Charles Sumner, 19 December 1867, Sumner Papers; Hopkins to William E. Chandler, 7 November 1867, William E. Chandler Papers; Foner, *Freedom's Lawmakers*, 38; *Manual of Georgia*, 4–5; *KKK Report*, Ga., 149–50.

questions of national politics." In 1867, he "favored the reconstruction measures as likely to afford the quickest relief to . . . the South." Bell perhaps
proved his sincerity as a Republican by naming his second son Ulysses S. Bell.[9]

Many antebellum settlers from the North won seats in the 1868 Georgia
constitutional convention, becoming, according to one scholar, its "most influential workers." Their influence derived from the factions they led, such as
with Bullock and Conley; the committees they chaired; and from their talent
as attorneys and debaters. On the average, these northern-born delegates had
resided in Georgia for more than a generation. Of the sixteen such men, only
Bullock had arrived shortly before the war. Amos T. Akerman of Elberton, a
Dartmouth graduate, and Henry K. McCay of Americus, a Princeton graduate, had both married southern belles after settling in the state as teachers.
Almost all opposed secession, but some later fought for the Confederacy, including General McCay and Colonel Akerman.[10]

Although a native of New Hampshire and a deeply religious man, Akerman
never questioned the legality or morality of slavery, even in his diary. He
turned later from teaching to law. His belief in the law ranked only slightly
below his faith. Like most northern-born Georgia scalawags, he was a Whig
before the war who believed that secession was misguided. But when secession
came, he yielded to what he thought to be "the irresistible" pressure of circumstances, including his upcoming marriage to "a Southern lady." He became "a heavy sufferer" because of the war, when his fortune fell from $15,000
to about $1,500. Akerman counted himself among Confederates who believed
that the war had settled once and forever the death of secession and slavery.
So he "urged [his] people to surrender all that was involved in the contest."
But they disliked his advice and many "became hostile." Because of his "com-
bativeness," he refused to yield "to such unreasonable condemnation." [11]

All in all, the convention attracted the best talent the Georgia Republican
Party had to offer. Several of the northern-born scalawags held office after the

9. Biographical File, Georgia Department of Archives and History; James Parrott to Andrew
Johnson, 21 July 1865, Johnson Papers; undated newspaper clipping in Henry P. Farrow Papers,
Hargrett Rare Book and Manuscript Library, University of Georgia, Athens; *Cyclopedia of Georgia*, 156–59; V. D. Lockhart, *Madison Bell: A Biographical Sketch of His Early Life and Education,
with a Brief Account of His Military and Official Career* (Atlanta, 1887), 25–26.

10. Coleman and Gurr, *Dictionary of Georgia Biography*, 1: 8–10, 218–19; *Manual of Georgia*,
4–5.

11. William S. McFeely, "Amos T. Akerman: The Lawyer and Racial Justice" in *Region, Race,
and Reconstruction*, 397–403.

convention ended, including Akerman, U.S. attorney general, and Bullock and Conley, governor. Others served as state cabinet officers and one, McCay, as a state supreme court justice. Many of the native scalawags in the convention later served as congressmen and high-ranking federal officeholders.

Originally the convention was to meet at Milledgeville, the small town that was Georgia's capital. But when General Pope learned the town's hotels would refuse rooms to black delegates, he commanded the convention to assemble on December 9 at Atlanta's city hall. As elsewhere, Republican delegates in Georgia divided into radicals and moderates. Moderate Republicans generally opposed unqualified black suffrage, officeholding by blacks, debtor relief measures, and widespread disfranchisement. They were smaller in numbers, unorganized, and less cohesive. But Democrats represented about one-fourth of the members, making it possible for moderates to win by gaining their support.[12]

On the issue of relief for debtors, intended to attract north Georgia and Wiregrass county voters, Republicans from those sections, as well as some of the area's Democrats, voted with the radicals. Radicals proved less successful on votes to guarantee the right of blacks to hold office, which they believed was implied in the right to vote. In exchange for unqualified black suffrage, radicals, including most blacks, voted against the disfranchisement of former Confederates. [13]

The Augusta Ring had the party caucus at the constitutional convention on March 7 rather than meet in a convention where they might be outnumbered by Henry P. Farrow's Union League followers. They nominated Bullock, endorsed the new constitution, and promised positions to individuals such as Brown, Angier, Akerman, and Farrow for pledges to back Bullock.[14] In the campaign that followed, relief and black officeholding became the major issues. Republicans played both to their advantage. Democrats helped by nominating former Confederate general John B. Gordon. Republicans concentrated much of their effort on winning the votes of farmers in north Georgia and in the Wiregrass counties of south Georgia. They reminded farmers that the

12. Nathans, *Losing the Peace*, 56–59, 64, 67–68; Hume, "'Black and Tan' Constitutional Conventions," 240–49; Conway, *Reconstruction of Georgia*, 153–54; Thompson, *Reconstruction in Georgia*, 193.

13. Nathans, *Losing the Peace*, 68–69; Thompson, *Reconstruction in Georgia*, 194–97.

14. Thompson, *Reconstruction in Georgia*, 201–2; *Atlanta New Era*, 6 March 1868; Nathans, *Losing the Peace*, 73–78; Farrow, *Hon. Henry P. Farrow*, 5.

Democrats opposed relief and that the new constitution guaranteed blacks the right to vote but not the right to hold office. At the same time, they told black voters they believed the constitution implied that blacks had the right to hold office.[15]

The constitution passed by almost 18,000 votes, while Bullock won by only 7,171 votes. Republicans won the state senate by a good margin, but carried the state house of representatives by only a slight one. Bullock won nine white majority counties in northeast Georgia, three in northwest Georgia, and another three on the state's southern border. Most of the north Georgia counties that voted Republican had large numbers of poor farmers on small plots. These counties had generally voted for Joseph E. Brown for governor in 1857. Bullock carried most of the majority black counties but by a smaller vote than in the convention.[16]

In Florida, Ossian B. Hart and others seeking to create a state party founded the probusiness Union Republican Club of Jacksonville in early 1867. Within six weeks, they recruited two hundred members from the town and the surrounding area. The members divided about equally into newcomers and longtime residents. The latter members were mostly wartime unionists, but they also counted some former secessionists, such as judges William Ledwith and Thomas T. Long, who were accused of being "blackhearted secesh . . . turned noisy republicans" to collect political plums. Because of his influence, Hart became state superintendent of voter registration. As elsewhere, in the Third Military District, Pope ordered Hart to give preference to civilians as registrars and to see that one of three registrars was a black. Hart combined his club responsibilities with his official ones. He appointed registrars, sent speakers to black rallies, and in myriad ways sought to further Reconstruction, such as by having the Union Republican Club sponsor a state convention in Tallahassee on July 11.[17]

Resentment of the Jacksonville club's influence, however, soon weakened Florida Republican unity. Antagonisms among Republicans surfaced when the Lincoln Brotherhood and the Union League competed to organize black voters. The brotherhood, led by politically moderate Freedmen's Bureau officers, including Thomas W. Osborn, bureau commander in Florida until June

15. Nathans, *Losing the Peace,* 88–101.
16. Ibid.
17. Davis, *Civil War and Reconstruction in Florida,* 472–73; Shofner, *Nor Is It Over Yet,* 165; *KKK Report,* Fla., 212–14, 255.

1866, won widespread black support in early 1867 before just as rapidly losing it to the more radical league. The league was led by a trio of northerners: William Sanders, a black former barber from Baltimore; Liberty Billings, a white minister possessed of a talent for "pulpitish political speeches"; and Daniel Richards, a former Illinois state senator with an influential friend back home, Congressman Elihu B. Washburne. For most of 1867, with funding from the Republican National Committee, they toured Florida in a mule-drawn wagon, which caused them to be called the "mule team." Richards only slightly exaggerated when he claimed they single-handedly "created the Republican Party in more than three-quarters" of the state.[18]

The Union League had been introduced during the war by others, including its first state president, A. A. Knight, a Lake City carpetbagger. But until 1867, its membership had been limited to whites in a few towns. Now black councils appeared throughout north Florida and league-sponsored rallies occurred often during spring 1867. By the end of April, chapters with blacks existed in over a dozen counties and in the towns of Tallahassee, Saint Augustine, Key West, and Pensacola. Night meetings included "musterings, haranguings and sermons, singing and praying, all looking to political results." Before summer's end, a council in opposition to the Union Republican Club appeared at Jacksonville as well as in almost every county. When the Republican convention of whites and blacks met at Tallahassee in July, the league controlled a majority of delegates. Billings attacked Hart, saying Hart had "lived too long in the atmosphere of slavery to be trusted." Then Osborn, supported by a black-white coalition, defeated Hart by a three-to-two margin for chairman. Hart boarded the next train back to Jacksonville.[19]

In spite of Richards's opinion that "two thirds, if not three fourths," of the delegates to Florida's constitutional convention at Tallahassee were "our friends," a conservative newspaper report estimating radicals at fewer than one-third eventually proved closer to the truth. Delegates divided almost equally into three groups: southern-born whites, northern-born whites, and blacks. When delegates elected Richards convention president by a vote of 22 to 21, moderate Republicans and conservatives bolted. They believed the vote also endorsed the proscriptive policies of the radicals. They reassembled at

    18. Davis, *Civil War and Reconstruction in Florida,* 470–71; Richards to Washburne, 11 November 1867, in George E. Osborn, ed., "Letters of a Carpetbagger in Florida, 1865–1869," *FHQ* 36 (January 1958): 260.
    19. Davis, *Civil War and Reconstruction in Florida,* 474–76.

Monticello, thirty miles northeast of Tallahassee by rail. There, in consultation with some of the state's conservative leaders, they wrote a constitution. Because neither convention had a quorum, General George C. Meade—then commander of the Third Military District—traveled by train from Atlanta to reorganize them into one. The reunited convention subsequently elected by a vote of 32 to 13 moderate Republican Horatio Jenkins, another Union army veteran with friends in the Congress. The convention soon adopted the Monticello version of the constitution by a vote of 28 to 16. Of the 16 who voted nay, 11 were blacks and the others were all wartime unionists.[20]

General Meade forwarded to Congress both versions of the constitution, endorsing the moderate one signed by a majority. Moderates required the governor to name state and local officeholders except for constables, allowed each county to have from one to four representatives, and required only an oath of future loyalty for voters. Both groups sent lobbyists to Washington.

The arguments of General Meade and the moderates won, and their document was presented to the people in a mid-May 1868 election. That election saw Harrison Reed and William H. Gleason defeat the conservative ticket and the radical ticket. Billings and Saunders, nominated by the radicals initially, saw their campaign fade after Billings's arrest by the military for making "incendiary speeches." Radicals replaced the candidates at the last minute with a ticket of two Florida scalawags, Samuel Walker for governor and William H. Christy, editor of the *Florida Times,* for lieutenant governor. Billings became the candidate for the state's sole congressional seat. Voters adopted the constitution by a vote of 14,520 to 9,491. Although several scalawags and blacks were elected to the legislature, all in all the election was a carpetbagger takeover.[21]

In Alabama, loyalists in the northern part of the state endorsed Congressional Reconstruction at Huntsville in March 1867. General Wager Swayne, the state's highest ranking military officer, a one-legged Medal of Honor winner whose father served on the Supreme Court, was there along with Freedmen's Bureau clerk John C. Keffer of Pennsylvania, who moonlighted as secretary of the state's Union League. Bothered by the presence of some Confederates, Swayne went so far as to offer a resolution that only true-blue un-

20. Richards to Washburne, 19 November 1867, in Osborn, "Carpetbagger in Florida," 263; Jerrell H. Shofner, "Florida: A Failure of Moderate Republicanism," in *Reconstruction and Redemption,* 20–23; Hume, "Florida Constitutional Convention," 16–21.

21. Shofner, "Florida," 23–26.

ionists should serve as leaders in the Reconstruction. A few politicians from the Black Belt attended, including the politically active Saffold brothers of Selma, Milton, who was practicing law in the nation's capital, and Benjamin, the military-appointed mayor of Selma who only two years before favored "colonization" for blacks. The latter was accused by a local newspaper of departing from his fine "record" and good "character . . . to fasten a negro government upon the white men of the state."[22]

Leaguers from throughout north Alabama rallied at nearby Decatur in April. White councils had been started during the war in Athens, Florence, and Huntsville, and in 1865 they spread into the surrounding area. By 1867, many members recognized the need for black councils as a part of a strategy to elect "delegates to [the] political convention to be held in Montgomery in June." Any white votes lost in north Alabama would be offset by black votes farther south. Most white Union League organizers in the state (176 of whom have been identified) were Freedmen's Bureau agents and planters; others included lawyers, schoolteachers, and physicians, all of whom had black constituencies. To a greater degree than elsewhere, scalawags in Alabama enlisted blacks into Union Leagues. For example, Dr. Thomas Haughey formed at least eleven chapters, totaling 550 members, and attorney Arthur Bingham recruited "about 100 [blacks] a week for the League."[23]

At the peak of Union League recruiting, a Freedmen's state convention met in Mobile to affirm the allegiance of blacks to the Republican Party. Afterward, Mobile witnessed flurries of political activity, culminating in a rally on May 14 in front of the courthouse, which was addressed by Congressman William D. Kelley of Pennsylvania, who was visiting the iron and coal industry being developed by him and other northern investors. Unfortunately, tensions surrounding the occasion precipitated a bloody race riot. Republicans blamed the town's police force, which was composed largely of former Confederate soldiers. General Pope removed the city council and the police force. He

22. Wiggins, *Scalawag in Alabama Politics*, 21; Willis Brewer, *Alabama: Her History, Resources, War Record, and Public Men, from 1540 to 1872* (Montgomery, 1872), 215; Fleming, *Reconstruction in Alabama*, 556; Michael W. Fitzgerald, "Wager Swayne, The Freedmen's Bureau, and the Politics of Reconstruction in Alabama," *Alabama Review* 48 (July 1995): 207.

23. Wiggins, *Scalawag in Alabama Politics*, 21; Albert Griffin to Swayne, 11 April 1867, ; Haughley to Swayne, 15 April 1867, A. Bingham to W. H. Smith, 11 April 1867, W. E. Connelly to Swayne, 15 April 1867, Swayne Papers; Ellison, *Bibb County*, 150–51; Loren Schweninger, "Alabama Blacks and the Congressional Reconstruction Acts of 1867," *Alabama Review* 31 (July 1978): 182–98.

placed the city under military rule and appointed as mayor Massachusetts-born Gustavus Horton, one of the town's wartime loyalists.[24]

Pope directed Swayne to divide Alabama into voter registration districts with boards composed of two whites, preferably civilians, and one black. Swayne, in turn, appointed scalawag William H. Smith general supervisor of registration on May 1. Swayne and Smith received recommendations for registrars from such individuals as the Reverend G. W. J. Chalfant, superintendent for missions of the Methodist Church (North) in Georgia and Alabama, Albert Griffin, editor of the influential *Mobile Nationalist,* and John C. Keffer, secretary of Alabama's Union League. Swayne and Governor Robert M. Patton, who were both striving to replace "known rebels" (a euphemism for anti-reconstructionists), appointed many scalawags to local offices.[25]

On June 3, 1867, General Swayne found his day "full of interruptions," because, he said, "tomorrow we shall organize the Republican State Convention of Alabama." The next day Governor Patton greeted the 150 party delegates. Scalawags accounted for most of the fifty whites, a majority of whom had opposed the Confederacy and their state government during 1865–67. They included those who were critical of President Johnson's policy previous to the Joint Committee on Reconstruction in early 1866, organizers of the Southern Loyalists Convention, individuals who attended earlier Republican meetings in north Alabama, and Montgomery Republicans, who were part of a local unionist underground during the war. Most delegates attended nightly Union League sessions. The league related to the party like "a wheel within [a] wheel"—it either initiated or ratified most of the party's major decisions. Shortly before adjourning, the delegates elected a party executive committee with a slight scalawag majority.[26]

Most Alabama scalawags identified with the Republicans during 1867. Many onetime peace party supporters saw cooperation with Republicans as the state's only way out. Considering what might have happened, including imprisonment and confiscation, a few men agreed with Benjamin F. Porter

24. Steele, "Aspects of Reconstruction in Mobile," 37, 41, 44–46; Horace Mann Bond, "Social and Economic Forces in Alabama Reconstruction," *Journal of Negro History* 23 (July 1938): 307; Loren Schweninger, "Alabama Blacks," 191.

25. Robert S. Rhodes, "The Registration of Voters and the Election of Delegates to the Reconstruction Convention in Alabama," *Alabama Review* 8 (April 1955): 121–25, 134–37; Swayne to Salmon P. Chase, 3 June, 8 July 1867, Chase Papers.

26. Wiggins, *Scalawag in Alabama Politics,* 21–23, 143; Fitzgerald, *Union League Movement,* 77–79.

of Greenville, who said the "Southern people ought to feel grateful for the exceedingly liberal construction given the Reconstruction act." Some former Johnson supporters, such as Joshua Morse, now thought it reasonable to act with the Republicans. Morse resented appeals for inaction and accused "old party leaders" of lacking "nerve," of having "forsaken the masses," and of engaging "in nursing a little ephemeral local popularity." Others, however, felt stymied. Benjamin Gardner of Barbour County, on one hand believed "Conservatives would lose all" because of their opposition to Congress, but on the other hand, he found Republicans "too radical on the Negro question." In Gardner's case, he swallowed his racism and turned Republican.[27]

Other scalawags considered their financial interests. Some, especially those from north Alabama, were pursuing war claims on property seized by Federals. A few former Confederates still feared the confiscation of their estates. This threat might have motivated Charles Hays of Green County, owner of "100,000 acres of the best land in the state." He claimed he had been forced into service by the Conscription Act. In 1865, Hays had quickly renewed his allegiance to the Union and appealed to President Johnson for a pardon. During 1867, he joined the Union League and crossed over to the Republican Party. Another possible explanation of Hays's decision to join the league and the party was that he had large "quantities of open land, and to secure laborers for another year," he felt it necessary to "render himself popular" to the blacks.[28]

One study has looked at five different inferential motivation categories of why Alabama whites (carpetbaggers and scalawags) became Republicans as indicated in their correspondence. Some mentioned more than one reason, others gave considerations that were difficult to categorize and only suggested by the "overtone" of the letter, such as lust for office or revenge for their treatment during the war. Thirty percent identified with the party because of their northern origin; this included carpetbaggers and some prewar settlers as well. About one-third (34 percent) identified with the Republican Party because of past party affiliation, either Whig (24 percent) or Union Democrat (10 per-

27. Porter to John Sherman, 7 March 1867, Sherman Papers; Morse to Andrew Johnson, 27 February 1866, Johnson Papers; Morse to Wager Swayne, 17 August 1867, Swayne Papers; Benjamin Gardner to Robert M. Patton, 3 July 1867, Governor Robert M. Patton Papers, Alabama Department of Archives and History.

28. William Warren Rogers Jr., *Black Belt Scalawag: Charles Hays and Southern Republicans in the Era of Reconstruction* (Athens, Ga., 1993), 20–23; Hays to Lewis E. Parsons, n.d., Parsons Papers.

cent). Only 10 percent joined the party strictly out of a desire to reconstruct the state and still fewer to moderate the party.[29]

Whites outnumbered blacks about five to four, but many whites refused to register and of those registering a large majority did not vote in the constitutional convention election of October 1867. They hoped thereby to thwart the Reconstruction Act requirement to hold the convention. Only about 24,500 whites voted. Of those, 18,500 voted in favor of holding the convention, probably representing the state's total number of white Republicans. The proconvention white vote came from several north Alabama counties, primarily from about a dozen of the most heavily white-populated and economically poor counties. There Republicans commanded from about 30 to 50 percent of white voters.[30]

Republicans swept the election of delegates. They elected former Whigs and Douglas Democrats, mostly from north Alabama, and carpetbaggers and blacks, primarily from the Black Belt. Although the conservative press described the delegates as being "wholly unknown to the people of Alabama," the Montgomery Advertiser admitted that many were "gentlemen and men of position and influence in their counties." To a greater degree than in other southeastern states, wartime loyalists were well represented.[31]

Delegates elected as convention president Elisha W. Peck of Tuscaloosa, a physically weak but strong-willed individual who was described as having denounced "secession at the first, in the middle, and at the end." They directed the old man, once "hung in effigy" by Confederates, to drape two United States flags over his chair. They also invited General Pope and General Swayne, as well as Governor Patton, to address them and to take seats in the convention. Taking a cue from party leaders in Washington, all delegates advocated moderation. After a few days of voting, it became clear that whites divided about equally into three groups: "extreme men, moderate men, and men who fluctuate[d]" according to their political advantage, voting with "whichever side seem[ed] to be the strongest." Extreme men consisted mostly of Freedmen's Bureau officials, some of whom were southerners, and their

29. Cash, "Alabama Republicans," 164.

30. Wiggins, Scalawag in Alabama Politics, 25; Michael W. Fitzgerald, "Radical Republicanism and the White Yeomanry during Alabama Reconstruction, 1865–1868," JSH 54 (November 1988): 585–86.

31. Fitzgerald, "Radical Republicanism," 585–86; KKK Report, Ala., 1850; Joseph C. Bradley to Wager Swayne, 24 April 1867, Swayne Papers.

black allies. Moderates were generally "men of standing, property, and good fame."[32]

The most outspoken radical was Daniel H. Bingham of Limestone County, federal register of bankruptcy at Athens since 1866. The New Yorker settled in the state before the war, bringing with him a high degree of Yankee idealism. Along with many of his neighbors, he opposed secession, and after being abused by Confederates, he left the state. He originally backed Johnson because he believed Johnson would punish the former Rebels. By summer 1866, he supported Congressional Reconstruction and the calling of the Southern Loyalists Convention at Philadelphia. Acting on his idealism as well as his bitterness, he championed blacks and poor white loyalists. He organized the Republican Party in Limestone County with "400 colored and 20 to 30 whites." As a result of his work with the Union League, black delegates regarded him as "their special leader."[33]

Original unionists turned Confederates led the moderates, men such as attorneys Henry C. Semple of Montgomery and Benjamin L. Wheelan of Hale County and headmaster Joseph H. Speed of Marion. They did not think that individuals such as themselves, forced to go with the Confederacy because of circumstances, should be punished for secession. Semple corresponded with a wide circle concerning his fight to prevent disfranchisement. Lewis E. Parsons told him that he could not "do a greater service than to defeat the adoption of the consti[tution]." Horace Greeley assured Semple of his support for opposition to "all proscriptions and disfranchisements."[34] Outgoing governor Patton also joined with others in attacking the constitution, fearing a black-carpetbagger takeover of the state. Wheelan, along with most moderates, later reconciled with the party. Many original unionists who supported the convention now denounced the party and its constitution. All of these boycotted the referendum on the constitution, taking advantage of the requirement that a majority of registered voters needed to participate for the document to be ratified. Semple led the fight against the adoption of the constitution.[35]

In the ratification election, the vote fell short of turnout needed to meet

32. Wiggins, *Scalawag in Alabama Politics*, 26; *New York Herald*, 29 November 1867.

33. Wiggins, *Scalawag in Alabama Politics*, 26–27; McMillan, *Constitutional Development*, 116–21; Fitzgerald, *Union League Movement*, 83.

34. Hume, "'Black and Tan' Constitutional Conventions," 20–31; McMillan, *Constitutional Development*, 122, 124–28.

35. Wiggins, *Scalawag in Alabama Politics*, 33.

the requirement. About 11,000 white Republicans who had voted for the convention failed to vote for the constitution. The greatest erosion occurred in north Alabama. Elsewhere, moderate Republicans failed to help get out the black vote. Beyond this, some Democratic-sponsored Ku Klux Klan activity decreased black turnout. Despite the success of the opponents, their strategy ultimately failed when Congress passed the Fourth Reconstruction Act on March 11, 1868, requiring a voting majority rather than a majority of registered voters. Congress readmitted Alabama as if the state had voted under the new act. Moderate Republicans still achieved a partial victory by seeing Smith, an antiproscription Republican, elected as governor. [36]

In South Carolina, General Daniel E. Sickles, a respected officer in charge there since 1865, received command of the Second Military District, which encompassed both Carolinas. Because the general found it difficult to find registrars of proven loyalty, he turned to Governor James L. Orr, a fellow Democratic congressman before the war with whom he had worked closely during the last two years.[37] Orr in turn wrote to local officeholders asking for the names of men who could take the loyalty oath of 1862. The responses illustrate the difficulty of locating literate and loyal registrars. One Camden correspondent suggested three young men, an "intelligent & trustworthy" fellow who "had lost his [left] arm before the war" and therefore did not serve in the Confederate army; another, a "friend" of his, "a clever . . . gentleman, [who] was in Europe during the whole war"; and a third who "taught school and 'drove cattle' during the war to keep himself out of the army and to preserve himself for the good of the whole country." Other officeholders, like Lemuel Boozer of Lexington, simply sent Orr some names—perhaps it took a loyalist to know one.[38]

Meanwhile, some of Orr's friends who supported Congressional Reconstruction asked him to move beyond his posture as law enforcer. Remarking that he felt "sick and tired of the uncertainty," John T. Green of Sumter, a prewar legislator whose illness kept him safely out of the Confederate army, warned Orr that if the state refused "the terms now offered," congressional

36. Fitzgerald, "Radical Republicanism," 590–95; Wiggins, *Scalawag in Alabama Politics*, 33–39.

37. Simkins and Woody, *South Carolina during Reconstruction*, 64–67.

38. Joel Williamson, *After Slavery*, 364; Boozer to James L. Orr, 3 May 1867, M. M. Benbow to Orr, 15 May 1867, Governor James Lawrence Orr Papers, South Carolina Department of Archives and History, Columbia.

radicals would demand more "onerous and oppressive measures." Christopher W. Dudley of Bennettsville, an assessor of internal revenue, told Orr that "no assumption of dignity" could protect South Carolina from "the consequences of rejecting what [was] offered." He urged Orr to "move boldly forward." Dudley believed former governor Benjamin F. Perry's collective inaction position was "lending influence in favor of anarchy." Orr also received mail from friends in and out of the state asking him to resist Congressional Reconstruction, either through the federal courts and/or by encouraging a boycott of the polls.[39]

Soon the governor spelled out his position. Speaking before the Charleston Board of Trade on April 2, he said he would accept the terms for Reconstruction, as "humiliating" as they were, and that he would "openly, fairly and squarely urge their adoption." He believed southerners could control black voters if they appealed to blacks personally. Fighting Congress, he said, would risk "the threat of confiscation." And the state's economy would remain unstable until "political relations" resumed with Washington. Orr blamed the current miasma on the national Democratic Party. Since 1860, he said, the party had misled the South on three occasions: during the secession crisis, during the 1866 National Union Convention (to which Orr was a party), and recently by advising rejection of the Howard Amendment (a proposal by Senator Jacob Howard of Michigan to grant the franchise to three classes of black males: the veterans, the literate, and those possessing at least $250 in property).[40]

Others now sought the governor's support for the state Republican Party, none more persistently than U.S. Marshal J. P. M. Epping, an entrepreneurial carpetbagger who owned businesses in Charleston and Columbia. Epping urged Orr to talk with him about the changed political situation, to address Republican rallies, and to help him recruit "decent Union men." He assured Orr that "the colored population [would] vote as a unit." But the governor refused to engage in partisan politics during 1867. Still, the fact that Orr endorsed cooperation with the national government and that he listened to them encouraged state Republicans.[41]

39. Green to Orr, 9 March 1867, Odell Duncan to Orr, 14 March 1867, Dudley to Orr, 27 April 27, 1867, Albert Voorhies to Orr, 6 March 1867, Orr Papers.

40. Simkins and Woody, *South Carolina during Reconstruction,* 83; Roger P. Leemhuis, *James L. Orr and the Sectional Conflict* (New York, 1979), 128–30.

41. Epping to Orr, 14, 25, 31 March, 14 May 1867, Orr Papers.

Following passage of the first Reconstruction Act, Charleston's black leaders, including that city's 1865 Negro convention members, joined whites to create the Union Republican Party of South Carolina. They approved a platform calling for free education, equality and enfranchisement for all regardless of race, officeholding by the "truly loyal," internal improvements, and benefits for the poor. Soon blacks were organizing throughout the state. John W. De-Forest said that blacks arrived in Greenville from ten to twenty miles away, "making a three days' job of it," to attend meetings of the Union League at the schoolhouse and hear "eloquent orators of the [Republican] party."[42] Whites gathered in such counties as Chesterfield, Georgetown, Lexington, and Pickens to accept what they saw as inevitable, universal manhood suffrage. At the Chesterfield County courthouse, a biracial rally agreed to nominate a common slate of black and white candidates for the state constitutional convention "for the sake of harmony between the two races."[43]

Manuel S. Corley of Lexington, who had corresponded for months with congressional Republicans, told Charles Sumner that the Reconstruction Acts were "sufficiently radical for practical purposes." Shortly thereafter, he penned a platform for a local freedmen's meeting, in which they pledged to back "the party that freed them" and to cooperate with "their old masters . . . upon a common platform of patriotic devotion to Congress and the nation." In April, he and other Lexington loyalists "of all colors" met, and in early July they elected Corley and Boozer, leaders in the state's Lutheran Church, as delegates to the state Republican convention. The number of whites attending those meetings so impressed William J. Armstrong, a touring white speaker from the North, that he told a Lexington crowd they lived "in the most loyal district in S. Carolina."[44]

Despite the partisan activity, only sixty-nine delegates from nine counties

42. Thomas Holt, *Black over White: Negro Political Leadership in South Carolina during Reconstruction* (Urbana, Ill., 1977), 27–28; Okon Edet Uya, *From Slavery to Public Service: Robert Smalls, 1839–1915* (New York, 1971), 46; Grady McWhiney, ed., *Reconstruction and the Freedmen* (Chicago, 1963), 38, 44–45.

43. Williamson, *After Slavery*, 366–69; C. Smith to James L. Orr, 25 April 1867, Orr Papers; John H. Moore, *The Juhl Letters to the "Charleston Courier": A View of the South, 1865–1871* (Athens, Ga., 1974), 153; E. G. Dudley to John A. Andrews, 31 July 1867, in Richard H. Abbott, ed., "A Yankee Views the Organization of the Republican Party in South Carolina, July 1867," *South Carolina Historical Magazine* 85 (July 1984): 248–49; Simeon Corley to Charles Sumner, 5 July 1867, Sumner Papers; Holt, *Black over White*, 28.

44. Corley to Charles Sumner, 14 March, 5 July, 25 November, 10 December 1867, Sumner Papers.

attended a Republican state convention at Charleston in May. According to Epping, it amounted to "a complete failure," because it was controlled by "designing" northerners of both races, and no one represented the Up Country, most likely to contribute white Republicans. Still some who attended became important party leaders and future officeholders. Seven of the nine scalawags soon became congressmen and/or legislators. Before adjourning, delegates elected a state central committee, with scalawag Christopher C. Bowen of Charleston as chairman, and agreed to try another state convention in July at Columbia. Soon Bowen reported to congressional leaders that the Republican Party had been organized in most towns but that little had been done in the countryside. He had men "ready, willing, and competent to perform the mission" if given sufficient funds.[45]

Bowen had the courage for the task at hand. One opponent described him as "not gifted, but bold; not discreet but voluble; not learned, but swaggering; not particular, but ambitious." According to Bowen, he was reared a Rhode Islander by his parents, who took him to Lee County, Georgia, where they died, leaving him "an orphan . . . with no resources but his own energies." He professed to have occupied himself thereafter "chiefly . . . in agricultural pursuits." Others claimed he made his living as a "faro dealer and gambler." In any event, he became a Charleston attorney during 1862 before becoming a captain in the Confederate Coast Guard. Then Bowen's life went from bad to worse. After being court-martialed in 1864, he was implicated for instigating the murder of his commanding officer and jailed for a year before being freed by Federals. Returning to the practice of law, he spent much of his time in what he called "gratuitous professional service for the poor," which eventually won him "a solid following among blacks." [46]

On July 24 at Columbia, sixty-six blacks and twenty-two whites, representing two-thirds of the state's counties, met for a three-day Republican convention. Spokesmen of both races warned freedmen to beware of radicalism. Scalawag Thomas J. Robertson of Columbia, a wealthy entrepreneur, called

45. J. P. M. Epping to James L. Orr, 14 May 1867, Orr Papers; Robert B. Elliott to Charles Sumner, 22 May 1867, Sumner Papers; C. C. Bowen to Benjamin F. Butler, 30 May 1867, Butler Papers.

46. Uya, *From Slavery to Public Service*, 11–15, 46; Barnes, *Fortieth Congress*, 2: 241–42; E. Culpepper Clark, *Francis Warrington Dawson and the Politics of Restoration: South Carolina, 1874–1889* (University, Ala., 1980), 41–45; Simkins and Woody, *South Carolina during Reconstruction*, 118–19.

for a platform "broad enough to accommodate the human race." But appeals for moderation failed except perhaps in one case, when blacks agreed to divide equally with whites the party's nominees for seats in the upcoming constitutional convention. Otherwise, delegates endorsed the radical platform earlier adopted, which for most whites meant "Democracy run mad." Before adjourning, the delegates, according to one of them, "instituted machinery by which the whole state [was] to be thoroughly canvassed and organized."[47]

Elbridge G. Dudley, a Massachusetts attorney and abolitionist turned Beaufort planter who was there to represent his county, pronounced the meeting "a most splendid success." He "was astonished at the amount of intelligence and ability shown by the colored men of the Convention." He did not seem the least bit concerned that the platform passed by the convention was "as Radical as it could be made." But scalawags expressed concern about the party's direction. W. W. Herbert of Winnsboro believed that having one-half of the party's candidates black would "drive off many white persons." Odell Duncan thought the convention represented neither "the white [nor the] colored population." He regretted that "prominent and good men" ready to support the party stayed away and that the platform had an "ultra radical character," because it recommended land taxes amounting to "confiscation."[48]

By the summer of 1867, "three parties" existed in South Carolina, according to Orr's confidant William Henry Trescot: those who like "Governor Perry oppose the call of the Convention"; those represented by the "Coloured Convention lately at Columbia," of which he thought the "white person belonging to it . . . an almost imperceptible infusion"; and finally those who believe the mistake of "universal suffrage" can be corrected only by teaching "the freedman how to discharge his duty," that is, the cooperation party. Trescot viewed most of the first position's leaders as being "above reproach." He predicted the third group of whites would be defeated because "the black vote of the State [was] united" by the Union League. The second group he described as being "directed by men whose only hope of power and profit is the perpetuation of . . . hostility between the races." Nonetheless, some of the state's origi-

47. Abbott, *Republican Party and the South*, 130–31; *New York Times*, 31 July 1867; Simkins and Woody, *South Carolina during Reconstruction*, 83, 117–18; Abbott, "A Yankee Views," 249; B. F. Randolph to Charles Sumner, 23 November 1867, Sumner Papers.
48. Abbott, "A Yankee Views," 246–49; Herbert to John Sherman, 30 July 1867, Sherman Papers; Odell Duncan to Charles Sumner, 6 August 1867, Sumner Papers.

nal unionists who initially supported President Johnson now crossed over to the Republicans, including the Mackeys of Charleston and the Moseses of Georgetown.[49]

The Mackeys—Dr. Albert G. Mackey, his brother Thomas, and his son, Edmund —were men of independence, courage, and talent. Dr. Mackey reasoned that since the Reconstruction Acts passed "by a two-thirds vote in both Houses of Congress," it was futile to deny their constitutionality. Consequently, he advocated their acceptance at public meetings throughout much of the state. Edmund, too young to have fought in the war, remained the most radical of the three, and Thomas, a Citadel graduate who had fought for the Confederacy, was the most conservative. Congressman Edmund Mackey was the only scalawag in this study to marry a black woman, Victoria Alice Sumter, described as "a pretty, well-educated octoroon from Sumter County . . . whom the Sumter family had reared as a lady's maid." Judge Thomas Mackey, always a man of humor, often jested, especially about Edgefield. He told of an Edgefield lad who left home for the Mexican War to escape his vicinity's violence. Once, while journeying to Edgefield, Mackey reported that "the fall shooting [was] about to commence." Speaking of the racial attitude of the county's whites, he said: "A great injustice has been done to the people of Edgefield. It is charged that they kill negroes on account of their political opinions. That is altogether a mistake; they do it for Sport."[50]

The Moses family supported President Johnson before 1867. Franklin J. Moses Jr., editor of the pro-Johnson *Sumter News* in 1866, supported the National Union Convention, which his father attended as a delegate. But suddenly, in spring 1867, his writing waxed radical, and he joined the Union League, summarily causing his dismissal as editor. In the fall, he won election as a constitutional convention delegate. He went on to serve as legislator and governor. His life became that of a stereotype scalawag, a turncoat who died in disgrace and dissipation. On the other hand, his father, state chief justice from 1868 to 1877, was a man "honored and respected alike by Radicals and Conservatives." He and his brother Montgomery, a circuit judge and "grand high priest of the Royal Arch Chapter of Masons of South Carolina," had been

49. Gailliard Hunt, "Letter of William Henry Trescot on Reconstruction in South Carolina, 1867," *American Historical Review* 15 (April 1910): 574–82.

50. Williamson, *After Slavery*, 374; *Proceedings of the Constitutional Convention of South Carolina*, 1: 16; *BDAC*, 1323; Gregorie, *History of Sumter County*, 344, 374; Edward L. Wells, *Hampton and Reconstruction* (Columbia, S.C., 1907), 159; Brooks, *Bench and Bar*, 196–202.

law partners for many years. Few expressed surprise when Montgomery followed his brother into the Republican Party.[51]

Almost all whites boycotted the election for holding a constitutional convention. The number of whites voting for the convention counted 2,350, fewer than 5 percent of total registered white voters. Other than those who lived in Charleston, most of these white Republicans resided in the mountain districts, which elected about two-thirds of the scalawag delegates. Carpetbaggers came from only a handful of heavily black-populated counties. Of the delegates elected, scalawags totaled only twenty-seven.[52]

Although scalawags represented a minority of delegates, everyone voted for Dr. Mackey. Other prominent scalawags included Robertson, the convention's wealthiest delegate, Lemuel Boozer of Lexington, and attorney James M. Rutland, an outright resister to the Confederacy. A few were young men from well-respected families and with good educations. Some were unknown beyond their own districts or beyond certain occupational or denominational circles, such as Boozer's friend Manuel S. Corley, a fine tailor and Lutheran leader. Others, however, were little-known individuals who had taken advantage of the situation. A few, unfortunately, were rough, disreputable men.[53]

At the beginning of the convention, several scalawags spoke in favor of moderation concerning economic policy and the treatment of former Confederates. Temporary chairman Robertson called for a "just and liberal constitution" free of "class legislation." Then Chairman Mackey set the tone, saying he was "a moderate man . . . opposed to all confiscations of property," because it would not promote the state's "political condition, or [advance] its commercial and agricultural prosperity." Furthermore, Mackey said, he opposed "any general disfranchisement" because it was "too late" and "to inflict it now would be only to gratify revenge." After a few attempts to revolutionize the state, the forward-looking constitution that passed represented what Mackey averred "followed in the progressive advancement of the age." [54]

51. *DAB*, 13: 275–76; Simkins and Woody, *South Carolina during Reconstruction*, 126–27, 142–43; Brooks, *Bench and Bar*, 195; Wells, *Hampton and Reconstruction*, 149; Elzas, *Jews of South Carolina*, 197–99; Moore, *Juhl Letters*, 107.

52. Hume, "'Black and Tan' Constitutional Conventions," 387–90, 429–67.

53. Ibid.; Simkins and Woody, *South Carolina during Reconstruction*, 93; *New York Times*, 23 January 1868; John Porter Hollis, *The Early Period of Reconstruction in South Carolina* (Baltimore, 1905), 83.

54. *Proceedings of the Constitutional Convention of South Carolina*, 1: 53, 60, 925–26; Leemhuis, *James L. Orr*, 146; Simkins and Woody, *South Carolina during Reconstruction*, 96–106; Hume, "'Black and Tan' Constitutional Conventions," 397–416.

A few days before the convention adjourned, Republicans met at Charleston to nominate candidates for state offices to run in the upcoming election. Most delegates at the same time were serving in the constitutional convention. Only one scalawag, Robertson, came under consideration for the gubernatorial nomination. When he withdrew because of lack of support, delegates nominated Robert K. Scott, a moderate Republican who headed the state's Freedmen's Bureau. He was respected even by conservatives. Democrats failed even to field an opposition ticket; instead they leveled an attack on the constitution. Republicans won the state races easily, and the constitution passed. [55]

Some of South Carolina's former secessionists went over to the Republicans in early 1868. One was William M. Thomas, a Charleston native who had settled in Greenville after graduating from South Carolina College in 1852. Since arriving in the Upland town, he had been a political enemy of Perry. The young lawyer thought that the former governor's idea of defeating Reconstruction by boycotting the elections, "masterly inactivity," as he called it, was senseless. Thomas's own path into the Republican Party, he claimed, began with an "about face" shortly after he showed his "gallantry" as a Confederate soldier on a Virginia battlefield. He had "been going *home* ever since: supporting Johnson's policy, then the [Fourteenth] constitutional amendment, and the reconstructing acts."

Still Thomas believed Congress had not gotten its Reconstruction legislation exactly right. He felt that middle ground should be found between disqualifying all former Confederates who, like himself, had been prewar officeholders and "removing all disabilities at once," which was a recipe for Republican defeat. In keeping with the path he had taken, he suggested that Congress "restore those who [were] penitent." Even Thomas's old black servant, as he admitted, found it difficult to believe the sincerity of his political conversion. Thomas indeed did intend to be a Republican. He campaigned for the new state constitution in spring 1868, became the Republican Party's choice for judge of South Carolina's sixth district as well as a member of the party's central committee and after returning to live in Charleston, became editor of one of the party's newspapers, the *Charleston Sun*.[56]

---

55. Current, *Those Terrible Carpetbaggers*, 100; Peggy Lamson, *The Glorious Failure: Black Congressman Robert Brown Elliott and the Reconstruction in South Carolina* (New York, 1973), 67–69; Simkins and Woody, *South Carolina during Reconstruction*, 112–46.

56. Brooks, *Bench and Bar*, 177; William M. Thomas to Charles Sumner, 2, 15 June 1868, Sumner Papers.

Meanwhile in Mississippi, General Edward O. C. Ord of Maryland, commander of the Fourth Military District of Mississippi and Arkansas, appointed a four-man military board, chaired by General Alvan C. Gillem of Tennessee, head of the state's Freedmen's Bureau, to arrange for a vote on the constitutional convention. He instructed the board to confer with "prominent and reliable Union men" about registrars. He told them to give preference to nonpartisans, because he believed there were not "intelligent republicans enough in Miss." Of 183 registrars appointed during spring 1867, about 100 had worn the Union blue, including a few blacks. The military board appointed a few "prominent and reliable" loyalists as registrars. Others could hardly be called nonpartisan. Ord appointed Alston Mygatt, whom Ord knew was president of Mississippi's Union League, and the vindictive Republican Abel Alderson of Jefferson County, who favored an extension of military rule in 1865.[57]

Mississippi's scalawags in early 1867 consisted mostly of wartime dissidents, turncoats, and deserters, men like Mygatt, a merchant and minister since 1837. Mygatt chaired the Republican Party's first state executive committee. Although a vocal antisecessionist before the war, he kept his antislavery feelings to himself. Following Vicksburg's fall to Federals, he headed the city's Union League, despite a lack of support from Union army officers, and in 1867, almost by default, he became state president of the league. He controlled the councils north and south of Vicksburg, but he exercised little authority in the state's interior. Mygatt hoped that the Republican Party would help bring to Mississippi small prosperous farms and improved agricultural methods; flourishing industry and growing towns, joined by internal improvements such as railroads; "free schools flourishing in every district"; and a government ruled by "loyal men."[58]

While other Mississippi scalawags helped organize leagues at home, few ventured beyond their local scene; this was true in other states as well. Outside organizers often worked as Freedmen's Bureau school supervisors and/or missionaries of northern denominations. Two visitors during summer 1867 contributed significantly to the growth of Mississippi chapters: Thomas W.

57. Garner, *Reconstruction in Mississippi*, 171–72; William C. Harris, *The Day of the Carpetbagger: Republican Reconstruction in Mississippi* (Baton Rouge, 1979), 67–70; Fitzgerald, *Union League Movement*, 46, 54, 86–87, 170; Sansing, "Role of the Scalawag in Mississippi," 55, 88; Harris, "Reconsideration of the Mississippi Scalawag," 15; Alderson to Andrew Johnson, 3 December 1865, Johnson Papers.

58. Fitzgerald, *Union League Movement*, 25, 31, 50, 87, 110–11.

Conway, former head of the Freedmen's Bureau in Louisiana, and his black traveling companion John Mercer Langston, son of a Virginia planter, who had his son educated in northern schools.[59]

Several early Mississippi Republicans included friends of the blacks. In addition to Mygatt, they included Judge Robert A. Hill, who supported the Freedmen's Bureau, and Robert W. Flournoy of Pontotoc County and Joshua S. Morris of Claiborne County, defenders of civil rights. Once Reconstruction came, Flournoy, through his newspaper *Equal Rights,* voiced his views against discrimination in public places and for an integrated school system. Testifying before a congressional committee, he said, "when children can play together, as black and white children do, I see no reason why it would poison them to go to school together." Morris believed the war had elevated freedmen to "absolute legal equality with the hitherto dominant class." Although less of an idealist than Flournoy, Morris, postmaster at Port Gibson in the 1850s, held strong convictions. He believed the South's "conduct toward the negro" made it necessary for the federal government, having this "elephant on its hands, to see that it should not die of starvation or perish from persecution." About himself, he said: "I felt like Daniel Defoe's gamecock . . . among the horses in the stable," who finding "no way for him to get out, . . . looked up and said to the horses, 'Gentlemen, let us not step on each other's toes.'"[60]

Other early Mississippi scalawags were reluctant rebels or less than loyal C.S.A. soldiers. Because attorney Charles A. Sullivan had in 1860–61 opposed secession, one of his neighbors wanted him hanged. After the war, Sullivan became a judge in the Freedmen's Bureau court and later served as a bureau agent. When Congressional Reconstruction came, he spoke at Starkville on March 23 to the "Old Whig and Union men," urging them to organize and to support "the congressional laws of reconstruction and the Constitutional Amendments." Sullivan went on to serve as a Republican state senator and judge. Some other individuals from prominent families, who had deserted the cause during the war, joined the party in 1867. Robert J. Alcorn and Elijah A.

59. Ibid., 240.

60. Wharton, *Negro in Mississippi,* 157; Harris, "Reconsideration of the Mississippi Scalawag," 11–14, 30–32, 37n; Harris, *Day of the Carpetbagger,* 186–87; *KKK Report,* Miss., 82, 91, 298, 15–25; James Whitfield to Commissioner of Freedmen's Bureau, 29 March 1867, G Robert Hill to Commissioner, 5 March 1867, J. H. F. Claiborne to Commissioner, 4 January 1867, Records of the Bureau of Refugees, Freedmen, and Abandoned Lands, RG 105; Robert W. Flournoy to Thaddeus Stevens, 20 November 1865, Stevens Papers; Joshua S. Morris petition, n.d., RG 233.

Peyton were the first of several members of their families who eventually affiliated with the party.[61]

Probate judge John McRae of Kemper County was his regiment's adjutant "until the summer of 1864," when according to his sister, "he came home and said his conscience would not permit . . . his continuing in a cause he abhorred." McRae and his friend Sheriff William W. Chisholm, who eventually controlled the county, rode to Republican meetings with fifteen to twenty of their former Confederate comrades. To some degree they were Republicans because only as members of that party could they, rather than their traditional enemies, control Kemper County. Former Confederate major Jefferson L. Wofford, a decorated hero, saw a new day dawning in Mississippi. Both as editor of the *Corinth Weekly News* and as a politician, he wrote and spoke in support of the Republican Party as the best means of bringing prosperity to north Mississippi. Some other whites must have agreed. One historian has shown that of the ten white Republican counties in the state, eight were situated along railroad lines that were opening up the lumber industry in north Mississippi.[62]

By summer 1867, state opinion makers tried to steer the course of Reconstruction. They took a stand for or against cooperating with the national government and the Republican Party. Most whites either wanted to cooperate without identifying with the party, which they considered too radical (cooperationists), or they desired to resist through a strategy of "masterly inactivity," keeping the required majority of voters away from the polls (conservatives). Others, much fewer in number, willingly supported the national Republican Party as well as Congressional Reconstruction. Both Republicans and cooperationists sought support from blacks; they differed, however, in what price they were willing to pay for that support. The latter would not accept black officeholding. During September and October of 1867, all three Mississippi groups organized into state political parties.[63]

Scalawags faced no difficulty in controlling the first statewide Republican Party meeting at Jackson on September 10, though blacks and carpetbaggers

61. G. C. Sullivan to John Sherman, 26 March 1867, Sherman Papers; Earnest F. Puckett, "Reconstruction in Monroe County," *Publications of the Mississippi Historical Society,* 11 (1910): 122–23.

62. James Madison Wells, *The Chisholm Massacre: A Picture of "Home Rule" in Mississippi,* 2d ed. (Washington, D.C., 1877), 15–20, 65; Lynch, *Kemper County Vindicated,* 21.

63. Harris, *Day of the Carpetbagger,* 83–96.

were well represented. Scalawags elected one of their own, Mygatt, as the convention's presiding officer, and they dominated the debate about the platform. But they were far from being united. Speaking for the radicals, Flournoy called for the political proscription of rebels, political rights for blacks, and free public schools for children of both races. Moderate and conservative scalawags opposed proscription of former rebels because they believed it would embitter whites against the Republican Party. After a lengthy debate, the platform adopted differed little from those passed elsewhere in the South during the summer of 1867. Moderates accepted the language of the platform for the sake of party harmony, but a few conservative scalawags, mostly little-known former Whig unionists, walked away from the convention never, with few exceptions, to return to the party.[64]

Two weeks later, a cooperationist group calling itself "the Reconstruction party of Mississippi" convened at Jackson. It adopted a platform that called the "Congressional plan of Reconstruction . . . oppressive," but the men gathered there accepted it as the law of the land. To reject it, they concluded, would only worsen matters. During the summer and fall of 1867, the Constitutional Union Party, taking the title of the 1860 political party, emerged to lead those determined to boycott the upcoming constitutional convention election.[65]

James L. Alcorn spelled out his belief in August 1867 in the pamphlet *Views of the Hon. J. L. Alcorn on the Political Situation of Mississippi*. He mentioned that only days before, an almost solid black vote had reelected Governor Brownlow in Tennessee and that voter registration figures in Alabama and Louisiana showed that blacks would soon elect Republican governors. He now believed it unlikely cooperationists could convince blacks to vote for southern conservatives. "The presence of the Loyal League," he said, now would counteract that. Bluntly he stated, "The 'old master,' gentlemen, has passed from fact to poetry." But there was hope, because the national Republican Party would welcome southern whites rather than be embarrassed by seeing a purely black man's party develop in the South. Yet Alcorn delayed until spring 1868 to declare his support for the Republican Party.[66]

64. Ibid., 103–6; Sansing, "Role of the Scalawag in Mississippi," 55.

65. Harris, *Day of the Carpetbagger*, 84–91.

66. James L. Alcorn, *Views of the Hon. J. L. Alcorn on the Political Situation of Mississippi* (Friar's Point, Miss., 1867); *New York Times*, 2 September 1867; Pereyra, *James Lusk Alcorn*, 90–93.

Thanks to the capable, albeit conservative, management leadership of Ord and Gillem, the constitutional convention election in early November occurred in an orderly manner. Out of the total registered voters, about one-half voted for the convention, including 6,000 whites, an indication of scalawag strength. For the most part, whites cast their ballots in large numbers only in counties with well-known candidates on the ticket; otherwise they boycotted the election. Of the delegates elected, about 80 percent were or soon became Republicans, over 50 percent of whom were scalawags.[67]

At the opening session of the convention on January 7, 1868, at Jackson, Mygatt gave an opening address. The delegates assembled, he said, to bring "to a final end that [economic] system that enriches the few at the expense of the many." The defense of that system of slavery through secession and war, he reminded them, had cost the state 30,000 lives, leaving "thousands of widows and orphans and a ruined economy." Those responsible for such loss, he said, must be shown the evil of their ways by being disfranchised, and their victims, loyal men of all colors, must be protected. The economy must also be rebuilt to support a good living and education for all.[68]

On the following day, Republicans elected as convention chairman a well-respected former Union army general who had accepted the surrender of Atlanta, Beroth B. Eggleston of Lowndes County, a "mild-mannered" man with a sense of fairness and a desire for efficiency. As in other black-and-tan conventions, the Republicans divided into radicals and moderates. In Mississippi the division largely developed on the issues of former Confederates voting and holding office. Several attempts had been made to group the delegates according to a roll analysis of key votes. One scholar found the convention as a whole to be made up of forty-five radicals, nineteen conservative radicals, and twenty-nine conservatives, which included a few Republicans.[69]

After weeks of debate, in mid-April the delegates passed a sweeping provision that prohibited anyone from holding office that had supported secession and/or the Confederacy. Then they moved on to continue the temporary disfranchisement of those not allowed to register to vote under the Reconstruc-

---

67. Harris, *Day of the Carpetbagger,* 108–16.

68. *Journal of the Proceedings in the Constitutional Convention of the State of Mississippi, 1868* (Jackson, Miss., 1871), 3–5.

69. Harris, *Day of the Carpetbagger,* 115–16; Currie, "Conflict and Consensus," 92–94; Hume, "'Black and Tan' Constitutional Conventions," 342–46; William A. Russ Jr., "Radical Disfranchisement in Mississippi, 1867–1870," *Mississippi Law Journal* 7 (October 1935): 373–74; *Journal of the Proceedings in the Constitutional Convention of the State of Mississippi, 1868,* 732–33.

tion Acts, leaving it to future legislatures to provide relief from this provision. Beyond these features, the constitution addressed several needed reforms. Altogether, the constitution was both good and enduring once the proscriptive clauses were removed.[70]

While the convention was still in session, Republicans met on February 5, 1868, to prepare for the upcoming general election. They gave the nominations to white delegates from black counties, four to carpetbaggers, including the almost unanimous selection of Eggleston for governor; and three to scalawags, including Robert J. Alcorn, James's cousin, for secretary of state; leaving blacks, who would be called upon to supply most of the votes, without a place on the ticket.[71]

Democrats also organized early in 1868. The Constitutional Union Party, which crashed in the convention election of November 1867, called a state convention on January 15 in Jackson. The group renamed itself the Mississippi Democratic Party. At a May convention, delegates chose Governor Benjamin G. Humphreys, a prewar Whig-unionist who had fought for the Confederacy, to head the ticket. The main election issue was the proscriptive provisions of the new constitution. Democrats left nothing to chance, using all means to win the election, including ostracism, intimidation, fraud, and violence.[72] These practices and moderate Republican opposition caused the defeat of the constitution by more than 15,000 votes.[73]

The nature of the birth of the Republican Party in the Southeast—South Carolina, Georgia, Florida, Alabama, and Mississippi—varied from state to state as well as from the creation of the party in the Upper South and Southwest, where better political foundations had already been laid. Some agencies for party building appeared in the Southeast during 1865–66—Union Leagues, loyalists, black newspapers, northern denominations, and some sympathetic Freedmen's Bureau agents—but these would have been of minimal political use without the help of north Republicans, who were reelected by a wide margin in fall 1866.

Initially the best hope for the party lay in Alabama, especially north Alabama, which had much in common with the Upper South during the war:

---

70. William C. Harris, "The Reconstruction of the Commonwealth 1865–1870," in *A History of Mississippi*, ed. Richard A. McLemore (Hattiesburg, 1973), 564.

71. Garner, *Reconstruction in Mississippi*, 208; Harris, *Day of the Carpetbagger*, 181–83.

72. Harris, *Day of the Carpetbagger*, 166–71; Garner, *Reconstruction in Mississippi*, 210–12.

73. Harris, *Day of the Carpetbagger*, 188–94; Garner, *Reconstruction in Mississippi*, 216.

occupation, local Union army recruits, and a relatively strong peace party movement. By 1866 north Alabama loyalists saw that they could combine their votes with those of blacks who were controlled by original unionists in the Black Belt to win state elections. In Georgia, by supporting Congressional Reconstruction, Brown helped to bring to the Republican Party hundreds of people in north Georgia who had disliked the Confederacy. Florida was greatly dependent on northerners of all types—prewar settlers, wartime federal appointees, and postwar newcomers—to create a Republican Party in the state. Loyalists in the Third Military district—Alabama, Georgia, and Florida—received strong support and encouragement from their military leaders to complete Reconstruction and to create a strong Republican Party. These officers placed voter registration in the hands of the loyalists by appointing prominent scalawags to oversee their state registration.

Many of the Mississippi and South Carolina scalawags entered the Republican Party after Reconstruction was well underway. Most initially supported President Johnson's approach. They broke with him only after his cause became hopeless and only when it became apparent that black voters would support no other party. James L. Orr of South Carolina and James L. Alcorn of Mississippi helped bring a small degree of respectability to the party, encouraging some who respected them to join the Republicans.

9

~

Turning the Corner Both Ways

Events during 1868 and 1869 encouraged some white southerners to become Republicans. Ulysses S. Grant's presidential campaign pledge to put
the past behind and look to the future appealed to moderates of both parties.
Others respected Grant because of his military ability and his nonpolitical
persona. This included a few former Confederate army officers like John S.
Mosby of Virginia and William H. Parson of Texas. The national party also
continued to move in the direction of moderation. The party opposed state
constitutions with proscriptive provisions penalizing former Confederates. In
June 1868, Congress relieved 1,431 individuals of their restrictions under the
Reconstruction Acts and the Fourteenth Amendment. Most had supported
Congressional Reconstruction, had affiliated with the Republican Party, and
had been elected, appointed, or considered for some public office. Other amnesty bills from 1868 to 1872 relieved many more former Confederates. Finally in spring 1872, Congress passed a general amnesty bill pardoning all but
a few hundred high-ranking former Confederates.[1]

Some pragmatic politicians became Republicans in 1868 to gain a seat at
the table. Joseph E. Brown of Georgia, James L. Alcorn of Mississippi, and
James L. Orr of South Carolina, who all cooperated with Congressional Reconstruction, now became full-fledged Republicans and soon accepted office

1. Abbott, *Republican Party and the South*, 215–17; Rembert W. Patrick, *The Reconstruction of the Nation* (New York, 1967), 165; Mosby, *War Reminiscences*, 6–7.

under that party. Their stand caused many of their friends to follow them into the party. As governor of Mississippi, Alcorn appointed many of his longtime colleagues to office. Known as Alcorn Republicans, they often supported the party and its platform with less than enthusiastic loyalty. Other coalition builders in Alabama—such as David P. Lewis, Lewis E. Parsons, and Alexander White—brought new leaders into that state's party. Most federal office-holders in the South declared their allegiance to Grant's party briefly before or shortly after his election. Some conservatives simply became so disgusted with their own party's reactionary policies during 1868–69 that they went over to the opposition. These included a number of North Carolina leaders such as Richmond M. Pearson and Samuel F. Phillips.[2]

The movement toward moderation by state Republican parties in the South made it easier for individuals to accept office under that party. To be a viable political party in any but the three states with well-organized black majorities—South Carolina, Mississippi, and Louisiana—white votes were needed. Republican moderates wanted native white leaders to bring the party respect, influence, prestige, and legitimacy. They also hoped such whites could curb the radical elements within the party. To attract whites, moderates emphasized economic policy, especially railroad construction, and downplayed the party's civil rights agenda. They also dangled patronage plums, especially judicial appointments. To a large degree, the number of converts varied because of each state's political dynamics.[3]

Many more forces, however, discouraged politicians from becoming Republicans. After keeping a low profile during 1867–69, a growing number of blacks gained public office in 1870–71, precluding whites from obtaining those positions, as did control of federal patronage by carpetbaggers. Party infighting, along with governmental corruption, also kept some out and caused others to return to the Democrats. The Liberal Republican Party of the early 1870s—a coalition of Republicans and conservatives with a reform agenda—provided "a bridge" by which some disappointed politicians could return to the conservative fold "without loss of face." Moderate Democrats saw no reason to leave their party once it took a "new departure," recognizing Reconstruction laws and progressive economic policy. Even more significant

2. Foner, *Reconstruction*, 298–99, 347; Pereyra, *James Lusk Alcorn*, 133; Miller, "Samuel Field Phillips," 263–80; Lancaster, "Scalawags of North Carolina," 224.

3. Foner, *Reconstruction*, 347; Michael Perman, *The Road to Redemption: Southern Politics, 1869–1879* (Chapel Hill, 1984), 24–26, 32–33, 35.

was the Democratic Party's ability to divide the parties along racial lines, making it the white man's party. Social pressures such as ostracism proved too severe for many to join the Republican Party.[4]

After 1868, only a small number of leaders from the Upper South appeared for the first time in the Republican ranks. These included a few original unionists who had received amnesty. Some felt ill-suited for a party led by former Confederates. Others saw that their state or local area could be better served by the party at the national level. This became true especially of new party converts in the mountainous areas of southwest Virginia, western North Carolina, and East Tennessee, where the Republican vote actually increased following Reconstruction.[5]

After Brownlow's election to the U. S. Senate in March 1869 and his replacement as governor by DeWitt C. Senter, a more friendly climate existed for converts to the Republican Party in Tennessee. Senter, nominated by moderates in his party and supported by a mellowed Brownlow, later defeated radical-backed William B. Stokes in an election in which conservatives (Democrats) supported Senter. During the weeks leading up to his election, Senter proposed universal manhood suffrage and promised if he were returned to office, he would remove all proscriptions on former Confederates. At this time, the state supreme court declared unconstitutional the governor's authority to set aside a county's registration where he found fraud. Senter, acting to guarantee his election, removed radical registrars in key counties and replaced them with conservatives. Some who deemed this the death of Brownlowism and who for one reason or another were dissatisfied with the conservatives soon found a home in the Republican Party.[6]

Following a failed gubernatorial campaign, Emerson Etheridge continued his Dresden law practice, and in 1869, running as a Democrat, he won a state senate seat. But after two years he became dissatisfied with his party's policies and resigned. In 1876, he supported the Republican Party and its presidential candidate, Rutherford B. Hayes. Knoxville attorney John Baxter opposed secession, then supported the Confederacy, then the Union as a Conservative

4. Perman, *Road to Redemption*, 25, 40, 42, 50–52; Foner, *Reconstruction*, 412–25; Alexander, "Persistent Whiggery," 322; Earle Dudley Ross, *The Liberal Republican Movement* (New York, 1910), 198.

5. Gordon B. McKinney, "The Mountain Republican Party-Army," *THQ* 32 (summer 1973): 125–27; McKinney, *Southern Mountain Republicans*, 62–63.

6. Corlew, *Tennessee*, 343–44.

Unionist during 1864–65. He stumped the state for Etheridge in 1868. Baxter became a halfway Republican when he, along with party regulars backing reform, supported the Liberal Republican Party in 1872. He exemplifies at least a few Democrats who took "the bridge" provided by that party into the Republican Party after Greeley's defeat. Former Confederate General George Maney of Nashville, another state senator elected in 1869, went over to the Republicans in the early 1870s. His position as president of the Tennessee and Pacific Railroad may well have related to his political conversion.[7]

Henry S. Foote, an influential antebellum politician in three states— Tennessee, Mississippi, and California—and pro-peace Confederate congressman from Nashville, joined the party after being out of politics for several years. Late in the war, Foote left Richmond to negotiate with Lincoln, offering him an unauthorized plan to exchange reunion for gradual emancipation. In 1869, Foote had his political restrictions under the Fourteenth Amendment removed. He wrote that he never gave "his sanction to . . . *secession*." At that time he supported Greeley's call for "universal suffrage and universal amnesty." Although Foote praised President Grant's inaugural address in 1869 as pointing the nation in the right direction, he voted for Greeley in 1872. By 1876, he was a Tennessee Republican and on that party's ticket as a presidential elector for Hayes.[8]

As seasoned politicians, these men quickly climbed the ladder in state party councils. Their influence was seen when in 1876 Etheridge, Foote, and Maney largely controlled the state's Republican Party convention. In 1876 and 1878, Etheridge and Maney became leading candidates for the party's gubernatorial nomination. Along the way, each received national party rewards: Etheridge became surveyor of customs at Memphis, Foote superintendent of the U.S. Mint at New Orleans, and Maney held several diplomatic posts in Latin America.[9]

Others supported the party in Tennessee once they were no longer disfranchised. Attorney William M. Randolph of Memphis, another former Confederate who like Foote had a mixed record during the war, became a Republican. Randolph, a Confederate district attorney in Little Rock, had gone over to the

7. *DAB*, 6: 501; Temple, *Notable Men of Tennessee*, 73–74; Lonnie E. Maness, "Emerson Etheridge and the Union," *THQ* 48 (summer 1989): 97–110; *Dictionary of the Confederacy*, 308; Ezra J. Warner, *Generals in Gray: Lives of the Confederate Commanders* (Baton Rouge, 1959), 210.

8. *DAB*, 6: 501; "Henry S. Foote Autobiographical Sketch," Claiborne Papers.

9. *DAB*, 6: 501; Temple, *Notable Men of Tennessee*, 74; Warner, *Generals in Gray*, 210.

unionists during 1864 and briefly backed the Murphy administration before moving to Memphis. Because of his disfranchisement under Tennessee law, Randolph refused to be involved in politics until he became eligible to vote in 1869. Once he did, he became a Republican. He served as the city's attorney from 1869 to 1874 and then ran a losing race as his party's candidate for Congress.[10]

Though in the minority after 1869, the Tennessee Republican Party could, on rare occasions, such as 1880, win a statewide election. That year, with the Democratic Party greatly divided over the state debt issue, Republican Alvin Hawkins of Huntingdon was elected governor. The strength of the Republican Party was, of course, in East Tennessee, which it almost invariably carried in state elections. The party generally carried a number of Tennessee River counties in West Tennessee—such as Carroll and Henderson—that had opposed secession. It also carried such predominantly black-populated counties as rural Fayette and Haywood and urban Shelby.[11]

In North Carolina during 1868–69, some affluent conservatives became so disgusted with their own party's unwillingness to meet Reconstruction halfway that they supported Grant for president. Before 1868, Pearson had abstained from public political statements because of his judicial position. Now he felt he could delay no longer. Pearson's letter of July 1868 in the *North Carolina Standard*, "An Appeal to the Calm Judgment of North Carolinians," urged conservative whites to participate in the state's November election as Republicans and not to leave the party to radical elements. Refusal by conservatives to vote or to accept the opposition as legitimate, he argued, amounted to "an open declaration of war" upon the political process.[12]

Nathaniel Boyden had supported President Johnson by leading his state's delegation to the National Union Convention in 1866. He had been elected on the Democratic ticket to Congress. After serving only a few months, however, he believed his party to be out of touch with the national situation. He decided to back Grant and the Republican Party as his state's best hope.[13] Phillips's doubts about conservatives dated from 1863–65, when they prolonged

10. O. F. Vedder, *History of the City of Memphis and Shelby County* (Syracuse, N.Y., 1888): 2: 56–62.

11. Corlew, *Tennessee*, 349.

12. Lancaster, "Scalawags of North Carolina," 224; *(Raleigh) North Carolina Standard*, 11 August, 16 September 1868; Thomas Settle to R. M. Pearson, 8 August 1868, Settle Papers.

13. *DNCB*, 1: 204.

the war "after all reasonable hope" had vanished. After serving as speaker of the state house in 1865–66, he retired from politics. Eventually, his growing disillusionment with friends mired in the past and his increased respect for Albion W. Tourgée, a new carpetbag friend, led Phillips back into politics. He voted for Grant in 1868 and was elected to the legislature as a Republican in 1870 before being defeated later that year in a contest for state attorney general.[14]

North Carolina's first Republican-controlled legislature met from July 1868 to March 1870. More than two-thirds of the 120 members of the lower house were Republicans, mostly scalawags. On the whole, the scalawags were unwilling to move beyond legal equality for blacks. Unlike blacks and a few carpetbaggers, they opposed social equality. They also proved to be slightly less proscriptive toward former Confederates than were their fellow partisans. During 1869, all three groups became less inclined to place restrictions on former Rebels. Other than some scandals, the Republican legislative record of reform was significant.[15]

Republicanism in North Carolina represented more than an "essentially . . . passing phase" created by a radical Congress. The party emerged in the state from a "well-established tradition of unionism, support for democratic reform, and opposition to the Confederacy, particularly in the area of civil liberty." The Union Party of 1865–66 accepting federal supremacy caused it to support Congressional Reconstruction and the Republican Party's agenda for "elevation of the Negro." By 1868, scalawags in the legislature championed reforms that distinguished them from the Democrats. Given the right situations, the party could retake control of the state's government into the 1880s and 1890s, as it did when Daniel L. Russell Jr. was elected governor in 1896.[16]

In Virginia, because General John M. Schofield opposed the new constitution's proscriptions, he delayed a referendum until July 1869, giving moderates time to mount a challenge. Conservative Party chairman Alexander Stuart took the initiative by calling a meeting of moderate conservatives, who, in turn, appointed the Committee of Nine to consult with moderate Republi-

14. Miller, "Samuel Field Phillips," 263–80; Phillips to K. P. Battle, 5 September 1865, 26 July, 16 August 1866, Battle Family Papers, Southern Historical Collection.

15. Allen W. Trelease, "Republican Reconstruction in North Carolina: A Roll-Call Analysis of the State House of Representatives, 1868–1870," *JSH* 42 (August 1976): 320–44.

16. Lancaster, "Scalawags of North Carolina," ii, 233, 396.

cans. Working together, the two groups acquired presidential and congressional backing to allow Virginians to vote separately on the disfranchisement provisions and the rest of the constitution. Moderate conservatives in return agreed to support the Republican ticket in the July 1869 state election if that party replaced Henry H. Wells, who had moved toward the radicals.[17]

Moderate Republicans, however, could not control their party. So when Wells received the nomination, they bolted. Afterward some of them met in Petersburg with Conservative Party moderate William Mahone and nominated former Union army officer Gilbert C. Walker, a Norfolk banker, on the "True Republican" ticket. The party represented mostly moderates led by John M. Botts (Francis H. Pierpont had returned to West Virginia). Now Virginia saw the strange sight of moderate Republicans and Conservatives voting for carpetbagger Walker for governor and for their own as legislators. Walker defeated Wells, but most legislative seats went to Conservatives. Finally, as was the plan, the constitution's proscriptions met defeat, while other parts of the constitution—which would endure for thirty years—were adopted.[18]

Some former Confederates now entered the Virginia Republican Party. Shortly after the November 1868 presidential election, General Samuel C. Armstrong, founder of Hampton Institute, reported that in eastern Virginia, "Republicans [were] increasing since the election of Grant, and [that] several southern gentlemen" in the Tidewater area were "much more radical" than himself. "Scores are getting down off the fence," he wrote, "and are rushing wildly to the Republican lines." They had, he commented, "already begun to talk of what they have suffered for their principles."[19] Noted cavalry commander John S. Mosby became a Republican in 1868. Mosby and Grant's mutual admiration undoubtedly led to Mosby's becoming a Republican. Mosby believed Grant would be reasonable concerning the South. After Mosby "canvassed Virginia" for Grant in 1872, the president was quoted as saying "that he owed the electoral vote of Virginia" to Mosby's campaigning.[20]

Robert W. Hughes, a states' rights Democrat who turned from law to jour

<hr />

17. Maddex, *Virginia Conservatives*, 67–85; Alexander H. H. Stuart, *A Narrative of the Leading Incidents of the Organization of the First Popular Movement in Virginia in 1865 to Re-Establish Peaceful Relations between the Northern and Southern States . . .* (Richmond, 1888), passim.

18. Ibid.

19. Fleming, *Documentary History of Reconstruction*, 1: 287; Maddex, "Virginia," 130.

20. Mosby to Jesse C. Green, 25 September 1888, John S. Mosby Papers, Small Special Collections Library, University of Virginia; Mosby, *War Reminiscences*, 6–7.

nalism during the 1850s, became the Republican Party's spokesman in 1869 through the *Richmond State Journal.* Although accused of opportunism, Hughes really was an independent thinker. For instance, he saw secession as legal but impractical, he backed the Confederacy but opposed President Davis, and he advocated reconciliation on congressional terms during 1865–66. But failing to generate support, he returned to the Democrats in 1868 before becoming a Republican in 1869. Through his newspaper, Hughes emphasized relief for debtors and economic development. He seemingly won some support for the party in the state. Grant carried Virginia in 1872, and Republicans won five of the state's nine seats in the U. S. House. Yet as the party's candidate for governor in 1873, he won only 43 percent of the vote.[21] Virginia's Republican Party continued to decline, only to be revived in the 1880s through its connection with the readjuster movement of dissatisfied conservatives who wanted to see the state's debt adjusted.[22]

In the Southeast from 1868 to 1870, whites becoming members of the Republican Party depended mostly on the influence of a few prominent converts. These included Brown of Georgia, who joined the party in spring 1868 and led the state's party delegation to the national convention that summer, and James L. Orr of South Carolina, who became a Republican shortly after stepping down as governor in summer 1868. Other whites associated with the party in Alabama when David P. Lewis and Lewis E. Parsons joined in early 1869. In Mississippi, Alcorn, who became governor in 1869, used both persuasion and patronage to attract whites to the Republican Party.[23]

Orr yielded to what he considered to be the best course for his state as well as for himself. In 1861, he accepted secession only as a last resort to save slavery and because of his loyalty to South Carolina. Then, as a Confederate senator, once defeat seemed inevitable, he, along with a handful of his congressional colleagues, asked for a negotiated peace. At the state's 1865 constitutional convention, because his course had appeared to be correct, Orr was "ready and forcible in debate." But some distrusted him because he sought to be the friend of all. Although as governor he marched in the forefront of the 1866 National Union Party movement, the Upland politician had a "virtue

21. Robert W. Hughes, *Papers Showing the Political Course of R. W. Hughes, the Republican Candidate for Governor, before and since the Fall of the Southern Confederacy in 1865; Prefixed by a Biographical Sketch* (Richmond, 1873), passim.

22. Maddex, "Virginia," 145–50; McKinney, "Mountain Republican Party-Army," 126, 139.

23. Foner, *Reconstruction,* 298–99.

possessed by no other South Carolinian," prominence. He could "change his mind on fundamentals when his sound sense of realism told him that this was necessary."[24]

During 1865–68, Governor Orr steered a moderate course. Regarding race relations, he persuaded legislators to modify the severe, unworkable black code they had passed earlier. By 1867, he even espoused black suffrage, with literacy and/or small property restrictions. When Congressional Reconstruction came, Orr refused to join other southern leaders before the federal courts or to back voter boycotts. Although he deferred becoming a Republican during 1867, he helped the military carry out Reconstruction.[25]

After he left office in July 1868, the newly elected Republican legislature selected Orr as one of the state circuit judges. Shortly thereafter, he became a Republican. The longtime politician did not "perceive any particular abandonment of principle in becoming a Republican." He thought "the white people of South Carolina, by joining the Republican party, . . . [could place] the control of the State in the hands of the intelligent and educated population." Several of Orr's friends and fellow National Democrats of the 1850s followed his example, including his law partner, Jacob P. Reed, a candidate for congress on the Democratic ticket in 1868, and the Melton brothers, Cyrus and Samuel, of York County.[26]

The Melton brothers had opposed secession but supported the Confederacy. Cyrus took "little part in public affairs" during the war and was "known . . . as a Union man." He barely missed winning election as president of the 1865 constitutional convention. After becoming a Republican in 1868, the scholarly man held several political posts. His more sociable brother, Samuel, often voiced his unionist opinion as an editor in the 1850s. Yet Samuel served with distinction on the battlefield and as assistant adjutant general of the Confederacy. Among other duties, according to a political enemy, Samuel issued an "order for burning Richmond" during the government's evacuation in 1865. A few months later, he became Governor Orr's chief of staff. After becoming a Republican, beginning in 1868 he served as circuit judge, state attor-

24. Andrews, *South since the War*, 49–50; Perman, *Reunion without Compromise*, 222–23; Simkins and Woody, *South Carolina during Reconstruction*, 77–79.

25. Leemhuis, *James L. Orr*, 122–30; Williamson, *After Slavery*, 77–79.

26. *KKK Report*, S.C., 14, 21; Brooks, *Bench and Bar*, 178–83, 191–94; Reynolds, *Reconstruction in South Carolina*, 295.

ney general, and federal district attorney. Like many South Carolina scalawags, he was a Methodist and a Mason.[27]

One of the most interesting latecomers to the Republican Party in South Carolina was Dr. John Winsmith of Spartanburg County, a wealthy longtime legislator. He served in the constitutional convention of 1865 and then the state senate. In 1868, the former fire-eater did an about-face. Although he considered himself a conservative, he backed Republican Robert K. Scott for governor. His course proved to be unpopular and costly. Receiving a night visit from about forty Klansmen, the stubborn old man seized his two out-dated single-shot pistols and ran into his yard firing at the night riders as they took cover. They were unharmed, but they returned fire, wounding him seven times. Still, he survived and thereafter they left him alone. Winsmith criticized the federal government for its inability to protect its citizens, but he stayed politically active.[28]

Some latecomers to the Republican Party in South Carolina included individuals who joined the party either shortly before or shortly after being appointed to state judicial posts. Robert F. Graham, who had excellent southern credentials—an honors graduate of the state university, Confederate colonel, postwar legislator, and Democratic presidential elector in 1868—"declared his adhesion to the Republican party in the summer of 1870." Soon thereafter he was elected as a circuit judge. Other latecomers included Thompson H. Cooke of Greenville, a Citadel graduate known as a man of "honesty and integrity," who was elected as a circuit judge in 1873, and John J. Maher of Barnwell, who was said to have accepted the circuit judge nomination in 1876 "at the solicitation of the Republican party."[29]

In Georgia, shortly after campaigning for the new constitution in the April 1868 ratification election, Brown became a full-fledged Republican. Showing its appreciation, the party selected him to lead its delegation to the Republican National Convention in May at Chicago. In a speech to the convention, Brown charmed delegates, telling them what they wanted to hear about his

27. Cyrus D. Melton petition, n.d., Amnesty Papers, RG 94; A. S. Wallace to Charles Sumner, 8 December 1866, 19 March 1867, Sumner Papers; Reynolds, *Reconstruction in South Carolina*, 158, 172, 229, 372; newspaper clipping, n.d., Benjamin F. Perry Papers, Rare Book, Manuscript, and Special Collections Library, Duke University.

28. Trelease, *White Terror*, 360.

29. Brooks, *Bench and Bar*, 187–90, 191–94, 206–7.

political conversion and the party in Georgia. He supported Congressional Reconstruction as the best terms the victorious North had to offer. He predicted that Georgia Republicans in November's presidential election would "roll up a majority for Gen. Grant." When Brown returned home, he played a leading role in the Central Grant Club of Georgia. In August, he spoke to an estimated crowd of seven thousand at a Grant-Colfax rally in Atlanta.[30]

Brown swept many admirers into the fold. Some friends following him into the party became officeholders, including two of his law partners, John D. Pope, a former Confederate later appointed U.S. attorney, and Judge Osborne A. Lochrane, Brown's successor on the state supreme court. Dawson A. Walker, who visited Washington with Brown in early 1867, also joined the party and later was its 1872 gubernatorial candidate.[31] Brown's motivation, like that of his friends insofar as they expressed it, was to stimulate Georgia's economic recovery by getting the state back in the Union and to direct the Republican Party along a moderate course. "Retrospecting dispassionately" on Brown's role in Reconstruction, a conservative friend averred, now "we can see how our righteous passion injured us, increased our difficulties, retarded our restoration, and created new and harder terms . . . the position of Gov. Brown was very logical."[32]

Three types of individuals were influenced by Brown: those who followed him in advocating Congressional Reconstruction and preceded him into the Republican Party; those who, like himself, supported the Reconstruction Acts but waited until 1868 to enter the party; and those who followed his guidance in 1867 but remained Democrats. Brown's former law partner Pope, judge of the Coweta Circuit, said he became a Republican early on "having voted for [the] convention, for the constitution, for Governor Bullock and for President Grant." Pope remained a Republican despite Democratic leaders and press engaging in "a systematic effort . . . to mortify, to slander, to disgrace, and to drive from society and from business, all white men who . . . avowed . . . republican principles."[33]

Dr. Samuel Bard became a Republican about the same time as his friend

30. Parks, *Joseph E. Brown*, 418–20; *Speech of Ex-Governor Brown of Georgia, Delivered in the National Republican Convention at Chicago in 1868* (n.p., n.d.); Taylor, "From the Ashes," 294; *Atlanta New Era*, 2 June 1868; *Proceedings of the Republican National Convention* (Chicago, 1868), 91–92.

31. Parks, *Joseph E. Brown*, 408, 467.

32. Avery, *History of the State of Georgia*, 377.

33. *The Condition of Affairs in Georgia* (Washington, D.C., 1869), 152–54.

Brown. Bard, an experienced journalist, had started the *Atlanta New Era* in 1866 as a pro-Johnson journal; he moved from a "wait and see" position in early 1867 to an "ardently reconstructionist" one later in the year, becoming "openly and candidly . . . Republican" in 1868. In the spring 1868 election campaign for the new constitution and for state officeholders, the *Atlanta New Era* called upon Georgia's "poor men" to elect Republicans as a means to bring "*Relief, Homesteads* and *Schools* for the people." Bard, afterward elected state printer, offered no idealistic rationale for his conversion. He candidly admitted he "accepted in good faith the Constitutional Amendment and Reconstruction Acts, not as the best measures for the South and the Union, but as the penalty of defeat." One radical claimed Bard was so conservative, he was "the only person . . . acquainted with himself that [knew] that he [was] a republican."[34]

V. A. Gaskill of Atlanta was a New Englander who came to Georgia "to teach school, and like most other Yankee boys found a girl [he] liked and stayed with her." He went on to practice law and edit the *Atlanta Intelligencer,* and he followed Brown into Reconstruction but not into the Republican Party. He campaigned for the new state constitution in north Georgia, "taking the position that suffrage was guaranteed" to blacks by the document, "but that office-holding was not." But he soon found the Republican Party too radical and attended the state Democratic convention in 1868. He claimed to occupy "the somewhat anamalous [*sic*] position of being called a 'reconstruction democrat' and was abused by the people on both sides."[35]

The greatest long-term defeat for the Georgia Republican Party came when a Democratic–moderate Republican combination successfully excluded thirty-two blacks from the legislature on the ground that the new constitution did not explicitly allow blacks to serve in public office. This position had been taken by several Republican leaders, including Brown, during the April election. Although congressional Republicans overturned the exclusion of the blacks in December 1869, politically the damage was done. Georgia Republicans could not make up in white votes what they lost in black votes. In the future, blacks would more likely vote for their own, stay home, or in some

---

34. Joseph E. Brown to Edward McPherson, 22 March 1867, McPherson Papers; Samuel Bard, *A Letter from Samuel Bard to President Grant on the Political Situation in Georgia* (Atlanta, 1870), 5; *Atlanta New Era,* 29 April 1868; Edwin Belcher to Charles Sumner, 15 December 1868, Sumner Papers.

35. *Condition of Affairs in Georgia,* 23–25.

cases vote Democratic, because white Republicans had proved they did not want to share political power with black leaders.[36]

Few Republican converts in Georgia who became party leaders emerged after the summer of 1868; most who did probably sought place and position. For example, one Republican characterized Judge William Gibson of Augusta as "a rampant rebel [and] colonel of a rebel regiment," as being "elected as a rebel judge over a Union man after the war," and as being initially "opposed to reconstruction in 1867." Another agreed that the circuit judge from Augusta was "suddenly converted to republicanism" shortly before the party's 1868 national convention, to which he was made a delegate because of his "supposed social standing." The same person said Gibson had a "love of office and [would] always be found on the strongest side."[37]

Others contemplating political conversion turned away when they did not receive a coveted office. This may have been a factor in four men's refusal to run as presidential electors in 1868, after they appeared at a Grant-for-president rally in Atlanta and after they were nominated by the state Republican Party. After failing to acquire a judgeship, Edward Harden of Athens declined to be a Grant presidential elector in 1868. "Gov. Brown, with all his pretended friendship sold [him] out," and Brown and Bullock "proved treacherous," he said, claiming he was "determined now to go with [his] race and [his] section and . . . vote for Seymour & Blair."[38]

Carpetbaggers deprived very few scalawags in Georgia of public office. According to one newspaper, the constitutional convention of 275 members contained only thirteen carpetbaggers. Reportedly eleven were "consistent members of Christian churches," leaving only two who were "given to profanity, intemperance, or the keeping of low company." Of the 214 members of the subsequent legislature, only "seven [had] become residents of the State since the war." Carpetbaggers and blacks combined composed no more than one-sixth of the membership of the constitutional convention or of the legislature following it. Of all former Confederate states, Georgia was probably freest of carpetbagger influence. There were northern-born Republicans of influence in the state who held significant state offices, but they had settled in the state before the Civil War.[39]

36. Nathans, *Losing the Peace,* 120–25.

37. *Report of the Committee on the Judiciary in Senate Reports,* 41st Cong., 2d sess., No. 175.

38. Harden to his Mother, 20 August 1868, Edward R. Harden Papers, Rare Book, Manuscript, and Special Collections Library, Duke University.

39. Thompson, *Reconstruction in Georgia,* 216–17; Conway, *Reconstruction of Georgia,* 161.

In Florida, despite being out of power, Conservative-Democratic leaders viewed the new constitution and Governor Harrison Reed's election optimistically. Charles Dyke, editor of the conservative *Tallahassee Floridian,* wrote to a fellow partisan that conservatives "ought to be grateful to Reed & Co." for controlling the "dangerous faction headed by Billings and for forming a Constitution so much more liberal than was expected" (obviously referring to the document's lack of proscription against former Confederates).[40] Reed reminded his former business partner David Yulee that "under our Constitution the Judiciary and State officers will be appointed," giving the governor almost complete control, and that the state's way of "apportionment will prevent a Negro Legislature." Finally, Reed saw his election as protecting the "material interest of the state" and as preventing a group of "conspirators" from destroying the state's railroads by wiping out their charters and taking control of them.[41]

Reed even made overtures to conservatives by appointing two of them— Robert J. Gamble and James D. Westcott—to his cabinet and by filling four of the seven circuit courts with conservative judges. But his actions recruited few Republican converts and he never came close to creating a coalition with the conservatives. Other than a few high-ranking appointments, Reed with rare exceptions named Republicans to state and local posts. The abuse of the conservative press, the violence of the Ku Klux Klan, and the disruptive methods used by conservative legislators caused Governor Reed to use any legal method possible to protect Republicans of both races. Moderate Republicans, mostly under carpetbag leadership, continued to control the state until 1877. During the 1870s, very little, if any, increase in the number of southern white Republicans occurred. When conservatives took over under Governor George F. Drew, the governor's appointive power and the state's apportionment laws almost enabled him to annihilate the state Republican Party.[42]

Some of Florida's fifteen hundred or so scalawags and its four hundred to five hundred carpetbaggers supported each of the different Republican factions in the state during Reconstruction. Most Jacksonville Republicans followed the moderate path of Hart and the Union Republican Club. But exceptions existed, such as William H. Christy and Calvin L. Robinson, who predicted that the Monticello constitution would bring conservative control.

40. Merlin G. Cox, "Military Reconstruction in Florida," *FHQ* 46 (January 1968): 232–33.
41. Ibid.
42. Shofner, "Florida," 25–27.

Several scalawags from the central part of the state, including some wartime deserters and refugees, were radicals. Scalawags failed to form a distinct faction. Generally they worked as well with carpetbaggers as carpetbaggers did with each other, and their resentment of newcomers seemed less flagrant than elsewhere. Although scalawags did not control the state administration, except for a few weeks under Hart, they divided other political plums almost equally with the carpetbaggers (both at the expense of blacks). Only two blacks received high-ranking offices in the state, Secretary of State Jonathan C. Gibbs and Congressman Josiah Walls.[43]

Many Alabama whites affiliated with the Republican Party after 1868. According to one study, which included blacks and carpetbaggers as well as scalawags, about one-third of the activists joined the party after 1868. Along with Mississippi, Alabama had the largest number of white Republican converts after 1868. Before the 1868 presidential campaign came to a close, David P. Lewis of Madison County, only a few months earlier a Democratic National Convention delegate, crossed over to the Republicans. He penned a series of newspaper articles defending national Republican Party policies and voted for Grant. He had a strange Civil War career, as a unionist at his state's secession convention, as a Confederate congressman who refused to take a loyalty oath to the Confederacy and resigned, and as a district judge and peace society member. When life in the state became unbearable, Lewis fled through Federal lines to Nashville in 1863. But Lewis opposed Congressional Reconstruction mainly because he felt it unfair to punish those "forced into rebellion against their votes, & their wishes." He believed that the Republican Party could grow in the South by appealing to the many "Douglas & Bell men" who in recent years had abstained from voting. The party could only succeed if it exempted from restrictions those who served the Confederacy for their own safety and who welcomed the state's restoration to the Union.[44]

After Grant's election, former governor Parsons took the attitude, if you can't lick 'em, join 'em. He had certainly tried to lick 'em. Following his failure to be seated as a United States senator during 1865–66, he became a leader of the pro-Johnson National Union Convention movement. He lobbied in Alabama against the Fourteenth Amendment and in Washington against

43. Shofner, *Nor Is It Over Yet,* 172–74, 213; *KKK Report,* Fla., 219; Hume, "'Black and Tan' Constitutional Conventions," 546–47, 553; Hume, "Florida Constitutional Convention," 12–13, 19–21.

44. Cash, "Alabama Republicans," 164; Wiggins, "Amnesty and Pardon," 240–48.

Congressional Reconstruction. When both became laws of the land, he joined others before the federal courts in questioning the constitutionality of the Reconstruction Acts. He also backed a boycott of southern elections, which tried to defeat Reconstruction by preventing a majority of registered voters from casting ballots for a convention as required by the initial legislation. In 1868, he led Alabama's delegation to the Democratic National Convention and campaigned for its presidential nominee. When Grant defeated Governor Horatio Seymour of New York, however, Parsons questioned his own dogmatism. He concluded that as long as southerners opposed Republicans, that party's leaders would be "suspicious of [their] intentions in regard to the Negro and the perpetuity of the Union." He saw it "would be better to make terms" with them and in "that way acquire their confidence." During spring 1869, Parsons urged Alabama audiences to put past political battles behind them. In September 1869, he announced his own conversion to the Republican Party.[45]

Parsons's law partner and longtime friend Alexander White, owner of extensive landholdings, also became a Republican about the same time. One contemporary felt that Parsons and White, leaders of other political movements—the Whigs for Douglas campaign in 1860 and the National Union effort of 1866—desired power and had decided "to reassemble the antebellum Whigs under the Republican banner." White wrote, "We need capital and we need labor," and neither the state nor the national Democratic Party could attract them to Alabama. Shortly after Grant's election in November 1868, White mailed an unsigned address, "To the Old Union Men of Alabama," urging them to accept the election results, the finality of black suffrage, and the need for northern capital. White also, like Lewis, advised national Republican leaders to remove the proscriptions on "the old Union men." His plan initially called for a third party, but when that effort failed, he became a Republican.[46]

Others followed Lewis, Parsons, and White into the Republican Party. Although few in number, such prominent converts threw party leadership to the scalawags. Scalawags, for example, made up 70 percent of their party's state presidential electors from 1868 to 1880. Although carpetbaggers claimed about one-third of high-ranking public offices, below that level they fared far

45. *KKK Report,* Ala., 77; Wiggins, "Five Men," 47, 50.
46. Wiggins, "Five Men," 47, 50; Wiggins, "Alabama Attitudes," 28–30.

more poorly. One study found individuals "elected to office in Alabama as Republicans between 1867 and 1880 were, in four-fifths of the instances, white ante-bellum residents of the state." Still scalawags constantly complained about carpetbaggers being given preference for some offices. Seeking to silence the clamor, the *(Montgomery) Alabama State Journal* in 1872 published a list of offices held by each group, showing 232 scalawag officeholders, compared with 49 carpetbaggers.[47]

Although scalawag David P. Lewis claimed that by 1868 "carpetbaggers [had] already landed everything that is Republican in Hell," if this had ever been the case, it certainly changed by 1872. That year a ticket of all scalawags, headed by Lewis, won the state election. Writing a generation later, former congressman Frederick G. Bromberg of Mobile, a successful attorney until his death despite his Republican politics, questioned the idea of the domination of the carpetbaggers. He wrote that of his thirty-two colleagues in the state senate in 1868, "only nine belonged to the class called 'carpetbaggers.'" The others, he said, included a white Democrat, a black Republican, and the remainder were all white Republicans of "advanced years" with large families. In the state house, he wrote, Democrats numbered from fourteen to sixteen, Negroes numbered no more than thirteen, and all others were white Republicans, including a few carpetbaggers. Almost all of the state's white majority counties, mainly the "central and northern counties," elected legislators who were either "natives, or old ante-bellum citizens," and those legislators elected one of their own, attorney B. F. McCraw of Pike County, as speaker of the state house of representatives. Elsewhere, some "aspiring negroes . . . and 'carpetbaggers'" briefly did control counties where "the negro was predominant in numbers."[48]

Before the beginning of Congressional Reconstruction, most Mississippi scalawags favored President Johnson's program. Even after, only about one-third of them affiliated with the Republican Party during 1867. Several factors caused Mississippi scalawags to delay identifying with the Republican Party, including the state's mild military rule from March 1867 to March 1869. Generals Edward O. C. Ord of Maryland and Alvan C. Gillem of Tennessee refused to replace conservative officeholders and prohibited those under their

---

47. Wiggins, "Five Men," 46, 48; Cash, "Alabama Republicans," 164; Wiggins, *Scalawag in Alabama Politics*, 132–33.

48. Frederick G. Bromberg, *The Reconstruction Period in Alabama* ([Mobile, Ala.], 1911–14), 1: 4–6.

command from engaging in partisan politics. The splintering of Mississippians into several factions from 1867 to 1869 slowed further scalawag enlistment. Before the initial meeting of the state Republican Party in September 1867, two other parties appeared, the Cooperationist, or Reconstruction, Party, and the Constitutional Union Party (named after the 1860 party). Scalawags who did not immediately identify with the Republican Party could be found in both camps, but most became Cooperationists hoping for immediate restoration without radical rule.[49]

After Grant's election as president in November 1868, several important Mississippians edged toward the Republican Party. Horatio Simrall, soon to be appointed by his old friend Governor Alcorn to the Mississippi Supreme Court, declared himself a Republican in spring 1869. He said he was "disposed to take [his] state from her isolation and hitch her onto the car of progress; to place her in such condition that the rich streams that flow out from the national treasury may not float past her." Simrall, who had served in the Kentucky as well as the Mississippi legislature, said he wanted "to open wide the door that people from the North, the East, and the West; from Europe, and if you please from Asia may . . . dwell amongst us." To attract capital and labor to Mississippi, he said, there would have to be "absolute freedom of opinion of the tongue and pen, [and] obedience to and enforcement of the laws." This he believed could best be brought about by the Republican Party.[50]

Encouraged by President Grant's willingness to follow a nonproscriptive course in Mississippi (as well as in Virginia), state moderates formed the National Union Republican Party of Mississippi. To enhance their position with Grant, they nominated his brother-in-law, Louis Dent, who was residing in the state. But after the new party fell under the influence of several former enemies of Congressional Reconstruction, Grant abandoned any notion of backing it. Instead, after being assured by the regular Republicans that they would now oppose proscription, the president endorsed them. At this point, Alcorn, who since 1865 had been a political voice crying in the wilderness, announced his willingness to support the Republican Party. He was in turn nominated as the candidate of the regulars, who opposed Dent. Alcorn, ac-

49. William C. Harris, "Mississippi: Republican Factionalism and Mismanagement," in *Reconstruction and Redemption*, 78–80; Harris, "Reconstruction of the Commonwealth," 568–69; Harris, *Day of the Carpetbagger*, 232.

50. Harris, *Day of the Carpetbagger*, 232.

cording to his biographer, aimed "to reassemble the antebellum Whig party" under the Republican banner.[51]

Meanwhile the military command in Mississippi underwent a significant change when General Adelbert Ames, a loyal Republican from New England, replaced conservative Tennessean Gillem. Ames did exactly what the state's Republicans had desired since the beginning of Congressional Reconstruction: he removed conservatives from office and named in their stead regular Republicans, who were expected to carry the election for their party. Altogether, Ames made more than two thousand changes in officeholders, and he named a new slate of registrars to guarantee his control of the election machinery. The combined elements of a more moderate Republican Party, the president's backing, the rewards of office for Republicans, the candidacy of an old respected Mississippian, and perhaps most important, the support of General Ames gave an impressive victory to Alcorn. Once he became governor, Alcorn appointed many of his 1869 opponents, especially his antebellum associates, most of whom identified with the Republican Party. Although Alcorn failed to attract prominent former Whigs in large numbers to the Republican Party, he did appoint many lesser-known ones. His administration became Whiggish enough to cause complaints from his party's former Union Democrats.[52]

During 1870–71, an increasing number of Mississippi leaders came to believe that a black majority at the polls would be a permanent situation in the state. According to one black, Congressman John R. Lynch of Natchez, his race had the opportunity after 1872 to choose from among many qualified white candidates. He believed it natural that Negroes preferred "the aristocrat of the past." Their relationship, he said, had been "friendly, cordial and amicable," while blacks' relationship to the "poor whites" had been just the opposite. "When the partiality of the colored man for the former aristocrats became generally known," he said, "the former aristocrats . . . began to come into the Republican party in large numbers . . . between 1872 and 1875."[53]

Among Mississippians entering the Republican fold during the 1870s was Orlando Davis of Tippah County, who became a circuit judge in 1870. He had

51. Harris, "Reconstruction of the Commonwealth," 569–70; Pereyra, *James Lusk Alcorn*, 90–93.

52. Garner, *Reconstruction in Mississippi*, 237–47; Degler, *Other South*, 199; James L. Alcorn to R. H. Waller, 1 August 1869, *Mississippi Pilot*, 25 September 1873, clipping, James L. Alcorn to his wife, n.d., Alcorn Papers; Sansing, "Role of the Scalawag in Mississippi," 151, 159; James L. Alcorn petition, n.d, RG 233.

53. Lynch, *Facts of Reconstruction*, 105–7.

been a delegate to the Democratic National Convention in 1868. Although he had strongly favored secession in 1861, once the war ended, he felt that since southern "arms . . . proved unsuccessful," it was his "duty to return . . . allegiance to the United States Government and yield to its policy a fair and candid support." His stand in 1870 was in keeping with that position. Davis was one of the state's many scalawag judges. Of the total number of Reconstruction Republican judges, scalawags accounted for fifty-five and carpetbaggers sixteen.[54]

Colonel James A. Lusk was another Republican convert for a while. Because of his respectability in his community, Lusk received a hero-like welcome from the predominately black local Republican club. Like many whites who joined the party in Mississippi during the 1870s, Lusk returned to the Democratic Party once white-line politics began. "No white man can live in the South in the future and act with any other than the Democratic fold unless he is . . . prepared to live a life of social isolation and remain in political oblivion," he said. By not being a Democrat, he told his black friends, he would hurt not only his own "political ambition" but any "future prospects" for his sons and he would bring the "humiliating consequences of . . . social ostracism" upon his daughters.[55]

Although Louisiana scalawags outnumbered carpetbaggers in the constitutional convention, in the legislatures that followed, scalawag numbers were small. The 1868 election saw Democrats win many of the seats in the larger towns and in the largely white-populated counties of the piney woods, winning 45 of 101 seats in the lower house and 16 of 36 in the senate. Predominately black districts elected either blacks or carpetbaggers, mostly former election supervisors, leaving scalawags only a few seats.

The first two speakers of the state house of representatives were southerners, but neither had resided in Louisiana very long: Mortimer Carr of Maryland, a young man "shrewd and wily in the extreme," and George W. Carter, a former Confederate colonel from Houston. Carter was a Methodist preacher and professor turned lawyer. He had successfully defended Warmoth in 1867 when he faced a charge in Galveston of embezzling $21,000. After Warmoth was elected, he convinced Carter to relocate to Louisiana. Warmoth appointed him judge for the newly created Cameron Parish. Soon thereafter, Carter was

54. Ibid., 107, 119–22, 128–29, 162; Sansing, "Role of the Scalawag in Mississippi," 176.
55. Lynch, *Facts of Reconstruction*, 119–23.

elected to the Louisiana house. Carter, a recent Republican, had tried in 1867 to persuade Houston blacks to support the Conservative Party. By now Carter was "old and rather deaf" but just as "shrewd and wily" as Carr. Carter's explanation for corruption in Louisiana politics was as good as any: "There seems to be something in the climate here that affects both parties."[56]

Only about two dozen scalawags received high-ranking state or federal posts in Louisiana before 1877. Seeking a federal job for his son Levi in 1867, former governor James Madison Wells, now practicing law in New Orleans, wrote that "nearly all the Federal appointments . . . have been filled by persons from other States . . . on the Score of loyalty." He thought that "all things being equal . . . preference should be given to those 'of the manor born' . . . who have lost everything by the war." This situation never changed appreciably. For the next eight years, only one-third of major federal officeholders serving in Louisiana resided there before 1861. Clearly control of the state's Republican Party passed into the hands of the carpetbaggers during 1867–68. Their vitality, camaraderie, and organizational skills—largely an outgrowth of army and Freedmen's Bureau experience—plus their influence with blacks and with Washington proved too formidable for their challengers.[57]

By the summer of 1867, former Democratic leaders in Arkansas had returned to the political scene. Robert W. Johnson, a former United States as well as Confederate senator, expressed his regrets about recent events in what he called the nation's "weakest state, counting wealth & numbers." He believed the Murphy administration was "mere shadows," that the military actually ruled. Johnson believed the new governor, Powell Clayton, was Murphy's opposite, having "greater audacity than Brownlow." Johnson estimated that altogether the Republicans represented "not over 500, if 250" leaders backed by "white followers not over 6000 consisting respectively of the corrupt, the criminal; & ignorant, or bewildered."[58]

During the state's decade of Reconstruction, scalawags held about half of the high-ranking offices, mostly during Murphy's tenure. A few received important Treasury and Justice Department appointments from President

56. Howard James Jones, "The Members of the Louisiana Legislature of 1868: Images of 'Radical Reconstruction' Leadership in the Deep South" (Ph.D. diss., Washington State University, 1975), 229–30; Lonn, Reconstruction in Louisiana, 8, 24n, 76, 88, 91n; Taylor, Louisiana Reconstructed, 213.

57. Taylor, Louisiana Reconstructed, 138; Wells to William E. Chandler, 18 May 1867, William P. Kellogg to Chandler, 17 April 1868, William E. Chandler Papers.

58. Robert W. Johnson to Johnson, 28 July 1868, PAJ, 14: 438–41.

Grant. But generally, after 1868 carpetbaggers monopolized prestigious posts.[59] Much of this was attributable to Clayton's power as governor and his influence later as a U.S. senator. Clayton goes to great lengths in *The Aftermath of the Civil War in Arkansas* to dispute charges that the period was a "Carpet-Bag Era." As he claims, such was not the case at the local level, where only 18 percent of 262 officials identified arrived in Arkansas during or following the war, or in the legislature, where over two-thirds of members were white southern natives. But the judiciary was about equally divided between carpetbaggers and scalawags, and significantly, carpetbaggers held most administrative, congressional, and federal positions.[60]

Arkansas Republican converts of importance after 1868 were almost non-existent. James F. Fagan of Saline County, an exception, was an unlikely candidate. Even though he had opposed secession, he recruited Confederate troops and became the state's highest-ranking general. He was a postwar Democratic Party leader until he became a Republican. Afterward, he headed a state militia divisions, served as a delegate to the constitutional convention of 1874, and was a U.S. marshal under appointment from President Grant. Fagan was one of several significant former Confederate commanders who became Republicans shortly after Grant's election in 1868. Others included Parson of Texas, Mosby of Virginia, and Maney of Tennessee. They respected Grant, his directness as a military man, and the way he appeared to be reaching out to southerners.[61]

In keeping with the mood of the Grant administration, the position of Texas moderates prevailed at Washington in all but one respect, that of wanting to hold the coming state election in July 1869. Confident of an approaching electoral triumph, Andrew J. Hamilton announced his gubernatorial candidacy from Washington, and soon he was campaigning in Texas. On April 20, the state Republican executive committee, meeting in Austin, voted against holding a state nominating convention and endorsed Hamilton for governor. Radicals met on June 7 at Houston to nominate Edmund J. Davis as governor. The Houston platform reflected a changed attitude on the part of most radicals: that the constitution represented the best possible document,

59. Orval Truman Driggs Jr., "The Issues of Powell Clayton Regime, 1868–1871" *ArkHQ* 8 (spring 1949): 59–75; Facts and Reminiscences, 25–27, Berry Papers.

60. Goodspeed, *Biographical and Historical Memoirs of Northwest Arkansas*, 961–62, 999–1000, 1075; Clayton, *Aftermath of the Civil War*, 298–304.

61. Warner, *Generals in Gray*, 85–86.

that its adoption was certain, and that therefore they must adjust to prevailing circumstances.[62]

The subdued position of radicals indicated to Grant that they wanted to unite the Texas party. Some moderates deserted Hamilton, and a number of high-ranking federal employees forwarded a petition to Washington condemning the Hamilton ticket as being supported primarily by Democrats. General Joseph J. Reynolds, once again commander of troops in Texas, initially favored moderate Republicans. By midsummer, however, he turned on them, either because of their failure to conclude a deal to back him for the U.S. Senate and/or because of their flirtation with white Democrats. At Reynolds's suggestion, Grant set the gubernatorial election late in 1869, allowing radicals a longer time to organize. He also purged the Hamilton-Pease federal officeholders, replacing them with radicals. Davis, with Reynold's aid, won by a small margin.[63]

By 1869, the issue in Texas was who would rule, moderates or radicals, rather than whose principles would prevail. Some individuals shifted from one group to another depending upon political advantage. The two wings differed little. The party platforms, political speeches, and private letters show concern about violence, civil rights, free public schools, internal improvements, and inducement for immigration. Though a few party leaders declared for social equality, most Republicans, blacks and whites, avoided the issue. The Texas Republican Party's primary weakness was not internal division. Rather the trouble was the party's inability to generate broad-based political support. The party's political power depended upon one or more highly unlikely circumstances: continued congressional support for radical government in the South, disfranchisement of a large number of white Texans, division of Texas into two or more states, adoption by the white majority of a new attitude regarding race, the winning of popular support by the highly unpopular Davis administration, and/or a rapid, heavy influx of northern and foreign immigrants into Texas.[64]

Scalawag latecomers to the Reconstruction Republican Party in Texas were few and far between. Of those scalawag leaders who joined the party after 1868, the best known included Lemuel D. Evans, a conservative unionist from Marshall who opposed the Republicans before and throughout his service in

62. *American Annual Cyclopaedia, 1869*, 674; Waller, *Colossal Hamilton*, 124–25.
63. Baggett, "Rise and Fall of the Texas Radicals," 105–7.
64. Baggett. "Birth of the Texas Republican Party," 20.

the constitutional convention of 1868–69. His failure to find a comfortable political home among former Confederates and his former association with many who became Republicans probably led to his support of the party after 1870. Governor Davis appointed him as chief justice of the Texas Supreme Court in 1870, and afterward he served as U.S. marshal for the state's eastern district. Others who came into the party were strong Confederates as long as the war lasted—men such as William Chambers, the party's gubernatorial candidate after Davis; Thomas Ochiltree of Galveston, who served as one of the state's immigration commissioners before being appointed by President Grant to replace Evans as U.S. marshal and being elected to Congress as an independent in 1883; and William H. Parson, a former Confederate army officer who supported Davis in 1869 and was elected to the state senate before becoming a state commissioner of immigration.[65]

In the Southeast and Southwest, which lacked good foundations for white Republicanism, the party's influence, along with many of its white followers, would disappear by 1880. Unlike the Upper South, where under the right circumstances the party could win statewide elections, the other two sections saw one state party after another after the 1870s become incapable of winning general elections. The Republican party there largely became a party of federal officeholders and conventioneers. The Republican strategy of moderation may have to a degree worked in the Upper South and briefly made the party viable in Alabama and Mississippi, but it was doomed in the Lower South as a new generation of Democrats came to the polls. Republicans did not lose to Democrats in the 1870s so much because of a decline in their voting base, composed primarily of blacks and a few thousand whites. They lost because of Democratic momentum and bulldozing, both driven by a renewed spirit of white supremacy.

65. W. H. Parson to James P. Newcomb, 7 October 1869, Newcomb Papers; *Reporter,* 3 September 1866; *BDAC,* 1007, 1600.

10

~

Summing Up the Scalawags

S cholars have assessed scalawags generally in one of three ways. Some have categorized them by motivations, such as bitterness, greed, opportunism, or even loyalty to the Union and a desire to help their state. Others see them as undergoing a progression from being members of unionist political parties or factions before the war, especially the Whigs, to opposing secession, being less than enthusiastic Confederates to outright resisters, to being members of unionist parties in 1865–66, to reluctantly accepting black suffrage and becoming Republicans during 1867–69. Finally a few individuals have placed them by location and as members of a certain class, planter Whigs who wanted to control black voters to prevent the rule of their enemies in the Democratic Party or contrarily poor whites who formerly supported the Democratic Party. A few writers have combined these approaches.

This present study of scalawag leaders was undertaken with the assumption that political conditions, and the social and geographic factors that caused them, differed enough from state to state to cause variances in their origins. It assumed that few individuals are political loners, that they act in concert with others, be they ever so few, which gives them some security in their decision making. It assumed that individuals act from a background, that those acts usually do not depart from stands they have previously taken, and that there is a progression in most political decision making. The past guides one's options or courses of action. This can be seen with original unionists, who drew on their past as antisecessionists as well as their past as Confederates, reluctant or otherwise. Scalawags—a great majority of whom claimed to have been reluctant Confederates or resisters to the Confederacy—had a different past than most southerners. Their past made them more disposed to join unionist parties during 1865–66 and the Republican Party in 1867.

Unlike northern founders of the Republican Party, southern founders did not identify with the party's antislavery beginnings in the 1850s. Only about one in twenty scalawags showed hostility toward slavery before the war. Those resided primarily in central North Carolina, with a few Quakers in eastern Virginia and Germans in the Southwest. One-half of the scalawags had held slaves, compared with two-thirds of redeemers. Scalawags also owned fewer slaves than did their opponents, which was largely a reflection of their being less wealthy. Although some scalawags had resented planters and the advantages given to planters in the South, especially during the war, others defended slavery both before and during the war. Even prewar settlers in the South did not claim to have become Republicans because of antislavery convictions. Rather, they pointed to their northern nativity, Whig politics, and nationalism as the reasons they opposed secession, accepted Congressional Reconstruction, and joined the Republican Party. As the war progressed, some scalawags changed their minds about slavery, especially as they formed alliances with the antislavery Lincoln administration. Some even freed their slaves before circumstances forced them to do so.

Overall, scalawags were less well-to-do than were redeemers. But exceptions existed. For example, in Alabama and Louisiana, 1860 estates of each group were about equal. In a few states, scalawags had accumulated more than redeemers had in others; those of North Carolina held property exceeding that of redeemers in half of the other states. Many in both groups reported small antebellum estates, an indication they had not come into their own financially and that numerous well-heeled officeholders ended their political careers with the war. The financial gap between scalawags and redeemers narrowed by 1865. Redeemers suffered a greater financial loss in the Lost Cause.

Scalawags also had less formal education than redeemers. But they acquired far more schooling than most southerners. Many had been teachers, and most were lawyers. Forty percent attended college, a large majority studied to practice professions, and some even achieved scholarly distinction. Neither group had arrived politically in 1860. But both were active in politics, either campaigning for themselves or for others or participating in rallies and conventions. Fewer scalawags had held office, had held more than one trust, or had obtained the highest positions. The widest margin of difference in experience appeared in the Upper South and the smallest in the Southwest. Both groups saw the most service in the Southeast. Less officeholding experience everywhere among scalawags is partially attributable to their having belonged mostly to the minority Whig Party or to the minority unionist faction in the Democratic Party.

The Republican Party barely penetrated the South by 1860. Only in Virginia did significant numbers of its antebellum members later become public officials. Former Whigs dominated both postwar parties in the Upper South, accounting for more than three-fourths of white Republicans. Former Democrats slightly outnumbered former Whigs among scalawags in other sections, but in the Southeast this happened only in one-party Democratic South Carolina. To a degree, the prewar party identity of scalawags derived from the composition of the Opposition Party (1857–59) within each section: from being wholly Whiggish in the Upper South, to mostly so in the Lower South, to being a Whig–Union Democratic fusion in the Southwest. Some scalawags had supported nationalist Stephen A. Douglas in 1860. Other than former Whigs, former Douglas Democrats were the most numerous prewar partisans in the Reconstruction Republican Party in the South. They were especially significant in North Carolina, Louisiana, and Texas.

Whatever their partisanship, scalawags still opposed secession after Lincoln's election, quite a contrast to the support given secession by a majority of redeemers. Scalawags spoke out against steps leading to secession, such as the seizure of federal property and the calling of conventions. Some served on unionist committees and others ran as antisecessionist candidates. Before Lincoln's threat of coercion, North Carolina's future Republicans continued to fight disunion, and even afterward those of East Tennessee attended area unionist conventions at Knoxville and Greeneville. When Federals invaded eastern North Carolina, they recruited two companies of troops, and later they enlisted troops in the western part of the state, with a total of more than 3,000 troops from the two sections. East Tennessee refugees formed Union army regiments in 1861–62, as did other future Republicans within the Volunteer State later, for a total of more than 30,000 soldiers. Altogether, more than 90 percent of the state's scalawags served either in the Union army and/ or as loyal state or federal officeholders during the war. Most of those who served in Virginia's government at Alexandria, formed after Pierpont moved from Wheeling, also soon became Republicans.

By 1863, peace movements developed in the South. In North Carolina, a peace wing of the former Whig-dominated Conservative Party sought peace through a negotiated settlement. Raleigh publisher Holden, a prewar Democrat and peace party leader, received the support of a host of lesser-known Whigs and some well-known Douglas Democrats (most of whom later became Republicans), as well as that of the antiaristocratic Heroes of America, one of several antiwar secret societies operating in the South. Peace party followers became the backbone of the Republican Party in the state. The party ran a strong, albeit losing, race for governor, with Holden heading the ticket, in 1864 and elected legislators and congressmen who continued to agitate for peace. The peace party movement and its followers witnessed carryover from 1864 in becoming the Union Party (Holdenites) of 1865–66, and the state's Republicans thereafter.

Another sort of peace movement developed in West Virginia and Tennessee, where Conservative Unionists broke with Lincoln over confiscation, emancipation, disfranchisement, and his unwillingness to pursue a peaceful reconciliation. They tried to stop the conflict by backing the 1864 Democratic Party presidential candidate, George B. McClellan. Unconditional unionists, on the other hand, supported Lincoln's reelection by sending proadministration delegates to the Republican National Convention and carrying the election for him and Andrew Johnson in the occupied areas (electoral votes, as it turned out, were not needed and not counted). Shortly after, Tennessee's ultraunionists rallied at Nashville on January 9, 1865, to abolish slavery and nominate a state administrative ticket headed by Brownlow as well as a legislative ticket, both running unopposed. When the ultraunionists accepted black suffrage in early 1867—mostly out of necessity—they became the state's Republican Party.

Limited anti-Confederate resistance in the Southeast increased after Federals invaded. Most north Alabama scalawags associated with the peace movement: some journeyed to Union-occupied Middle Tennessee, and more than 2,500 joined the United States Army. Those becoming Federals soon associated with Union army officers who would later settle in their state. Some Georgia and Mississippi scalawags renewed their allegiance to the United States when Federals occupied their area. A few served as Union army scouts and spies. Of those who officially served the Union in the Southeast, Floridians had the highest percentage, because the captured coastal towns became centers of refuge. A combination of newcomers and prewar residents of northern birth supported by federal employment emerged, foreshadowing Florida's Reconstruction leadership. At times, unionist undergrounds existed in Georgia, in Atlanta and Columbus; in Florida, in Jacksonville and Tampa; and in Alabama, in Montgomery and Mobile. Many underground members later became Republicans. In South Carolina, wartime Republican Party activity was limited to a few northerners and Sea Islands blacks, who sent delegates to the 1864 Republican National Convention. Despite the fact that more scalawags from the Southeast than elsewhere served the Confederacy, still twice as many of its redeemers, two-thirds compared with one-third, donned gray uniforms, showing that some scalawags avoided Confederate army service any way they could.

Of the Southwest scalawags, most reluctantly bowed to the Confederacy; others, however, refused. Some retired from public life, a few resisted, and many fled. Many from Texas traveled to Mexico, then boarded boats bound for New Orleans. Others from Louisiana also took refuge in the Crescent City. Most of these refugees soon supported the Lincoln administration. When they returned to Texas, they became some of their state's most prominent figures in the Republican Party. In Texas counties where Germans represented a majority, future Republicans led the resistance. Some anti-Confederate activity occurred in Louisiana's western parishes, where resisters included a few prominent families, who soon joined the Republican Party. From 1863 to 1865, nearly one-third of Arkansas scalawags joined the Union army, primarily as officers of local regiments. Altogether, more than 8,000 Arkansas men wore the Union blue. Several Texans, from among the almost 2,000 who soldiered in the Union army, later were among another group of significant Republicans, which included two future governors, Andrew J. Hamilton and Edmund J. Davis. Davis raised the First and Second Texas (Union) Cavalry, several of whose officers became Republican politicians.

After the capture of south Louisiana and north Arkansas, at least half of the scalawags from those states held office under loyal wartime administrations, which were initially established by the military and later by constitutional conventions. Most of these men made their first connection with the Republican Party when they attended May 1864 rallies in Little Rock and New Orleans to elect national convention delegates. Loyal legislatures met in these two states, and conservative and radical factions formed that would continue into the postwar years. Radical factions laid the foundation for the Republican Party in these states.

Following the war in the Upper South, future Tennessee Republicans generally favored the disfranchisement of former Confederates, but that single issue did not solidify political party lines. Fall 1865 congressional elections aided party building because candidates took a stand for or against Brownlowism. After a year of jockeying and sparring, the Fourteenth Amendment fixed party lines: those for it identified with the Republicans and Governor Brownlow, those opposed with the Democrats and President Johnson. Nationally, too, the amendment divided politicians, causing opponents to convene different weeks during the summer of 1866 at Philadelphia, each group hoping to influence fall congressional elections in the North. Because Tennessee adopted the amendment, the Republican majority Congress allowed it to bypass Congressional Reconstruction.

In Virginia, following the government's move from Alexandria to Richmond, unionists split into moderates, mostly former Whigs who supported Governor Pierpont, and radicals of assorted antecedents who saw Pierpont's policy as a sellout to Confederates and called for male suffrage "without regard to color." Many Virginia Republicans testified before the Joint Committee on Reconstruction, which was established to discredit Johnson. Some began publishing weeklies the first two years after the war, a few edited by scalawags, such as James W. Hunnicutt of the *Richmond New Nation*. After the Reconstruction Acts in March 1867, white radicals and black leaders formed Union League councils to instruct blacks how and for whom to vote. But Virginia moderates were encouraged when national Republican Party chiefs, seeing the need to attract southern whites, furthered a milder brand of Dixie Republicanism. Some former Confederates accepted the appeal for a cooperation movement. Still, the steadfast allegiance of blacks to the radicals doomed the moderate cause, and radicals went on to control the next Virginia Republican convention and the 1868 state constitutional convention. Following the constitutional convention, however, moderate Republicans and conservative Democrats defeated a referendum on the proscriptive provision in the new constitution and elected as governor Republican moderate Gilbert C. Walker, along with a Democratic legislature. Afterward a few former Confederates entered the moderate wing of the Republican Party.

In North Carolina during 1865, conservatives and former secessionists combined against followers of Holden, who as provisional governor used patronage and pardons to increase his power base. Of the 1865–66 lawmakers who supported Holden and who later remained politically active, most of the constitutional convention delegates and many of the legislators became Republicans. In the western mountain area, ultraunionists continued the Heroes of America, or in some cases with northern newcomers formed councils of the Union League. During the fall of 1866, Holdenites and members of these "strait sects" joined to endorse the Fourteenth Amendment. State scalawags, led by Holden, successfully controlled the Republican Party during 1867 by preventing a takeover from the left by a carpetbagger-black coalition and from the right by a group of the state's prewar free soilers. Still, ideologically the state's Republican Party split into several wings—radicals, reformists, moderates, and conservatives—as it mostly did elsewhere in the South.

In the Southwest during 1865, despite loyalist attempts to stabilize their position, divisions occurred within the ranks. In Louisiana, they remained divided into radicals and moderates of the Free State Party (Republican Party), and Conservative Unionists. Governor James Madison Wells headed two November 1865 tickets, the losing Conservative Unionists and the victorious national Democratic Party, both of which needed his influence with President Johnson. Crushed by the outcome, some Conservative Unionists crossed over into the Republican Party, eventually even Wells. Wells found it increasingly difficult to deal with former Confederates in the legislature, who undermined changes made by wartime unionists. Moderates, with Wells's connivance, decided on a desperate coup d'etat: to reconvene the 1864 constitutional convention and legalize black suffrage, an attempt that caused a bloody race riot. After the advent of black suffrage in 1867 as part of Congressional Reconstruction, new factions arose: one, the pure radicals, dominated by free men of color, the other, the compromisers, led by carpetbaggers, whose chief, Henry Clay Warmoth, a young Yankee veteran, became governor in 1868. Thereafter, carpetbaggers controlled the party and few significant scalawags entered, although some continued to acquire important state posts.

In postwar Arkansas as elsewhere, unionists differed about the best approach for dealing with Confederates. Most, including Governor Murphy, favored a mild reconciliation, which would nonetheless bestow preference upon unionists. Two groups of former Confederates pursued contradictory courses regarding the Murphy administration, until the state's supreme court voided the wartime loyalty oath, legally allowing former Confederates to win most of the offices. By 1868, as in Louisiana, the Arkansas Republican Party belonged to the carpetbaggers, a majority of whom arrived earlier as army officers, including Governor Powell Clayton. Thereafter important scalawag converts became almost nonexistent. During the state's decade-long Reconstruction, scalawags held about half of the high-ranking offices, but most came during Murphy's tenure.

In postwar Texas, hundreds of refugees returned, including Governor Andrew J. Hamilton, who, with his longtime friends in the Austin clique, ruled for a few months. Although the 1866 constitutional convention clearly lay in the hands of those who had served the Confederacy, it brought together unionists who later helped create the state's Republican Party. After losing the June 1866 general election, Texas loyalists turned their attention toward Washington. They accepted Negro suffrage, some reluctantly, some readily, as the sole avenue to power. During 1867, the military appointed hundreds of loyalists to local offices. The 1868 constitutional election swept blacks, who previously were spectators, and carpetbaggers into the political arena, but their role remained one of collaboration rather than control. Scalawags controlled the Republican Party in Texas, but differences caused bitter division in the party.

In the Southeast during 1865, other than newcomers, about the only Republicans resided along the east coast of Florida. Although ignored by provisional governor William Marvin, their numbers increased as northern settlers arrived to plant and to profit as entrepreneurs. These individuals and loyalists elsewhere in the state formed the Union Party in 1866. Following the first Reconstruction Act, the head of the Union Party, Ossian B. Hart, organized the probusiness Union-Republican Club of Jacksonville. The club quickly recruited two hundred nearby residents, sent speakers to black rallies, and sponsored a state convention in July at Tallahassee. Opposition to the club, however, rapidly emerged. The opposition centered around the Lincoln Brotherhood, led by some Freedmen's Bureau officers, which in turn lost out to the more radical Union League. At the time of the 1868 constitutional convention, confrontation erupted when Hart's moderate Republicans joined conservatives to draft a document later adopted by the voters. Each Republican faction received support from some of the fifteen hundred or so Florida scalawags, who did fairly well in dividing the plums with their carpetbag allies who ruled Florida until 1877.

In postwar Alabama, ultraunionists looked to create a winning coalition. During 1865–66, many were elected to office; nearly a third of the members of the state convention and the legislature that followed later became Republicans. Opposition to the Johnson administration came from out-of-office radi-

cals, some of whom, along with a few Freedmen's Bureau agents, held
meetings in north Alabama in early 1867 before enlisting blacks through the
Union League. By year's end, many scalawags who later obtained higher office
were recruited by the military as voter registrars, constitutional convention
delegates, and local officials. One-fourth of them entered the party after the
1868 presidential contest, mostly former Whigs from the Black Belt. Altogether, scalawags received nearly two-thirds of the top one hundred positions
and fared even better in acquiring lesser posts.

In Georgia during 1865–66, newly arrived whites and blacks, sustained
mostly by federal or denominational employment, joined hard-line unionists
in establishing Union League councils and chapters of the Georgia Equal
Rights Association and in publishing a few newspapers. Antebellum settlers
from the North who became Republicans cropped up in several places, including Atlanta and Augusta, where they linked up with former Whig mayors
to fashion political machines. All of Georgia's scalawags were by no means
former Whigs, however; several significant Douglas Democrats also became
Republicans, some of whom originally supported President Johnson's policies. During 1867–68, these former Douglas Democrats were joined by former
governor Brown, who supported Congressional Reconstruction before becoming a Republican in 1868, and some of his friends. In Georgia, as elsewhere, the Reconstruction Acts accelerated party formation and the
recruitment of candidates and officeholders, and individuals with records of
loyalty to the Union or disloyalty to the Confederacy received preference. The
issue of debt relief may have caused some north Georgia political leaders to
join the Republican Party.

In South Carolina, hardly any loyalists existed with whom to build a unionist party, and the conservative generals who commanded there appointed
few likely Republicans. Blacks organized quickly in 1865, but until 1867 there
was little cooperation between them and white radicals. In spring 1867,
Charleston, Beaufort, and Columbia became bases for the proliferation of the
party as carpetbaggers and black clergymen, especially those affiliated with the
educational department of the Freedmen's Bureau, organized black voters
through Union Leagues. Unlike elsewhere, blacks in South Carolina almost
single-handedly started the state's Republican Party. Scalawags and carpetbaggers entered in significant numbers later, during the fall 1867 constitutional
convention campaign. Some of the state's scalawags had opposed the Confederacy, but most, albeit against secession, fought for the South and initially

favored Johnson's Reconstruction plan. Shortly after leaving office in 1868, the ever pragmatic Governor Orr, who earlier cooperated with the military in carrying out Congressional Reconstruction, went over to the Republicans. As happened with Brown of Georgia, many of Orr's friends followed him into the party. Most of the state party's latecomers were lawyers who received judicial appointments.

A majority of Mississippi scalawags supported the Johnson administration. Only a handful showed any inclination to identify with the Republican Party before 1867, and many delayed until after the 1868 presidential election. Nearly as many Mississippi scalawags as those of Alabama became 1865–66 candidates and/or officeholders. Among the few whites who embraced Republicanism early on were wartime dissidents, turncoats, and deserters. Alcorn was an 1868 convert who wanted "to reassemble the antebellum Whig party." Once he was elected governor, Alcorn named to high office many former Whig associates, who campaigned against him in the 1869 election. As in South Carolina, few loyalists existed in Mississippi as a nucleus for party formation. Other factors also delayed many from identifying with the Republican Party, especially the state's rule by generals who refused to recruit unionists for office and the diffusion of partisans into several factions from 1867 to 1869.

The Upper South states contain those mountain counties V. O. Key has called "the great spine of Republicanism [that] runs down the back of the South." These states accounted for more white Reconstruction Republicans than could be found in all other former Confederate states combined. Only in this region did white Republicans outnumber black Republicans. Also, scalawag leaders greatly outnumbered the recently arrived carpetbag leaders, and high-ranking black GOP officeholders were almost nonexistent. Only here— because of the concentration of white Republicans—was Democratic hegemony ever threatened in the decades following Reconstruction, with the election of Republican slates in the 1880s and 1890s.

Upper South states had similar patterns of intrastate sectionalism, which were caused by geographical divisions. They also shared some of the same political developments. One commonality was a stable but competitive antebellum two-party system. In North Carolina, opposition to Jefferson Davis's leadership and eventually to the war itself culminated in continued two-party competition. Conservatives and Confederates combined to defeat Holden's peace party. Largely because of early occupation, these states provided more white Union army recruits than all the remaining seceded states: more than 40,000 soldiers, many of whom became postwar Republicans. Union-occupied areas and unoccupied East Tennessee continued to elect U.S. congressmen, and in June 1864 these states, with the exception of North Carolina, sent delegates to the Republican National Convention in Baltimore. Significant to the evolution of political leadership, most members of the wartime Union Party in Virginia and Tennessee and the peace party in North Carolina later formed their states' Republican parties.

Whereas in the Upper South a majority of the scalawags were prewar Whigs, in the Southwest most had identified with the Douglas wing of the Democratic Party. They had become alienated from their state parties either during the latter part of the 1850s in Texas and Louisiana or during 1860–61 in Arkansas. Northern-born and foreign-born prewar settlers shared in the leadership of Reconstruction much more extensively in the Southwest than elsewhere. Almost one-third of the region's scalawags were born outside the slave states. Other circumstances resembled those in the Upper South. Many Southwest scalawags initially resisted the Confederacy and most eventually rejected the Lost Cause during the war. The great majority of anti-Confederates hailed from less affluent areas or from urban areas, where slavery was weakest. Federal forces occupied enormous parts of northwest Arkansas and southern Louisiana during 1861–64. Several future scalawags became Union officers. Unionists in occupied areas also instituted loyal governments and elected U.S. congressmen (not all of whom were seated). In 1864, they sent delegates to the Republican National Convention. State Republican parties in Arkansas and Louisiana were formed mostly by wartime Union Party leaders and in Texas by refugees and resisters.

Southeast scalawags differed from those of the other regions in that they were composed almost equally of prewar Whigs and Democrats, although for the most part they had been opposed to the dominant wing of the state Democratic Party and many had been active in the 1850s unionist fusion parties. Also they differed, despite their antisecessionism, in that once the break came, most quickly and quietly accepted it and eventually served the Confederacy. Later occupation of the region and its greater proportional population of blacks partly accounted for this difference. Very few Southeast scalawags identified with the Republican Party during the war, and most failed to do so until the Congressional Reconstruction Acts were nearly a fait accompli.

Despite regional differences and varying circumstances, common factors predisposed a large majority of scalawags to join the Reconstruction Republican Party, and those factors ranged along a line moving from left to right. The farther an individual is placed along that line, the greater the odds that he became a Republican. The line moves as follows: an 1860 antisecessionist Breckinridge supporter / 1860 Bell or Douglas supporter / 1860 anti-secessionist / passive wartime unionist / peace party advocate / active wartime unionist / postwar Union party supporter.

Where this was not the case, that scalawag was the exception rather than the rule. A few scalawags were disillusioned Confederates confused by their times. Henry C. Niles of Mississippi said, "I have ever since [the war] seemed to myself broken off from mankind: a kind of solitary wanderer in the wild of life, without any direction, or fixed point of view; a gloomy gazer on the world to which I have little relation." But most, like Osborne A. Lochrane, thought they saw a new day dawning. They called for an "enlightened civilization," governed by a desire for "improvement," to replace one controlled by symbols from the past. "We must be men not monuments," Lochrane said, "Let not pride, prejudice, and folly blind us and lead us stumbling backward over a wilderness of graves."[1]

1. Henry C. Niles Diary, 1869–71, last page, n.p, n.d., Scrapbook, Jason Niles Diaries, Journals, and Scrapbook, Southern Historical Collection; Duncan, *Entrepreneur for Equality*, 20.

Appendix

Tables on Status and Political Background

TABLE 1
Status Categories of Upper South Scalawags and Redeemers (in percentages)

	1860 Estate (thousands)			Slaveholdings in 1860			Educational Level			Primary Vocation		
	0–10	10–20	20+	0	1–20	20+	Elem	Sec	Coll	Agri	Bus	Prof
Scalawags												
North Carolina (N82)	41	19	40	55	27	18	26	22	52	11	13	76
Tennessee (N81)	57	15	28	67	32	1	42	17	41	12	16	72
Virginia (N54)	65	9	26	59	37	4	30	22	48	17	24	59
West Virginia (N60)	62	23	15	87	13	0	50	17	33	8	25	67
Total (%) (N277)	55	17	28	66	27	7	36	20	44	12	19	69
Redeemers												
North Carolina (N76)	33	22	45	40	39	21	8	8	84	4	4	92
Tennessee (N88)	47	19	34	48	42	10	24	15	61	3	8	89
Virginia (N60)	38	25	37	40	38	22	24	13	63	7	5	88
West Virginia (N50)	48	26	26	70	26	4	30	18	52	4	8	88
Total (%) (N274)	42	22	36	48	38	14	21	13	66	5	6	89
Difference in Totals (%)	+13	−5	−8	+18	−11	−7	+15	+7	−22	+7	+13	−20

Note: Percentages are based on the known only. For each category the number of persons for which information was found (scalawags or redeemers) ranged from 90% to 95%.

TABLE 2

Past Political Categories of Upper South Scalawags and Redeemers (in percentages)

	Antebellum Officeholding			1850s Party Affiliation			Secession Stand		Civilian and Military Service	
	Local	Party	St/Fed	Dem	Whig	Rep	Anti	Pro	Union	Conf
Scalawags										
North Carolina (N82)	38	12	10	26	74	0	92	8	8	73
Tennessee (N81)	33	9	6	9	91	0	97	3	91	5
Virginia (N54)	27	11	2	13	76	11	93	7	65	24
West Virginia (N60)	35	8	10	26	60	14	100	0	91	4
Total (%) (N287)	34	10	7	18	76	6	95	5	64	26
Redeemers										
North Carolina (N76)	65	12	20	30	70	0	70	30	0	96
Tennessee (N88)	57	23	14	48	52	0	59	41	21	71
Virginia (N60)	60	15	15	52	48	0	52	48	4	93
West Virginia (N50)	44	8	8	58	42	0	56	44	32	45
Total (%) (N274)	58	15	15	45	55	0	61	39	14	76
Difference in Totals (%)	−24	−5	−8	−27	+21	+6	+34	−34	+50	−50

Note: Percentages are based on the known only. Officeholding and party affiliation were located a minimum of 80% of the time for each state's scalawags and redeemers; for secession stand and civilian and military service, the percentage located for each of the groups was from 90% to 95%. Some individuals did not serve under either government.

TABLE 3

Status Categories of Southeast Scalawags and Redeemers (in percentages)

	1860 Estate (thousands)			Slaveholdings in 1860			Educational Level			Primary Vocation		
	0–10	10–20	20+	0	1–20	20+	Elem	Sec	Coll	Agri	Bus	Prof
Scalawags												
Alabama (N65)	35	28	37	33	52	15	33	26	41	5	12	83
Florida (N35)	52	29	19	55	39	6	45	29	26	19	23	58
Georgia (N59)	50	20	30	52	37	11	32	26	42	7	21	72
Mississippi (N64)	57	18	25	36	36	28	35	19	46	4	5	91
South Carolina (N47)	57	19	24	52	31	17	27	20	53	19	10	71
Total (%) (N270)	50	22	28	45	39	16	34	24	42	10	13	77
Redeemers												
Alabama (N52)	43	21	36	41	40	19	13	17	70	8	4	88
Florida (N31)	36	28	36	52	32	16	33	26	41	11	7	82
Georgia (N51)	28	26	46	31	43	26	11	17	72	6	4	90
Mississippi (N53)	37	21	42	34	38	28	23	15	62	6	2	92
South Carolina (N50)	31	22	47	27	38	35	9	13	78	14	4	82
Total (%) (N237)	35	23	42	36	39	25	16	16	68	9	4	87
Difference in Totals (%)	+15	−1	−14	+9	0	−9	+18	+8	−26	+1	+9	−10

Note: Percentages are based on the known only. For each category the number of persons for which information was found (scalawags or redeemers) ranged from 90% to 95%.

TABLE 4
Past Political Categories of Southeast Scalawags and Redeemers (in percentages)

	Antebellum Officeholding			1850s Party Affiliation			Secession Stand		Civilian and Military Service	
	Local	Party	St/Fed	Dem	Whig	Rep	Anti	Pro	Union	Conf
Scalawags										
Alabama (N65)	59	9	6	48	52	0	91	9	9	63
Florida (N35)	13	3	7	60	40	0	94	6	29	32
Georgia (N59)	40	11	6	43	57	0	94	6	6	49
Mississippi (N64)	51	8	6	33	67	0	76	24	4	70
South Carolina (N47)	38	7	7	95	5	0	74	26	5	55
Total (%) (N270)	43	8	6	54	46	0	84	16	9	56
Redeemers										
Alabama (N52)	38	11	15	84	16	0	25	75	0	75
Florida (N31)	65	11	32	37	63	0	32	68	0	76
Georgia (N51)	52	22	26	80	20	0	35	65	0	96
Mississippi (N53)	35	8	29	57	43	0	34	66	0	84
South Carolina (N50)	64	7	20	100	0	0	4	96	0	90
Total (%) (N237)	50	12	24	75	25	0	26	74	0	89
Difference in Totals (%)	−7	−4	−18	−21	+21	0	+58	−58	+9	−33

Note: Percentages are based on the known only. Officeholding and party affiliation were located a minimum of 80% of the time for each state's scalawags and redeemers; for secession stand and civilian and military service, the percentage located for each of the groups was from 90% to 95%. Some individuals did not serve under either government.

TABLE 5
Status Categories of Southwest Scalawags and Redeemers (in percentages)

	1860 Estate (thousands)			Slaveholdings in 1860			Educational Level			Primary Vocation		
	0–10	10–20	20+	0	1–20	20+	Elem	Sec	Coll	Agri	Bus	Prof
Scalawags												
Arkansas (N40)	66	17	17	69	25	6	44	31	25	11	11	78
Louisiana (N65)	54	23	23	76	17	7	29	19	52	7	12	81
Texas (N80)	57	21	22	65	29	6	39	24	37	8	11	81
Total (%) (N185)	59	20	21	69	25	6	38	24	38	9	11	80
Redeemers												
Arkansas (N50)	47	22	31	54	33	13	42	27	31	2	2	96
Louisiana (N51)	52	26	22	54	38	8	26	22	52	2	9	89
Texas (N54)	41	18	41	45	41	14	25	14	61	10	4	86
Total (%) (N155)	47	22	31	51	37	12	31	21	48	5	5	90
Difference in Totals (%)	+12	−2	−10	+18	−12	−6	+7	+3	−10	+4	+6	−10

Note: Percentages are based on the known only. For each category the number of persons for which information was found (scalawags or redeemers) ranged from 90% to 95%.

TABLE 6
Past Political Categories of Southwest Scalawags and Redeemers (in percentages)

	Antebellum Office holding			1850s Party Affiliation			Secession Stand		Civilian and Military Service	
	Local	Party	St/Fed	Dem	Whig	Rep	Anti	Pro	Union	Conf
Scalawags										
Arkansas (N40)	42	0	8	56	41	3	95	5	73	25
Louisiana (N65)	36	12	12	43	57	0	93	7	60	22
Texas (N80)	39	4	15	67	33	0	93	7	22	40
Total (%) (N185)	41	5	10	58	41	1	93	7	36	32
Redeemers										
Arkansas (N50)	44	3	22	69	31	0	40	60	6	67
Louisiana (N51)	39	4	24	65	35	0	21	79	0	70
Texas (N54)	76	17	22	86	14	0	29	71	0	96
Total (%) (N155)	52	8	23	73	27	0	30	70	2	78
Difference in Totals (%)	−11	−3	−13	−15	+16	+1	+63	−63	+34	−46

Note: Percentages are based on the known only. Officeholding and party affiliation were located a minimum of 80% of the time for each state's scalawags and redeemers; for secession stand and civilian and military service, the percentage located for each of the groups was from 90% to 95%. Some individuals did not serve under either government.

Bibliography

MANUSCRIPT COLLECTIONS

Alabama Department of Archives and History, Montgomery

Dustan, Charles W. Papers.
Parsons, Governor Lewis E. Papers.
Patton, Governor Robert M. Papers.
Swayne, [Military] Governor Wager. Papers.

Arkansas History Commission, Little Rock

Berry, James R. Papers.
Bliss, Calvin C. Papers.

Atlanta Historical Society, Atlanta

Conley, Benjamin F. Papers.

Austin History Center, Austin Public Library, Austin

Bartholomew, Eugene C. Papers.
Graham, R. Niles, and Elisha Marshall Pease. Collection.
Kuechler, Jacob. Papers.

Center for American History, University of Texas at Austin

Brown, Frank. Collection.
Duval, Thomas H. Diaries.
Hamilton, Andrew Jackson. Papers.

Haynes, John L. Papers.
Newcomb, James Pearson, Jr. Papers.

Hargrett Rare Book and Manuscript Library, University of Georgia, Athens

Brown, Joseph E. Collection.
Farrow, Henry P. Papers.

Houghton Library, Harvard University, Cambridge, Mass.

Sumner, Charles. Papers.

Library of Congress, Washington, D.C.

Butler, Benjamin F. Papers.
Chandler, William E. Papers.
Chandler, Zachariah. Papers.
Chase, Salmon P. Papers.
Denison George S. Papers.
Johnson, Andrew. Papers.
Lincoln, Abraham. Papers.
McPherson, Edward. Papers
Sherman, John. Papers.
Stevens, Thaddeus. Papers.

Louisiana and Lower Mississippi Valley Collections,
Louisiana State University Libraries, Baton Rouge

Flanders, Benjamin F. Papers.
Taliaferro, James G., and Family. Papers.

Louisiana State Museum Historical Center, New Orleans

Wells, James Madison. Papers.

Mississippi Department of Archives and History, Jackson

Alcorn, James L. Papers.
Garner, James Wilford. Papers.

National Archives, Washington, D.C.

Amnesty Papers. Records of the Adjutant General's Office. RG 94.
Eighth Census of the United States, 1860. Census Office. RG 29.
Index to Compiled Service Records of Volunteer Union Soldiers Who Served in Orga-
    nizations from Southern States. Records of the Adjutant General's Office. RG 94.
Letters of Application and Recommendation. General Records of the Department of
    Treasury. RG 56.
Petitions for the Removal of Legal and Political Disabilities Imposed by the Fourteenth
    Amendment. Records of the Adjutant General's Office. RG 233.

Records of the Bureau of Refugees, Freedmen, and Abandoned Lands. RG 105.

Records of the Commissioners of Claims (Southern Claims Commission), 1871–80. General Records of the Department of Treasury. RG 56.

Records Relating to the Appointment of Federal Judges, Marshals, and Attorneys. General Records of the Justice Department. RG 60.

North Carolina Division of Archives and History, Raleigh

Graham, William A. Papers.

Hale, Edward J. Papers.

Rare Book, Manuscript, and Special Collections Library, Duke University, Durham, N.C.

Bryant, John Emory. Papers.

Harden, Edward R. Papers.

Longstreet, James. Papers.

Perry, Benjamin F. Papers.

Woodruff, Joseph. Diary.

South Carolina Department of Archives and History, Columbia

Orr, James Lawrence. Papers of Governors.

Southern Historical Collection, Wilson Library,
University of North Carolina at Chapel Hill

Barringer, Daniel M. Papers.

Battle Family. Papers.

Claiborne, John Francis Hamtramck. Papers.

Niles, Jason. Diaries, Journals, and Scrapbook.

Orr, Jehu A. Papers.

Perry, Benjamin F. Papers.

Settle, Thomas. Papers.

Warmoth, Henry Clay. Papers.

Tennessee State Library and Archives, Nashville

Brownlow, William G. Governors' Papers.

Texas State Library and Archives Commission, Austin

Executive Record Books 281–83

Muster Rolls of the First and Second Texas Cavalry in the Union Army

Texas Voter Registration List, 1867–68

Tracy W. McGregor Library, Albert H. Small Special Collections Library,
University of Virginia Library, Charlottesville

Akerman, Amos Tappan. Papers.

Barbour, B. J. Papers.

Mosby, John S. Papers.

University of Chicago, Chicago, Ill.

Douglas, Stephen A. Papers.

University Archives and Special Collections, University of Tennessee, Knoxville

Temple, Oliver P. Papers.

West Virginia and Regional History Collection, West Virginia University, Morgantown

Pierpont, Francis H. Papers.

GOVERNMENT DOCUMENTS AND PUBLICATIONS

Consolidated Index of Claims Reported by the Commissioner of Claims to the House of Representatives from 1871 to 1880. 3 vols. Washington, D.C., 1892.

Debates and Proceedings of the Convention which Assembled at Little Rock, January 7th, 1868, under the Provisions of the Act of Congress of March 2d, 1867, and the Acts of March 23d and July 19th, 1867. Supplementary Thereto, to Form a Constitution for the State of Arkansas. Little Rock, 1868.

Debates in the Convention for the Revision and Amendment of the Constitution of the State of Louisiana Assembled at Liberty Hall, New Orleans, April 6, 1864. New Orleans, 1864.

The Laws of Texas, 1822–1897. 10 vols. Austin, 1898.

Journal of the Constitutional Convention which Convened at Alexandria on the 13th day of February, 1864. Alexandria, Va., 1864.

Journal of the Constitutional Convention of the State of North Carolina, at Its Session 1868. Raleigh, 1868.

Journal of the Convention of Delegates of the People of Arkansas. Assembled at the Capitol, January 4, 1864. Little Rock, 1870.

Journal of the House of Delegates of the State of Virginia for the Extra Session, 1861. Richmond, 1861.

Journals of the House of Representatives of the Sessions of 1864, 1864–65, and 1865. Little Rock, 1870.

Journal of the North Carolina Constitutional Convention. Raleigh, 1865.

Journal of the Proceedings and Debates in the Constitutional Convention of the State of Mississippi, August, 1865. Jackson, Miss., 1865.

Journal of the Proceedings in the Constitutional Convention of the State of Mississippi, 1868. Jackson, Miss., 1871.

Journal of the Proceedings of the Convention of the State of Alabama, Held in the City of Montgomery, on Tuesday, September 12, 1865. Montgomery, 1865.

Journal of the Reconstruction Convention of the State of Texas. Austin, 1866.

Journal of the Senate of North Carolina, 1866–67. Raleigh, 1867.

Official Register of the United States, Containing a List of the Officers and Employees in the Civil, Military, and Naval Services. Washington, D.C., 1861–80.

Proceedings of the Constitutional Convention of South Carolina Held at Charleston, S.C., beginning January 14th and ending March 17th, 1868. 2 vols. Charleston, 1868.

Report from the Select Committee to Investigate the Assault upon the Hon. W. D. Kelley. Washington, D.C., 1864.

Report of the Adjutant General of Arkansas for the Period of the Late Rebellion and to November 1, 1866. Washington, D.C., 1867.

Report of the Adjutant General of the State of Tennessee on the Military Forces of the State from 1861 to 1866. Nashville, 1866.

Report of the Committee on the Judiciary in Senate Reports, 41st Cong., 2d sess., No. 175. Washington, D.C.

Report of the Joint Committee on Reconstruction. Washington, D.C., 1866.

Report of the Joint Select Committee to Inquire into the Condition of Affairs in the Late Insurrectionary States. 13 vols. Washington, D.C., 1872.

Report of the Select Committee, Memphis Riots and Massacres. Washington, D.C., 1866.

Report of the Select Committee on the New Orleans Riots of July 30, 1866. Washington, D.C., 1867.

Summary Reports in All Cases Reported to Congress as Disallowed under the Act of March 3, 1871. 4 vols. Washington, D.C., 1876–81.

Tennessee *House Journal.* 33d GA, 2d sess. Nashville, 1861.

Tennessee *Senate Journal.* Brownlow Assembly, 2d adj. sess. Nashville, 1867.

The War of the Rebellion: A Compilation of the Official Records of the Union and Confederate Armies. Ed. Robert N. Scott et al. 128 vols. Washington, D.C., 1880–1901.

White, Robert H. *Messages of the Governors of Tennessee 1796–1907.* 8 vols. Nashville, 1952–1972.

Newspapers, Periodicals, and Annuals

Alexandria Gazette. 1865.

The American Annual Cyclopaedia and Register of Important Events of the Year, Embracing Political, Civil, Military, and Social Affairs; Public Documents; Biography; Statistics; Commerce; Finance; Literature; Science; Agriculture and Mechanical Industry. 15 vols. (1860–76). New York, 1864–78.

Atlanta New Era. 1867–68.

Augusta Tri-Weekly Constitutionalist. 1865–67.

Austin Daily Republican. 1868–69.

Austin Southern Intelligencer. 1860–61, 1865–67.

Dallas Herald. 1865–66.

Flake's Galveston Bulletin. 1860–61, 1865–69.

Galveston Daily News. 1860–61.

Harper's Weekly. 1865–69.

Knoxville Whig. 1860–61, 1865–69.

Little Rock Unconditional Union. 1864.

Marshall Harrison Flag. 1860–61.

Nashville Union. 1861, 1864.

Nashville Dispatch. 1865–66.

New Orleans Era. 1863–64.

New Orleans Picayune. 1864–65.

New Orleans Times. 1863–67.

New Orleans Tribune. 1865–67.

New Orleans Delta. 1859–61.

New Orleans True Delta. 1859–60.

New York Herald. 1865–69.

New York Times. 1862–70.

New York Tribune. 1861–70.

(Raleigh) North Carolina Standard. 1860–68.

The Reporter: A Periodical Devoted to Religion, Law, Legislation, and Public Events. 1866.

San Antonio Daily Express. 1860–61, 1867–70.

Texas Almanac. 1859–60, 1865–66.

Wheeling Intelligencer. 1860–61.

Winston Sentinel. 1867.

Contemporary Publications and Published Documents

Abbott, Richard H., ed. "A Yankee Views the Organization of the Republican Party in South Carolina, July 1867." *South Carolina Historical Magazine* 85 (July 1984): 244–50.

Alcorn, James L. *Views of Hon. J. L. Alcorn on the Political Situation of Mississippi.* Friar's Point, Miss., 1867.

Allen, Albert H. *Arkansas Imprints, 1821–1876.* New York, 1947.

Andrews, Sidney. *The South since the War as Shown by Fourteen Weeks of Travel and Observation in Georgia and the Carolinas.* Boston, 1866.

An Appeal to Republican Senators by Wealthy and Influential Republican Leaders of Georgia. Washington, D.C., 1870.

Atkinson, George A., and Alvaro F. Gibbens. *Prominent Men of West Virginia.* Wheeling, W. Va., 1890.

Avery, I. W. *The History of the State of Georgia from 1850 to 1881, Embracing the Three Important Epochs: The Decade before the War of 1861–5; The War; The Period of Reconstruction.* New York, 1881.

Bailey, William H. *The Effects of the Civil War upon the Rights of Person and Property.* Raleigh, 1867.

Bard, Samuel. *A Letter from Samuel Bard to President Grant on the Political Situation in Georgia.* Atlanta, 1870.

Barnard, John D., ed. "Reconstruction on the Lower Mississippi." *Mississippi Valley Historical Review* 21 (December 1934): 387–96.

Barnes, William H. *The Fortieth Congress of the United States: Historical and Biographical.* 2 vols. New York, 1870.

Barrett, Thomas. *The Great Hanging at Gainesville, Cooke County, Texas, October, A.D. 1862.* Gainesville, Tex., 1885.

Bartlett, John Russell. *Dictionary of Americanisms: A Glossary of Words and Phrases Usually Regarded as Peculiar to the United States.* 2d ed. Boston, 1859.

Basler, Roy P., ed. *The Collected Works of Abraham Lincoln*. 11 vols. New Brunswick, N.J., 1953–90.

Beale, Howard K., ed. *The Diary of Edward Bates, 1859–1866*. Annual Report of the American Historical Association for 1930. Vol. 4. Washington, D.C., 1933.

———.ed. *Diary of Gideon Welles, Secretary of the Navy under Lincoln and Johnson*. 3 vols. New York, 1960.

Billings, Edward C. *The Struggle between the Civilization of Slavery and That of Freedom, Recently and Now Going On in Louisiana*. Hatfield, Mass., 1873.

Biographical Encyclopaedia of Texas of the Nineteenth Century. New York, 1880.

Botts, John M. *The Great Rebellion: Its Secret History, Rise, Progress, and Disastrous Failure*. New York, 1866.

Brewer, Willis. *Alabama: Her History, Resources, War Record, and Public Men, from 1540 to 1872*. Montgomery 1872.

Brooks, U. R. *South Carolina Bench and Bar*. Columbia, S.C., 1908.

Brownlow, William G. *Sketches of the Rise, Progress, and Decline of Secession: With a Narrative of Personal Adventures among the Rebels*. Philadelphia, 1862.

Caldwell, John H. *Slavery and Southern Methodism: Two Sermons Preached in the Methodist Church in Newnan, Georgia*. Newnan, Ga., 1865.

Chase, Salmon P. *Diary and Correspondence of Salmon P. Chase*. Annual Report of the American Historical Association, 1902. Washington, D.C., 1903.

Claiborne, John F. H. *Mississippi, as a Province, Territory, and State, with Biographical Notices of Eminent Citizens*. Jackson, Miss., 1880.

Clayton, W. W. *History of Davidson County, Tennessee, with Illustrations and Biographical Sketches of Its Prominent Men and Pioneers*. Nashville, 1880.

The Condition of Affairs in Georgia. Washington, D.C., 1869.

Confederate Records of the State of Georgia. 6 vols. Atlanta, 1909–11.

Constitution of Union League of the State of Texas. Austin, 1867.

Convention of Southern Unionists. Washington, D.C., n.d.

Cyclopedia of Eminent and Representative Men of the Carolinas of the Nineteenth Century. 2 vols. Madison, Wis., 1892.

Dennett, John Richard. *The South as It Is, 1865–1866*. Ed. Henry M. Christman. New York, 1965.

Donald, David H., ed. *Inside Lincoln's Cabinet: The Civil War Diaries of Salmon P. Chase*. New York, 1954.

Dostie, A. P. *Freedom Versus Slavery: Address Delivered before the Free State Union Association, of New Orleans, January 2, 1864*. New Orleans, 1864.

Douglas, Stephen A. *Letters*. Ed. Robert W. Johannsen. Urbana, Ill., 1961.

Fleming, Walter L. *Documentary History of Reconstruction: Political, Military, Social, Religious, Educational, and Industrial, 1865 to the present time*. 2 vols. New York, 1906.

Foote, Henry S. *War of the Rebellion; or, Scylla and Charybdis: Consisting of Observations upon the Causes, Course, and Consequences of the Late Civil War in the United States*. New York, 1866.

Goodspeed. *Biographical and Historical Memoirs of Eastern Arkansas* . . . Chicago, 1889.

Goodspeed. *Biographical and Historical Memoirs of Louisiana* . . . 3 vols. Chicago, 1892.

Goodspeed. *Biographical and Historical Memoirs of Mississippi* . . . 2 vols. Chicago, 1891.

Goodspeed. *Biographical and Historical Memoirs of Northwest Arkansas.* Chicago, 1889.

Goodspeed. *Biographical Souvenir of the States of Georgia and Florida* . . . Chicago, 1889.

Goodspeed. *History of Tennessee from the Earliest Time to the Present* . . . Nashville, 1886.

Goodspeed. *Northern Alabama, Historical and Biographical.* Birmingham, 1888.

Graf, Leroy P., and Ralph W. Haskins, eds. *The Papers of Andrew Johnson.* Knoxville, 1967–.

Hahn, Michael. *What Is Unconditional Unionism?* New Orleans, 1863.

Hallum, John. *Biographical and Pictorial History of Arkansas.* Albany, N.Y., 1887.

Hamilton, J. G. de Roulhac, ed. *The Correspondence of Jonathan Worth.* 2 vols. Raleigh, 1909.

Hamilton, J. G. de Roulhac, and Max R. Williams, eds. *The Papers of William Alexander Graham.* 8 vols. Raleigh, 1957–92.

Hay, John. *Lincoln and the Civil War in the Diaries and Letters of John Hay.* Selected and with an introduction by Dennett Tyler. New York, 1939.

Hayes, John D., ed. *Samuel Francis DuPont: A Selection from His Civil War Letters.* 3 vols. Ithaca, N.Y., 1969.

Hempstead, Fay. *A Pictorial History of Arkansas, from Earliest Times to the Year 1890* . . . Saint Louis, 1890.

Hesseltine, William B., ed. *Three against Lincoln: Murat Halstead Reports the Caucuses of 1860.* Baton Rouge, 1960.

Hunnicutt, James W. *The Conspiracy Unveiled: The South Sacrificed; or the Horrors of Secession.* Philadelphia, 1863.

Hunt, Gailliard. "Letter of William Henry Trescot on Reconstruction in South Carolina, 1867," *American Historical Review* 15 (April 1910): 574–82.

Jones, Alexander H. *Knocking at the Door: Alex H. Jones, Member-Elect to Congress; His Course before the War, during the War, and after the War.* Washington, D.C., 1866.

Keating, John M. *History of the City of Memphis.* 2 vols. Syracuse, N.Y., 1888.

Lang, Theodore F. *Loyal West Virginia from 1861 to 1865.* Baltimore, 1895.

Lewis, Virgil A., ed. *How West Virginia Was Made: Proceedings of the First Convention of the People of Northwestern Virginia at Wheeling, May 13, 14, and 15, 1861, and the Journal of the Second Convention of the People of Northwestern Virginia at Wheeling, which Assembled June 11th, 1861.* Charleston, W. Va., 1909.

Lockhart, V. D. *Madison Bell: A Biographical Sketch of His Early Life and Education, with a Brief Account of His Military and Official Career.* Atlanta, 1887.

Lowe, Richard. "Virginia's Reconstruction Convention: General Schofield Rates the Delegates." *VMHB* 80 (July 1972): 341–60.

Lufkin, Charles L. "West Tennessee Unionists in the Civil War: A Hawkins Family Letter." *THQ* 46 (spring 1987): 33–42.

Lynch, James D. *The Bench and Bar of Mississippi*. New York, 1881.

——. *Kemper County Vindicated, and a Peep at Radical Rule in Mississippi*. New York, 1879.

Maloney, Walter C. *A Sketch of the History of Key West, Florida*. Gainesville, Fla., 1968.

Martin, Isabella D., and Myrta L. Avery, eds. *A Diary from Dixie, as Written by Mary Boykin Chesnut* . . . Boston, 1949.

Marshall, Jessie Ames, ed. *Private and Official Correspondence of Gen. Benjamin F. Butler during the Period of the Civil War*. 5 vols. Norwood, Mass., 1917.

McPherson, Edward. *The Political History of the United States of America during the Great Rebellion* . . . 2d ed. Washington, D.C., 1865.

——. *The Political History of the United States of America during the Period of Reconstruction, from April 15, 1865, to July 15, 1870* . . . 3d ed. Washington, D.C., 1880.

McWhiney, Grady, ed. *Reconstruction and the Freedmen*. Chicago, 1963.

Merrill, Walter M., and Louis Ruchames, eds. *The Letters of William Lloyd Garrison*. 4 vols. Cambridge, Mass., 1971–81.

Moore, Frank, ed. *The Rebellion Record: A Diary of American Events* . . . 11 vols. New York, 1861–71.

Moore, John H. *The Juhl Letters to the "Charleston Courier": A View of the South, 1865–1871*. Athens, Ga., 1974.

Newcomb, James P. *Sketch of Secession Times in Texas and Journal of Travels in Mexico*. San Francisco, 1863.

Nicolay, John G., and John Hay. *Abraham Lincoln: A History*. 10 vols. New York, 1890.

Niven, John, ed. *The Salmon P. Chase Papers*. 5 vols. Kent, Ohio, 1993–98.

Nolte, Eugene A. "Downeasters in Arkansas: Letters of Roscoe G. Jennings to His Brother." *ArkHQ* 18 (spring 1950): 1–25.

Official Report of the Proceedings of the Republican State Convention Held at Fort Worth, Texas, April 29 and 30 and May 1, 1884. Austin, 1884.

Olsen, Otto H., and Ellen Z. McGrew, eds. "Prelude to Reconstruction: The Correspondence of State Senator Leander Sams Gash, 1866–1867." *NCHR* 60 (January 1983): 37–88; (April 1983): 206–38; (July 1983): 333–66.

Osborn, George E., ed. "Letters of a Carpetbagger in Florida, 1866–1869." *FHQ* 36 (January 1958): 239–85.

Padgett, James A., ed. "Some Letters of George Stanton Denison, 1854–1866." *LHQ* 23 (October 1940): 1132–240.

Parker, Granville. *The Formation of the State of West Virginia and Other Incidents of the Late Civil War* . . . Wellsburg, W. Va., 1875.

Parton, James. *General Butler in New Orleans: History of the Administration of the Department of the Gulf* . . . Boston, 1864.

Paschal, George W. *A Digest of Decisions of the Supreme Court of Texas and of the United States upon Texas Law*. 3 vols. Washington, D.C., 1872–75.

Pease, Theodore C., ed. *Collections of the Illinois State Historical Library*. Vol. 18. Springfield, Ill., 1923.

Pitkin, J. R. G. Letter of JRG Pitkin of New Orleans, La. to Hon. B. F. Butler. Pamphlet. N.p., n.d.

Phillips, Ulrich B., ed. *The Correspondence of Robert Toombs, Alexander H. Stephens, and Howell Cobb*. Vol. 2 of the Annual Report of the American Historical Association for the Year 1911. Washington, D.C., 1913.

Powell, E. A. "Fifty-five Years in West Alabama," *AlaHQ* 4 (winter 1942): 636–41.

Proceedings of the Annual Meeting of the Grand National Council, Union League of America. Washington, D.C., 1863, 1869.

Proceedings of the Convention of the Republican Party of Louisiana Held at Economy Hall, New Orleans, September 25, 1865; and the Central Executive Committee of the Friends of the Universal Suffrage of Louisiana, now the Central Executive Committee of the Republican Party of Louisiana. N.p., n.d.

Proceedings of the First Three Republican National Conventions, 1856, 1860, and 1864, as Reported by Horace Greeley. Minneapolis, 1893.

Proceedings of the Freedmen's Convention of Georgia, Assembled at Augusta, January 10, 1866. Augusta, Ga., 1866.

Proceedings of the Republican State Convention Assembled at Austin, August 12, 1868. Austin, 1868.

Reed, Emily Hazen. *The Life of A. P. Dostie; or, The Conflict of New Orleans*. New York, 1868.

Reid, Whitelaw. *After the War: A Southern Tour, May 1, 1865, to May 1, 1866*. Cincinnati, 1866.

Report of Proceedings of Conference in Richmond. New York, 1867.

Saffold, Milton J. *Address to Native White Republicans, October 1870*. N.p., n.d.

St. Clair Abrams, A. *Manual and Biographical Register of the State of Georgia for 1871–1872*. Atlanta, 1872.

Savage, John. *The Life and Public Services of Andrew Johnson: Including His State Papers, Speeches, and Addresses*. New York, 1866.

Scarborough, William K., ed. *The Diary of Edmund Ruffin*. 3 vols. Baton Rouge, 1972–89.

Simon, John Y. *The Papers of Ulysses S. Grant*. Carbondale, Ill., 1967–.

Smart, James G., ed. *A Radical View: The "Agate" Dispatches of Whitelaw Reid 1861–1865*. 2 vols. Memphis, 1976.

Speech Delivered by Hon. E. M. Pease at Turner Hall, Galveston, Texas, July 12th, 1880. Galveston, 1880.

Speech of Ex-Governor Brown of Georgia, Delivered in the National Republican Convention at Chicago in 1868. N.p., n.d.

Speer, William S. *Sketches of Prominent Tennesseans: Containing Biographies and Records of Many of the Families Who Have Obtained Prominence in Tennessee*. Nashville, 1888.

Temple, Oliver P. *East Tennessee and the Civil War*. Cincinnati, 1899.

———. *Notable Men of Tennessee, from 1833 to 1875: Their Times and Their Contemporaries*. Compiled by Mary B. Temple. New York, 1912.

Torbert, Noble J., ed. *The Papers of John Willis Ellis*. 2 vols. Raleigh, 1964.

Vedder, O. F. *History of the City of Memphis and Shelby County*. 2 vols. Syracuse, N.Y., 1888.

Wells, James Madison. *The Chisolm Massacre: A Picture of "Home Rule" in Mississippi*. 2d ed. Washington, D.C., 1878.

Williams, R. H., and John W. Sanson. *Massacre on the Nueces River*. Grand Prairie, Tex., 1965.

Winkler, Ernest W. *Check List of Texas Imprints*. 2 vols. Austin, 1949–63.

Woody, Robert H., ed. "Behind the Scenes in the Reconstruction Legislature of South Carolina: Diary of Joseph Woodruff." *JSH* 2 (May 1936): 233–59.

Worley, Ted R., ed. "Elisha Baxter's Autobiography." *ArkHQ* 14 (summer 1955): 172–73.

MEMOIRS, REMINISCENCES, AND AUTOBIOGRAPHIES

Boutwell, George S. *Reminiscences of Sixty Years in Public Affairs*. 2 vols. New York, 1902.

Bromberg, Frederick G. *The Reconstruction Period in Alabama*. 2 vols. [Mobile, Ala.], 1911–14.

Caldwell, John H. *Reminiscences of the Reconstruction of Church and State in Georgia*. Wilmington, Del., 1895.

Carrigan, Alfred Holt. "Reminiscences of the Secession Convention." Publications of the Arkansas Historical Association. Little Rock, 1906–17. 1: 306–14.

Clayton, Powell. *The Aftermath of the Civil War in Arkansas*. New York, 1915.

Cox, Samuel S. *Union—Disunion—Reunion: Three Decades of Federal Legislation, 1855 to 1885* . . . Providence, R.I., 1885.

Cypert, Jesse N. "Secession Convention." Publications of the Arkansas Historical Association. Little Rock, 1906–17. 2: 315–26.

Douglass, Frederick. *Life and Times of Frederick Douglass Written by Himself*. Rev. ed. Boston, 1892.

Farrow, Henry P. *Hon. Henry P. Farrow, United States Senator Elect. What Are His Antecedents?* Pamphlet. Washington, D.C., 1870.

Flippin, Percy S., ed. "From the Autobiography of Herschel V. Johnson, 1856–1867." *American Historical Review* 30 (January 1925): 311–36.

Guinn, James M. K. "History of Randolph County." *AlaHQ* 4 (fall 1942): 291–413.

Hallum, John. *The Diary of an Old Lawyer; or, Scenes behind the Curtain*. Nashville, 1895.

Harrell, John M. *The Brooks and Baxter War: A History of the Reconstruction Period in Arkansas*. Saint Louis, 1893.

Herbert, Hilary A., ed. *Why the Solid South? Or Reconstruction and Its Results*. Reprint. New York, 1969.

Holden, William W. *Memoirs of W. W. Holden*. Introduction by William K. Boyd. Durham, N.C., 1911.

Houzeau, Jean-Charles. *My Passage at the New Orleans "Tribune": A Memoir of the Civil War Era.* Ed. David C. Rankin. Baton Rouge, 1984.

Hughes, Robert W. *Papers Showing the Political Course of R. W. Hughes, the Republican Candidate for Governor, before and since the Fall of the Southern Confederacy in 1865; Prefixed by a Biographical Sketch.* Richmond, 1873.

Longstreet, James. *From Manassas to Appomattox: Memories of the Civil War in America.* Philadelphia, 1896.

Lynch, John R. *The Facts of Reconstruction.* New York, 1913.

McClure, Alexander K. *Abraham Lincoln and Men of War-Times.* Philadelphia, 1892.

Mosby, John S. *Mosby's War Reminiscences and Stuart's Cavalry Campaigns.* Boston, 1887.

Stephens, Alexander H. *A Constitutional View of the Late War between the States: Its Causes, Character, Conduct, and Results, Presented in a Series of Colloquies at Liberty Hall.* 2 vols. Philadelphia, 1868–70.

Stuart, Alexander H. H. *A Narrative of the Leading Incidents of the Organization of the First Popular Movement in Virginia in 1865 to Re-Establish Peaceful Relations between the Northern and Southern States . . .* Richmond, 1888.

Tunnell, Ted, ed. *Carpetbagger from Vermont: The Autobiography of Marshall Harvey Twitchell.* Baton Rouge, 1989.

Warmoth, Henry Clay. *War, Politics, and Reconstruction: Stormy Days in Louisiana.* New York, 1930.

Books

Abbott, Richard H. *The Republican Party and the South, 1855–1877: The First Southern Strategy.* Chapel Hill, 1986.

Alexander, Roberta Sue. *North Carolina Faces the Freedmen: Race Relations during Presidential Reconstruction, 1865–1867.* Durham, N.C., 1985.

Alexander, Thomas B. *Political Reconstruction in Tennessee.* Nashville, 1950.

———. *Thomas A. R. Nelson of East Tennessee.* Nashville, 1956.

Alexander, Thomas B., and Richard E. Beringer. *The Anatomy of the Confederate Congress: A Study of the Influences of Member Characteristics on Legislative Voting Behavior, 1861–1865.* Nashville, 1972.

Ambler, Charles H. *Francis H. Pierpont: Union War Governor of Virginia and Father of West Virginia.* Chapel Hill, 1937.

Ambler, Charles H., and Festus P. Summers. *West Virginia, the Mountain State.* 2d ed. Englewood Cliffs, N.J., 1958.

Ash, Stephen V. *When the Yankees Came: Conflict and Chaos in the Occupied South, 1861–1865.* Chapel Hill, 1995.

Bakhtin, Mikhail M. *Speech Genres and Other Late Essays.* Trans. Vern W. McGee. Ed. Michael Holquist and Caryl Emerson. Austin, Tex., 1986.

Barkley, Mary Starr. *History of Travis County and Austin, 1839–1899.* Waco, 1963.

Barney, William L. *The Secessionist Impulse: Alabama and Mississippi in 1860.* Princeton, N.J., 1974.

Belz, Herman. *Emancipation and Equal Rights: Politics and Constitutionalism in the Civil War Era.* New York, 1978.

————. *Reconstructing the Union: Theory and Policy during the Civil War.* Ithaca, N.Y., 1969.

Benedict, Michael L. *A Compromise of Principle: Congressional Republicans and Reconstruction, 1865–1869.* New York, 1974.

Biographical Directory of the American Congress, 1774–1971 . . . Washington, D.C., 1971.

Brewer, J. Mason. *Negro Legislators of Texas and Their Descendants: A History of the Negro in Texas Politics from Reconstruction to Disfranchisement.* Dallas, 1935.

Brock, William R. *An American Crisis: Congress and Reconstruction, 1865–1867.* New York, 1963.

Brown Jr., Canter. *Ossian Bingley Hart: Florida's Loyalist Reconstruction Governor.* Baton Rouge, 1997.

Buenger, Walter L. *Secession and the Union in Texas.* Austin, 1984.

Burnham, Walter Dean. *Presidential Ballots: 1836–1892.* Baltimore, 1955.

Campbell, Mary E. R. *The Attitude of Tennesseans toward the Union, 1847–1861.* New York, 1961.

Campbell, Randolph B. *Grass-Roots Reconstruction in Texas, 1865–1880.* Baton Rouge, 1997.

Capers, Gerald M. *Occupied City: New Orleans under the Federals, 1862–1865.* Lexington, Ky., 1965.

Cappon, Lester J. *Virginia Newspapers, 1821–1935: A Bibliography with Historical Introduction and Notes.* New York, 1936.

Carman, Harry J., and Reinhard H. Luthin. *Lincoln and the Patronage.* New York, 1943.

Carter, Dan T. *When the War Was Over: The Failure of Self-Reconstruction in the South, 1865–1867.* Baton Rouge, 1985.

Carter, Hodding. *The Angry Scar: The Story of Reconstruction.* Garden City, N. Y., 1959.

Casdorph, Paul. *A History of the Republican Party in Texas, 1865–1965.* Introduction by Dwight D. Eisenhower. Austin, 1965.

Cashin, Edward J. *The Story of Augusta.* Augusta, Ga., 1980.

Caskey, Willie Malvin. *Secession and Restoration of Louisiana.* Baton Rouge, 1938.

Channing, Steven A. *Crisis of Fear: Secession in South Carolina.* New York, 1970.

Chesson, Michael B. *Richmond after the War, 1865–1890.* Richmond, 1981.

Cimbala, Paul A. *Under the Guardianship of the Nation: The Freedmen's Bureau and the Reconstruction of Georgia, 1865–1870.* Athens, Ga., 1997.

Clark, E. Culpepper. *Francis Warrington Dawson and the Politics of Restoration: South Carolina, 1874–1889.* University, Ala., 1980.

Coleman, Kenneth, and Charles S. Gurr, eds. *Dictionary of Georgia Biography.* 2 vols. Athens, Ga., 1983.

Conway, Alan. *The Reconstruction of Georgia.* Minneapolis, Minn., 1966.

Corlew, Robert E. *Tennessee: A Short History.* 2d ed. Knoxville, 1981.

Coulter, E. Merton. *William G. Brownlow, Fighting Parson of the Southern Highlands.* Chapel Hill, 1937.

Cox, LaWanda, and John H. Cox. *Politics, Principle, and Prejudice, 1865–1866: Dilemma of Reconstruction America.* New York, 1963.

Crenshaw, Ollinger. *The Slave States in the Presidential Election of 1860.* Baltimore, 1945.

Crofts, Daniel W. *Reluctant Confederates: Upper South Unionists in the Secession Crisis.* Chapel Hill, 1989.

Current, Richard N. *Lincoln's Loyalists: Union Soldiers from the Confederacy.* Boston, 1992.

————. *Those Terrible Carpetbaggers.* New York, 1988.

Current, Richard N., et al., eds. *The Encyclopedia of the Confederacy.* 4 vols. New York, 1993.

Currie-McDaniel, Ruth. *Carpetbagger of Conscience: A Biography of John Emory Bryant.* Athens, Ga., 1987.

Curry, Richard Orr. *A House Divided: A Study of Statehood Politics and the Copperhead Movement in West Virginia.* Pittsburgh, 1964.

————, ed. *Radicalism, Racism, and Party Realignment: The Border States during Reconstruction.* Baltimore, 1969.

Dabney, Virginius. *Virginia, the New Dominion.* New York, 1971.

Davis, William Watson. *The Civil War and Reconstruction in Florida.* New York, 1913.

Degler, Carl N. *The Other South: Southern Dissenters in the Nineteenth Century.* New York, 1974.

Denman, Clarence Phillips. *The Secession Movement in Alabama.* Montgomery, 1933.

Dictionary of American Biography. Under the auspices of the American Council of Learned Societies. 22 vols. New York, 1928–58.

Dictionary of American History. Rev. ed. 8 vols. New York: Scribner, 1976.

Dixon, Thomas. *The Sins of the Fathers: A Romance of the South.* New York, 1912.

Dorris, Jonathan T. *Pardon and Amnesty under Lincoln and Johnson: The Restoration of the Confederates to Their Rights and Privileges, 1861–1898.* Chapel Hill, 1953.

Dougan, Michael B. *Confederate Arkansas: The People and Policies of a Frontier State in Wartime.* University, Ala., 1976.

Drago, Edmund L. *Black Politicians and Reconstruction in Georgia: A Splendid Failure.* Baton Rouge, 1982.

Du Bois, W. E. B. *Black Reconstruction in America.* New York, 1935.

DuBose, John Witherspoon. *Alabama's Tragic Decade: Ten Years of Alabama, 1865–1874.* Ed. James K. Greer. Birmingham, 1940.

Dumond, Dwight Lowell. *The Secession Movement, 1860–1861.* New York, 1931.

Duncan, Russell. *Entrepreneur for Equality: Governor Rufus Bullock, Commerce, and Race in Post–Civil War Georgia.* Athens, Ga., 1994.

Dunning, William Archibald. *Reconstruction: Political and Economic, 1865–1870.* New York, 1907.

Durrill, Wayne K. *War of Another Kind: A Southern Community in the Great Rebellion.* New York, 1990.

Dyer, Thomas G. *Secret Yankees: The Union Circle in Confederate Atlanta.* Baltimore, 1999.

Eckenrode, Hamilton James. *The Political History of Virginia during the Reconstruction.* Baltimore, 1904.

Elliott, Claude. *Leathercoat: The Life History of a Texas Patriot.* San Antonio, 1938.

Ellison, Rhoda Coleman. *Bibb County, Alabama: The First Hundred Years, 1818–1918.* University, Ala., 1984.

Elzas, Barnett A. *The Jews of South Carolina, from the Earliest Times to the Present Day.* Philadelphia, 1905.

The Encyclopedia of the New West . . . Chicago, 1880.

Evans, W. McKee. *Ballots and Fence Rails: Reconstruction on the Lower Cape Fear.* Chapel Hill, 1967.

Fehrenbacher, Don E., ed. *History and American Society: Essays of David M. Potter.* New York, 1973.

Ficklen, John Rose. *History of Reconstruction in Louisiana, through 1868.* Baltimore, 1910.

Finley, Randy. *From Slavery to Uncertain Freedom: The Freedmen's Bureau in Arkansas, 1865–1869.* Fayetteville, 1996.

Fitzgerald, Michael W. *The Union League Movement in the Deep South: Politics and Agricultural Change during Reconstruction.* Baton Rouge, 1989.

Fleming, Walter L. *Civil War and Reconstruction in Alabama.* New York, 1905.

———. *The Sequel of Appomattox: A Chronicle of the Reunion of the States.* New Haven, 1919.

Folk, Edgar E., and Bynum Shaw. *W. W. Holden: A Political Biography.* Winston-Salem, N.C., 1984.

Foner, Eric. *Reconstruction: America's Unfinished Revolution, 1863–1877.* New York, 1988.

Foner, Eric, ed. *Freedom's Lawmakers: A Directory of Black Officeholders during Reconstruction.* Baton Rouge, 1996.

Ford, Lacy K., Jr. *Origins of Southern Radicalism: The South Carolina Upcountry, 1800–1860.* New York, 1988.

Franklin, John Hope. *Reconstruction: After the Civil War.* Chicago, 1961.

Fraser, Walter J., Jr., and Winfred B. Moore Jr., eds. *The Southern Enigma: Essays on Race, Class, and Folk Culture.* Westport, Conn., 1983.

Garner, James Wilford. *Reconstruction in Mississippi.* New York, 1901.

Garrett, Franklin M. *Atlanta and Environs: A Chronicle of Its People and Events.* 4 vols. Athens, Ga., 1954–87.

Garrett, Jill K., and Marise P. Lightfoot. *The Civil War in Maury County, Tennessee.* Columbia, Tenn., 1966.

Gillette, William. *Retreat from Reconstruction, 1869–1879.* Baton Rouge, 1979.

Green, Fletcher M. *The Role of the Yankee in the Old South.* Athens, Ga., 1972.

Gregorie, Anne King. *History of Sumter County, South Carolina.* Sumter, S.C., 1954.

Griffith, Louis T., and John E. Talmadge. *Georgia Journalism, 1763–1950.* Athens, Ga., 1951.

Gunderson, Robert G. *Old Gentlemen's Convention: The Washington Peace Conference of 1861.* Madison, Wis., 1961.

Hall, Clifton R. *Andrew Johnson, Military Governor of Tennessee.* Princeton, N.J., 1916.

Hall, Granville D. *The Rending of Virginia: A History.* Chicago, 1902.

Hamer, Philip M. *Tennessee: A History, 1673–1932.* 2 vols. New York, 1933.

Hamilton, J. G. de Roulhac. *Reconstruction in North Carolina.* New York, 1914.

Harrington, Fred Harvey. *Fighting Politician: Major General N. P. Banks.* Philadelphia, 1948.

Harris, William C. *The Day of the Carpetbagger: Republican Reconstruction in Mississippi.* Baton Rouge, 1979.

———. *Presidential Reconstruction in Mississippi.* Baton Rouge, 1967.

———. *William Woods Holden: Firebrand of North Carolina Politics.* Baton Rouge, 1987.

Hesseltine, William B. *Confederate Leaders in the New South.* Baton Rouge, 1950.

Hollis, John Porter. *The Early Period of Reconstruction in South Carolina.* Baltimore, 1905.

Holt, Thomas. *Black over White: Negro Political Leadership in South Carolina during Reconstruction.* Urbana, Ill., 1977.

Hoole, William Stanley. *Alabama Tories: The First Alabama Cavalry, U.S.A., 1862–1865.* Tuscaloosa, 1960.

Hunt, Thomas. *The Life of William H. Hunt.* Brattleboro, Vt., 1922.

Hyman, Harold. *The Era of the Oath: Northern Loyalty Tests during the Civil War and Reconstruction.* Philadelphia, 1954.

Jones, Jacqueline. *Soldiers of Light and Love: Northern Teachers and Georgia Blacks, 1865–1873.* Chapel Hill, 1980.

Johns, John E. *Florida during the Civil War.* Gainesville, Fla., 1963.

Key, V. O., Jr. *Southern Politics in State and Nation.* New York, 1949.

Klingberg, Frank W. *The Southern Claims Commission.* Berkeley, Calif., 1955.

Knight, Oliver. *Fort Worth: Outpost on the Trinity.* Norman, Okla., 1953.

Kousser, J. Morgan, and James M. McPherson, eds. *Region, Race, and Reconstruction: Essays in Honor of C. Vann Woodward.* New York, 1982.

Lamson, Peggy. *The Glorious Failure: Black Congressman Robert Brown Elliott and the Reconstruction in South Carolina.* New York, 1973.

Leemhuis, Roger P. *James L. Orr and the Sectional Conflict.* New York, 1979.

Litwack, Leon F. *Been in the Storm So Long: The Aftermath of Slavery.* New York, 1979.

Lonn, Ella. *Desertion during the Civil War.* New York, 1928.

———. *Reconstruction in Louisiana after 1868.* New York, 1918.

Lowe, Richard. *Republicans and Reconstruction in Virginia, 1856–1870.* Charlottesville, 1991.

Maddex, Jack, Jr. *The Virginia Conservatives, 1867–1879: A Study in Reconstruction Politics.* Chapel Hill, 1970.

Mantell, Martin E. *Johnson, Grant, and the Politics of Reconstruction.* New York, 1973.

Marten, James. *Texas Divided: Loyalty and Dissent in the Lone Star State, 1856–1874.* Lexington, Ky., 1989.

Maslowski, Peter. *Treason Must Be Made Odious: Military Occupation and Wartime Reconstruction in Nashville, Tennessee, 1862–1865.* Millwood, N.Y., 1978.

McBride, Robert M., and Dan M. Robison, comps. *Biographical Directory of the Tennessee General Assembly.* Vols. 1, 2. Nashville, 1975.

McCrary, Peyton. *Abraham Lincoln and Reconstruction: The Louisiana Experiment.* Princeton, N.J., 1978.

McFeely, William S. *Yankee Stepfather: General O. O. Howard and the Freedmen.* New Haven, 1968.

McKinney, Gordon B. *Southern Mountain Republicans, 1865–1900: Politics and the Appalachian Community.* Chapel Hill, 1978.

McKitrick, Eric L. *Andrew Johnson and Reconstruction.* Chicago, 1960.

McMillan, Malcolm Cook. *Constitutional Development in Alabama, 1798–1901: A Study in Politics, the Negro, and Sectionalism.* Chapel Hill, 1955.

McPherson, James M. *Ordeal by Fire: The Civil War and Reconstruction.* 2d ed. New York, 1993.

Moneyhon, Carl H. *The Impact of the Civil War and Reconstruction on Arkansas: Persistence in the Midst of Ruin.* Baton Rouge, 1994.

———. *Republicanism in Reconstruction Texas.* Austin, 1980.

Nathans, Elizabeth Studley. *Losing the Peace: Georgia Republicans and Reconstruction, 1865–1871.* Baton Rouge, 1968.

National Cyclopaedia of American Biography. Vols. 1–13. New York, 1892–1906.

Netherton, Nan, et al. *Fairfax County, Virginia: A History.* Fairfax, Va., 1978.

Nevins, Allan. *The Emergence of Lincoln.* 2 vols. New York, 1950.

———. *The War for the Union.* 4 vols. New York, 1959–60.

Northen, William J., ed. *Men of Mark in Georgia: A Complete and Elaborate History of the State from Its Settlement to the Present Time.* 6 vols. Atlanta, 1907–12.

Oberholtzer, Ellis P. *A History of the United States since the Civil War.* 5 vols. New York, 1917–37.

Olsen, Otto H. *Carpetbagger's Crusade: The Life of Albion Winegar Tourgée.* Baltimore, 1965.

———, ed. *Reconstruction and Redemption in the South.* Baton Rouge, 1980.

Owen, Thomas McAdory. *History of Alabama and Dictionary of Alabama Biography.* 4 vols. Chicago, 1921.

Parks, Joseph H. *Joseph E. Brown of Georgia.* Baton Rouge, 1977.

Patrick, Rembert. *The Reconstruction of the Nation.* New York, 1967.

Patton, James Welch. *Unionism and Reconstruction in Tennessee, 1860–1869.* Chapel Hill, 1934.

Perdue, Robert E. *The Negro in Savannah, 1865–1900.* New York, 1973.

Pereyra, Lillian A. *James Lusk Alcorn: Persistent Whig.* Baton Rouge, 1966.

Perman, Michael. *Reunion without Compromise: The South and Reconstruction, 1865–1868.* New York, 1973.

———. *The Road to Redemption: Southern Politics, 1869–1879.* Chapel Hill, 1984.

Piston, William Garrett. *Lee's Tarnished Lieutenant: James Longstreet and His Place in Southern History.* Athens, Ga., 1987.

Potter, David M. *Lincoln and His Party in the Secession Crisis.* New Haven, 1942.

Powell, Lawrence N. *New Masters: Northern Planters during the Civil War and Recon-struction*. New Haven, 1980.

Powell, William S., ed. *Dictionary of North Carolina Biography*. 6 vols. Chapel Hill, 1979–96.

Quarles, Benjamin. *Frederick Douglass*. New York, 1968.

Ramsdell, Charles W. *Reconstruction in Texas*. New York, 1910.

Randall, James G., and David H. Donald. *The Civil War and Reconstruction*. 2d ed. Boston, 1961.

Randall, James G., and Richard N. Current. *The Last Full Measure*. Vol. 4 of *Lincoln the President*. New York, 1955.

Ransleben, Guido E. *A Hundred Years of Comfort in Texas: A Centennial History*. San Antonio, 1954.

Raper, Horace W. *William W. Holden: North Carolina's Political Enigma*. Chapel Hill, 1985.

Reynolds, Donald E. *Editors Make War: Southern Newspapers in the Secession Crisis*. Nashville, 1970.

Reynolds, John S. *Reconstruction in South Carolina, 1865–1877*. Columbia, S.C., 1905.

Richardson, Joe M. *The Negro in the Reconstruction of Florida, 1865–1877*. Tallahassee, 1965.

Richter, William L. *The Army in Texas during Reconstruction*. College Station, Tex., 1991.

Rickels, Milton. *Thomas Bangs Thorpe: Humorist of the Old Southwest*. Baton Rouge, 1962.

Riddleberger, Patrick W. *1866: The Critical Year Revisited*. Carbondale, Illinois, 1979.

Roberts, Derrell C. *Joseph E. Brown and the Politics of Reconstruction*. University, Ala., 1973.

Rogers, William Warren, Jr. *Black Belt Scalawag: Charles Hays and the Southern Repub-licans in the Era of Reconstruction*. Athens, Ga., 1993.

Rose, Willie Lee. *Rehearsal for Reconstruction: The Port Royal Experiment*. Indianapolis, Ind., 1964.

Ross, Earle Dudley. *The Liberal Republican Movement*. New York, 1910.

Rowland, Dunbar, ed. *Encyclopedia of Mississippi History: Comprising Sketches of Coun-ties, Towns, Events, Institutions, and Persons*. 2 vols. Madison, Wis., 1907.

Russell, James Michael. *Atlanta, 1847–1890: City Building in the Old South and the New*. Baton Rouge, 1988.

Sears, Louis M. *John Slidell*. Durham, N.C., 1925.

Sefton, James E. *The United States Army and Reconstruction, 1865–1877*. Baton Rouge, 1967.

Seip, Terry L. *The South Returns to Congress: Men, Economic Measures, and Intersec-tional Relationships, 1868–1879*. Baton Rouge, 1983.

Sewell, Richard H. *Ballots for Freedom: Antislavery Politics in the United States, 1837–1860*. New York, 1976.

Shadgett, Olive Hall. *The Republican Party in Georgia, from Reconstruction through 1900*. Athens, Ga., 1964.

Shofner, Jerrell H. *Nor Is It Over Yet: Florida in the Era of Reconstruction, 1863–1877*. Gainesville, Fla., 1974.

Shugg, Roger W. *Origins of Class Struggle in Louisiana: A Social History of White Farmers and Laborers during Slavery and after, 1840–1875*. Baton Rouge, 1939.

Simkins, Francis Butler, and Robert Hilliard Woody. *South Carolina during Reconstruction*. Chapel Hill, 1932.

Smith, John I. *The Courage of a Southern Unionist: A Biography of Isaac Murphy, Governor of Arkansas, 1864–1868*. Little Rock, 1979.

Squires, W. H. T. *Unleashed at Long Last: Reconstruction in Virginia, April 9, 1865, to January 26, 1870*. Portsmouth, Va., 1939.

Stampp, Kenneth M. *The Era of Reconstruction, 1865–1877*. New York, 1965.

Staples, Thomas S. *Reconstruction in Arkansas, 1862–1874*. New York, 1923.

Tatum, Georgia Lee. *Disloyalty in the Confederacy*. Chapel Hill, 1934.

Taylor, Joe Gray. *Louisiana Reconstructed, 1863–1877*. Baton Rouge, 1974.

Tennessee Civil War Centennial Commission. *Tennesseans in the Civil War: A Military History of the Confederate and Union Units with Available Rosters of Personnel*. 2 vols., Nashville, 1964.

Thomas, David Y. *Arkansas in War and Reconstruction, 1861–1874*. Little Rock, 1926.

Thompson, C. Mildred. *Reconstruction in Georgia: Economic, Social, Political, 1865–1872*. New York, 1915.

Trefousse, Hans L. *The Radical Republicans: Lincoln's Vanguard for Racial Justice*. Baton Rouge, 1968.

Trelease, Allen W. *White Terror: The Ku Klux Klan Conspiracy and Southern Reconstruction*. New York, 1971.

Tunnell, Ted. *Crucible of Reconstruction: War, Radicalism, and Race in Louisiana, 1862–1877*. Baton Rouge, 1984.

Uya, Okon Edet. *From Slavery to Public Service: Robert Smalls, 1839–1915*. New York, 1971.

Vandal, Gilles. *The New Orleans Riot of 1866: Anatomy of a Tragedy*. Lafayette, La., 1983.

Vincent, Charles. *Black Legislators in Louisiana during Reconstruction*. Baton Rouge, 1976.

Wakelyn, Jon L. *Biographical Dictionary of the Confederacy*. Westport, Conn., 1977.

Walker, Peter F. *Vicksburg: A People at War, 1860–1865*. Chapel Hill, 1960.

Waller, John L. *Colossal Hamilton of Texas: A Biography of Andrew Jackson Hamilton, Militant Unionist and Reconstruction Governor*. El Paso, 1968.

Warner, Ezra J. *Generals in Gray: Lives of the Confederate Commanders*. Baton Rouge, 1959.

Webb, Walter Prescott, et al., eds. *The Handbook of Texas*. 3 vols. Austin, 1952–76.

Wells, Edward L. *Hampton and Reconstruction*. Columbia, S.C., 1907.

Wharton, Vernon Lane. *The Negro in Mississippi, 1865–1890*. Chapel Hill, 1947.

White, Howard A. *The Freedmen's Bureau in Louisiana*. Baton Rouge, 1970.

Wiggins, Sarah Woolfolk. *The Scalawag in Alabama Politics, 1865–1881*. Tuscaloosa, 1977.

Williamson, Joel. *After Slavery: The Negro in South Carolina during Reconstruction, 1861–1877.* Chapel Hill, 1965.

Woody, Robert H. *Republican Newspapers of South Carolina.* Charlottesville, 1936.

Wooster, Ralph A. *The Secession Conventions of the South.* Princeton, N.J., 1962.

ARTICLES

Abbott, Richard H. "Yankee Farmers in Northern Virginia, 1840–1860." *VMHB* 66 (January 1968): 56–63.

Alexander, Thomas B. "Persistent Whiggery in the Confederate South, 1860–1877." *JSH* 27 (August 1961): 305–29.

———. "Whiggery and Reconstruction in Tennessee." *JSH* 16 (August 1950): 291–305.

Auman, William T., and David D. Scarboro. "The Heroes of America in Civil War North Carolina." *NCHR* 58 (autumn 1981): 327–63.

Avillo, Philip J., Jr. "Ballots for the Faithful: The Oath and the Emergence of Slave State Republican Congressmen, 1861–1867." *Civil War History* 22 (June 1976): 164–74.

Baggett, James Alex. "Birth of the Texas Republican Party." *SwHQ* 78 (July 1974): 1–20.

———. "The Constitutional Union Party in Texas." *SwHQ* 82 (January 1979): 233–64.

———. "Origins of Early Texas Republican Party Leadership." *JSH* 40 (August 1974): 441–54.

———. "Origins of Upper South Scalawag Leadership." *Civil War History* 29 (March 1983): 53–73.

Bentley, George R. "The Political Activity of the Freedmen's Bureau in Florida." *FHQ* 28 (July 1949): 28–37.

Biesele, Rudolph L. "The Texas State Convention of Germans in 1854." *SwHQ* 33 (April 1929): 247–61.

Binning, F. Wayne. "Carpetbaggers' Triumph: The Louisiana State Election of 1868." *LH* 14 (winter 1973): 21–39.

Blankinship, Gary. "Colonel Fielding Hurst and the Hurst Nation." *WTHSP* 34 (1980): 71–87.

Bond, Horace Mann. "Social and Economic Forces in Alabama Reconstruction." *Journal of Negro History* 23 (July 1938): 290–348.

Boyd, William K. "William W. Holden." *Annual Publication of Historical Papers Published by the Historical Society of Trinity College.* 3 (1899): 39–130.

Bryan, Charles F. "A Gathering of Tories: The East Tennessee Convention of 1861." *THQ* 39 (spring 1980): 27–48.

Cason, Roberta F. "The Loyal League in Georgia." *GHQ* 20 (June 1936): 125–53.

Copeland, Fayette. "The New Orleans Press and the Reconstruction." *LHQ* 30 (January 1947), 149–337.

Cox, Merlin G. "Military Reconstruction in Florida," *FHQ* 46 (January 1968): 219–33.

Crow, Jeffrey. "Thomas Settle Jr., Reconstruction, and the Memory of the Civil War." *JSH* 62 (October 1996): 700–20.

Curry, Richard Orr. "A Reappraisal of Statehood Politics in West Virginia." *JSH* 28 (November 1962): 403–21.

Dailey, Douglass C. "The Election of 1872 in North Carolina." *NCHR* 40 (summer 1963): 338–60.

Darden, David L. "Alabama Secession Convention." *AlaHQ* 3 (fall and winter 1941): 269–451.

Davis, Donald W. "Ratification of the Constitution of 1868—Record of Voters." *LH* 6 (summer 1965): 301–5.

Davis, Granville. "Arkansas and the Little Giant." *WTHSP* 22 (1968): 28–51.

Delaney, Norman C. "Charles Henry Foster and the Unionists of Eastern North Carolina," *NCHR* 37 (July 1960): 344–66.

Dew, Charles B. "The Long Lost Returns: The Candidates and Their Totals in Louisiana Secession Convention." *LH* 10 (fall 1969): 364–68.

Donald, David H. "Communication to the Editor of the *Journal of Southern History.*" *JSH* 30 (May 1964): 254–56.

———. "The Scalawag in Mississippi Reconstruction." *JSH* 10 (November 1944): 447–60.

Driggs, Orval Truman, Jr. "The Issues of the Powell Clayton Regime, 1868–1871." *ArkHQ* 8 (spring 1949): 1–75.

Durham, Walter T. "How Say You, Senator Fowler?" *THQ* 42 (spring 1983): 39–57.

Ellem, Warren A. "Who Were the Mississippi Scalawags?" *JSH* 38 (May 1972): 217–40.

Elliott, Claude. "Union Sentiment in Texas, 1861–1865." *SwHQ* 50 (April 1946): 449–77.

Farmer, Fanny Memory. "Legal Education in North Carolina, 1820–1860." *NCHR* 28 (July 1951): 271–97.

Fitzgerald, Michael W. "Radical Republicanism and the White Yeomanry during Alabama Reconstruction, 1865–1868." *JSH* 54 (November 1988): 565–96.

———. "Wager Swayne, The Freedmen's Bureau, and the Politics of Reconstruction in Alabama." *Alabama Review* 48 (July 1995): 188–218.

Fowler, Russell. "Chancellor William Macon Smith and Judicial Reconstruction: A Study of Tyranny and Integrity." *WTHSP* 48 (1994): 35–59.

Futch, Ovid L. "Salmon P. Chase and Civil War Politics in Florida," *FHQ* 32 (January 1954), 163–88.

Garner, Stanton. "Thomas Bangs Thorpe in the Gilded Age: Shifty in a New Country." *Mississippi Quarterly* 36 (winter 1982–83): 35–52.

Gonzales, John E. "Henry Stuart Foote in Exile." *JMH* 15 (January 1953): 90–98.

Govan, Gilbert E., and James W. Livingood. "Chattanooga under Military Occupation, 1863–1865." *JSH* 17 (February 1951): 23–47.

Greer, James K. "Louisiana Politics, 1845–1861." *LHQ* 13 (July 1930): 614–56.

Grob, Gerald N. "Reconstruction: An American Morality Play." In *American History: Retrospect and Prospect,* George A. Billias and Gerald N. Grob, eds. New York, 1971. 191–231.

Harris, William C. "Lincoln and Wartime Reconstruction in North Carolina, 1861–1863." *NCHR* 63 (April 1986): 149–68.

———. "A Reconsideration of the Mississippi Scalawag," *JMH* 32 (February 1970): 3–42.

———. "The Reconstruction of the Commonwealth, 1865–1870." In *A History of Mississippi*, Richard A. McLemore, ed. Hattiesburg, 1973.

———. "The Southern Unionist Critique of the Civil War." *Civil War History* 31 (March 1985): 39–56.

Henry, Milton. "What Became of the Tennessee Whigs?" *THQ* 11 (March 1952): 57–98.

Holley, Peggy Scott. "The Seventh Tennessee Volunteer Cavalry: West Tennessee Unionists in Andersonville Prison." *WTHSP* 42 (1988): 39–58.

Hume, Richard L. "Membership of the Arkansas Constitutional Convention of 1868: A Case Study of Republican Factionalism in the Reconstruction South." *JSH* 39 (May 1973): 183–206.

———. "Florida Constitutional Convention of 1868." *FHQ* 51 (July 1972): 1–21.

James, Joseph B. "Southern Reaction to the Proposal of the Fourteenth Amendment." *JSH* 22 (November 1956): 477–97.

Johnston, Angus J., II. "Disloyalty on Confederate Railroads in Virginia." *VMHB* 63 (October 1955): 410–26.

Jordan, Weymouth T. "Noah B. Cloud and the *American Cotton Planter*." *Agricultural History* 31 (October 1957): 44–49.

Kibler, Lillian A. "Unionist Sentiment in South Carolina in 1860." *JSH* 4 (August 1938): 346–66.

Kolchin, Peter. "Scalawags, Carpetbaggers, and Reconstruction: A Quantitative Look at Southern Congressional Politics, 1868–1872." *JSH* 45 (February 1979): 63–76.

Lang, Herbert H. "J. F. H. Claiborne at 'Laurel Wood' Plantation, 1853–1870." *JMH* 18 (October 1956): 1–17.

Lathrop, Barnes F. "Disaffection in Confederate Louisiana: The Case of William Hyman." *JSH* 24 (August 1958): 308–18.

Long, Durwood. "Unanimity and Disloyalty in Secessionist Alabama." *Civil War History* 11 (September 1965): 257–74.

Lowe, Richard. "Another Look at Reconstruction in Virginia." *Civil War History* 32 (March 1986): 56–76.

———. "Francis Harrison Pierpont: Wartime Unionist, Reconstruction Moderate." In *The Governors of Virginia, 1860–1978*, Edward Younger, ed. Charlottesville, 1982.

———. "The Republican Party in Antebellum Virginia, 1856–1860." *VMHB* 81 (July 1973): 259–79.

Lowrey, Walter M. "The Political Career of James Madison Wells." *LHQ* 31 (October 1948): 995–1123.

Maness, Lonnie. "Emerson Etheridge and the Union." *THQ* 48 (summer 1989): 97–110.

Martin, Richard A. "Defeat in Victory: Yankee Experience in Early Civil War Jacksonville." *FHQ* 53 (July 1974): 1–32.

McDonough, James L. "John Schofield as Military Director of Reconstruction in Virginia." *Civil War History* 15 (September 1969): 237–56.

McKinney, Gordon B. "The Rise of the Houk Machine in East Tennessee." *ETHSP* 45 (1973): 61–77.

———. "Southern Mountain Republicans and the Negro, 1865–1900." *JSH* 51 (November 1975): 493–516.

———. "The Mountain Republican Party-Army," *THQ* 32 (summer 1973): 124–39.

McWhiney, Grady. "Were the Whigs a Class Party in Alabama?" *JSH* 23 (November 1957): 510–22.

Mering, John V. "The Slave-State Constitutional Unionists and the Politics of Consensus." *JSH* 43 (August 1977): 395–410.

Miller, Robert D. "Samuel Field Phillips: The Odyssey of a Southern Dissenter." *NCHR* 43 (July 1981): 263–80.

Miscamble, Wilson D. "Andrew Johnson and the Election of William G. ('Parson') Brownlow as Governor of Tennessee." *THQ* 37 (fall 1978): 308–20.

Moore, Frederick W. "Representation in the National Congress from the Seceding States, 1861–1865." *American Historical Review* 2 (January 1897): 279–93, 461–71.

Mulhollan, Paige E. "The Arkansas General Assembly of 1866 and Its Effect on Reconstruction." *ArkHQ* 20 (winter 1961): 331–44.

Olsen, Otto H. "Albion W. Tourgée: Carpetbagger." *NCHR* 40 (autumn 1963): 434–54.

———. "Reconsidering the Scalawags." *Civil War History* 12 (December 1966): 304–20.

Palmer, Paul C. "Miscegenation as an Issue in the Arkansas Constitutional Convention of 1868." *ArkHQ* 24 (summer 1965), 99–119.

Parks, Joseph H. "Memphis under Military Rule, 1862 to 1865." *ETHSP* 14 (1942): 31–58.

Peek, Ralph L. "Military Reconstruction and the Growth of the Anti-Negro Sentiment in Florida, 1867." *FHQ* 47 (April 1969): 380–400.

Puckett, Earnest F. "Reconstruction in Monroe County." *Publications of the Mississippi Historical Society.* 11 (1910): 103–62.

Queener, Verton M. "The Origin of the Republican Party in East Tennessee." *ETHSP* 13 (1941): 66–90.

Rankin, David C. "The Origins of Black Leadership in New Orleans during Reconstruction." *JSH* 40 (August 1974): 417–40.

Raper, Horace W. "William W. Holden and the Peace Movement in North Carolina." *NCHR* 31 (October 1954): 493–516.

Reynolds, Donald E. "The New Orleans Riot of 1866, Reconsidered," *LH* 5 (winter 1964): 5–28.

Rhodes, Robert S. "The Registration of Voters and the Election of Delegates to the Reconstruction Convention in Alabama." *Alabama Review* 8 (April 1955): 119–42.

Richter, William L. "James Longstreet: From Rebel to Scalawag." *LH* 11 (summer 1970): 215–30.

———. "Tyrant and Reformer: General Griffin Reconstructs Texas, 1865–1866." *Prologue* 10 (winter 1978): 225–41.

———. "'Must Rubb Outt and Begin Anew': The Army and the Republican Party in Texas Reconstruction, 1867–1870." *Civil War History* 19 (December 1973): 334–52.

Russ, William A., Jr. "Radical Disfranchisement in Mississippi (1867–1870)." *Mississippi Law Journal* 7 (April 1935): 365–77.

———. "Radical Disfranchisement in Texas, 1867–1870." *SwHQ* 38 (July 1934): 40–52.

———. "Registration and Disfranchisement under Radical Reconstruction." *Mississippi Valley Historical Review* 21 (September 1934): 163–80.

Schweninger, Loren. "Alabama Blacks and the Congressional Reconstruction Acts of 1867." *Alabama Review* 31 (July 1978): 182–98.

Scroggs, Jack B. "Carpetbagger Constitutional Reform in the South Atlantic States, 1867–1868." *JSH* 27 (November 1961): 475–93.

———. "Southern Reconstruction: A Radical View." *JSH* 24 (November 1958): 407–29.

Shadgett, Olive Hall. "James Johnson, Provisional Governor of Georgia." *GHQ* 36 (March 1952): 1–21.

Shanks, Henry T. "Disloyalty to the Confederacy in Southwestern Virginia, 1861–1865," *NCHR* 21 (April 1944): 118–35.

Shook, Robert W. "Toward a List of Reconstruction Loyalists." *SwHQ* 76 (January 1973): 315–20.

Shugg, Roger W. "A Suppressed Co-operationist Protest against Secession," *LHQ* 19 (January 1936): 199–203.

Simpson, Amos, and Vaughan Baker. "Michael Hahn: Steady Patriot." *LH* 13 (summer 1972): 229–52.

Smith, George Winston. "Carpetbag Imperialism in Florida, 1862–1868." *FHQ* 27 (October 1948): 99–130; *FHQ* 28 (January 1949): 260–99.

Smyrl, Frank H. "Texans in the Union Army, 1861–1865." *SwHQ* 65 (October 1961): 234–50.

———. "Unionism in Texas, 1856–1861." *SwHQ* 68 (October 1964): 172–95.

Somers, Dale A. "James P. Newcomb: The Making of a Radical." *SwHQ* 72 (April 1969): 449–69.

Steelman, Joseph F. "Daniel Reaves Goodloe: A Perplexed Abolitionist during Reconstruction." In *Essays in Southern Biography*. East Carolina College Publications in History (Greenville, N.C., 1965) 2: 77–93.

Stone, Lawrence. "Prosopography," *Daedalus* 100 (winter 1971): 46–79.

Stuart, Meriwether. "Colonel Ulric Dahlgren and Richmond's Union Underground, April 1864." *VMHB* 72 (April 1964): 152–204.

Trelease, Allen W. "Who Were the Scalawags?" *JSH* 29 (November 1963): 445–68.

———. "Republican Reconstruction in North Carolina: A Roll-Call Analysis of the State House of Representatives, 1868–1870." *JSH* (August 1976): 319–44.

Uzee, Philip D. "The Beginnings of the Louisiana Republican Party." *LH* 12 (summer 1971), 197–211.

Wagstaff, Thomas. "The Arm-in-Arm Convention." *Civil War History* 14 (June 1968): 101–19.

Ward, Judson C. "The Republican Party in Bourbon Georgia, 1872–1890." *JSH* 9 (May 1943): 196–209.

Watkins, Beverly. "Efforts to Encourage Immigration to Arkansas, 1865–1874." *ArkHQ* 38 (spring 1979): 32–62.

White, Kenneth B. "Wager Swayne: Racist or Realist?" *Alabama Review* 31 (April 1978): 92–109.

White, Laura A. "The National Democrats in South Carolina, 1852 to 1860." *South Atlantic Quarterly* 28 (October 1929): 370–89.

Wiggins, Sarah Woolfolk. "Alabama Attitudes toward the Republican Party in 1868 and 1964." *Alabama Review* 20 (January 1967): 27–33.

———. "Amnesty and Pardon and Republicanism in Alabama." *AlaHQ* 26 (summer 1964): 240–48.

———. "Five Men Called Scalawags." *Alabama Review* 17 (January 1964): 45–55.

———. "What Is a *Scalawag*?" *Alabama Review* 25 (January 1972): 57–58.

Williams, E. Russ. "John Ray: Forgotten Scalawag." *Louisiana Studies* 13 (fall 1974): 241–62.

Williams, Max R. "The Foundations of the Whig Party in North Carolina: A Synthesis and a Modest Proposal." *NCHR* 47 (spring 1970): 115–29.

Woody, Robert H. "Franklin J. Moses Jr., Scalawag Governor of South Carolina, 1872–1874." *NCHR* 10 (April 1933): 111–32.

Dissertations, Theses, and Papers

Adams, William H. "The Louisiana Whig Party." Ph.D. dissertation, Louisiana State University, 1960.

Baggett, James Alex. "The Rise and Fall of the Texas Radicals, 1867–1883." Ph.D. dissertation, University of North Texas, 1972.

Benson, Harry K. "The Public Career of Adelbert Ames, 1861–1876." Ph.D. dissertation, University of Virginia, 1975.

Breese, Donald H. "Politics in the Lower South during Presidential Reconstruction, April to November, 1865." Ph.D. dissertation, University of California, 1964.

Bryan, Charles F. "The Civil War in East Tennessee: A Social, Political, and Economic Study." Ph.D. dissertation, University of Tennessee, 1978.

Carrier, John P. "A Political History of Texas during the Reconstruction, 1865–1874." Ph.D. dissertation, Vanderbilt University, 1971.

Casdorph, Paul. "Texas Delegations to Republican National Conventions, 1860–1896." Master's thesis, University of Texas, 1961.

Cash, William McKinley. "Alabama Republicans during Reconstruction: Personal Characteristics, Motivation, and Political Activity of Party Activists, 1867–1880." Ph.D. dissertation, University of Alabama, 1973.

Currie, James T. "Conflict and Consensus: Creating the 1868 Mississippi Constitution." Master's thesis, University of Virginia, 1969.

Darrah, Marsha Young. "Political Career of Col. William B. Stokes of Tennessee." Master's thesis, Tennessee Tech University, 1968.

deTreville, John R. "Reconstruction in Augusta, Georgia, 1865–1868." Master's thesis, University of North Carolina, 1979.

Ellenburg, Martha Ann. "Reconstruction in Arkansas." Ph.D. dissertation, University of Missouri, 1967.

Griffin, Roger A. "Connecticut Yankee in Texas: A Biography of Elisha Marshall Pease." Ph.D. dissertation, University of Texas, Austin, 1973.

Gunter, Charles R., Jr. "Bedford County during the Civil War." Master's thesis, University of Tennessee, 1963.

Harahan, Joseph P. "Politics, Political Parties, and Voter Participation in Tidewater Virginia during Reconstruction, 1865–1900." Ph.D. dissertation, Michigan State University, 1973.

Hardison, Edwin T. "In the Toils of War: Andrew Johnson and the Federal Occupation of Tennessee, 1862–1865." Ph.D. dissertation, University of Tennessee, 1981.

Hooper, Ernest W. "Memphis, Tennessee: Federal Occupation and Reconstruction, 1862–1870." Ph.D. dissertation, University of North Carolina, 1957.

Hume, Richard L. "The 'Black and Tan' Constitutional Conventions of 1867–1869 in Ten Former Confederate States: A Study of Their Membership." Ph.D. dissertation, University of Washington, 1969.

Jones, George L. "The Political Career of Henry Pattillo Farrow, Georgia Republican, 1865–1904." Master's thesis, University of Georgia, 1966.

Jones, Howard James. "The Members of the Louisiana Legislature of 1868: Images of 'Radical Reconstruction' Leadership in the Deep South." Ph.D. dissertation, Washington State University, 1975.

Lancaster, James L. "The Scalawags of North Carolina, 1850–1868." Ph.D. dissertation, Princeton University, 1974.

McGee, Edward H. "North Carolina Conservatives and Reconstruction." Ph.D. dissertation, University of North Carolina, 1972.

Meador, John Allen. "Florida Political Parties, 1865–1877." Ph.D. dissertation, University of Florida, 1964.

Mills, Wynona Gillmore. "James Govan Taliaferro, 1798–1876: Louisiana Unionist and Scalawag." Master's thesis, Louisiana State University, 1964.

O'Brien, John Thomas, Jr. "From Bondage to Citizenship: The Richmond Black Community, 1865–1867." Ph.D. dissertation, University of Rochester, 1974.

Phillips, Paul D. "The Freedmen's Bureau in Tennessee." Ph.D. dissertation, Vanderbilt University, 1964.

Sansing, David G. "The Role of the Scalawag in Mississippi Reconstruction." Ph.D. dissertation, University of Southern Mississippi, 1969.

Scarborough, Jane Lynn. "George W. Paschal, Texas Unionist and Scalawag Jurisprudent." Ph.D. dissertation, Rice University, 1972.

Shook, Robert W. "Federal Occupation and Administration of Texas, 1865–1870." Ph.D. dissertation, University of North Texas, 1970.

Smith, Allen C. "The Republican Party in Georgia, 1867–1871." Master's thesis, Duke University, 1937.

Stabler, John B. "A History of the Constitutional Union Party: A Tragic Failure." Ph.D. dissertation, Columbia University, 1954.

Steele, Roberta. "Some Aspects of Reconstruction in Mobile, 1865–1875." Master's thesis, Auburn University, 1937.

Swift, Charles J., Jr. "James Lusk Alcorn," in James Lusk Alcorn Papers, Mississippi Department of Archives and History.

Taylor, Arthur R. "From the Ashes: Atlanta during Reconstruction, 1865–1876." Ph.D. dissertation, Emory University, 1973.

Wetta, Francis J. "The Louisiana Scalawags." Ph.D. dissertation, Louisiana State University, 1977.

Young, David N. "The Mississippi Whigs, 1834–1860." Ph.D. dissertation, University of Alabama, 1958.

Zuber, Richard Lee. "The Role of Rufus Brown Bullock in Georgia Politics." Master's thesis, Emory University, 1957.

Index

Washington National Intelligencer, 56
Washington Union Club (Memphis), 101
Watts, Thomas H., 74
Wayland, Francis, 21
Webb, Lewis W., 96–97
Webster, Daniel, 41, 54
Welles, Gideon, 203
Wells, Henry H., 184, 187, 242
Wells, James Madison: as a resister, 76, 112; as a refugee, 113; as governor, 140–45, 196, 266; mentioned, 17, 194, 256
Wells, Levi, 256
Wells, Thomas M., 116
Wellsburg (Va.) Herald, 36
Westcott, James D., 249
West Virginia, 11, 29, 36, 58–59, 95–96, 137
Wheelen, Benjamin L., 220
Wheeling, W.Va., 57–58
Wheeling Intelligencer, 36
Whigs: in nation, 33; in South, 19, 31–41, 260–62; in Ala., 36, 162, 218–19; in Ark., 39—40, 120; in Fla., 19; in Ga., 19, 36–37; in La., 39; in Miss., 5, 19, 36, 47, 253–54, 269; in N.C., 20, 32, 34, 61, 90–91, 132, 188–90, 263; in Tenn., 34–35, 110, 127, 129; in Tex., 37–38; in Va., 34, 97, 184–85, 265

White, Alexander, 237, 251
White-line politics, 255
White Terror, 6
"Who Were the Scalawags?" 5
Wickham, William C., 89, 130
Wiggins, Sarah Woolfolk, 6
Willey, Waitman T., 58
Wilmington, N.C., 135
Wilson, Alexander N., 52, 168
Wilson, Henry, 184–85, 195, 209
Wilson, Lemuel, 67, 159
Williamson, Joel, 176
Wing, Warren W., 96–97
Winsmith, John, 245
Winston, John A., 162
Winston County, Ala., 50–51, 165
Wisener, William H., 101
Wofford, Jefferson L., 231
Worth, Jonathan, 134–35, 189
Worthington, John, 81
Wrotnowski, Stanislas, 76

Yancey, William L., 57
Yorkville, S.C., 30
Yorkville (S.C.) Inquirer, 30
Yulee, David, 249